T0206943

Lecture Notes in Computer Science 13193

More information about this subseries at https://link.springer.com/bookseries/7409

Malte Smits (Ed.)

Information for a Better World: Shaping the Global Future

17th International Conference, iConference 2022
Virtual Event, February 28 – March 4, 2022
Proceedings, Part II

Editor
Malte Smits
Humboldt-Universität zu Berlin
Berlin, Germany

ISSN 0302-9743 ISSN 1611-3349 (electronic)
Lecture Notes in Computer Science
ISBN 978-3-030-96959-2 ISBN 978-3-030-96960-8 (eBook)
https://doi.org/10.1007/978-3-030-96960-8

LNCS Sublibrary: SL3 – Information Systems and Applications, incl. Internet/Web, and HCI

This Springer imprint is published by the registered company Springer Nature Switzerland AG
The registered company address is: Gewerbestrasse 11, 6330 Cham, Switzerland

Preface

This year's iConference looked at building post-COVID realities in a world that has adapted to home offices and connecting in digital spaces and that gave us many reasons to reflect on our approach to research, information technology, and communication. In these challenging and difficult times researchers from all over the world came together and worked on current issues, trying to understand more of what we need when it comes to social justice, sustainability, government, and the workplace. What can we improve together? How does a better world look to us?

iConference 2022 was hosted by the iSchools at Kyushu University, University College Dublin, and the University of Texas at Austin under the motto "Information for a Better World: Shaping the Global Future", encouraging a positive and enthusiastic view on the coming years – shared and discussed by attendants in a plethora of presentations, interactive events, and colloquiums. It was the seventeenth event in the iConference series and the third to be held virtually, taking place online between February 28 and March 4, 2022.

The conference chairs accepted a total of 32 full research papers and 29 short research papers along with 35 posters. The submissions were reviewed, scored, and reworked with the help of 255 active peer reviewers in a double-blind review process. Participants also hosted 10 workshops to share information and discuss various topics. Similarly, the Doctoral Colloqium, the Early Career Colloquium, and the Student Symposium held a total of 73 presentations and meetings.

For the fifth time the full and short research papers are published in Springer's Lecture Notes in Computer Science (LNCS). The proceedings are sorted into the following seven categories: Library and Information Science, Information Governance and Ethics, Data Science, Human-Computer Interaction and Technology, Information Behaviour and Retrieval, Health Informatics, and Communities and Media.

We would like to thank all the reviewers for their invaluable effort, expertise, and work. A big thank you also goes to the other chairs for their hard work and prowess. Without them this conference would not have been possible. Our gratitude goes out to everyone who worked on this conference and those who joined and participated in any way, shape, or form.

With a bright and hopeful vision, the iConference again brought researchers together and created and empowered connections between scholars and scientists to grow something that is way bigger than the sum of its parts. Together we explored "Information for a Better World: Shaping the Global Future".

January 2022

Malte Smits
Kristin Eschenfelder
Lihong "Nick" Zhou
Makoto Kato
Henriette Roued-Cunliffe
Michael Twidale

Organization

iConference 2022 was organized by the iSchools at Kyushu University, Japan; University College Dublin, Ireland; and the University of Texas at Austin, USA.

Conference Chairs

Amber Cushing	University College Dublin, Ireland
Kenneth R. Fleischmann	University of Texas at Austin, USA
Emi Ishita	Kyushu University, Japan
Eric Meyer	University of Texas at Austin, USA
Kalpana Shankar	University College Dublin, Ireland
Yoichi Tomiura	Kyushu University, Japan

Full Research Paper Chairs

Kristin Eschenfelder	University of Wisconsin-Madison, USA
Lihong "Nick" Zhou	University of Wuhan, China

Short Research Paper Chairs

Makoto Kato	University of Tsukuba, Japan
Henriette Roued-Cunliffe	University of Copenhagen, Denmark
Michael Twidale	University of Illinois Urbana-Champaign, USA

Poster Chairs

Preben Hansen	Stockholm University, Sweden
Pengyi Zhang	Peking University, China

Interactive Events Chairs

Gillian Oliver	Monash University, Australia
Virginia Ortíz-Repiso	Universidad Carlos III de Madrid, Spain

Doctoral Colloquium Chairs

Ben Cowan	University College Dublin, Ireland
Mohammad Jarrahi	University of North Carolina at Chapel Hill, USA
Atsuyuki Moroshima	University of Tsukuba, Japan

Student Symposium Chairs

Koraljika Golub	Linnaeus University, Sweden
Colin Rhinesmith	Simmons University, USA
Di Wang	Wuhan University, China

Early Career Colloquium Chairs

Doug Oard	University of Maryland, USA
Natalie Pang	University of Singapore, Singapore
António Lucas Soares	University of Porto, Portugal

Social Activity Chairs

Shaobo Liang	Wuhan University, China
Ulrike Liebner	Humboldt-Universität zu Berlin, Germany

Proceedings Chair

Malte Smits	Humboldt-Universität zu Berlin, Germany

Conference Coordinators

Executive Director

Michael Seadle	iSchools Organization

Director of Communications

Clark Heideger	iSchools Organization

Business Manager

Slava Sterzer	iSchools Organization

Program Manager

Katharina Toeppe	iSchools Organization

Social Media

Cynthia Ding	iSchools Organization

Additional Reviewers

Jacob Abbott
Waseem Afzal
Noa Aharony
Jae-wook Ahn
Isola Ajiferuke
Bader Albahlal
Nicole D. Alemanne
Daniel Gelaw Alemneh
Hamed Alhoori
Reham Alhuraiti
Anas Hamad Alsuhaibani
Xiaomi An
Misita Anwar
Muhmammad Naveed Anwar
Catherine Arnott-Smith
Leif Azzopardi
Cristina Robles Bahm
Alex Ball
Zoe Bartliff
Andrew Berry
Nanyi Bi
Toine Bogers
Maria Bonn
Sarah Bratt
Jo Ann M. Brooks
Sarah A. Buchanan
John Budd
Julia Bullard
Yao Cai
Biddy Casselden
Tamy Chambers
Wayland Chang
Tiffany Chao
Hsin-liang Chen
Jiangping Chen
Chola Chhetri
Rachel Ivy Clarke
Anthony Joseph Corso
Andrew Cox
Sally Jo Cunningham
Amber L. Cushing
Rebecca Davis
Shengli Deng
Bridget Disney
Brian Dobreski
Philip Doty
Kedma Duarte
Ricardo Eito-Brun
Avsalom Elmalech
Heidi Enwald
Kristin Eschenfelder
Bruce Ferwerda
Rachel Fleming-May
Fred Fonseca
Henry Alexis Gabb
Maria Gäde
Chunmei Gan
Victor Garcia-Font
John Gathegi
Tali Gazit
Yegin Genc
Susan Elizabeth German
Dion Goh
Patrick Thomas Golden
Melissa Gross
Michael Gryk
Kailash Gupta
Ayse Gursoy
Lala Hajibayova
Carina Hallqvist
Jenna Hartel
Bruce Hartpence
Daqing He
Jiangen He
Viviane Hessami
Alison Hicks
Kelly M. Hoffman
Chris Holstrom
Liang Hong
Kun Huang
Ching Yin Huang
Shuiqing Huang
Isto Huvila
Aylin Imeri (Ilhan)
Sharon Ince
Charles Inskip

Yvette Iribe Ramirez
Vanessa Irvin
Wei Jeng
Tingting Jiang
Michael Jones
Heidi Julien
Nicolas Jullien
Jaap Kamps
Unmil Karadkar
Páraic Kerrigan
Heikki Keskustalo
Jigya Khabar
Yeolib Kim
Vanessa Kitzie
Bart Knijnenburg
Kyungwon Koh
Kolina Koltai
Adam Kriesberg
Keeheon Lee
Jian-Sin Lee
Kijung Lee
Lo Lee
Myeong Lee
Noah Lenstra
Shijuan Li
Guangjian Li
Kai Li
Meng-Hao Li
Ying Li
Louise Limberg
Jenny Lindberg
Henry Linger
Zack Lischer-Katz
Ping Liu
Xiaobin Lu
Kun Lu
Ana Lucic
Christopher Lueg
Haakon Lund
Haiqun Ma
Jinxuan Ma
Lai Ma
Craig MacDonald
Jin Mao
Kate Marek
Matthew S. Mayernik
Philipp Mayr-Schlegel
Claire McGuinness
Pamela Ann McKinney
David McMenemy
Shuyuan Ho Metcalfe
Shawne Miksa
A. J. Million
J. Elizabeth Mills
Stasa Milojevic
Chao Min
Lorri Mon
Camilla Moring
Valerie Nesset
Chaoqun Ni
David M. Nichols
Jan Nolin
Rebecca Noone
Casey O'Donnell
Sanghee Oh
Benedict Salazar Olgado
Peter Organisciak
Felipe Ortega
Abraham Oshni Alvandi
Kathleen Padova
Min Sook Park
Sohyun Park
Hyoungjoo Park
Bo Pei
Diane Pennington
Vivien Petras
Bobby Phuritsabam
Mary Pietrowicz
Ola Pilerot
Alex Poole
Jennifer Proctor
Jian Qin
Marie L. Radford
Arcot Rajasekar
Susan Rathbun-Grubb
Ming Ren
Gabby Resch
Angela U. Rieks
Milly Romeijn-Stout
Philip Romero-Masters

Howard Rosenbaum
Ariel Rosenfeld
Vassilis Routsis
Ehsan Sabaghian
Ashley Sands
Madelyn Rose Sanfilippo
Sally Sanger
Anindita Sarker
Steve Sawyer
Laura Sbaffi
Kirsten Schlebbe
Rainforest Scully-Blaker
Michael Seadle
Ryan Shaw
Stephen C. Slota
Mads Solberg
Shijie Song
Clay Spinuzzi
Beth St. Jean
Gretchen Renee Stahlman
Hrvoje Stancic
Caroline Stratton
Besiki Stvilia
Shigeo Sugimoto
Tanja Svarre
Sue Yeon Syn
Anna Maria Tammaro
Yi Tang
Andrea Karoline Thomer
Chunhua Tsai
Tien-I Tsai
Yuen-Hsien Tseng
Pertti Vakkari
Frans van der Sluis
Nitin Verma
Travis Wagner
Jieyu Wang
Lin Wang
Xiangnyu Wang
Xiaoguang Wang
Yanyan Wang
Yi-Yu Wang
Xiaofei Wei
Martin Weiss
Brian Wentz
Rachel Williams
R. Jason Winning
Dietmar Wolfram
Adam Worrall
Steven John Wright
I-Chin Wu
Qiuhui Xiao
Juan Xie
Iris Xie
Lifang Xu
Shenmeng Xu
Xiao Xue
Hui Yan
Erjia Yan
Gal Yavetz
Ayoung Yoon
Sarah Young
Bei Yu
Chuanming Yu
Liangzhi Yu
Xianjin Zha
Chengzhi Zhang
Chenwei Zhang
Jinchao Zhang
Mei Zhang
Xiaojuan Zhang
Xinyu Zhang
Yan Zhang
Ziming Zhang
Yiming Zhao
Yuxiang (Chris) Zhao
Qinghua Zhu
Zhiya Zuo

Contents – Part II

Information Behaviour and Retrieval

Contents – Part I

Information Governance and Ethics

Data Science

Human-Computer Interaction and Technology

Information Behaviour and Retrieval

An Initial Analysis of E-Procurement Search Behaviour

Stuart Mackie[1(✉)], Leif Azzopardi[2], and Yashar Moshfeghi[2]

[1] BiP Solutions Limited, Glasgow, Scotland, UK
stuart.mackie@bipsolutions.com
[2] University of Strathclyde, Glasgow, Scotland, UK
{leif.azzopardi,yashar.moshfeghi}@strath.ac.uk

Abstract. Procurement or tender search is where suppliers seek opportunities for providing goods, works or services that authorities, organisations and businesses require. Such opportunities are listed as procurement contract notices for which suppliers can submit tenders. Typically, an E-Procurement system is used to help find and carry out one or more of the stages involved in the procurement process (from finding potential opportunities, bidding on such opportunities, to delivering the goods, works or services, i.e. find, win, deliver). Such systems are crucial in enabling suppliers to efficiently search through the available listings of procurement contract notices listed across various public and commercial portals. However, little research has investigated how end-users search for such opportunities. In this paper, we perform a descriptive analysis of the professional search behaviours of suppliers using a bespoke e-procurement system. Our analysis is based on a sub-sample of six months of search log interaction data. First, we provide an overview of the usage patterns of our sample of users before investigating how the behaviour of searchers is influenced by the type of search form used (quick vs advanced), user expertise (new vs experienced), and the domain of the procurement notices (General, Defence, Medical, etc.). Our findings highlight that more experienced searchers appear to be more strategic than less experienced searchers and that searchers behave differently depending on the domain in terms of querying and assessing behaviours. This analysis suggests that e-procurement search engines need to be mindful of the differences across searchers and between domains when designing a system to help support their users.

Keywords: Professional search · Procurement search

1 Introduction

Procurement is the activity of tax-funded authorities, organisations and companies purchasing supplies, services, or works. By and large, a majority of procurement opportunities are provided through tax-funded authorities such as national and local government, health, education, police, and defence authorities. Within

M. Smits (Ed.): iConference 2022, LNCS 13193, pp. 3–12, 2022.
https://doi.org/10.1007/978-3-030-96960-8_1

the European Union (EU), for example, the annual procurement spend accounts for approx. 14% of EU's GDP[1]. Government institutions are increasingly being obliged by law to publish descriptions of public contracts, called, "*requests for tenders*" or "*call for bids*". These documents specify the details of the goods, services and/or works required to be supplied and are essentially invitations to suppliers to submit a tender and bid on the contract. Moreover, such public procurement is a highly regulated activity[2]. Public procurement legislation aims to ensure transparency, promote competition, and achieve value for money for taxpayers. Increasingly, commercial organisations are also publishing descriptions of contracts in order to provide greater transparency and increased efficiency. As such, more and more procurement notices are being posted on various and distributed forums (e.g. on local and central government sites, and commercial procurement portals, etc.).

Suppliers that wish to supply to the market can submit bids (i.e. tender) for such procurement contracts. However, prior to a business submitting a tender for a procurement contract, they must first search for and find a relevant opportunity [5,6]. The search and recommendation tasks within the procurement contracts search domain can be characterised as a professional search task [10,12] – as the search task has a high financial value associated with it, and the process of searching through all the different opportunities from the disparate platforms comes at a high cost. To this end, various e-procurement systems and search technologies have been developed aimed at helping suppliers identify opportunities for which they can bid on by aggregating the opportunities from the different portals [1–3,8,9]. Such systems play a vital role in making the market more efficient in matching suppliers with those in need of goods, services and works [7]. Despite their importance, little is known about how suppliers use and engage with such search systems to find relevant opportunities on such bespoke customised search platforms. Such systems are often more complex than web search interfaces [4] and require more expertise to use effectively [13].

In this paper, we present an initial analysis of the search behaviours of professional procurement searchers – people who actively search for opportunities so that their company can submit tenders to win business. Specifically, we present highlights of search user behaviour mined from a large-scale log analysis conducted within the context of a commercial procurement contracts search engine[3].

To gain a better understanding of search user behaviour within procurement contracts search, we instrumented the search engine and collected user log data over a six-month period [11]. The analysis reported in this paper is based on a 6-month period from January–June 2020, where we sample all queries and clicks over this time. In Sect. 2, we first discuss the search context, users, and queries. Then, in Sect. 3, we analyse customer queries based on the different types of search form used (i.e. advanced vs quick search) and examine the

[1] ec.europa.eu/growth/single-market/public-procurement_en.

[2] ec.europa.eu/growth/single-market/public-procurement/rules-implementation_en.

[3] trackerintelligence.com.

differences between experienced and inexperienced users. Finally, in Sect. 4, we analyse customer queries across industry domains (i.e. healthcare vs defence).

2 Search Context, Users, and Queries

Several online procurement portals exist for the purpose of publishing procurement notices, such as Contracts Finder[4], Tenders Electronic Daily[5], or SAM.gov[6]. Within the market, aggregated search services combine feeds from different country and authority specific portals to reduce the burden on business users of repeatedly searching multiple portals. Within the domain of procurement search, the documents being search for are split into two main categories: contract notices and procurement awards.

Contract notices specify the supplies, services, or works required by the purchasing organisation. Procurement awards disclose which business successfully won a previously advertised contract. Procurement notices are structured documents, with metadata fields denoting the purchaser, location of supply, value of the contract, nature of the contract (i.e. works, services, or supplies), Further, contracts are annotated with the Common Procurement Vocabulary[7] (CPV), an EU-wide procurement classification system used to assign numerical codes to represent the supplies, services, or works subject to procurement. This metadata is in addition to the contract's full-text natural language description. Within the 6-month period of the log sample we analyse in this paper, we observed that the search engine indexed over 100,000 new contract notices and awards each month. Further, we also noted a marked increase in the volume of contracts published in March 2020, which may correspond to the financial end-of-year or tax-funded authorities publishing procurement tenders related to the COVID-19 pandemic (e.g. for personal protective equipment, etc.).

In contrast to ad-hoc web search [4], we characterise procurement contract search as a professional search task [10,12]. This particular search task involves business users (i.e. employees or business owners) searching for economic opportunities, with significant economic value associated with the success of their search tasks. Figure 1 shows the different sizes of the businesses within our sample that submitted queries to the search engine in this period. As can be seen by the distribution over the customer-reported number of employees (captured on sign-up), the search system is used by small, medium, and large businesses – which may impact on the relevance of contract opportunities sought. Additionally, in Fig. 1, we illustrate the timestamp of queries and clicks logged. We observe that the temporal pattern of user interaction is directly aligned with traditional business hours (i.e. Monday–Friday 9–5pm) – highlighting that professional searchers are primarily engaged in search activity within the office environment. Taken together, Fig. 1 provides us with an initial understanding of the demographics and activities of professional searchers within this domain.

---

4 contractsfinder.service.gov.uk.

5 ted.europa.eu/TED.

6 beta.sam.gov.

7 simap.ted.europa.eu/web/simap/cpv.

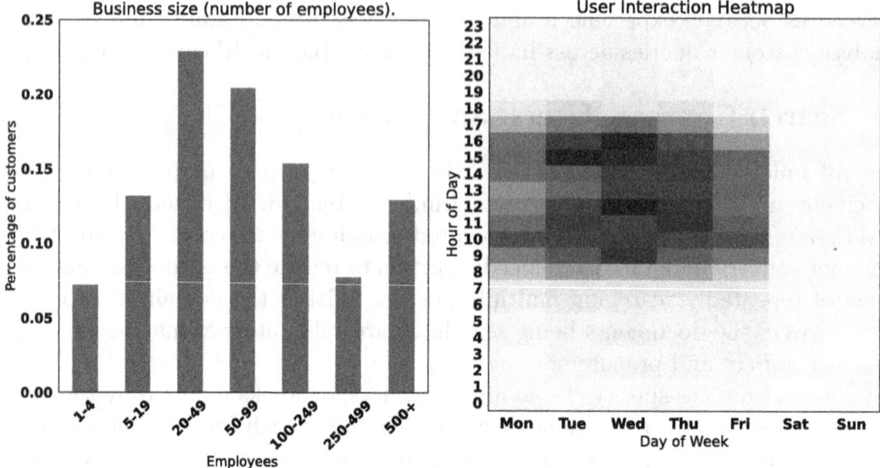

Fig. 1. An illustration of the characteristics of the population of professional searchers within the domain of procurement contracts search. The system is used by customers from a diverse range of business sizes, and is predominately accessed by such users during office hours.

Table 1. Summary statistics of search user behaviour within the domain of procurement contract search.

Terms per-query	Clicks per-query	Click depth	Dwell time	Queries per-session	Session length
11.2	3.0	39.3	72.3 s	1.9	8 m 49 s

We present summary statistics of search user behaviour within the domain of procurement contracts search in Table 1. In Table 1, we report the mean number of terms issued per-query, the mean number of clicks observed per-query, the mean click depth into the SERP rankings, mean dwell time, and then two session-based summary statistics – the number of queries per session and the mean session length. Compared to Web search [4], from Table 1 we note that procurement searchers regularly issue queries with more than ten terms (11.2 vs. 2.35 in Web search), tend to view more pages (3.0 vs. 2.2 in Web search), click on results that are further down the ranking (39.3 vs. half of users not clicking beyond the first Web SERP) and issue more queries in a session (1.9 vs. approx. two-thirds with a single Web search query). We also note the mean dwell time per document examined was approximately one minute while the mean time spend on the search result pages was over eight minutes (across the session), indicating that procurement searchers invest significant amounts of time and effort into searching.

In Fig. 2, we illustrate the distribution of total queries over the 6-month log sample, and the distribution of queries observed over different search forms. From Fig. 2, we observe that a quarter of all queries within the sample occurred in March 2020, with a sustained increase in search traffic through April, May,

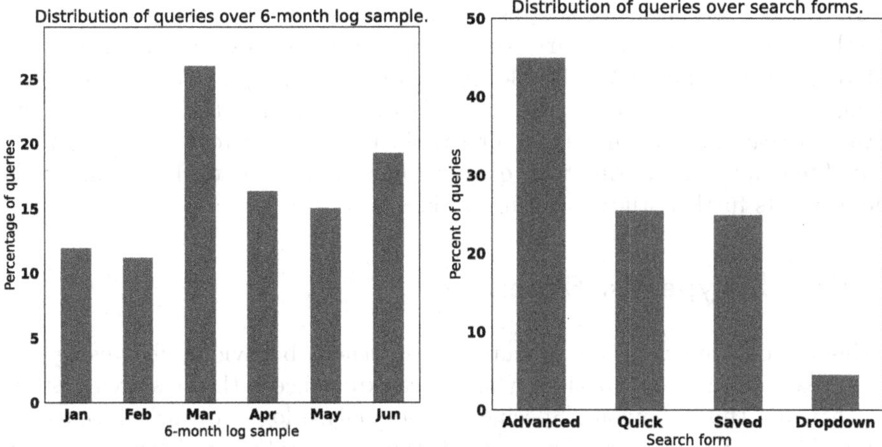

Fig. 2. The distribution of queries over the 6-month log sample, and the distribution of queries over the 4 different search forms offered to users of the system.

and June. This marked increase in the overall number of queries in March 2020 may potentially be related to the financial end-of-year (with tenders for contracts being related to annual budgets) or the COVID-19 pandemic.

Further from Fig. 2, we illustrate the distribution of customer queries submitted to different search forms provided by the system. "*Advanced*" search is a complex interaction, where the user can specify several search filters when submitting their query, as opposed to "*Quick*" search where the user simply issues query terms (but can specify an ALL or ANY Boolean condition). "*Saved*" search allows the user to store a curated query to be executed on the system on a regular basis – and is based on the advanced search form. "*Dropdown*" search is the simplest form, where the query is expressed as simple query terms with no facility for controlling Boolean operators. From Fig. 2, we observe that advanced search is used more frequently than quick search and saved search, with dropdown search accounting for under 5% of queries submitted to the system. This preference for advanced search further illustrates the investment of time and effort professional searchers are making into this particular search task.

Table 2. Distribution of search form usage over the 6-month log sample.

Search form	Jan	Feb	Mar	Apr	May	June
Advanced	51%	49%	50%	41%	38%	45%
Quick	25%	26%	22%	26%	30%	27%
Saved	21%	22%	24%	28%	27%	24%
Dropdown	03%	04%	04%	05%	05%	04%

In Table 2, we illustrate the distribution of search form usage over the 6-month log sample. From January–March, advanced searches account for approx. half of all queries. Post-COVID19 lockdown (March 2020), we observe a marked change in search behaviour, with a decrease in the monthly proportion of advanced searches, and increases for saved and quick searches. This may be related to employees altering their querying behaviour while working from home and warrants further study in future work.

3 Search Type Vs. Experience

In this section, we investigate procurement searcher's behaviour when using different search forms, and consider what effect experience with the search system may have on this behaviour. Specifically, we analyse log data for "*Advanced*", "*Quick*", and "*Saved*" search form usage for customers who have been subscribed to the system for less than one year (new users), and customers who have been subscribed for more than one year (experienced users). Our research question is: are there observable differences in the characteristics of procurement search behaviour over different search interfaces and user experience levels?

Table 3. Search user behaviour statistics for new and experienced users across the different search type.

Interaction	New users			Experienced users		
	Quick	Advanced	Saved	Quick	Advanced	Saved
Query distribution	7.8	12.5	9.5	18.0	**40.5**	10.0
Query terms	2.0	8.3	21.8	1.6	10.0	**33.5**
CPV codes	–	3.2	7.9	–	1.5	**13.3**
Query formulation	32 s	53 s	**2 m 38 s**	36 s	1 m 28 s	1 m 39 s
Items retrieved	675	1920	567	226	707	218
Clicks per query	2.0	2.6	3.0	1.7	2.3	**3.6**
Rank click depth	33.6	**64.5**	64.1	15.8	31.0	38.8
Dwell time (s)	77.93	73.93	73.97	56.18	**111.2**	76.59

Table 3 reports search user behaviour summary statistics for quick, advanced, and saved search for new users and experienced users. We report the per-form query distribution (i.e. usage), mean number of terms and CPV codes used in queries, the mean time to enter and issue the query (query formulation time), the mean number of items retrieved per-query, the mean number of clicks per-query, the mean of the rank of the last click (rank depth), and the mean of the time spend examining the documents that the user clicked on (dwell time).

In terms of querying behaviour, from Table 3, we first note that 40% of the total number of queries are for advanced search from experienced users.

Over both customer segments, advanced search exhibits the most usage. Beyond advanced search, for new users, there is a moderate preference for saved searches, but for the more experienced users, there is a marked shift towards quick search usage over saved search. Over both customer segments, the number of search terms and CPV codes used in queries increases with the complexity of the search form (i.e. quick>advanced>saved). Specifically, for quick search we see a small number of query terms (with CPV codes being unavailable in quick search), a moderate number of query terms and small number of CPV codes being used for advanced search, and a larger number of query terms and increased number of CPV codes for saved searches. Between the two customer segments, we see the new users enter more terms in quick search and more CPV codes in advanced search than the more experienced users. For the more experienced users, we see marked increases in the number of query terms and CPV codes used in curated saved searches. For query formulation time, we see that the time taken to submit queries generally follows the complexity of the search interaction. Advanced search users who have more experience with the system appear to take longer while formulating these searches than novice users, but appear to not spend as much time as novice users curating their saved searches.

In terms of on-SERP behaviour, from Table 3, we note that new users tend to submit queries that return more documents than experienced users. This suggests that experienced users could be obtaining better precision in their results. For clicks per-query, we observe that increases in the number of clicks follows the complexity of the search interaction (i.e. quick>advanced>saved). For click depth, we observe that across each corresponding search form less experienced users tend to click further into the ranking than experienced users, and for both user experience levels the more complex search interactions see increased click depths. The on-document dwell time for new years is similar across search form usage. However, for the more experienced users, there is a marked shift in dwell time between quick search and advanced search. This indicates that more experienced users are being more strategic and are taking less time to assess contracts found via quick search than those found via advanced search – i.e. the amount of time spent assessing is proportional to the amount of time they spend investing in a good query. Table 3 gives us an initial understanding of search user behaviour within the domain of procurement search. From this, we can conclude that there are indeed observable differences in the characteristics of procurement search behaviour over different search interfaces and user experience levels that highlight opportunities for future work.

4 Query Classification by Industry Sector

In this section, we analyse customer queries over different industry domains. The mechanism we use to investigate search user behaviour across industry domains is through categorising queries (and subsequent search interactions) into industry verticals using the CPV codes in queries. CPV codes are added to procurement contracts to indicate the subject of the works, services, or supplied that are to be procured from the market. The categorisation of CPV codes into specific industry domains has been undertaken by procurement experts within the company. Specifically, each CPV code has been mapped to 9 industry verticals: "*General*","*Defence*","*Education & Culture*","*Energy & Environment*","*Health & Care*","*Infrastructure & Construction*","*Professional Services*","*Technology & Communications*", and "*Transport & Logistics*". Our research question is: are there are observable differences in the characteristics of procurement search behaviour over different industry groupings?

Table 4. Search user behaviour statistics - based on industry domain.

Industry	Terms	CPV	Q. Form	Clicks	Depth	Dwell
General	22.3	28.2	1 m 49 s	5.2	33.8	60 s
Defence	25.5	**51.0**	1 m 38 s	6.5	41.7	42 s
Education & Culture	34.3	22.0	2 m 3 s	3.7	40.9	60 s
Energy & Environment	**63.3**	25.0	1 m 50 s	6.5	37.5	40 s
Health & Care	29.1	24.4	1 m 26 s	5.9	56.7	**70 s**
Infra. & Construction	42.5	23.6	1 m 34 s	5.6	71.9	45 s
Professional services	44.5	20.6	1 m 37 s	5.2	47.1	47 s
Tech. & Comms	31.1	29.1	**2 m 21 s**	4.1	38.6	53 s
Transport & Logistics	29.4	36.7	2 m 14 s	**6.9**	**104.7**	62 s

Table 4 reports search user behaviour summary statistics for queries in 9 different industry domains. We report the mean number of terms in queries, the mean number of CPV codes used in queries, the mean query formulation time, the mean number of clicks per-query, the mean rank depth, and mean dwell time. From Table 4, we observe than there is considerable variation in search user behaviour across industry verticals. Specifically, the minimum number of query terms is seen in the "*General*" category, while the maximum number of query terms is seen in the "*Energy & Environment*" category. The "*Defence*" grouping sees the highest CPV code usage, while the "*Professional Services*" grouping see the lowest usage of CPV codes in queries. Users who submit queries to the "*Education & Culture*" grouping tend to take the longest to formulate queries. Users who submit queries to the "*Transport & Logistics*" grouping tend to click the most documents per-query and click furthest into the ranking. Users who submit queries to the "*Health & Care*" grouping tend to take the longest to assess contracts. Table 4 gives us a further understanding of search user behaviour within the domain of procurement search. From this, we can conclude that there are indeed observable differences in the characteristics of procurement search behaviour over industry verticals that again highlight opportunities for future work.

5 Summary and Future Work

In this paper, via a log study, we have presented an initial overview of search user behaviour of professional searchers within procurement contracts search. We have highlighted interesting differences in demographics and usage that are distinct from general web search, examined the effect that user system experience has on search behaviour, and noted a divergence in behaviour across users within specific industry domains. In doing so, we have ascertained that there are discernible patterns of search user behaviour particular to this professional search task.

The findings presented suggest that specific support is needed for novice searchers so that they can better craft queries and focus their attention when searching for contracts. Moreover, our findings also suggest that the different industry domains in which procurement contracts are categorised could also benefit from additional support. However, further work is required to probe more deeply into what mechanism and interventions would best support the searching activities of procurement searchers. Aside from expertise, the notion of relevance also takes on different dimensions: topical and commercial. While traditionally topical relevance is important (i.e. is the document related to type of business opportunities the company is looking?), another important factor is around commercial relevance (i.e. is this opportunity relevant to the business?). While a contract may match a given customer's query and be on topic, a core question is whether the business can actually fulfil the contract, and if they can how profitable or valuable would that contract be to the business? So a small business may not be able to fulfil a large order, while a small order may not worthwhile for a larger businesses. However, such issues around topical relevance and commercial relevance also require further investigation and analysis.

In summary, this work presents one of the first studies providing insights into the search behaviours of users searching for opportunities. And more work is required to better understand the difficulties and challenges in finding and identifying relevant opportunities in order to make the procurement activities more economically efficient, competitive and fair.

Acknowledgments. The collaboration between BiP Solutions Limited and the University of Strathclyde is supported by Innovate UK (Knowledge Transfer Project 11464).

References

1. Alvarez-Rodríguez, J., Labra Gayo, J., Silva, F., Alor-Hernández, G., Sanchez-Ramirez, C., Luna, J.: Towards a pan-european e-procurement platform to aggregate, publish and search public procurement notices powered by linked open data: the moldeas approach. Int. J. Softw. Eng. Knowl. Eng. **22**, 365–384 (2012)
2. Doring, S., Fischer, S., Kiessling, W., Preisinger, T.: Optimizing the catalog search process for e-procurement platforms. In: International Workshop on Data Engineering Issues in E-Commerce, pp. 39–48 (2005)

3. Döring, S., Kießling, W., Preisinger, T., Fischer, S.: Evaluation and optimization of the catalog search process of e-procurement platforms. Electron. Comm. Res. Appl. **5**(1), 44–56 (2006). International Workshop on Data Engineering Issues in E-Commerce (DEEC 2005)
4. Jansen, B.J., Spink, A., Bateman, J., Saracevic, T.: Real life information retrieval: a study of user queries on the web. In: ACM SIGIR Forum (1998)
5. Mackie, S., Azzopardi, L., Moshfeghi, Y.: Search user behaviour within the procurement contracts domain. In: European Conference on Information Retrieval, Industry Day (ECIR) (2020).
6. Mackie, S., Macdonald, D., Azzopardi, L., Moshfeghi, Y.: Looking for opportunities: challenges in procurement search. In: Proceedings of the Conference on Research and Development in Information Retrieval (SIGIR) (2019)
7. Mehrbod, A., Zutshi, A., Grilo, A.: A vector space model approach for searching and matching product e-catalogues. In: Proceedings of the Eighth International Conference on Management Science and Engineering Management, pp. 833–842 (2014)
8. Mehrbod, A., Zutshi, A., Grilo, A., Cruz-Machado, V.: Evaluation of an e-catalogue matching mechanism in public procurement notice search. **502**, 1237–1247 (2017)
9. Mynarz, J., Svátek, V., Di Noia, T.: Matchmaking Public Procurement Linked Open Data, pp. 405–422 (2015)
10. Russell-Rose, T., Chamberlain, J., Azzopardi, L.: Information retrieval in the workplace: a comparison of professional search practices. Inf. Process. Manag. (2018)
11. Silvestri, F.: Mining query logs: turning search usage data into knowledge. Found. Trends Inf. Retriev. (2010)
12. Verberne, S., et al.: First international workshop on professional search. SIGIR Forum **52**(2) (2018)
13. White, R.W., Dumais, S., Teevan, J.: Characterizing the influence of domain expertise on web search behavior. In: WSDM 2009 (2009)

Mobile Devices as Information Discovery Tools for Young Children

A Multi-method Study on Children's and Parents' Perspectives

Kirsten Schlebbe(✉)

Humboldt-Universität zu Berlin, Unter den Linden 6, 10099 Berlin, Germany
schlebbe@ibi.hu-berlin.de

Abstract. With the increased use of mobile devices by young children, the question arises whether these devices also serve as tools for information discovery for this age group. This study examines how children aged four to six years use mobile devices, especially tablets, and whether this use includes activities that are linked to the discovery of information. In addition, it investigates whether aspects related to children's information behavior play a role in parents' and children's perceptions of tablet use. A multi-method and interactive research approach, following the *Mosaic approach*, was adopted for data collection with families from Germany. The results show that mobile devices play a role in the discovery of information by young children. Via tablets, children discover information rather accidentally while watching videos or playing with game applications. For the intentional discovery of information, mainly smartphones are used, with parents or older siblings acting as information mediaries for young children. Regarding parents' and children's perceptions of tablet use, it appears that the devices are mainly associated with entertainment activities, although parents in particular also recognize the potential of the devices in the area of learning and information discovery. Overall, this study offers a multi-perspective and diverse insight into young children's use of mobile devices and adds to the research on children's digital information behavior. Of specific value is the inclusion of young children's perspectives, which are understudied in information behavior research.

Keywords: Children · Information behavior · Mobile devices · Parents

1 Introduction

Mobile devices like tablets and smartphones offer almost unlimited access to digital information. Whether it is a quick search for specific information via a search engine or browsing various Websites: The potential of these devices as tools for discovering information is immense [1]. With the increased use of mobile devices by young children [2], the question arises whether these devices also serve as tools for information discovery for this age group.

Previous studies have shown that the information behavior of children aged six years or younger differs from that of older children, adolescents or adults: Parents and other individuals often play an important role as sources of information and search

M. Smits (Ed.): iConference 2022, LNCS 13193, pp. 13–31, 2022.
https://doi.org/10.1007/978-3-030-96960-8_2

assistants [3, 4]. Furthermore, young children's encounter with information is often rather unintended. As a consequence, models of information behavior research that focus on intentional forms of information seeking are of limited use for the study of young children's information behavior [4]. Therefore, this study primarily uses Wilson's [5] typology of information discovery, which includes both the intentional and accidental discovery of information, to examine children's information behavior in connection with mobile devices. Overall, this paper aims to answer the following research questions:

- *RQ1:* How do children aged four to six years use mobile devices, especially tablets, and does this use include activities that can be linked to the discovery of information?
- *RQ2:* What are parents' and children's perceptions of children's tablet use and do aspects related to children's information discovery play a role in these perceptions?

To answer these questions, this study uses the *Mosaic approach* [6], a multi-method and interactive framework for data collection with young children. The study focuses on German children from four to six years of age. The upper age limit was determined by the standard elementary school enrollment age in Germany. The lower age limit was intended to avoid an overly wide age range and to ensure that the children have the linguistic abilities to participate in the study. The study focused on tablet use, especially during data collection with the children. However, children's use of other mobile devices was also investigated to capture the overall context.

The paper is organized as follows. Section 2 presents literature about the connection between young children's information behavior and mobile devices as well as studies on parents' and children's perceptions of mobile device use. Section 3 describes the study's research design. Section 4 presents the results, which are then discussed in Sect. 5 and summarized in Sect. 6.

2 Literature Review

2.1 Young Children's Information Behavior and Mobile Devices

The adult user has been in the focus of information behavior research for many years. Although there were some important examples in earlier years that dealt with the information behavior of children (*e.g.*, [7–9]), it was not until the beginning of the 21st century that a greater interest in this age group emerged. But even then, the focus was mostly on school-aged children and adolescents (*e.g.*, [10–15]). Therefore, the user group of younger children was long underrepresented in information behavior research. This is problematic because early studies including younger participants suggested that their information behavior differs from that of older children [16, 17].

In recent years, research on the user group of young children has been increasing. For example, in her survey with 31 parents and caregivers of children between the ages of four and eight years from Canada and the U.S., Barriage [4] found that the most mentioned ways of children's information seeking were interpersonal interactions, books, the Internet and television use. Furthermore, her results showed that parents often assist their children in the process of finding information.

Further research has focused on examining the relationship between children's information behavior and digital technology. For example, Agarwal [18] investigated the use of touch devices in a single case study with a child between two and four years of age. His results show that the tasks the child spent most of her time with were watching videos as well as playing with educational applications and games. Given *et al.* [19] examined the everyday information seeking with information technologies of 15 Australian children aged three to five years old. Their results show that the children use the devices for a variety of activities that can be seen as "early steps in the 'mastery of life' that define an individual's everyday information behaviors" (p. 346), including artistic and sociodramatic play as well as early literacy and numeracy activities.

2.2 Parents' and Young Children's Perceptions of Mobile Device Use

Different studies investigated parents' motivations and perceptions of their young children's use of mobile devices. For example, an interview study of Chen *et al.* [20] with eleven Singapore parents of children aged one to five years found that parents' primary motivations for children's use of digital devices were an interest in children's learning, tension release, and bonding through co-use. Similarly, a survey of Papadakis *et al.* [21] with 293 Greek families with children between four and six years found the improvement of learning outcomes and entertainment to be important motivations for children's use of mobile devices. The results of an interview study of Chaudron *et al.* [22] with seventy families with children up to eight years from seven countries (Belgium, Czech Republic, Finland, Germany, Italy, Russia, UK) also showed that parents value digital and mobile devices primarily for their entertainment and occupational character. However, they also reported appreciating the learning opportunities and information offered via the devices.

With regard to children's perceptions of mobile devices, the same study [22] indicates that children have a positive view of digital technologies and relate them primarily to entertainment and fun, although some of the interviewed children also associated the technologies with sharing or seeking information or learning opportunities. However, this only applied to the older children in the sample. In their study with 43 children between four and six years in the U.S., Eisen and Lillard [23] found that only about half of the children stated that tablets can be used for reading and learning, while most children associated the device with the activities of taking photos, playing games and watching videos. A study of Dias and Brito [24] with 25 Portuguese families with at least one child aged three to eight years also showed that young children have a very positive view of digital devices and perceived tablets as "a source of entertainment and fun" (p. 23).

In summary, earlier studies show that digital and mobile devices seem to play a role in young children's intentional and accidental discovery of information. In addition, previous research suggests that parents perceive mobile devices as tools for learning and information discovery, while especially younger children seem to associate the devices mainly with entertainment and fun. This study aims to further investigate the use and perception of mobile devices as tools for information discovery for young children, with an increased emphasis on children's perspectives.

3 Research Design

This study is part of a larger research project investigating the information behavior of young children in relation to their use of mobile devices. While previous research [3, 25] focused on parents' perspectives, the goal of the present study was to include the children and their perspectives as well.

For data collection, a combination of etic and emic approaches [26] was used, gathering data from parents as well as from the children themselves. As part of an initial exploratory implementation of the research design, eight German families with children aged four to six years participated in the study over a two-month period in 2021. A multi-method research approach, following the *Mosaic approach*, was adopted for data collection with the children. The *Mosaic approach* is a framework thought as participatory, reflexive, focused on children's experiences, and multi-method [27]. Besides observing and talking to children, creative tools like photography or drawing are suggested as a method to "enable young children to communicate their ideas and feelings" (p. 25) [6].

Due to the COVID-19 pandemic, the data collection had to be conducted without direct personal contact. For this purpose, a so-called "research book" was created and sent to the families by mail. The book contained four creative tasks for children and parents around the topic of tablet use. In addition, at least one parent of the family participated in a semi-structured interview.

The instruments of data collection were pretested with one family. Additionally, the research book was discussed with two other parents.

As part of informed consent, the parents gave consent for their child's participation as well as their own participation in the study. To address the specific ethical aspects of research with children, all children were informed about the aim of the study and their rights within a short video and asked for their assent. It was also explicitly explained to all parents that the completion of the tasks could also be done only partially, depending on the individual interests and abilities of the child. For participating in the study, all families received a 50.00 EUR voucher, allowing them to choose from a small selection of stores and leisure activities for families. In addition, the children received a sweet treat and a certificate of participation.

3.1 Sample

A combination of convenience and snowball sampling was used for the recruitment of the families. The final sample consisted of eight families with a child aged four to six years who had prior experience using a tablet. All families live in Berlin, Germany, or the surrounding area. Table 1 describes the study sample in detail.

Table 1. Description of the study sample.

Fam	Children[a] (age in years)	Parents (*interviewee/s*)	Siblings (age in years)
A	Ada (4) ♀	Father & *Mother*	Brother (1)
B	Ben (4) ♂	Father & *Mother*	Brother (<1)
C	Cara (6) ♀	*Father & Mother*	Sister (8), Sister (12), Brother (14)
D	Denise (5) ♀	*Father & Mother*	
E	Elias (5) ♂	Father & *Mother*	Sister (9)
F	Felix (4) ♂	Father & *Mother*	Brother (1)
G	Gina (4) ♀	Father & *Mother*	Brother (1)
H	Henrik (6) ♂	Father & *Mother*	

[a]For the purpose of anonymization, the children were given pseudonyms.

All children live in a household with a father and a mother. Four children are female and four children are male. Half of the children were four years old, with the youngest child, Gina, having just turned four. Two children were five years old and two were six years old. For these two children, study participation coincided with the time of elementary school enrollment. Six children have younger or older siblings, Denise and Henrik are only children.

All data were collected in German. Quotes included in this paper were translated from German into English.

3.2 Data Collection

Parent Interview. In two cases, both parents were interviewed. In six families, only the mother participated in the interview. Due to the COVID-19 pandemic, all interviews were conducted via the videoconferencing service *Zoom*. The length of the interviews ranged from thirty to ninety minutes. All interviews were audio-recorded.

The aim of the interview was to find out more about children's use of mobile devices, especially tablets. Furthermore, the parents' personal attitudes towards children's use of mobile devices were investigated. For the interview guide, a part of the questions was adopted from an earlier study on children's information behavior in connection with mobile devices [3]. In addition, questions regarding parents' perceptions in relation to the devices, especially as a tool for learning and acquiring information, were added. A trcanslated version of the basic interview guide can be found in Appendix 1.

Research Book. The "research book" contained four creative tasks for the children and parents around the topic of tablet use. The families should solve the tasks in free order over a period of about two to four weeks. Figure 1 describes the different elements of the book.

INTRODUCTION Greeting, reference to the informational video and instructions for the tasks.	
MINI-QUESTIONNAIRE Rating of various activities with the tablet (depending on the answers during the parent interview) using green and red sticky dots.	**PHOTO-TOUR** Documentation of places in the home where the child has already used the tablet and description of activities. For privacy reasons, taking photos was optional and could also be replaced by a short description of the places.
PARENT-CHILD-INTERVIEW The parents ask their child four open questions about the child's perceptions of and experiences with the tablet. A translated version of the interview questions can be found in Appendix 2.	**DREAM TABLET** The children are to imagine that they can do magic and build their "dream tablet" of which they should draw a picture or craft something. After creating the work, they explain it to their parents.
CONCLUSION A large free space for further notes or drawings and thanks for participation.	

Fig. 1. Elements of the research book.

Recordings and photos for the research book were taken by the families and sent to the researcher by email or via a mobile messenger of parents' choice. After completion, the book was sent to the researcher by mail and then digitized.

The goal of the research book was to include the children's perspective on the devices in the study and to allow for triangulation. The various tasks were designed to discover what activities the children associate with the device and what perceptions they have of the tablet in general.

Figure 2 provides an overview of the different types of data collection during the study and, thus, shows the individual "mosaic pieces" that are intended to provide a multi-perspective view of children's tablet use. Due to the large amount of data collected, only a limited insight into the various results can be provided within the scope of this paper.

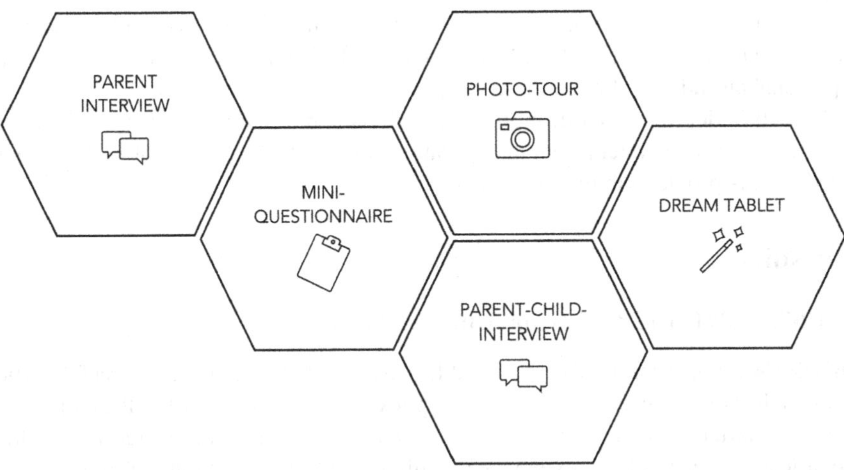

Fig. 2. Different types of data collection during the study.

3.3 Data Analysis

After data collection, all data was organized, transcribed and analyzed using the qualitative data analysis software *MAXQDA Plus 2020* (version 20.4.1). For data analysis,

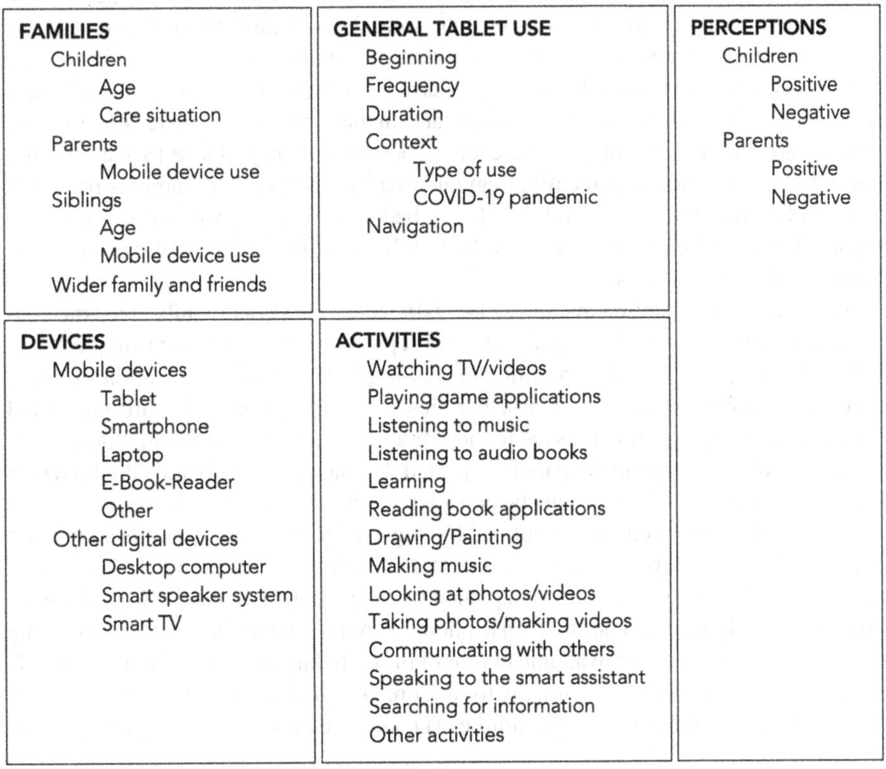

FAMILIES
- Children
  - Age
  - Care situation
- Parents
  - Mobile device use
- Siblings
  - Age
  - Mobile device use
- Wider family and friends

GENERAL TABLET USE
- Beginning
- Frequency
- Duration
- Context
  - Type of use
  - COVID-19 pandemic
- Navigation

PERCEPTIONS
- Children
  - Positive
  - Negative
- Parents
  - Positive
  - Negative

DEVICES
- Mobile devices
  - Tablet
  - Smartphone
  - Laptop
  - E-Book-Reader
  - Other
- Other digital devices
  - Desktop computer
  - Smart speaker system
  - Smart TV

ACTIVITIES
- Watching TV/videos
- Playing game applications
- Listening to music
- Listening to audio books
- Learning
- Reading book applications
- Drawing/Painting
- Making music
- Looking at photos/videos
- Taking photos/making videos
- Communicating with others
- Speaking to the smart assistant
- Searching for information
- Other activities

Fig. 3. Code system (level 1–3).

a combination of inductive and deductive coding methods was used with a focus on descriptive and values coding [28], to examine the device use and its context as well as the personal attitudes of the families.

Due to the adoption of questions from an earlier interview study [3], it was possible to use a part of the code system from that research. A simplified overview of the developed code system is provided in Fig. 3.

4 Results

4.1 Children's Use of Tablets and Other Mobile Devices

General Use. Since children's use of a tablet was one of the sampling criteria for participation in the study, the use of this device applies to all children. Most of the children in the sample started using the tablet at around two to three years of age. Thus, all children have at least one year of use experience, while the oldest children in the sample, Cara (6) and Henrik (6), have been using the device for more than four years.

Several families reported that the frequency and duration of children's use vary over time, for example, depending on the weather or children's current interests. The frequency of use in the sample differs from weekly to daily use. The duration of use is generally determined by the parents. In some families, this is a fixed maximum length of use of, for example, 15 min per day; in other families, the time of use is decided on a situational basis or according to the activity with the device.

The tablet is used in various contexts and situations. One situation mentioned several times is the use while traveling. For some children, this was also the first context of use with the tablet. Furthermore, parents report that the device is sometimes used to keep children occupied, for example, at the pediatrician's appointment or when visiting a restaurant. Some children use the tablet regularly in the early morning when other family members are still asleep, others in the evening before bedtime to listen to audio books. During the photo tours, documenting regular places of use at home, families primarily photographed the family sofa and the child's bed. The parents' bed, the child's room in general, the kitchen table as well as the families' garden, balcony or car were also documented as places of use.

It is important to mention that the COVID-19 pandemic strongly influenced the context of this study. Except for Family D, who reported that Denise's (5) frequency of mobile device use increased very little during the pandemic, all other families experienced an increased use. In most of these families, the combination of daycare and school closures and parents' occupations led to more frequent and longer use of mobile devices by the children. Although many parents reported that the use normalized with the return to daycare, the general impact must be considered when interpreting the data.

In all families, children use not only tablets but a range of different mobile and digital devices. All children have already used smartphones. In Families E and H, this contact is limited to a few activities and accompanied by the parents. In contrast, Cara (6) from Family C recently received her first smartphone. Parents' laptops are rarely used by the children. E-book readers are available in four of the eight families, but only in Families C and F, the E-book reader is occasionally used for reading aloud to the children by parents or older siblings. Additionally, two families (D and E) own special digital cameras for children that can be used to take photos and play with game applications. Other digital devices used by the children that do not have a screen or are mobile only to a limited extent are game consoles (Families C and F) or a digital audio player designed for children called *Toniebox* (Families D, F and G). Another special case is the educational game *Tiptoi*, which is used via a digital pen and paper (Family A, B, D and F). A smart speaker system is available in Families F and H and is also used by Felix (4) and Henrik (6). Denise (5) is also familiar with such a system, but only through the use at neighbors of Family D.

Activities. The children use different mobile devices for a wide range of activities. Apart from Gina (4), the tablet is used by all children for watching videos, usually a small selection of TV series or occasionally movies for children. Playing with game applications is also done via the tablet by almost all children, except for Denise (5). The children usually have a small selection of game applications that are often linked to the children's topics of interest, such as horses or dinosaurs. Another playful activity with the tablet is digital painting or coloring, which a majority of the children has already done.

Dedicated educational learning applications are used primarily by the older children in the sample, Cara (6) and Henrik (6), but four-year-old Felix has also experience with applications of this kind. Some other parents also see individual learning aspects in the game applications that their children use, but overall, they tend to assign the applications to the area of play. Particularly among the families with younger children, some parents indicate that they have been reserved about learning applications so far but would be open to using them in the future, for example, when their children start school.

Reading digital books together via the tablet is not practiced by any family. Instead, all families mainly use analog books for reading aloud. Families C and F also use an E-book reader for this purpose. In most families, listening to music or audio books tends to be done via smartphones or special devices such as the already mentioned *Toniebox* or classic CD players. Exceptions here are Families E and H, where listening to audio books via the tablet is a frequent activity.

Taking photos or making videos and looking at photos or watching self-recorded videos is popular among many children. In most families, this tends to be done via parents' smartphones. An exception here is Henrik (6), who uses the tablet to create and edit his own photos and videos. For communication activities, most families also primarily use smartphones. Almost all children have experience with video calls or sending messages in the form of emojis. However, these communicative activities are usually supervised and guided by the parents. Watching videos, listening to audiobooks or playing with game applications via the tablet, however, is usually done relatively independently by the children, although specifically the younger children still need parental support in some cases.

The smart assistant of the mobile devices is hardly used by the children. Only Henrik (6), who is also familiar with the family's smart speaker system, has also used the mobile device assistant *Siri*. In Family F, that also uses a smart speaker system, Felix' (4) interaction is limited to these devices; he does not use the assistant on the tablet or smartphone. Most parents also explicitly point out that they do not use the smart assistant function themselves.

When asked if the families use mobile devices to search intentionally for information for their children, almost all parents answered positively. In Family A, however, this type of use is very limited as Mother A reports that she can answer the majority of Ada's (4) questions herself and usually does not need to refer to digital sources for this purpose. The father of Family C also describes the impression that a digital information search for his daughter's questions is often not necessary or, if so, is taken over by her older siblings, but Mother C reports that she has used the mobile devices in the presence of her daughter to answer her questions. In the other families, parents also report that they occasionally use mobile devices to answer children's questions or search for suitable digital images or videos: *"...he also says things like 'Can you Google this, Mama?', yes. So, it's totally, it often happens when he wants to know...the other day he asked, 'How is electricity made?' and then...I just looked it up"* (Mother B).

However, mainly due to the children's limited writing and reading skills, the search is carried out by parents or older siblings who mainly use the search engine *Google* for this purpose. The discovered videos or images are then shown to the children. Most parents report that they tend to use their smartphones for these purposes. In most families, the tablet is rarely used for parents' systematic information searches for their children. In Families F and H, the smart speaker system helps to overcome the problem of children's limited reading and writing skills for search. Both families' mothers report that their sons, Felix (4) and Henrik (6), occasionally turn to the system's smart assistant with questions: *"he communicates with them...really casually and, well...it's mainly to play children's songs or just to ask, 'How does the animal do?' or 'How does the T-Rex do?'. So, mainly dinosaur questions, right?"* (Mother F).

4.2 Parents' and Children's Perceptions of Tablet Use

Parents' Perceptions. When asked about the general advantages and disadvantages of tablet use for their child, the parents named different aspects. One advantage that almost all parents perceive, especially from their point of view, is the aspect of children's occupation by the device. Many parents report that they use this time to complete their own tasks or take care of younger siblings. However, some parents also pointed out that they do take advantage of this opportunity, but do not necessarily feel good about it. Another advantage mentioned by the majority of parents is the introduction of children to the digital world through the use, as it is important for them that their children develop digital skills. Easy access to a wide range of fun and diverse entertainment options is also stated as a benefit by many parents. In addition, the mobility of the device, the development of personal interests, and the encouragement to focus on a particular activity are mentioned by individual parents as benefits of tablet use.

Learning opportunities, as well as the discovery of information, are also perceived as positive aspects of the devices by a large majority of parents. In this context, explicit learning applications, but also the content of videos or game applications play a role. Parents mentioned, for example, educational TV shows or explanatory videos for children, as well as applications that provide knowledge about colors, shapes or everyday life activities. But it is important to mention that, specifically with younger children, who often do not yet use explicit learning applications, parents strongly limit the importance of the devices in the overall context of learning and perceive it as a minor additional contribution to other learning opportunities: *"So, in comparison to the other things she does, for example, what she learns at daycare or what she learns at home, a very minor role. So, yes, there are learning aspects as well, but they play a relatively minor role"* (Mother A).

The parents also see negative aspects of children's tablet use. All parents mentioned that they limit the amount of children's time of use because otherwise the children often become restless, frustrated or tired. Since many of the children would like to use the devices for longer, this sometimes leads to conflicts. Some parents also mention the risk of online content that is not suitable for children. As their children's use of the devices is currently very limited, they do not see this as an urgent problem but feel that they will need to address it at a later time.

Children's Perceptions. In general, the children have a very positive perception of the tablet. They like most of the activities with the device, especially watching videos, playing with game applications and taking photos or making videos, which no child, who already engaged in these activities, rated negatively. Individual activities that are evaluated negatively by some children include communicating with others via mobile devices. In the case of Henrik (6), this explicitly applies only to talking to other people, but he likes sending emojis. Ben (4) and Elias (5) expressed that they do not like listening to music via the device. Other activities such as drawing, learning with learning applications or listening to audio books were each rated negatively in individual cases. This is consistent with the descriptions during the parent interviews, which gave the impression that the children usually enjoy using the equipment very much.

The positive perception is also confirmed by the short parent-child-interviews. When asked what they like about the tablet and what their favorite activity with the device is, all children responded with activities they do frequently with the devices and rated positively during the mini-questionnaire. When asked what they do not like about the tablet, some children answered exclusively or at first that there is nothing they do not like about the device. When pointed out by their parents, a few children agreed that they sometimes have trouble navigating the devices. Furthermore, some children named individual activities that they do not like with the tablet, which is consistent with the evaluation of activities during the questionnaire. Henrik (6) is only bothered by the fact that he often drops the tablet, and his following answer shows that, overall, he likes using the tablet very much: *"What I find stupid about the iPad is that Mama always says…I'm not allowed to watch iPad while eating"* (Henrik).

The last question of the parent-child-interview was related to the aspect of learning and knowledge acquisition via the tablet, asking the children if they had ever learned something new through the device and, if so, what this was. This question was not easy to answer for many children, possibly due to the abstract nature of the concept of learning. However, Ben (4) and Denise (5) were able to think of something they had learned through the tablet: Ben had learned via a video how human muscles work and shared that he now does muscle training himself. Denise remembered that her mother had looked up for her that the sea wasp is one of the most dangerous animals in the world. With the help of their parents, other children were also able to remember things they had learned using the tablet, such as animal sounds or general information about animals and their way of life*: "Haven't you watched some documentaries…?"* (Father C) *"Yes! Right. About cheetahs"* (Cara). A few children also thought of things they had learned about using the tablet, such as the access code or that it should not get wet. However, some children also answered this question negatively or could not think of an example of something they learned through the device.

The "dream tablets" designed by the children also provide interesting insights into their perspectives on the devices. Due to the heterogeneity and complexity of the related data, this task can only be presented very briefly here. Generally, it can be stated that many of the children based their creations on topics, applications or activities that they positively associate with the devices. Some of the children also developed ideas for game applications or added features to their devices that the regular tablet does not have, such as magical powers. Figure 4 shows the example of Denise's (5) "dream tablet", which she would like to use for watching videos, painting pictures and doing magic, but also for learning more about numbers and characters.

Fig. 4. "Dream tablet" created by Denise (5).

5 Discussion

Similar to earlier research [22], the results show that the families in the sample use mobile devices for intentional information search activities for their children. Most parents consider online services, such as search engines and educational videos that can be accessed via mobile devices, to be helpful to address their children's information needs. However, the interviews with the parents show that, mainly due to the children's limited writing and reading skills, these search activities are carried out by parents or older siblings, acting as information mediaries [29] for the children. Furthermore, the families predominantly use smartphones instead of tablets for this purpose. An interesting topic in the context of children's intentional information search with digital devices is the use of smart speaker systems based on voice interaction. In the families where such devices are used by the children, they occasionally turn to the devices with questions. With the further distribution of these devices, an interesting field of research in connection with children's intentional information discovery may emerge, as initial studies [30, 31] already show.

Some of the families, especially those with older children, also use tablets for explicit learning activities, such as first math or alphabet exercises. The process of learning is clearly related to the topic of information behavior and must, therefore, also be considered in this context.

Regarding accidental information discovery, the exchange with parents and children indicates that children also gain new information via the tablet through entertaining activities such as watching educational TV programs and documentaries for children or playing with game applications that deal with everyday life topics. As argued by the author before [3], this shows that the boundaries between entertainment and information are fluid and that these activities should also be regarded as part of children's information behavior.

These results show that the distinction emphasized by Wilson [5] between intentional and accidental discovery of information can be applied to children's information behavior in the context of mobile device use.

In relation to parents' and children's perceptions of the tablet, both seem to perceive the device primarily as an entertainment medium which is in line with previous studies [20–24]. Overall, the children expressed very positive perceptions, which are strongly shaped by their favorite entertainment activities. The possibility of learning new things does not yet seem to be strongly associated with the devices for most of the children but some of them were able to name, either independently or with the support of their parents, examples of things they learned through the tablet.

Most parents' statements were also dominated by children's entertainment activities with the tablet. Furthermore, they mentioned the aspect of children's occupation by the device as a general advantage of use. Parents also see the tablet as a tool for discovering information and learning but many of them rate the importance of the device in this area as being rather low, compared to interpersonal interactions or analog media as sources of information. In some interviews, it became apparent that this may be partly due to the young age of the children, and that some parents can imagine an increased use of the device for learning as well as for a more independent acquiring of information at an advanced age.

6 Conclusion

This study examined how children aged four to six years use mobile devices, especially tablets, and whether this use includes activities that can be linked to the discovery of information. Furthermore, it investigated whether aspects related to children's information behavior play a role in parents' and children's perceptions of tablet use. The multi-method and interactive *Mosaic approach* was applied for an exploratory data collection with eight families from Germany.

The results show that mobile devices play a role in the discovery of information by young children. Via the tablet, children primarily discover information rather accidentally while watching videos or playing with game applications. For the intentional discovery of information, smartphones are more likely to be used, with parents or older siblings acting as information mediaries. This is primarily explained by children's limited writing and reading skills, which indicates that an increased adoption of smart speaker systems may lead to interesting developments in this area. With regard to the perceptions of tablet use by parents and children, it appears that the devices are mainly associated with entertainment and fun, although parents in particular also recognize the potential of the devices in the area of learning and information discovery.

The limitations of this study also have to be mentioned. The small and relatively homogenous sample does not allow for the generalization of the results. All participating families were relatively well equipped with mobile devices. The parents interviewed were all regular users of such devices and had generally positive attitudes towards their children's device use. For families with lower levels of technology equipment and parental use, different results may be found. Furthermore, the COVID-19 pandemic led to various limitations in relation to the recruitment of participants as well as the data collection. For example, parents' interviewing and guiding of the data collection may have influenced the results. Opportunities for reflexive discussion of the results with the families were also limited by the pandemic situation. Regarding data analysis, it should be noted that the coding was performed by only one researcher.

Nevertheless, this study offers a multi-perspective and diverse insight into young children's use of mobile devices and adds to the research on children's digital information behavior. Of particular value is the inclusion of young children's perspectives, which are still understudied in information behavior research. Therefore, this study will serve as a starting point to apply the developed instruments of data collection on a larger scale to further increase the inclusion of young children's voices in this field.

Acknowledgements. The author gratefully acknowledges the financial support of *Humboldt-Innovation*, a subsidiary-company of Humboldt-Universität zu Berlin, for this study. The author would like to thank the families who volunteered for this study.

Appendix 1: Parent-Interview Guide

Introduction of the Family

– At the beginning of this interview, would you please introduce your family to me?

Child(ren) *(ask if necessary)*

- How old is your child (in months)?
- How is your child cared for in day-to-day life? Does he/she go to kindergarten or daycare?

  – Are digital devices used with the children at these places?

- Do you have other children?
- How old are they (in months)?

Parents *(ask if necessary)*

- Do you have a partner who also takes care of the children?

Use of and Attitude Toward Digital Mobile Devices by Parents

– There are many different digital mobile devices in most households now, *e.g.*, smartphones, tablets, laptops, e-book readers, etc. How would you describe your own use of digital mobile devices? *(Checklist I)* (Table 2)

Table 2. Checklist I: Use of digital mobile devices by parent/s and child.

Mobile device	Parent/s	Child
Tablet		
Smartphone		
Laptop		
E-book-reader		
Other?		

– And how would you describe your attitude toward the use of digital devices in general?
– *(If applicable)* Is this similar in the case of your partner or different?

Use of Digital Mobile Devices, Especially Tablet, by Child

- We just talked about your use of digital mobile devices. What mobile devices does your child use at home? *(Checklist I)*
- Are there other places where your child uses digital mobile devices? *If yes:* Which digital mobile devices? What does your child do with these devices?
- In this interview, I want to focus primarily on your child's use of the tablet. However, if it makes sense to you, feel free to mention other digital mobile devices. How long has your child been using the tablet, approximately?
- How often does your child typically use the tablet, approximately?
- And how long does your child typically use the tablet at a time, approximately?
- Does your child usually use the tablet independently or together with you?
- How do you assess your child's skills in using the tablet?
- What does your child do with the tablet, either independently or together with you (also with other digital mobile devices)? *(Checklist II)*

Checklist II: Child's Activities

- ☐ Watching videos, movies or TV series
- ☐ Looking at photos or watching videos you have taken yourself
- ☐ Playing with game apps
- ☐ Listening to music
- ☐ Listening to audio books
- ☐ Reading or reading aloud
- ☐ Taking photos or making videos
- ☐ Painting or drawing
- ☐ Making music
- ☐ Learning, *e.g.*, with educational apps
- ☐ Searching for information, *e.g.*, via search engines like *Google* or other Websites
  - ☐ *If yes:* What were you and your child searching for?
- ☐ Talking or texting with other people
- ☐ Talking with *Siri*, *Alexa* or *Google*, *i.e.*, the smart assistant

- What would you say is your child's current favourite activity with the tablet?
- Have there been any developments in this context since your child started using the device? If yes, could you describe them to me?
- Have there been any changes in your child's use of the tablet as a result of the COVID-19 pandemic? If yes, could you describe them to me?

Parents' Perceptions of Their Child's Tablet Use

- From your perspective as (a) parent(s), are there any positive aspects of your child's use of the tablet for you? If yes, what are they?
- And do you see any negative aspects of its use? If yes, can you describe them to me in more detail?

The Tablet as a Learning and Information Environment

- Do you think the tablet plays a role for your child in learning new things?
  - *If yes:* In what ways?
  - *If no:* Why not?
- And what about acquiring new information or knowledge? Do you think the tablet plays a role here?
  - *If yes:* In what ways?
  - *If no:* Why not?

Conclusion

- Is there anything else you would like to know from me or you would like to add?

Appendix 2: Questions for Parent-Child-Interview

1. What do you like about the tablet?
2. What is your favorite thing to do with the tablet?
3. Is there anything you don't like about the tablet?
4. Have you ever learned something new through the tablet? If so, what was that?

References

1. Burford, S., Park, S.: The impact of mobile tablet devices on human information behaviour. J. Document. **70**(4), 622–639 (2014)
2. Rideout, V., Robb, M.B.: The Common Sense Census: Media Use by Kids Age Zero to Eight. Common Sense Media, San Francisco (2020)
3. Schlebbe, K.: Watching, playing, making, learning: young children's use of mobile devices. In: Sundqvist, A., Berget, G., Nolin, J., Skjerdingstad, K. (eds.) Sustainable Digital Communities. iConference 2020, LNCS, vol. 12051, pp. 288–296. Springer, Cham (2020). https://doi.org/10.1007/978-3-030-43687-2
4. Barriage, S.: 'Talk, talk and more talk': parental perceptions of young children's information practices related to their hobbies and interests. Inf. Res. **21**(3), 721 (2016)

5. Wilson, T.D.: Exploring Information Behavior: An Introduction. Preliminary edn. T.D. Wilson, Sheffield (2020)
6. Clark, A.: Listening to Young Children. The Mosaic Approach. 3rd edn. Jessica Kingsley Publishers, London (2017)
7. Farrell, D.G.: Library and information needs of young children. In: Cuadra, C.A., Bates, M.J. (eds.) Library and Information Service Needs of the Nation: Proceedings of a Conference on the Needs of Occupational, Ethnic, and Other Groups in the United States, pp. 1421–1454. US Government Printing Office, Washington (1974)
8. Walter, V.A.: The information needs of children. Adv. Librariansh. **18**, 111–129 (1994)
9. McKechnie, L.: Opening the "preschoolers' door to learning": an ethnographic study of the use of public libraries by preschool girls. Doctoral Dissertation, University of Western Ontario, London, Ontario (1996)
10. Agosto, D.E., Hughes-Hassell, S.: People, places, and questions: an investigation of the everyday life information-seeking behaviors of urban young adults. Libr. Inf. Sci. Res. **27**(2), 141–163 (2005)
11. Bilal, D., Kirby, J.: Differences and similarities in information seeking: children and adults as Web users. Inf. Process. Manage. **38**(5), 649–670 (2002)
12. Cooper, L.Z.: A case study of information-seeking behavior in 7-year-old children in a semistructured situation. J. Am. Soc. Inform. Sci. Technol. **53**(11), 904–922 (2002)
13. Foss, E., et al.: Children's search roles at home: implications for designers, researchers, educators, and parents. J. Am. Soc. Inform. Sci. Technol. **63**(3), 558–573 (2012)
14. Meyers, E.M., Fisher, K.E., Marcoux, E.: Making sense of an information world: the everyday-life information behavior of preteens. Lib. Quart. **79**(3), 301–341 (2009)
15. Vanderschantz, N., Hinze, A., Cunningham, S.J.: "Sometimes the internet reads the question wrong": children's search strategies and difficulties. Proc. Am. Soc. Inf. Sci. Technol. **51**(1), 1–10 (2014)
16. Shenton, A.K., Dixon, P.: Just what is information anyway? Some findings of research with school pupils. Educ. Libr. J. **46**(3), 5–14 (2003)
17. Spink, A., Heinström, J.: Information behaviour development in early childhood. In: Spink, A., Heinström, J. (eds.) New Directions in Information Behaviour, pp. 245–256. Bingley, Emerald (2011)
18. Agarwal, N.K.: Use of touch devices by toddlers or preschoolers: observations and findings from a single-case study. In: Bilal, D., Beheshti, J. (eds.) New Directions in Children's and Adolescent's Information Behavior Research, pp. 3–37. Bingley, Emerald (2014)
19. Given, L., Winkler, D.C., Willson, R., Davidson, C., Danby, S., Thorpe, K.: Watching young children "play" with information technology: everyday life information seeking in the home. Lib. Inf. Sci. Res. **38**(4), 344–352 (2016)
20. Chen, W., Teo, M.H., Nguyen, D.: Singapore parents' use of digital devices with young children: motivations and uses. Asia Pac. Educ. Res. **28**, 239–250 (2019)
21. Papadakis, S., Zaranis, N., Kalogiannakis, M.: Parental involvement and attitudes towards young Greek children's mobile usage. Int. J. Child-Comput. Interact. **22**, 1–14 (2019)
22. Chaudron, S., et al.: Young Children (0–8) and Digital Technology: A Qualitative Exploratory Study Across Seven Countries. EUR 27052. Publications Office of the European Union, Luxembourg (2015)
23. Eisen, S., Lillard, A.S.: Young children's thinking about touchscreens versus other media in the US. J. Child. Media **11**(2), 167–179 (2017)
24. Dias, P., Brito, R.: "The Tablet Is My Best Friend!": Practices and perceptions of young children and their parents. In: Holloway, D., Willson, M., Murcia, K., Archer, C., Stocco, F. (eds.) Young Children's Rights in a Digital World. CWIR, vol. 23, pp. 17–28. Springer, Cham (2021). https://doi.org/10.1007/978-3-030-65916-5_2

25. Schlebbe, K.: Support versus restriction: parents' influence on young children's information behaviour in connection with mobile devices. In: Proceedings of ISIC, the Information Behaviour Conference, Information Research, vol. 25, no. 4, isic2006 (2020)
26. Shenton, A.K.: Etic, emic, or both? A fundamental decision for researchers of young people's information needs. New Rev. Child. Literat. Librariansh. **16**(1), 54–67 (2010)
27. Clark, A.: Listening to and involving young children: a review of research and practice. Early Child Dev. Care **175**(6), 489–505 (2005)
28. Saldaña, J.: The Coding Manual for Qualitative Researchers, 2nd edn. Sage, Thousand Oaks (2013)
29. Abrahamson, J.A., Fisher, K.E.: 'What's past is prologue': towards a general model of lay information mediary behaviour. Inf. Res. **12**(4), Colis15 (2007)
30. Oranç, C., Ruggeri, A.: "Alexa, let me ask you something different" Children's adaptive information search with voice assistants. Hum. Behav. Emerg. Technol. **3**(4), 595–605 (2021)
31. Radford, M., Floegel, D., Barriage, S., Houli, D.: "Alexa, where do babies come from?" Investigating children's practices with intelligent personal assistants. In: ALISE 2019 Conference Proceedings, pp. 148–152 (2019)

Conversational Interaction with Historical Figures: What's It Good For?

Xin Qian(✉), Douglas W. Oard, and Joel Chan

University of Maryland, College Park 20740, USA
{xinq,oard,joelchan}@umd.edu

Abstract. Historical records can tell us about the knowledge, opinions, and actions of individuals, but direct use of historical records is a complex process that is better attuned to the needs of scholars than the interests of the general public. This paper explores the potential for conversational interaction with representations of historical figures that are constructed from primary and secondary source materials. An interview study, supported by a computational prototype as a provocation, is used to elicit expert assessments of the potential uses of such systems in historical museums. Qualitative analysis of study results reveals three broad classes of design implications: situating design in archival assurance, creating immersive user experiences, and supporting active inquiries.

Keywords: Information retrieval · Question answering · Digital archives · Cultural institutions · Natural language dialogue

1 Introduction

Over the last two decades of the 20th century, the General Electric corporation advertised using the slogan "We bring good things to life!" By this, they meant both that they gave life to good things (precisely, machines), and that those good things could enrich people's lives. Now, two decades after GE retired the slogan, we stand at the verge of a third possible meaning as we begin to draw on the vast digital and digitizable traces that people have left behind to reanimate some aspects of their lives. In particular, we are interested in providing the possibility of conducting meaningful and informative conversations with historical figures who are no longer alive, and thus no longer able to speak for themselves.

Since the inception of writing, people have left written traces of some of their activities. Over time, those traces have been enriched in many ways, both in content and form, to the point where today we have not just written records but also spoken records and vast stores of digital activity records. Not all of this makes it into the future in a usable form, but today's profusion of digital content, coupled with the rapidly declining costs of storage, make it likely that very substantial quantities will. The usual way of using this information involves three distinct steps: first finding that which might be expected to be useful, then assimilating what actually is useful from among what's found, and

M. Smits (Ed.): iConference 2022, LNCS 13193, pp. 32–49, 2022.
https://doi.org/10.1007/978-3-030-96960-8_3

finally using what has been learned in some way [26]. Iteratively applying such a process effectively is an acquired skill, and thus it is no surprise that doctoral students are typically better at it than high school students [14,19]. There are, however, many more high school students than there are doctoral students, suggesting that there might be a market for approaches that allow people to interact somewhat more naturally with the historical record. The search-assimilate-apply process dates back a few millennia to the invention of archives [18], and later of libraries [40]. However, humans have been optimized by evolution to acquire and assimilate information through conversation since perhaps hundreds of millennia before that. Our goal, therefore, is to support conversational interaction with representations of historical figures from our past.

When a conversational agent emulates the interaction style of someone who is no longer alive, this has been called "virtual immortality" [5]. Early systems that demonstrated the potential for conversations with historical figures such as Charles Darwin [50] or Richard Nixon [12] were hand-engineered, able to support a conversation with a specific figure on a limited range of topics. However, two technologies are now converging to permit broader support for these kinds of conversational interaction. One thread is a type of knowledge-grounded conversational agent that has led to systems that are today popularly referred to as "retrieval-based chatbots" [55]. The key idea in a retrieval-based chatbot is that when the system reaches a point in a conversation where it needs some information, it turns to a search engine to find what it needs [15]. For a simple example, ask Amazon's Alexa where the third-largest pyramid is; Alexa will tell you that it found the answer on the Web. The second thread is a line of work on automated style rewriting in which the goal is to transform written or spoken content into forms of expression that more closely resemble those of some specific person. A third piece of the puzzle that makes it possible to connect these two lines of work is the increasing availability of content in both digital and digitized primary and secondary sources. We can use all of that content as a basis for retrieval, and we can use the first-person writing and speaking we find there as a basis for rewriting retrieved content into a form that the person we wish to represent might actually have produced.

The fact that we could now build such systems leads to the question of whether we should. That question, in turn, raises at least two concerns. First, what would we do with such a system—what purposes could it serve? Our principal goal in this paper is to explore that question in the context of one type of cultural heritage institution: a history museum. A second equally important question is how best to navigate the critical ethical questions that arise. We would, after all, essentially be putting words in the mouth of the historical figure, and we would be doing so with imperfect technology that might sometimes hallucinate things that they would not actually have said. We largely leave questions about how best to address such concerns to future work, noting here only that Amazon's Alexa points to one possible approach—be clear with those who use your system, what you are doing, and how you are doing it.

With that as background, the remainder of this paper is organized as follows. The next section reviews related work on virtual immortality, retrieval-based chatbots, and style rewriting. We then describe a text collection, and a system to retrieve content from that collection that we created to illustrate what might be possible. We used the system as a boundary object [51] to facilitate an interview study in which four academic experts in libraries, archives, and museums reacted to our vision, and to our initial prototype's embodiment of some aspects of that vision, offering their ideas on how such systems might actually be used. We conclude with a qualitative analysis of the results of that study.

2 Related Work

In this section, we review related work on virtual immortality, retrieval-based chatbots, and style rewriting.

2.1 Virtual Immortality Demonstration Systems

Virtual immortality is a rather grand name for systems that have sought to demonstrate the potential for conversing with representations of specific people, specifically historical figures or fictitious characters [5,38,47]. To date, all such systems have been hand-engineered, with curated content that is designed to answer questions that the designers anticipate might be asked. Prominent examples include a systems that can respond with recordings of actors playing Charles Darwin's [50] or Albert Einstein's ghost [33], a virtual President Nixon [12], interactive storytelling by Holocaust survivors [2,3,52], a representation of the playwright August Strindberg serving as a tour guide for Stockholm [6,24], and a fictional character (Sergeant Blackwell) who answers questions after a training session [31]. Figure 1 summarizes some the characteristics of these systems.

2.2 Retrieval-Based Chatbots

Retrieval-based chatbots are a flexible approach to building automated systems for conversational text interactions that can converse knowledgeably with people on a range of topics. The responses generated by a retrieval-based chatbot are typically based on existing material found in some text collection(s), perhaps augmented by content from a database or knowledge graph [54]. There has been evolutionary development from single-turn question answering [15,41,54] to multi-turn conversations [55]. One approach to developing such systems has therefore been to first build systems that do well at retrieving the right response for a single turn, and then to extend that system to interpret subsequent user requests in the context of prior user requests and system responses. The key to that first step, successfully retrieving a suitable response, lies in matching user requests with candidate responses from the collection. The matching problem is core to research in information retrieval (IR), and in particular the sub-field of open-domain question answering (QA) [53]. State-of-the-art QA systems build

	Charles Darwin's Ghost (Same applies to Albert Einstein's)	Ask the President	New Dimension in Testimony (NDT)	August System	Sergeant Blackwell
Figure	Charles Darwin	President Nixon	Holocaust survivors	August Strindberg	Sergeant Blackwell
Real records?	Curated: writers create the narratives	Video sequences	Yes, elicited w/ protocol in film studios	Curated	Fictional
Scope of answerable questions	Any of 199 questions, from philosophical to personal	Any of 280 questions	Questions that are answerable by recorded dialogs	Restaurants and facilities in Stockholm, information about KTH, the research, the system, and August Strindberg	57 pre-defined subject lines including the identity of the character, its origin, and questions about the training

Fig. 1. Virtual immortality demonstration systems.

on neural "deep learning" BERT (Bidirectional Encoder Representations from Transformers) models that use self-attention to model both the linguistic context of each question and document term and relationships between terms that appear in questions and terms that appear in documents [16]. These deep learning models are trained on massive quantities of language use, including many examples of questions and answers, and they have demonstrated substantially better accuracy [32] than traditional retrieval techniques based on question rewriting and term matching [46]. However, the massively interconnected self-attention networks in BERT result in slower system response, so the usual approach is to do an initial rapid search and then further refine that smaller set of search results using BERT. This is the approach taken by monoBERT [36], which we use in Sect. 3.

2.3 Style Rewriting

The general goal of style rewriting is to change the form of a passage of text or speech to match specific style requirements of an application [20]. Early work on this task used hand-crafted rules to perform, for example, paraphrase and simplification [11]. More recent models have used statistical approaches, for example, guided by a word co-occurrence graph learned from a large collection of text in the desired style [4,28]. As with QA, the most recent work uses Transformer-based models for sequence-to-sequence transfer, treating style rewriting in a manner akin to the way that modern systems like Google Translate convert text from one language to another. Such techniques have been used to transfer text into styles used by characters from "Star Trek" [28] or those of more abstract personas [49]. Similar techniques have also been used to rewrite text with specific degrees of formality [42] or to obfuscate gender [43]. We have not implemented style rewriting for the prototype described in Sect. 3, but such a capability will ultimately be necessary for deployed systems.

3 A Chatbot Prototype

To illustrate some of the capabilities we ultimately envision providing to participants in our interview study, we started by assembling a text collection for one historical figure whom we expected our participants would know sufficiently well. We first describe the materials that we collected, and then how we used those materials to build a single-turn retrieval-based chatbot.

3.1 President Reagan Collection

In the United States, presidential libraries typically co-locate a historical museum built around the legacy of a presidential administration with the National Archives and Records Administration (NARA) staff that manages the records of that administration. Materials from these presidential libraries are naturally of interest to scholars (e.g., [34,45]), but for our present purpose it is the museum function of a presidential library that most interests us. The libraries of more recent presidents hold larger quantities of digital and digitized records, but it is the records of administrations further in the past that are able to provide access to the largest fractions of their holdings. There is thus currently a sweet spot that starts roughly with the Carter administration and continues through roughly the Clinton administration from which substantial digital or digitized materials are now available. Among that window, we chose to work with records from the Reagan administration, the first of the two-term (i.e., 8-year) administrations.

Table 1. Statistics of the President Reagan collection.

Document type	Count
Public papers documents	8,148
Personal diary entries	2,902
Interview transcripts	248

The Ronald Reagan Presidential Library and Museum website[1] contains records of the Reagan Administration from 1981 to 1989, such as speeches and reports, records of the President's daily activities, and donated personal collections. Additionally, there are a number of secondary sources on President Reagan that draw on these materials, including a biography [7] and an annotated collection of Reagan's letters [48] that can be used for research purposes (without public redistribution) under the fair use provisions of U.S. copyright law. We

[1] https://www.reaganlibrary.gov/.

Table 2. Some questions that could be asked of the President Reagan collection.

Question type	Example
Domestic policy	*What do you think employment levels will be next year?*
International policy	*How will the United States deal with Cuba?*
News event	*What do you think of Doonesbury's critiques of you?*
Personal affairs	*How would you like to be remembered?*

assembled from these Web and published materials a diverse text collection of substantial size that can provide different types of insights into President Reagan's thinking and his statements. Table 1 gives statistics of the collection that we assembled.

3.2 A Prototype Single-Turn Chatbot

The goal of the chatbot that we created for this study was to retrieve content relevant to user questions for a single conversation turn. Given a user question, the system uses two sequential components, the first of which seeks to find passages (i.e., parts of documents) that contain an answer, and the second of which seeks to extract the best answer from a retrieved passage. Figure 2 illustrates this framework. A user question can be on any aspect of Reagan's experiences or attitudes that are documented in the collection (see Table 2 for examples).

Retrieval. The retrieval component first uses non-neural relevance matching to get an initial set of highly ranked passages, and then it reranks those passages with a neural text matching model [37]. To accommodate the length limitations of the computationally complex reranker, all documents in the collection are first segmented into 300-word passages, which are indexed for efficient term-matching retrieval using ElasticSearch v.6.5.4. Reranking is performed using monoBERT [36], a neural, Transformer-based BERT text matching model [16].

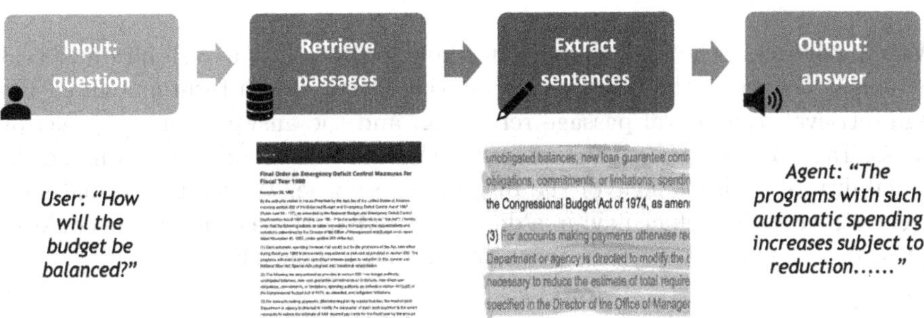

Fig. 2. The chatbot prototype uses two sequential components, retrieve and extract.

monoBERT is fine-tuned on the MS MARCO passage retrieval task, and therefore re-purposed for pointwise classification of passage relevance. We use a BERT-base version of monoBERT as the reranker, made available by the original authors.[2] The inputs to the reranker are a concatenation of the user's question with each passage. The reranker cross-encodes the inputs. The output is a matching score for that question-passage pair. Passages that had been ranked highly by ElasticSearch get reranked by the reranker. The scores by the reranker are sorted such that passages most likely to contain an answer are at the top of the resulting ranked list.

Extraction. The second component extracts relevant sentences from retrieved passages. We model our approach on techniques used in the Machine Reading Comprehension (MRC) task in open-domain question answering [13], which seeks to extract relevant spans from a specified text as answers to an input question. While the more general MRC setting allows spans of arbitrary length (but usually just several words) as answers, our current implementation extracts spans at the sentence level, as an answer sentence selection task [56]. Since the participants in our study could examine sentences that precede and follow the selected sentence, we felt that a sentence selection task would suffice to support our study. For an answer sentence selection task, WikiQA [56] provides a suitable data collection to train a model for this component. It includes 3,047 questions from Wikipedia-related user questions sampled from Bing query logs, paired with a total of 29,258 sentences from summary paragraphs in Wikipedia pages. The extraction model to train on this data collection is again a neural, Transformer-based BERT text matching model. We use the Huggingface's transformers library[3] v2.4.1 to fine-tune it as a classification task ourselves, with the default training procedure and hyperparameters. Same as how the retrieval component's neural text matching model gets fine-tuned, the extraction model cross-encodes the user's question with each sentence from a passage, and then predicts a label. At inference time, the model works with the user's question and each sentence from retrieved passages of the Presidential Reagan collection. We use spaCy [27] v2.2.4, specifically its Sentencizer module, to identify the sentences in each passage.

Web Interface. The final component of our prototype is a Web interface that incrementally shows the results of the initial ElasticSearch term-matching passage retrieval, the neural passage reranking, and the answer sentence selection stages. Table 3 summarizes the typical time between issuing the question and the availability of each element of the displayed response. We focus here on effectiveness rather than efficiency; in a deployed system, these components could be optimized for efficient response, with sub-second latency (Fig. 3).

[2] https://github.com/nyu-dl/dl4marco-bert.
[3] https://huggingface.co/transformers/.

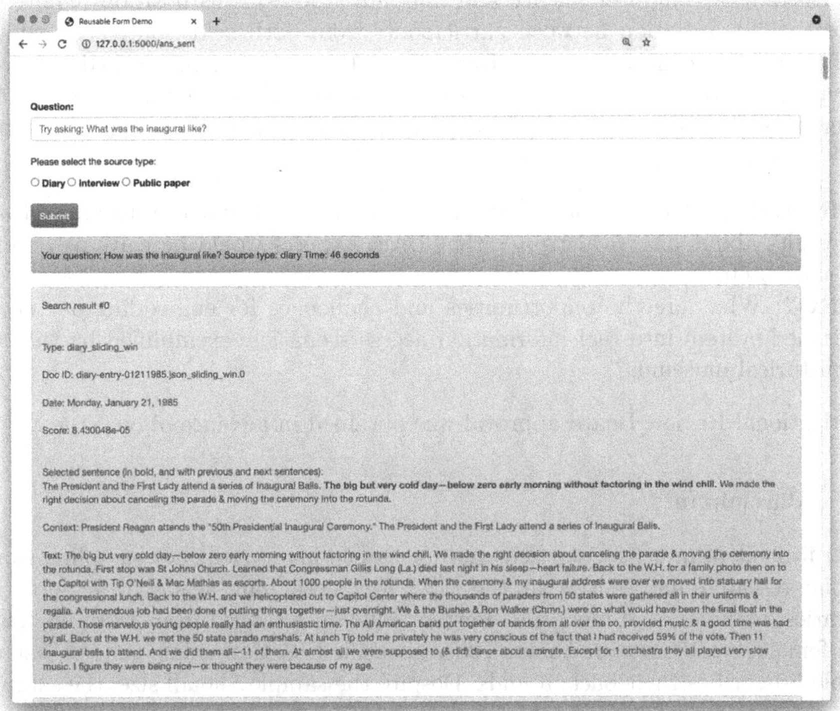

Fig. 3. The prototype Web interface. This screenshot shows the final stage, answer sentence selection, on diaries.

4 Expert Interviews

Historical museum exhibits impart a presentation of history to visitors to fulfill a role of public education, to which selected artifacts from the collection of historical figures contribute. We chose a presidential library as a putative setting for our envisioned system. This setting occupies a middle ground in a continuum of scenarios for accessing the legacy of historical figures, ranging from formal learning, to everyday entertainment. How can systems of the type we envision support information access in this setting? The system also sits at an

Table 3. Empirical differences between three elements of the prototype.

	Passage retrieval		Answer sentence selection
	Non-neural term-matching	Neural reranking	
Format	Passage of up to 300 words		Single sentence
Response time	~0 s	10–15 s	~60 s

intersection of computer science and museum studies. This position requires a substantial translation between participants from both fields, only after which a shared vision can emerge [51]. To facilitate this translation, we used our prototype as a boundary object to support in-depth, semi-structured, contextual interviews [17,30] with academic experts in libraries, archives, and museums (LAM). Our research questions were:

- **RQ1:** Could the envisioned system, as demonstrated by our prototype, return results about historical figures that LAM experts would perceive as potentially useful?
- **RQ2:** What are the opportunities and challenges for embedding our envisioned system into real information access scenarios, exemplified by that of historical museums?

Institutional Review Board approval was obtained in advance of our study.

4.1 Participants

Recruitment of interview participants was based on convenience sampling from public research universities in the US. We chose four academic experts in libraries, archives, and museums. Participants' ages ranged from 18 to 66. Two are female, while two are male. Three identified as Caucasian, one as Asian. Table 4 describes their backgrounds. Despite the sample's small size, the sample has diversity regarding individual expertise.

Table 4. Biographical sketch and research focus (rephrased for anonymity) for each participant.

ID	Biographical sketch	Research focus
P1	Female, Ph.D., English literature	Designing digital systems for trans-media storytelling in the virtual world
P2	Male, J.D.	Public access to archival materials, including presidential library materials
P3	Male, Ph.D., Information Studies; Graduate certificate in Museum Studies	Understanding, access and use of cultural heritage collections
P4	Female, Ph.D., Museum Anthropology	How technologies could enable heritage institutions to share knowledge with communities

4.2 Interview Protocol

Each participant scheduled a one-to-one interview with the first author of this paper through email, and the interview was conducted remotely using Zoom. Interviews were audio- and screen-recorded. Each interview lasted approximately 45 min, with no monetary compensation.

The interview began with a tutorial video about the prototype system. The participant then tried the live system, but verbally speaking questions that the interviewer typed on their behalf. The participant and the interviewer then together inspected the results from each stage as they appeared. Participants were asked to think aloud to give their reactions to the results.

After using the prototype, the interviewer and participant began a semi-structured interview conversation. The conversation began with a general question about their impression towards the system: *"What kind of challenges and/or value do you see in a system like this?"* To foster a natural conversational flow, the interviewer often prompted participants to elaborate on their answers from perspectives related to their own expertise. In addition to questions tailored to participants' experience, the interview also included a small set of more general questions that could be asked wherever appropriate, often as follow-ups to capture participants' passing thoughts in earlier responses. For example, *"How do museums engage visitors, of whom a large body only made a single visit, in a longer connection to the museum's subject?"* could be asked if the participant mentioned museum visitors; *"Text answers can be in the form of long-form narratives. What strategies do museums use to efficiently and effectively present them,"* could be asked if the conversation reached a visual aspect of museum exhibitions; or *"Museum visitors receive information from curated contents on display, how do museums decide those contents?"* could be asked if topics related to curation arose. These procedures were documented in an interview guide.

4.3 Analysis Approach

Overall, the analysis approach was based on iterative open-coding. The data for this was four interviews of a total duration of 3 h and 7 min, auto-transcribed. An initial pass of memoing happened during and right after each interview, where the interviewer took margin notes and then created a bullet-point summary on the printed interview guide. The notes include questions answered versus skipped, terms mentioned in participants' responses to describe or pinpoint references, and general observations. Answered interview questions from early interviews partially informed the types of questions answerable and interesting for later interviews, especially for experts with similar research directions (e.g., P3 to P4).

The four interview transcripts were imported to NVIVO v.1.4.1, then each was open-coded in separate sessions and in reverse order of interviewing (i.e., P4 to P1), to identify themes. In these open-coding sessions, the first author of this paper tagged related text spans with initial codes. Operations included creating new codes or grouping spans into existing codes. Some initial codes adopted the exact wording as noted in memos. Grouping into existing codes often involved cross-checks with the code's existing text spans, and slight updates to the code. The author decided span boundaries usually as turn-taking points, or at transition phrases, such as *"and I think [PAUSE]"* or *"if that makes sense"*. Some initial codes from these sessions included *"controversy in archives: ownership"* and *"archives need language (later revised as, cross-lingual) support"*. Each open-coding session was considered completed when the author perceived both a reasonable coverage of coded spans and an exhaustion of discovering existing or new codes throughout an entire transcript.

A more focused coding session was then conducted on the tagged initial codes. This was an iterative process that aimed towards highest-level implications, engaging with the raw text spans as "data", in the context of each participants' background and interests. It yielded a nested structure from the initial codes, where top-level codes are close to the implications we summarize below in Sect. 4.6. A more refined sort-through adjusted that structure into a temporal or spatial logic sensible for presentation [8]. For example, P2 described a process for the inquiring users, while P3 and P4 thought through the question of who are the users. The author subsequently made the former code subsidiary to the later code.

The qualitative interviewing methodology requires describing the author's position as the research investigator, i.e., reflecting the researcher as the "instrument" for producing knowledge from personal narratives [8]. While the author doing the coding has expertise in system design and development and has been influenced by views of technologies as socially constructed [39], they lack systematic training in museum studies. A syllabus in museum studies[4] also informed the analysis.

4.4 Replicability

We acknowledge an inherent complexity in our interview study protocol, where the study both uses a computational prototype (an instrument novel in design), and recruits academic experts with specific expertise. Given these considerations, conceptual replication [1] would be appropriate. To support conceptual replication, we describe the prototype configuration (Sect. 3) and summarize domain experts' backgrounds and demographics (Sect. 4.1), while keeping confidential actual participant identities pursuant to our IRB-approved study protocol.

4.5 Results from the Prototype Exploration

On average, participants spent 11.3 min interacting with the system, and issued 1.5 questions. Participants asked questions impromptu (i.e., from the top of their minds) based on their past knowledge. Participants rarely commented directly about result quality being good, bad, relevant, or irrelevant. Instead, they often dug directly into result contents and spoke about insights. For example, upon seeing results that matched their expectation, P3 showed a contented smile and added that, *"Yeah, so say no to drugs was a popular slogan during the Reagan administration. So it was the Reagan project."* Subsequent conversations were positive towards the robustness of results. Half of the participants proactively connected or compared-and-contrasted the system with mainstream search engines (P1: *"If I were querying Google, I would expect to get many news*

[4] HIST 691: Museum Studies by Dr. Spencer R. Crew from George Mason University.

reports. What I might be able to extract from this system that I could not from Google is searching certain genres or types of information. And the addition of diaries could be very valuable..."; P2: "*Google and others have done smaller-scale projects... It seems that your project as the digitization initiatives scale up, would become much more interesting for researchers, but you have enough.*")

Despite the promising results, one noteworthy instance of poor results came in response to one question by P2. The question involved a named entity with a common English first name. Results mentioned a different person from Reagan's cabinet. P2 attached IR relevance as the meaning of result quality in the protocol, and pinpointed those results as "*false positives*". The error suggests that the system should adequately handle named entities due to the specificity of social circles in the materials of historical figures.

Overall, participants expressed a generally positive impression towards the system. P1 affirmed the value of a system that "*speaks from primary source information.*" P4 associated the system's functionality with a recent, massive full-text search tool—a platform that digitized books.[5] All participants articulated potential use cases for the system, including the system being a display for users to wrap up with summative questions at the end of an exhibition (P1), being an automated desk assistant in a museum library for locating materials in binder books (P2 and P3) and being an interface that indigenous leaders could use to distill cultural values from indigenous archive collections (P4). We unify these cases into themes to be taken as implications, and characterize the target user population throughout Sect. 4.6.

4.6 Design Implications

Analysis of the interview study identified three design implications.

Implication 1: Creating Immersive Experiences. Selecting museums as the venue underscores the importance of user experience design. P3 reflected that any possible means of visual design accompanying the textual content would enhance the system's value as a museum exhibit. P3 further suggested incorporating "*pictures, videos, maps, rather than just text,*" implying the multi-sensory requirement for effective interaction.

Some recent literature supplements P3's suggestion and highlights the importance of museums exhibiting continuity of time and place [10, 44] to contextualize the history, which we summarize as "in-the-moment." That phrasing differentiates this idea from well-implemented "of-the-moment" displays, such as the Colonial Williamsburg Visitor Center for the eve of the American Revolution. Featuring an "in-the-moment" experience might be appropriately sensible for a museum subject of historical figures. For example, visitors to the US Holocaust Memorial Museum in Washington, DC receive "identification cards" of Holocaust experiencers, to align their visit with experiencers' life narratives in

[5] https://opentexts.world/about.

sequence. If museum text materials have metadata annotations describing time and place, that could help instantiate several instances of our envisioned system for distribution across the physical museum layout. P1, an expert in digital humanities, directly pictured an "in-the-moment" system competency as if the retrieval system had provided time-travel immersion. Reading from retrieved texts, they reported that the system restored intensive memory, as if bringing them *"right back in a very emotional way"* to their earlier memories of the Reagan administration's silence on the AIDS epidemic.

Implication 2: Considering Archival Assurance. *Assurance* refers to steps that prove item value or physical existence, and records item information [21]. Reacting to the results of a query on Reagan's Berlin Wall address, P3 critiqued the contents for being potentially unverifiable by the user of such a system since *"no visitors in the museum will be actually in that Berlin Wall address!"*.

The diversity of issues that might arise precludes any universal solution. For example, arranging manuscripts into a public-facing collection sometimes involves more sensitive factors than the obvious format conversion operations [22]. Developing a conversational system on top of those public-facing collections without awareness of these factors could be problematic. P4 provided an example of this, noting that indigenous materials could have been illegally confiscated from tribal groups and removed from their original cultural contexts [25], and that *"the records are usually described by predominantly white institutions and white systems and often colonial systems, i.e., systems of power that do not tend to highlight those stories or those historical figures"*.

On a related point, gaps in the records that are available for digital processing could also be a concern. Digitization remains a continuing strategic challenge for archives [35]. Nowadays, public access to archives in a National Archives and Records Administration (NARA) research room still employs a system of notebooks and finding aids, making only limited use of computer databases (P2). Consistently, P4 noted that working with digitized text would be the first challenge, that currently *"very few archival collections are digitized ... at all, let alone transcribed or ... text searchable in any way."* On the other hand, there has been a significant focus on the processing of personal papers and manuscripts [22], where the duty is not exclusive to archivists. For example, between 1987 to 2018, the Einstein Papers Project[6] released multiple volumes of Einstein's writing and correspondence.

Implication 3: Engaging Inquiring Museum Visitors into Community-Based Scholar Roles. Many museums include a library room or reading room that provides access to related materials [9,23]. Visitors who read in these libraries are a specific population, active community members willing to spend additional time for more in-depth inquiry. For convenience, we describe them as "library room" scholars.

[6] https://www.einstein.caltech.edu/index.html.

Our envisioned system provides a progression point that could entice single-visit visitors to become library room scholars. P1 also imagined visitors to *"come across the system at the end of the exhibition... primed to ask, well-formulated queries based on the knowledge acquired."* P1 further suggested that museum curators might well want to collaborate closely with the system designers to foster just this sort of synergy. As much as the system could provide a successful initial interaction of single-visit visitors with the archival content, a growing sense of curiosity or resonance could move some of the people towards long-term, scholarly work. For example, P2 pointed out that *"having a narrative"* would be beneficial to the younger population who learn history through mass media instead of books with details, who *"frankly are not well versed in history, of what happened in the Cuban Missile Crisis or the assassination of Martin Luther King."*

Connecting this with Implication 2, we could imagine community-based library room scholars reciprocating in archival assurance. P4 acknowledged the system being intriguing for *"genealogists as a huge portion of users, trying to reconstruct their family histories, e.g., Black or Latin community members."* For example, one recent change at the Smithsonian's National Anthropological Archives has been welcoming indigenous researchers to correct metadata and description in archives when they came across errors in the reading room [9].

5 Conclusion and Future Work

In the movie *Field of Dreams*, a voice invites us to imagine that "if you build it, they will come." In our study, we have sought to replace, or at least to augment, that voice with the voice of experience. We have drawn on the insights of experts in libraries, archives, and museums. The insights help us imagine how systems that would allow museum visitors to converse with a representation of an actual historical figure might actually be used, and what issues might arise in the context of that use. To do this, we found it helpful to actually build it, at least in prototype form. We see this intersectionality between the technical and the applied as both useful inspirations for our next steps, and as emblematic of the value of bringing different types of expertise together to capitalize in reflective ways on emerging opportunities.

Records of prominent historical figures provide enduring traces of their life. Seeing a convergence of conversational technologies, we explored the possibility of conversational interactions with historical figures, as represented in their records. We assembled a text collection for Ronald Reagan, and developed a prototype retrieval-based chatbot as a boundary object to support interviews with academic experts. Our study yielded implications addressing immersive experiences, assurance, and supporting a continuum of use that could help some visitors engage more deeply with the content over time.

While this interview study offers preliminary insight into how our envisioned system might be used, there remains a gap between our ultimate vision and our current prototype. Thus, we plan next to focus our technical work on style rewriting, and then on multi-stage dialog management. We also plan to focus on the ethical concerns that arise from systems posthumously representing historical figures; for this we hope to conduct a similarly structured interview study with ethicists. Looking further ahead, we might also explore other applications of this technology, such as interactive textbooks [29] that might embed our envisioned system in a sidebar allows spontaneous questions scaffolded from course materials. And perhaps one day, we might be able to bring historical figures to a Reddit "Ask Me Anything" session. If we are able to build *that*, then perhaps they will come.

Acknowledgements. The authors are grateful to the anonymous participants in our research study, who contributed their time and expertise to this study. This research has been supported in part by the National Science Foundation under grant number 1618695. Any opinions, findings, and conclusions or recommendations expressed in this material are those of the authors and do not necessarily reflect the views of the National Science Foundation.

References

1. Aguinis, H., Solarino, A.M.: Transparency and replicability in qualitative research: the case of interviews with elite informants. Strateg. Manag. J. **40**(8), 1291–1315 (2019)
2. Artstein, R., Gainer, A., Georgila, K., Leuski, A., Shapiro, A., Traum, D.: New dimensions in testimony demonstration. In: Proceedings of the 2016 Conference of the North American Chapter of the Association for Computational Linguistics: Demonstrations, pp. 32–36 (2016)
3. Artstein, R., et al.: Time-offset interaction with a holocaust survivor. In: Proceedings of the 19th International Conference on Intelligent User Interfaces, pp. 163–168 (2014)
4. Banerjee, S., Biyani, P., Tsioutsiouliklis, K.: Transforming chatbot responses to mimic domain-specific linguistic styles. In: Second Workshop on Chatbots and Conversational Agent Technologies (2016)
5. Bell, G., Gray, J.: Digital immortality. Commun. ACM **44**(3), 28–31 (2001)
6. Bell, L., Gustafson, J.: Utterance types in the August dialogues. In: ESCA Tutorial and Research Workshop (ETRW) on Interactive Dialogue in Multi-Modal Systems (1999)
7. Brands, H.W.: Reagan: The Life. Anchor, New York (2016)
8. Brinkmann, S.: Qualitative Interviewing. Oxford University Press, Oxford (2013)
9. Buchanan, R., et al.: Toward inclusive reading rooms: recommendations for decolonizing practices and welcoming indigenous researchers (2021)
10. Cafaro, F., Ress, S.A.: Time travelers: mapping museum visitors across time and space. In: Proceedings of the 2016 ACM International Joint Conference on Pervasive and Ubiquitous Computing (UbiComp'16): Adjunct, pp. 1492–1497 (2016)
11. Carroll, J., Minnen, G., Canning, Y., Devlin, S., Tait, J.: Practical simplification of English newspaper text to assist aphasic readers. In: Proceedings of the AAAI-98 Workshop on Integrating Artificial Intelligence and Assistive Technology, pp. 7–10 (1998)

12. Chabot, L.: Nixon Library Technology Lets Visitors 'Interview' Him (1990). https://www.latimes.com/archives/la-xpm-1990-07-21-mn-346-story.html. Accessed 12 Apr 2021
13. Chen, D., Fisch, A., Weston, J., Bordes, A.: Reading Wikipedia to answer open-domain questions. In: Proceedings of the 55th Annual Meeting of the Association for Computational Linguistics (Volume 1: Long Papers), pp. 1870–1879 (2017)
14. Cole, C.: Inducing expertise in history doctoral students via information retrieval design. Libr. Q. Inf. Commun. Policy **70**(1), 86–109 (2000)
15. Dalton, J., Xiong, C., Callan, J.: TREC CAsT 2019: the conversational assistance track overview (2020)
16. Devlin, J., Chang, M.W., Lee, K., Toutanova, K.: BERT: pre-training of deep bidirectional transformers for language understanding. arXiv preprint arXiv:1810.04805 (2018)
17. Dixon, E., Lazar, A.: Approach matters: linking practitioner approaches to technology design for people with dementia. In: Proceedings of the 2020 CHI Conference on Human Factors in Computing Systems, pp. 1–15 (2020)
18. Duff, W.M., Johnson, C.A.: Accidentally found on purpose: information-seeking behavior of historians in archives. Libr. Q. Inf. Commun. Policy **72**(4), 472–496 (2002)
19. Fidel, R., et al.: A visit to the information mall: web searching behavior of high school students. J. Am. Soc. Inf. Sci. **50**(1), 24–37 (1999)
20. Fu, Z., Tan, X., Peng, N., Zhao, D., Yan, R.: Style transfer in text: exploration and evaluation. In: Proceedings of the AAAI Conference on Artificial Intelligence, vol. 32, no. 1, April 2018
21. Glazer, A.S.: Auditing Museum Collections (1991). http://archives.cpajournal.com/old/11287210.htm. Accessed 12 Apr 2021
22. Greene, M., Meissner, D.: More product, less process: revamping traditional archival processing. Am. Arch. **68**(2), 208–263 (2005)
23. Griffin, C.: The museum library. Univ. Mus. Bull. **19**(2), 23–27 (1955)
24. Gustafson, J., Lindberg, N., Lundeberg, M.: The August spoken dialogue system. In: Sixth European Conference on Speech Communication and Technology (1999)
25. Harth, M.L.: Learning from museums with indigenous collections: beyond repatriation. Curator Mus. J. **42**(4), 274–284 (1999)
26. Hjørland, B.: Epistemology and the socio-cognitive perspective in information science. J. Am. Soc. Inform. Sci. Technol. **53**(4), 257–270 (2002)
27. Honnibal, M., Montani, I., Van Landeghem, S., Boyd, A.: spaCy: Industrial-strength Natural Language Processing in Python (2020). https://doi.org/10.5281/zenodo.1212303
28. Jena, G., Vashisht, M., Basu, A., Ungar, L., Sedoc, J.: Enterprise to computer: star trek chatbot. arXiv preprint arXiv:1708.00818 (2017)
29. Koike, H., Sato, Y., Kobayashi, Y., Tobita, H., Kobayashi, M.: Interactive textbook and interactive Venn diagram: natural and intuitive interfaces on augmented desk system. In: Proceedings of the SIGCHI Conference on Human Factors in Computing Systems (CHI'00), pp. 121–128 (2000)
30. Kvale, S.: Doing Interviews. SAGE, New York (2008)
31. Leuski, A., Pair, J., Traum, D., McNerney, P.J., Georgiou, P., Patel, R.: How to talk to a hologram. In: Proceedings of the 11th International Conference on Intelligent User Interfaces, pp. 360–362 (2006)
32. Lin, J., Nogueira, R., Yates, A.: Pretrained Transformers for Text Ranking: BERT and Beyond (2020)

33. Marinelli, D., Stevens, S.: Synthetic interviews: the art of creating a ‘dyad’ between humans and machine-based characters. In: Proceedings 1998 IEEE 4th Workshop Interactive Voice Technology for Telecommunications Applications (IVTTA’98), pp. 43–48 (1998)
34. McGranahan, C.: A presidential archive of lies: racism, Twitter, and a history of the present. Int. J. Commun. **13**, 19 (2019)
35. National Archives: Strategy for digitizing archival materials (2014). https://www.archives.gov/digitization/strategy.html. Accessed 12 Apr 2021
36. Nogueira, R., Cho, K.: Passage re-ranking with BERT. arXiv preprint arXiv:1901.04085 (2019)
37. Nogueira, R., Yang, W., Cho, K., Lin, J.: Multi-stage document ranking with BERT. arXiv preprint arXiv:1910.14424 (2019)
38. Parkin, S.: Back-up brains: the era of digital immortality (2015). https://www.bbc.com/future/article/20150122-the-secret-to-immortality. Accessed 12 Apr 2021
39. Pinch, T.J., Bijker, W.E.: The social construction of facts and artefacts: or how the sociology of science and the sociology of technology might benefit each other. Soc. Stud. Sci. **14**(3), 399–441 (1984)
40. Prabha, C., Connaway, L.S., Olszewski, L., Jenkins, L.R.: What is enough? Satisficing information needs. J. Doc. **63**(1), 74–89 (2007)
41. Radlinski, F., Craswell, N.: A theoretical framework for conversational search. In: Proceedings of the 2017 Conference on Computer Human Information Interaction and Retrieval, pp. 117–126 (2017)
42. Rao, S., Tetreault, J.: Dear sir or madam, may I introduce the GYAFC dataset: corpus, benchmarks and metrics for formality style transfer. In: Proceedings of the 2018 Conference of the North American Chapter of the Association for Computational Linguistics: Human Language Technologies, Volume 1 (Long Papers), New Orleans, Louisiana, pp. 129–140, June 2018
43. Reddy, S., Knight, K.: Obfuscating gender in social media writing. In: Proceedings of the First Workshop on NLP and Computational Social Science, Austin, Texas, pp. 17–26. Association for Computational Linguistics, November 2016
44. Ress, S., Cafaro, F., Bora, D., Prasad, D., Soundarajan, D.: Mapping history: orienting museum visitors across time and space. J. Comput. Cult. Herit. **11**(3), 1–25 (2018)
45. Riley, R.L.: Presidential oral history: the Clinton presidential history project. Oral Hist. Rev. **34**(2), 81–106 (2007)
46. Robertson, S., Zaragoza, H.: The probabilistic relevance framework: BM25 and beyond. Found. Trends Inf. Retr. **3**(4), 333–389 (2009)
47. Savin-Baden, M., Burden, D.: Digital immortality and virtual humans. Postdigit. Sci. Educ. **1**(1), 87–103 (2018). https://doi.org/10.1007/s42438-018-0007-6
48. Skinner, K.K., Anderson, A., Anderson, M.: Reagan: A Life in Letters. Simon and Schuster, New York (2004)
49. Song, H., Wang, Y., Zhang, W.N., Liu, X., Liu, T.: Generate, delete and rewrite: a three-stage framework for improving persona consistency of dialogue generation. In: Proceedings of the 58th Annual Meeting of the Association for Computational Linguistics, pp. 5821–5831, July 2020
50. Spice, B., Sloss, E.: Carnegie Mellon’s Synthetic Interview Technology Enables Virtual Chats with Darwin’s Ghost (2009). https://www.cmu.edu/news/archive/2009/February/feb5_darwininterview.shtml. Accessed 23 Feb 2021
51. Star, S.L., Griesemer, J.R.: Institutional ecology, translations’ and boundary objects: amateurs and professionals in Berkeley’s Museum of Vertebrate Zoology, 1907–39. Soc. Stud. Sci. **19**(3), 387–420 (1989)

52. Traum, D., et al.: New Dimensions in testimony: digitally preserving a Holocaust survivor's interactive storytelling. In: Schoenau-Fog, H., Bruni, L.E., Louchart, S., Baceviciute, S. (eds.) ICIDS 2015. LNCS, vol. 9445, pp. 269–281. Springer, Cham (2015). https://doi.org/10.1007/978-3-319-27036-4_26
53. Voorhees, E.M., et al.: The TREC-8 question answering track report. In: TREC, vol. 99, pp. 77–82 (1999)
54. Wang, H., Lu, Z., Li, H., Chen, E.: A dataset for research on short-text conversations. In: Proceedings of the 2013 Conference on Empirical Methods in Natural Language Processing, Seattle, Washington, USA, pp. 935–945. Association for Computational Linguistics, October 2013
55. Wu, Y., Wu, W., Xing, C., Zhou, M., Li, Z.: Sequential matching network: a new architecture for multi-turn response selection in retrieval-based chatbots. In: Proceedings of the 55th Annual Meeting of the Association for Computational Linguistics (Volume 1: Long Papers), Vancouver, Canada, pp. 496–505, July 2017
56. Yang, Y., Yih, W.T., Meek, C.: WikiQA: a challenge dataset for open-domain question answering. In: Proceedings of the 2015 Conference on Empirical Methods in Natural Language Processing, pp. 2013–2018 (2015)

Hybrid Digital Card Sorting: New Research Technique or Mere Variant?

Elke Greifeneder(✉) and Paulina Bressel

Berlin School for Library and Information Science, Humboldt-Universität zu Berlin, Berlin, Germany
greifeneder@ibi.hu-berlin.de

Abstract. Card sorting is a method to evaluate and build information architectures. This article describes hybrid digital card sorting and discusses its characteristic traits: as a new method, as a new research technique or as a mere variation of physical card sorting. The article presents the research designs, the approaches for analysis as well as selected results of two hybrid digital card sorting case studies. The evaluation of differences and similarities between the two case studies and between other forms of card sorting such as physical, open or closed card sorting reveal that hybrid digital card sorting requires different data collection techniques than physical card sorting. Hybrid digital card sorting demands quantitative analysis approaches using cluster analysis such as dendrograms with only few qualitative elements. Since it is the opposite of physical card sorting, it deserves to be called a new research technique.

Keywords: Card sorting · Hybrid card sorting · Standardization · Method · Research technique

1 Introduction

Card Sorting is a standard method in user experience research and user experience design to evaluate information architectures [41]. The method provides "insight into how users categorize and cluster information" [11, 34] and helps understanding mental models of those using information systems [8, 11, 17]. In its origins, card sorting used to be a method that required an on-site setting, in which a small discussion group took part in the study. The research design did not require a high level of expertise and the analysis was mostly qualitative in nature.

Card sorting turned online relatively early [1], mostly by repurposing other tools, for example task management tools like *Trello* [56] or *Asana* [3]. Today, there are a vast number of vendors selling online card sorting tool services such as *UserZoom* [59], Proven by Users [45] or *Optimal Workshop* [40], most offering services for research design and analysis. There are few open source tools available such as *cardSORTER* [9] and *Kardsort* [31], neither of which offer in-build analysis tools.

In this article, we present two case studies applying hybrid digital card sorting testing that answer the following research question: is hybrid digital card sorting a variant of

M. Smits (Ed.): iConference 2022, LNCS 13193, pp. 50–67, 2022.
https://doi.org/10.1007/978-3-030-96960-8_4

the standard, physical, card sorting method, or is it, in fact, a new research technique or even a new research method? According to Pickard [44] a research method is the overall approach, or as she puts it the strategy, and is defined by the driving purpose of the investigation. Research techniques, in contrast, are "the individual data collection techniques applied within a method" [44, p. XIX]. The same research method, for example a survey, can have different research techniques as approaches to data collection, i.e. questionnaires or surveys. Different research methods and techniques require distinct rules for research design and analysis. A variant, in contrast, is an alteration to a research technique without impacting the design or the type of analysis. Coming back to the research question, this article postulates that if hybrid digital card sorting counts as a new research method or technique, it would require (new) distinct rules for research design and analysis.

After a literature review on closed and open card sorting, hybrid digital card sorting and their applications in information science, we present two case studies, where we applied hybrid digital card sorting. We base our arguments on those case studies and use them as research data. We answer the research question by comparing research designs and data analysis in both case studies with the approaches used in standard, physical, card sorting studies.

2 Background

Card sorting supports the understanding of how users categorize and cluster information [11, 34] based on their individual context and mental models [8, 11, 17, 35, 42]. It is used in the LIS-field and other research areas, like psychology and engineering [11] to evaluate and optimize the usability of Information Architectures and is therefore used while (re-)designing and (re-)organizing websites, software and products [8, 22, 41]. Figure 1 shows a model of the various card sorting research techniques, which will be explained in detail below.

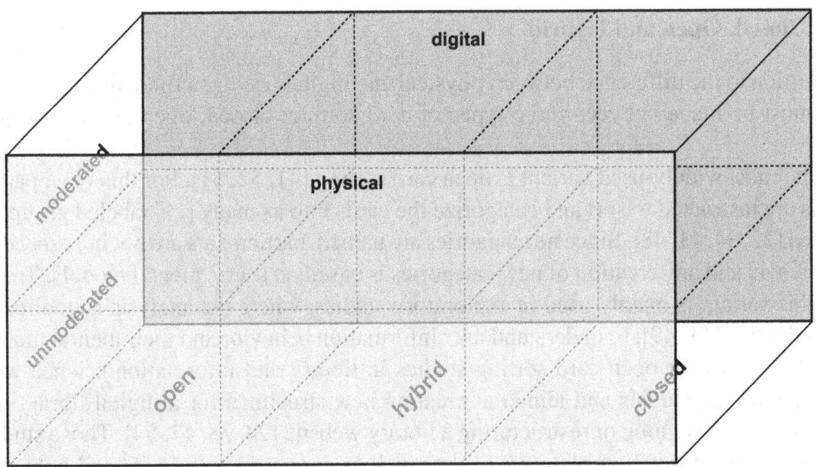

Fig. 1. Three-dimensional model of card sorting research techniques (source: authors)

2.1 Physical and Digital Card Sorting

Card sorting can be done digitally or physically, the latter being the standard so far, which means that the study is influenced by criteria like location, date, number of participations and design setup. While testing physically requires more planning activity for the researcher in addition to the moderating the test, digital card sorting is mostly unmoderated and enables time and location independence. This results in different card sorting implementations [22]. Card sorting can be moderated (for example in group-settings or interviewer + subject) leading to discussions and exchange of ideas during the test, and consequently more standardized results. Card sorting can also be unmoderated with individuals taking the test separately (e.g. digital or in person). In past research, physical testing seems to be the usual form, while digital testing was seldom done in scholarly research [2, 11, 14].

For the physical variant a representative sample typically contains 15 to 20 participants [39, 41, 57] and the analysis is often done qualitatively [50, 60]. During the test, researchers can ask for the participants' thoughts while listening to their discussions. If questions occurred, researchers could help directly [34].

In contrast to physical testing, participants are on their own during digital card sorting and cannot engage in discussions with other participants or ask researchers for help [34]. To what extent this influences the results, still has to be researched [11]. The analysis of digital card sorting is done by using special software, which supports the quantitative analysis afterwards [11, 48, 60]. Statistical tools like dendrograms show how many people agree that cards are similar and belong in the same group. This agreement is indicated by an "agreement level". In simplified terms, 100% agreement means that all users agree that two or more cards belong together, an agreement level of zero means that nobody links two specific cards together. Beside dendrograms other methods like cluster analysis and similarity matrix are also commonly used [43, 50, 58]. With no need for participants to take the test at the same time or in the same location, more participants can be involved.

2.2 Closed, Open and Hybrid

In addition to the difference between physical and digital testing, a fundamental distinction must be made between three types of card sorting: closed, open and hybrid [41, 48].

The most widely-used variant is open card sorting [41, 52, 61]. For this type, participants are instructed to sort and categorize the cards into as many self-labeled groups as desired [22, 34, 41, 48]. Since no categories are named, participants are not influenced by researchers and any creation of new categories is based on users' mental models. Therefore this variant is mainly used in exploratory studies, where the analysis is qualitative and inductive [11, 49], to understand user information behavior and their mental models [54]. Examples for open card sorting studies in library and information science were mainly physical studies and aimed at creating new structures for a digital library [6], rebranding, redesigning or restructuring a library website [24, 38, 47, 54]. Those studies developed an information platform [42] as well as supporting guide [5] and helped to understand the correlation of navigation structures and mental models [50].

Closed card sorting, sometimes referred to as fixed card sorting [11], in contrast provides predefined categories, to which participants assign the cards [34, 41]. The given categories cannot be renamed and the creation of new categories is not part of the test [21]. While open card sorting is helpful for creating and designing new products, closed card sorting tests are used for existing structures, which need to be redone or need to validate menu structures and labels [54]. Previous library and information science studies applied closed physical card sorting for usability tests for existing library and university websites [21, 34, 60] or information platforms [42].

The third type of card sorting is the hybrid form, sometimes also referred to as semi-closed or semi-open card sorting [26, 48]. As the name implies, this variant comprises a combination of open and closed card sorting, in which participants sort cards with both predefined and unlimited new categories [41]. Sometimes the cards are open or user-created [11] and participants are also allowed to rename and delete categories, in order to obtain an optimal usable information structure [48]. Based on previous research, the hybrid variant seems to be applied especially for the evaluation and revision of user groups with special needs, such as blind persons, whose web usability needs were often neglected [48] or people with disorders like strokes [33]. Otherwise nearly no research has yet been done with this card sorting variant.

All three variants are independently feasible, and can also be complementary with other research methods. In the past, especially focus groups, interviews and thinking aloud were carried out as complementary methods, because of the possibility to interact with participants and to ask about their thoughts and reasons behind their actions [5, 11, 42].

2.3 Moderated and Unmoderated

Online research techniques are on the rise and we can see that today nearly all traditional methods have a matching online part. Diaries are transformed into digital text diaries [30] or being done as video diaries [32]. YouTube [53] or Zoom [25] are used to conduct online observations. Think-aloud-protocols have become moderated or unmoderated usability tests [18]. Physical interviews are done as online synchronous interviews [7, 29], but also as asynchronous interviews [4, 12, 23]. Focus groups can be conducted synchronously [55], but can be converted into asynchronous online discussions [46].

Those examples show that the online shift in most cases includes two distinct variants: first, the synchronous or moderated variant of the traditional, physical, method. It may use other tools and objects, but its research design and analysis does not differ significantly from the physical counterpart. The asynchronous or unmoderated variant requires a different setup, and different rules and approaches for analysis. Ferguson [13] examined asynchronous interviews and discovered that there are substantial differences. Interviewees have time to consider their answers and can choose the time for responses. Asynchronous interviews are not conducted synchronously Participants can choose to answer one question at a time, take a break and respond to another question later. Participants can also provide supplementary materials. Those data differ from synchronous interview data where answers are much more spontaneous, where there is a time limit, and where the interviewer decides on the order of questions. Those differences ought to be reflected for research design setup and directives for analysis. Greifeneder [18] examined unmoderated online usability tests in a natural environment and a laboratory setting and discovered that unmoderated online usability tests require different directives for research design. She outlines, for example, the necessity for defining success-URLs and to avoid tasks that distract participants by being too intriguing, which lead to experiences where participants paused the test and went exploring. Greifeneder also discovered that asynchronous usability tests require different indicators for data interpretation. She suggested that completion time and the number of page views need to be interpreted differently than in a physical usability test.

3 Presentation of Case Studies

The following part presents the two case studies. For each case study, we will outline the context of the information system that was examined, the primary goal of the card sorting test, the tool that was used, the research design setup and results.

3.1 Case Study 1

Case study one [20] examined the specialised information services' portal for German philology [15]. The specialised information services programme is funded by the German Research foundation and aims at providing "information aligned to the special need of research subject areas, principally digital information irrespective of location." [51]. Its users are highly specialized German researchers, who may live in Germany, but also live abroad. The portal for German philology researchers is called "Germanistik im Netz", officially shortened to GiN. At present, it is only available in German. GiN is provided by the library of Goethe University Frankfurt and was developed between 2018 and 2020. It will go through a planned redesign in 2022, because, among other issues, users criticized the structure of the website. The authors of this article were asked to conduct a user study as independent and objective observers to the system.

The goal of the user study was to improve the information architecture of GiN so card sorting seemed the obvious methodological choice. Since GiN users are located at many German and international research institutions, we quickly opted for an online test setting. In its current structure, GiN has four major entries into the portal, called subsequently top categories. Those categories represent the philological activities *publish, inform, seek, research* [16]. All items that are structured below these categories are called subcategories. For example, under the category *publish* users find the subcategories *e-journal hosting* and *institutional repository*. The two research questions for the study were:

(1) Which subcategories assign GiN's users to existing top categories?
(2) Which top and subcategories are misleading or incomprehensible?

Research Design for Case Study 1
We used the commercial product *OptimalSort* provided by *Optimal Workshop* [40][1] to conduct the study. *OptimalSort* allows closed, open and hybrid digital card sorting implementations. Pre- and post-study questionnaires in all variants from closed to open questions are possible. Top- and subcategories can be entered manually or as a bulk import. Participants receive an online link for participation and can take part in the card sorting remotely and asynchronously, either using the Browser version of a desktop PC or on any mobile application. The installation of software is not necessary. *OptimalSort* offers the raw data for download and diverse online analyses options such as dendrograms, similarity matrix, and survey responses. It further allows the selection of participants and allows for the exclusion of, for example, drop-outs. In the hybrid or open variant, user-developed categories can be grouped together and renamed.

The research design was kept relatively short to recruit enough participants and intentionally simple so that participants did not require long instructions in the unmoderated setting. We chose 17 subcategories as cards to be sorted and used the four existing categories plus the start page as top categories. In the hybrid unmoderated test setting, participants could create new categories and could, but did not have to, use the existing top categories. Participants were free to leave the card sorting activity before all cards were sorted. We asked participants three short questions before the card sorting activity regarding their disciplinary background, their level of expertise with the portal and their seniority. After the activity, we asked another set of four questions about missing cards, misleading cards and further comments about those. We closed with a question about the need for tutorials, which was added because of a bid by GiN's providers and was not linked to the card sorting per se. Figure 2 shows the card sorting activity interface for case study 1.

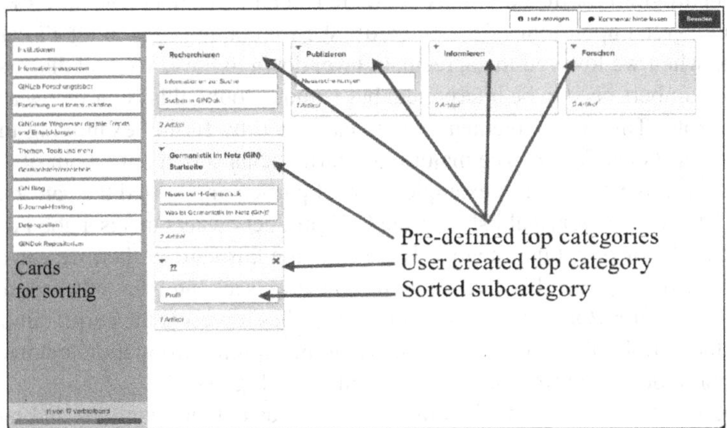

Fig. 2. Card sorting activity interface for case study 1.

The card sorting test was available between July 7 and July 26 2021 and was distributed to a specialized mailing list for German philology via Twitter and the GiN blog.

[1] *Optimal Workshop* granted us free use of their software for thin non-commercial research study.

92 participants completed the study and needed on average six minutes for completion. The majority of participants (80%) came from Germany, but we also identified participants from nine other countries. This shows that users access GiN worldwide and that an online method was an appropriate choice. Regarding seniority, participants were approximately evenly distributed between senior professors (26%), PostDocs (20%) and PhD students holding a researcher position (21%). The other participants were distributed across a variety of smaller groups, including specialized groups such as lecturer positions, junior professors or students. In contrast, the experience level with the portal GiN was very low with 30% who never use GiN or rarely (36%). A quarter uses the portal at least once a month. Only 9% use GiN on a regular basis. Summarizing the demographic information on the study participants, a large sample took part in the study, which allows for quantitative analyses. The majority (46%) were experienced researchers with a seniority level of at least six years and most have no or very limited experience using the portal.

Results of Case Study 1

For both case studies we will present results about user-developed categories, card-categories matches, cluster size and frequency, missing and misleading cards. In the GiN case study, 92 participants attended, 11 of them did not sort any cards. The majority, 79 participants, sorted cards only to the predefined five top categories. 13 participants created 30 additional distinct categories, on average they created additional 3 categories. The maximum were 5 additional categories. We were able to regroup those 30 new categories into 12 different thematic groups. Some regroupings were straightforward such as categories like "*unknown*" or "*I do not know*" or "*unclear*". For others, we suggested a new group under one of the user-named categories and offer a detailed list as appendix to the full study report.

The dendrogram for the GiN study shows that at an agreement level of 69%, participants only agreed upon four of the 17 cards. We were able to group all 17 cards into ten groups when we lowered the agreement level down to 35%. We will discuss below how those numbers need to be interpreted, but without doubt, this is far below a desired agreement rate. This low agreement can be explained by further examining the standardization grid (see Fig. 3). The majority of participants sorted only 8 out of 17 cards into one clear top category. For example, 68% of participants sorted the card *e-journal hosting* to the top category publish. For the GiN product owners this is a good indicator that this card belongs in this category. If we examine this card further, we can see that another 9% would expect this card under the category seek, and that others sorted it to inform or to research. Only five of those major matches represent the current implementation on the portal. This is a clear indicator that the current information architecture of the GiN portal does not reflect users' mental models (Fig. 3).

The results that we presented so far were given as default diagrams and tables by *OptimalSort* and could be edited by regrouping categories. It is tempting for researchers and User Experience designers to focus entirely on those quick quantitative analyses, as Robbins et al. [47] pointed out as well. The results suggest that the unstructurdness of the portal can be solved by first adding more categories. Since participants added on average five additional categories, one could argue that users want to have ten major

Name	Research	GiN homepage	Inform	Publish	Seek	Current	Digital Options	New releases	Networking	Profile	Unklear
Data sources	11	2	6		54						2
E-Journal-Hosting	2	2	2	63	8		2				
Research and Communication	68	1	4	1					2		1
Germanist directory	4	8	43	1	21				2		
GiN blog	2	35	21	15	1	1					
GiNDok repository	10	8	3	26	27						
GiNGuide digital trends and developments	13	13	34	7	4	2	1				1
GiNLab research laboratoy	70	4							1		1
Search information	2	13	11		51						1
Information resources	1	3	34	1	37						2
Institutions	9	10	45	2	7				1		1
New releases	2	8	19	24	23			4			
Latest by H-Germanistik		34	41		1	3					
Profile	2	55	12	2		1				4	1
Research in GiNDok	1	16	1	4	56						
Topics, Tools and more	9	26	22	3	13	1	1				2
What is Germanistik im Netz (GiN)?		67	9			1					

= given upper categories
= new created upper categories

Fig. 3. Standardization grid of selected categories for case study 1.

categories. Secondly, using the above similarity matrix one might suggest a new information architecture based on the respective major matches. We suggest that this result may improve the portal, but it would not solve the underlying problem of the portal.

Only 2 of the 92 participants explicitly created a category "unclear", which means that the majority of participants felt confident sorting the cards to a category. On the other hand, 92% of the participants stated in the post-activity survey that at least one card was incomprehensible. The main "incomprehensible" cards were *database, e-journal hosting, repository, research lab, profile*, and *seeking in GiN*. Except for *profile* card, all cards are library vocabulary. We infer that the feeling that GIN is unstructured can only be solved by helping users interact in the online library vocabulary world and that the restructuring as described above is only one of two steps to solve the problem. In conclusion of case study 1, only 15% of participants reported missing cards with the most frequently mentioned missing sub-category for this community being networking opportunities. Several comments stated that the 17 cards were already more than enough.

3.2 Case Study 2

Case study two [19] also took place within a library portal context and with highly specialized researchers as users. Case study 2 examined the new German National Manuscript Portal [28], abbreviated as HSP (in German: Handschriftenportal), which is currently under development. The new portal will serve as a central resource for information on medieval and early modern manuscripts [27]. Its users are highly specialized international researchers working with and researching manuscripts. The HSP portal will replace the database Manuscripta Mediaevalia [37]. The HSP is developed by the four manuscript centers in Germany, the National Library in Berlin – Prussian Cultural Heritage (SBB-PK), the Leipzig University Library (UBL), the Herzog August Library Wolfenbüttel (HAB) and the Bavarian State Library Munich (BSB). The authors of this article were added in 2020 as sub-partners to the project to examine the usability of the new portal, which led to several sub-studies of which hybrid card-sorting was the first one.

The goal of the hybrid card sorting study was to develop the structure of the complex filter system in the HSP. The portal will offer a wide range of filter functionalities and the project developers wanted insight if the proposed organization of those filters would fit the usage of their target group. The study had three research questions:

(1) How do HSP users create groups of filters to make them findable?
(2) Which filters are misleading or incomprehensible?
(3) Which filters are missing?

Research Design of Case Study 2

Case study 2 was conducted using only open source programs. We used the open source software *Kardsort* to conduct the study. *Kardsort* was developed at the University of Paderborn and is maintained by Kailaash Balachandran. *Kardsort* also allows closed, open and hybrid digital card sorting implementations and pre- and post-study questionnaires in all variants from closed to open questions are possible. Researchers can add additional information to cards and categories, which helps users understand the context of a card or a category. Participants receive an online link for participation and can take part in the card sorting remotely and asynchronously either using the Browser version of a desktop PC or on any mobile application[2]. The installation of software is not necessary. *KardSort* does not offer ready-made analyses. The raw data needs to be downloaded and analyzed using appropriate tools. Results can be exported to.csv, SynCaps and Casolysis format. We used *LibreOffice* and *Casolysis 2.0* for analysis [10]. *Casolyiss* is a free card sort evaluation programme, also developed by researchers at the university of Paderborn. Data cleaning and category regrouping had to be done manually outside of Kardsort.

The research design was also kept short with an average duration of ten minutes. Instead of website subcategories like in case study 1, we examined filter options, so the cards were the future filters. We chose 36 cards and offered participants three 3 example categories. Those three categories belong to a list of possible categories developed by the portal developers and were binding, ownership and metadata description. They were chosen as starters to offer participants orientation for possible categories. In the hybrid unmoderated test setting, participants could create new categories and could, but did not have to, use the existing top categories. Due to a restriction by *Kardsort*, participants had to sort all cards before continuing with the study, so we told participants that, if need be, they could create a category in which they put cards they did not want or could not sort. We asked participants three short questions before the card sorting activity

[2] Participants reported that the mobile version did not work properly, but this may have been due to a change in the software during data collection and may work better now. We did not experience any issues with the mobile version.

regarding their motivation, their level of expertise with manuscript portals and if they have experience with the alpha version of the HSP. After the activity, we asked questions about missing and misleading cards and further comments about those. Figure 4 shows the card sorting activity interface for case study 2.

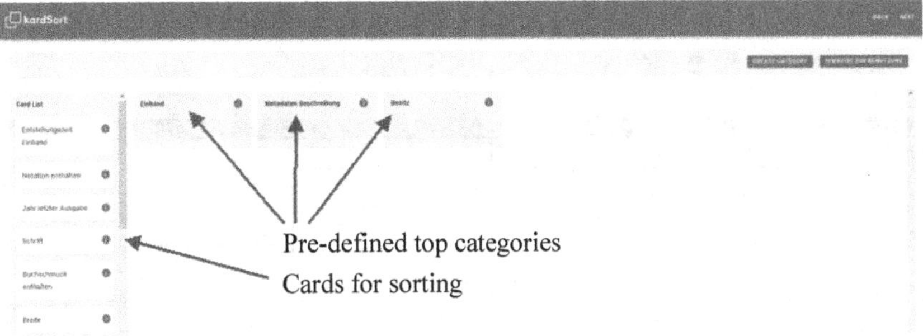

Fig. 4. Card sorting activity interface for case study 2.

The card sorting test was available between April 21 and May 2 2021 and was distributed to a specialised mailing list *diskus*, via the blog of the HSP project and individual mouth to mouth communication through members of the advisory council and leaders of the manuscript centers. 56 participants completed the study of which 68% have already experimented with the alpha version of the new portal. The participants are clearly experts at using digital services in their daily research work. 51% of participants work at least once a week with a virtual catalogue such as e-codices or Handschriftenzenzus and another 23% work between once a week and once a month with virtual catalogues. 27% use those catalogues rarely or never. *Kardsort* did not offer information on location, so we can only conclude that all participants were German speaking since the study setup was in German.

Results of Case Study 2

Similar to above, for case study 2 we present results about user-developed categories, card-category matches, cluster size and frequency, missing and misleading cards. In the HSP case study, 55 participants sorted cards to the predefined three top categories, and one participant decided to use only self-created categories. Participants created 160 additional categories, which could be grouped together to 85 distinct additional categories.[3] The 56 participants created on average 2,9 additional categories. Most participants used the given category *metadata description* as a big container and sorted on average 25 filter cards into this one big container. There is only one user-created category that received similar interest, which was a category called "*content*". The full report explains in detail why the three given categories should not be pursued anymore. Apart from the one big container category, participants sorted between three to five filter cards per category, which seems to be a good indicator for the depth of the categories. We grouped the user-created categories into 12 different sub-themes and grouped those again into four big

[3] *OptimalSort* automatically merges identical categories whereas researchers have to do that manually in *KardSort.*

blocks: block 1: exterieur of the manuscript; block 2: equipment of manuscript; block 3: origins of manuscript; and block 4: content of manuscript. Thus, the final suggestion for an information architecture for the filters is entirely based on users' suggestions for category names.

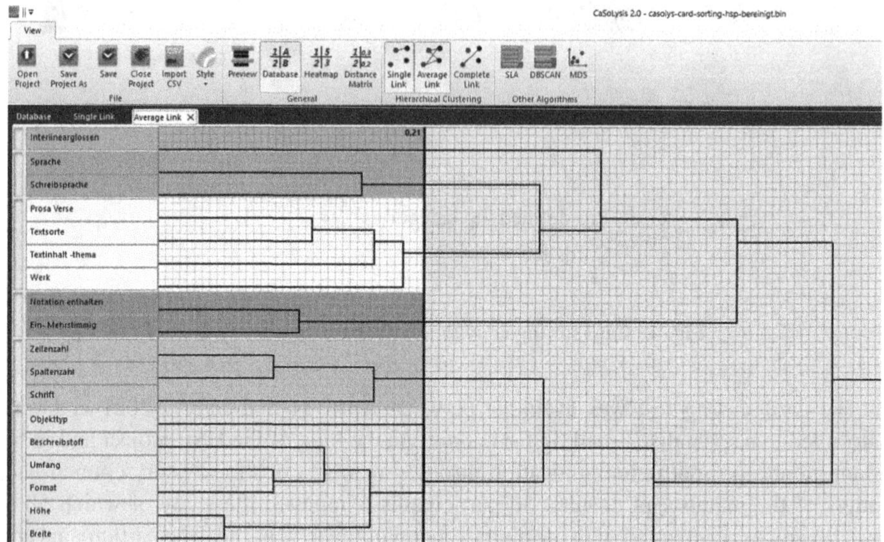

Fig. 5. Example of dendrogram from case study 2.

The dendrogram (see Fig. 5) for the HSP study shows that an agreement level of 82%[4], thirty of the 36 filter cards were clustered into nine groups. At an agreement level of 64%, all filters could be assigned to six clusters. The six unclustered filter cards from the first clustering were the same cards that were mentioned most frequently in response to the question about misleading or incomprehensible cards. Most frequently, participants criticized a filter for not being precise enough, for example the filter "*place*" might be interpreted as place of location, place of discovery, place named in title etc. 59% of users commented on misleading or incomprehensible cards. We asked participants if filters were missing and 43% of participants listed additional desired filters, some naming more than ten, highly specialized, filters. Concluding case study 2, we can observe that the participants of the HSP are highly motivated to co-develop the future filter system because they will use it frequently in their daily researchers' life. This higher degree of familiarity and usage motivation with library portals lead to a much higher agreement rate in the clustering. Cards were misleading and not incomprehensible. It is worth noting that while the requested missing cards were highly specialized terms such as fascicle, fleuroné or rubricator, the user-suggested names for the top categories were

[4] *Casolysis* allows for both single linkage and average linkage clustering. In the article, we refer to the results of the single linkage clustering. *OptimalSort* does not state which cluster procedure has been used.

very simple terms such as content, exterior, origins that also novices in the research area understand.

4 Discussion of Findings

The two case studies have given insights into how to apply hybrid digital card sorting. We will first summarize similarities and differences and will then compare the results with physical card sorting.

4.1 Summary of Case Studies

The aim of the two case studies matches the core idea behind card sorting: to understand how users categorize and cluster information. Both studies took place online, unmoderated, and used a hybrid form of card sorting. In both cases, we examined a library portal and worked with specialized researchers. Table 1 below shows the key differences between the two case studies. In contrast to case study 1, case study 2 was intentionally conducted with an open source program to examine the feasibility of hybrid card sorting tests using an open science toolbox.

Both datasets were first analyzed using the available quantitative instruments and then examined more closely using a qualitative approach, mostly by examining the open questions asked in the pre- and post-survey and comparing them with sorting activities. For both groups, the result was a relatively large group of top categories with a low number of sub-categories in each of them, thus a very broad entry to the information architecture. It must be discussed if this result helps the portal operators, because such a high number of top categories is virtually impossible for mobile designs.

We hypothesize that the more experience and more motivation users have with the object of study, the higher the agreement level on similar cards. In our studies, the dendrograms and similarity matrices helped first of all to uncover problematic cards and only secondly to determine potential groups. If participants do not understand the cards themselves, as in case study 1, the clusters suggested by dendrograms or similarity matrices become random artefacts and must be critically examined.

Table 1. Summary of key differences between the two case studies

	Case study 1: GiN	Case study 2: HSP
Goal	Improve main portal structure	Develop a new filter structure
Structure of website	Exists	In development
Participants	92	56
Experience with website	Low or no experience	High experience
Duration time	6 min	10 min

(continued)

Table 1. *(continued)*

	Case study 1: GiN	Case study 2: HSP
Software	Commercial product	Open source
Cards	17	36
Predefined categories	5	3
User created categories	30	85
Average number of new categories per user	3	2,9
Final thematic groups	12	12 + 4 main thematic blocks
Agreement rate for all available cards	35%	64%; 82% excluding misleading cards
Incomprehensible cards mentioned	92% of participants	59% of participants
Missing cards mentioned	15% of participants	43% of participants

Both studies have shown that the given categories, which mostly serve as an example for participants to understand how the test setup works, have a huge impact on the results. It is worth spending time on the best choice of the predefined categories.

4.2 Differences Between Card Sorting Research Designs

This research seeks to answer the question of how hybrid digital card sorting differs from other forms of card sorting by presenting the research designs and results from two case studies. It is important to remember that neither hybrid card sorting tests are new, nor are digital, unmoderated, card sorting tests. It is the combination that is unique and that has not been discussed.

The online setting usually requires a short duration and is kept as simple as sensible in its tasks, because participants do not receive external help from researchers. The three recruitment advantages - short, easy to do, easily accessible from everywhere - lead to a higher number of participants. While physical card sorting, be it closed, hybrid or open, rarely has more than 20 participants in total, both online case studies had a much larger sample.

A larger sample is important for the study's validity, because it compensates for the lack of any discussion among the participants. In a moderated and generally physical setting, participants discuss the cards, discuss names for new categories and discuss the sorting. Most importantly, participants have to agree to one suggestion for an information architecture. In the hybrid, unmoderated setting, this is totally different. Participants take part individually, thus there is no discussion. In a hybrid unmoderated setting, the researchers have to suggest which cards belong together and how categories ought to be named based on a very careful analysis of the data. But as the two case studies have shown, the proposition of one ideal information architecture for the target group is difficult. Researchers can use dendrograms or similarity matrices as indicators, but there is no defined standard about which factor is acceptable for grouping information elements within an information architecture. The final grouping is biased towards researchers' perspective and may not represent users' intention. For example, in case study 1, we grouped user-named categories together such as *e-journal hosting* and *digital options* or *data sources* and *sources*. It was our interpretation that those categories have the same meaning and can be grouped together and consequently used as one category.

The missing discussion leads to another difference between unmoderated and moderated settings. In the hybrid unmoderated setting, we lacked people's arguments about why cards were sorted the way they were. We lack an understanding of users' reasoning. Of course, if no one in the physical settings records the discussions, this data is also missing. In our case studies, we compensate for this lack of arguments by asking post-activity questions and we suggest that this should be a requirement for future hybrid digital card sorting studies. On the other hand, the hybrid setting in case study 1 has shown that the problem lies in the use of library vocabulary. The physical test setting might not yield that information, because if one participant had asked what a term means, someone else would have explained it. Hybrid digital settings help to decipher the severity of a problem.

Not all physical card sorting studies are group discussions. Especially those who use open or hybrid physical settings opt for individual participation, followed by interviews or a questionnaire to collect data on participants' reasoning. We can see that it is the factor of single-participation that leads to the creation of a high number of user-created categories and not necessarily greater openness. In an open physical card sorting study Capra's ten participants created 77 new categories where the "individual participants created between 4 and 13" new categories. [8]. Conrad and Tucker [11] report that their 12 participants created around a hundred new categories. Lewis et al.' [34] participants created in their study 199 new categories. Compared to those numbers, the 30 and respectively 85 new categories in our case studies appear small. It is also an indication that hybrid produces fewer user-created categories than the open variant in physical settings.

The fundamental difference between a hybrid digital card sorting test and any form of physical test with a smaller sample is the data analysis. Textbooks tell us that card sorting analysis is mostly qualitative in nature, being the analysis of the group discussion or of the interviews and the final product of the card sorting activity. Card sorting is advertised as an easy method that does not require a high level of expertise [36]. None of this is true for hybrid digital card sorting. Its analysis is mostly quantitative in nature, requiring researchers to read and understand dendrograms and similarity matrices, compute statistical data and to carefully consider clusters.

5 Conclusion

This article asked at the outset what hybrid digital card sorting really is. It presented the research designs, the approaches for analysis as well as selected results of two hybrid digital card sorting case studies. The evaluation of differences and similarities between the two case studies and between other forms of card sorting such as physical, open or closed card sorting revealed that hybrid digital card sorting requires different data collection techniques than physical card sorting. It requires first a different research setup, which takes the fact into account that participants cannot ask for clarification, is shorter and compensates for the lack of a group discussion. Hybrid digital card sorting demands quantitative analyses approaches using hierarchical cluster analysis such as dendrograms with only few qualitative elements; quite the opposite of physical card sorting. The differences between hybrid digital and open physical card sorts are less distinctive. Both techniques produce user-created categories. The major difference lies in group-card sorting with a group discussion versus individual, unmoderated participation.

We help no one if we treat hybrid card sorting as a mere variant of the group-based physical card sorting, because this leads to needless surprises when it comes to the actual implementation and completion of the study. It is important to acknowledge that hybrid digital card sorting is a distinct research technique. It requires separate rules for data collection and analysis. This article is a first step towards implementation of such rules.

This article questions if hybrid card sorting should be considered as a different method than physical card sorting. There are arguments that favor this hypothesis including the fact that the outcome of a group-based physical card sort activity is a single final user-developed suggestion for a new information structure, whereas hybrid card sorting provides a researcher-developed suggestion based on user research data. But the core strategy, as Pickard puts it, remains: evaluating information architectures. Hybrid card sorting is a challenging new research technique, but it is not a new method.

References

1. Albert, B., Tullis, T., Tedesco, D.: Beyond the usability lab. In: Conducting Large-Scale Online User Experience Studies. Elsevier, Kaufmann, Amsterdam (2010)
2. Allen, E.: Mastering Card Sorting: How to Use Research to Organize Information Intuitively. O'Reilly Media, Online (2018). https://www.oreilly.com/videos/mastering-card-sorting/9781492037675/. Accessed 14 Sept 2021
3. Asana Online Tool. https://asana.com/. Accessed 14 Sept 2021
4. Bampton, R., Cowton, C., Downs, Y.: The E-interview in qualitative research. In: Sappleton, N. (ed.) Advancing Research Methods with New Technologies, pp. 329–343. IGI Global (2013)
5. Barker, A., Hoffman, A.: Student-centered design: creating libguides students can actually use. CRL (2021). https://doi.org/10.5860/crl.82.1.75
6. Bostian, S.J.: Organizing interpretive text for a digital library: how user testing found the lost frontier. Slavic East Eur. Inf. Resour. (2005). https://doi.org/10.1300/J167v06n02_08
7. Bressel, P.: Die übergangenen Patient*innen. Eine qualitative Analyse der Informationsbedarfe von jungen Erwachsenen mit Krebs in Deutschland. Humboldt-Universität zu Berlin. Master thesis (2021). https://doi.org/10.18452/22913
8. Capra, M.G.: Factor analysis of card sort data: an alternative to hierarchical cluster analysis. Proc. Human Factors Ergonom. Soc. Annu. Meet. (2005). https://doi.org/10.1177/154193120504900512
9. cardSORTER Beta. https://github.com/victordibia/cardsorter. Accessed 14 Sept 2021
10. Casolysis Installer. https://drive.google.com/file/d/1UvDtmOGiMRltUqVGMOwWpfPeAX_Ug1F7/view?usp=sharing. Accessed 14 Sept 2021
11. Conrad, L.Y., Tucker, V.M.: Making it tangible: hybrid card sorting within qualitative interviews. J. Document. **75**(2), 397–416 (2019). https://doi.org/10.1108/JD-06-2018-0091

12. Debenham, M.: Computer mediated communication and disability support: addressing barriers to study for undergraduate distance learners with long-term health problems. The Open University. PhD thesis (2001). https://doi.org/10.21954/ou.ro.0000b48f
13. Ferguson, R.: The construction of shared knowledge through asynchronous dialogue. The Open University. PhD thesis (2009). https://doi.org/10.21954/ou.ro.00004dc4
14. Ford, E.: Is digital better than analog? Considerations for online card sort studies. Coll. Res. Libr. News **74**(5), 258–261 (2013)
15. GiN Homepage. https://www.germanistik-im-netz.de/. Accessed 14 Sept 2021
16. GiN – Über uns. https://www.germanistik-im-netz.de/ueber-uns. Accessed 14 Sept 2021
17. Goodman, E., Kuniavsky, M., Moed, A.: Observing the user experience. In: A Practitioner's Guide to User Research, 2nd edn. Interactive Technologies. Morgan Kaufmann Elsevier, Amsterdam (2012)
18. Greifeneder, E.: The effects of distraction on task completion scores in a natural environment test setting. J. Assn. Inf. Sci. Technol. **67**(12), 2858–2870 (2016). https://doi.org/10.1002/asi.23537
19. Greifeneder, E., Bressel, P.: Studie zur Präsentation der Facetten auf dem Handschriftenportal (2021). https://doi.org/10.18452/23232
20. Greifeneder, E., Bressel, P.: Ergebnisbericht. Studie zur Webseitenstruktur des Fachinformationsdienstes "Germanistik im Netz". urn:nbn:de:hebis:30:3-646114
21. Guay, S., Rudin, L., Reynolds, S.: Testing, testing: a usability case study at University of Toronto Scarborough Library. Lib. Manag. **40**(1/2), 88–97 (2019). https://doi.org/10.1108/LM-10-2017-0107
22. Harloff, J.: Multiple level weighted card sorting. Methodology (2005). https://doi.org/10.1027/1614-2241.1.4.119
23. Hawkins, J.: The practical utility and suitability of email interviews in qualitative research. TQR (2018). https://doi.org/10.46743/2160-3715/2018.3266
24. Hepburn, P., Lewis, K.M.: What's in a name? Using card sorting to evaluate branding in an academic library's web site. CRL (2008). https://doi.org/10.5860/crl.69.3.242
25. Howlett, M.: Looking at the 'field' through a Zoom lens: methodological reflections on conducting online research during a global pandemic. Qual. Res. (2021). https://doi.org/10.1177/1468794120985691
26. Hudson, W.: Card sorting. In: Soegaard, M., Dam, R.F. (eds.) The Encyclopedia of Human-Computer Interaction, 2nd edn. Interaction Design Foundation, Online (2013). https://www.interaction-design.org/literature/book/the-encyclopedia-of-human-computer-interaction-2nd-ed/card-sorting
27. HSP Project Homepage. https://en.handschriftenzentren.de/handschriftenportal/. Accessed 14 Sept 2021
28. HSP Website. https://alpha.handschriftenportal.de/. Accessed 14 Sept 2021
29. Janghorban, R., LatifnejadRoudsari, R., Taghipour, A.: Skype interviewing: the new generation of online synchronous interview in qualitative research. Int. J. Qual. Stud. Health Well Being (2014). https://doi.org/10.3402/qhw.v9.24152
30. Jarrahi, M.H., Goray, C., Zirker, S., Zhang, Y.: Using digital diaries as a research method for capturing practices in situ. In: Symon, G., Pritchard, K., Hine, C. (eds.) Cover Research Methods for Digital Work and Organization. Oxford University Press, Oxford (2021)
31. Kardsort Online Tool. https://kardsort.com/. Accessed 14 Sept 2021
32. Kaur, H., Saukko, P., Lumsden, K.: Rhythms of moving in and between digital media: a study on video diaries of young people with physical disabilities. Mobilities **13**(3), 397–410 (2018). https://doi.org/10.1080/17450101.2017.1355349
33. Kerr, J., Hilari, K., Litosseliti, L.: Information needs after stroke: What to include and how to structure it on a website. A qualitative study using focus groups and card sorting. Aphasiology **24**(10), 1170–1196 (2010). https://doi.org/10.1080/02687030903383738

34. Lewis, K.M., Hepburn, P.: Open card sorting and factor analysis: a usability case study. Electron. Libr. (2010). https://doi.org/10.1108/02640471011051981
35. Lyon, L., Mattern, E., Jeng, W., He, D.: Investigating perceptions and support for transparency and openness in research: using card sorting in a pilot study with academic librarians. Proc. Assoc. Info. Sci. Tech. (2016)
36. Martin, B., Hanington, B.: Card sorting. In: Universal Methods of Design: 100 Ways to Research Complex Problems, Develop Innovative Ideas, and Design Effective Solutions. Rockport Publishers, Beverly (2012)
37. Manuscripta Mediaevalia Homepage. http://www.manuscripta-mediaevalia.de/. Accessed 14 Sept 2021
38. McHale, N.: Toward a user-centered academic library home page. J. Web Librariansh. (2008). https://doi.org/10.1080/19322900802205825
39. Nielsen, J.: Card sorting: How Many Users to Test. NN/g (2004). https://www.nngroup.com/articles/card-sorting-how-many-users-to-test/. Accessed 14 Sept 2021
40. OptimalSort. https://www.optimalworkshop.com/. Accessed:14 Sept 2021
41. Pampoukidou, S., Katsanos, C.: Test-retest reliability of the open card sorting method. In: Kitamura, Y., Quigley, A., Isbister, K., Igarashi, T. (eds.) Extended Abstracts of the 2021 CHI Conference on Human Factors in Computing Systems. CHI 2021: CHI Conference on Human Factors in Computing Systems, Yokohama Japan, 8 May 2021 to 13 May 2021, pp. 1–7. ACM, New York (2021). https://doi.org/10.1145/3411763.3451750
42. Pestana, C., Barros, L., Scuri, S., Barreto, M.: Can HCI help increase people's engagement in sustainable development? A case study on energy literacy. Sustainability (2021). https://doi.org/10.3390/su13147543
43. Petrie, H., Power, C., Cairns, P., Seneler, C.: Using card sorts for understanding website information architectures: technological, methodological and cultural issues. In: Campos, P., Graham, N., Jorge, J., Nunes, N., Palanque, P., Winckler, M. (eds.) INTERACT 2011. LNCS, vol. 6949, pp. 309–322. Springer, Heidelberg (2011). https://doi.org/10.1007/978-3-642-23768-3_26
44. Pickard, A.: Research Methods in Information, 2nd edn. Routledge Taylor & Francis, Oxfordshire (2007)
45. Proven By Users Online Tool. https://provenbyusers.com/. Accessed 14 Sept 2021
46. Reisner, S.L., et al.: Sensitive health topics with underserved patient populations: methodological considerations for online focus group discussions. Qual. Health Res. **28**(10), 1658–1673 (2018). https://doi.org/10.1177/1049732317705355
47. Robbins, L.P., Esposito, L., Kretz, C., Aloi, M.: What a user wants: redesigning a library's web site based on a card-sort analysis. J. Web Librariansh. (2008). https://doi.org/10.1080/19322900802111346
48. Robles, T.d.J.Á., Rodríguez, F.J.Á., Benítez-Guerrero, E., Rusu, C.: Adapting card sorting for blind people: evaluation of the interaction design in TalkBack. Comput. Stand. Interfaces (2019). https://doi.org/10.1016/j.csi.2019.103356
49. Saunders, M.N.: Using mixed methods – combining card sorts and in-depth interviews. In: Lyon, F., Möllering, G., Saunders, M. (eds.) Handbook of Research Methods on Trust, pp. 134–144. Edward Elgar Publishing, Cheltenham (2015)
50. Schmettow, M., Sommer, J.: Linking card sorting to browsing performance – are congruent municipal websites more efficient to use? Behav. Inf. Technol. (2016). https://doi.org/10.1080/0144929X.2016.1157207
51. SIS Programme Website. https://www.dfg.de/en/research_funding/programmes/infrastructure/lis/funding_opportunities/specialised_info_services/index.html. Accessed 14 Sept 2021
52. Spencer, D.: Card Sorting. Designing Usable Categories. Rosenfeld Media, Brooklyn (2009)

53. Sumiala, J., Tikka, M.: Imagining globalised fears: school shooting videos and circulation of violence on YouTube. Soc. Anthropol. **19**(3), 254–267 (2011). https://doi.org/10.1111/j.1469-8676.2011.00158.x
54. Sundt, A., Eastman, T.: Informing website navigation design with team-based card sorting. J. Web Librariansh. (2019). https://doi.org/10.1080/19322909.2018.1544873
55. Stewart, D.W., Shamdasani, P.: Online focus groups. J. Advert. (2017). https://doi.org/10.1080/00913367.2016.1252288
56. Trello Online Tool. https://trello.com/. Accessed 14 Sept 2021
57. Tullis, T., Wood, L.: How many users are enough for a card-sorting study? In: CONVERENCE 2004. Usability Professionals Association (UPA), Minneapolis (2004)
58. Tullis, T., Albert, B.: Measuring the user experience. In: Collecting, Analyzing, and Presenting Usability Metrics. Elsevier/MK Morgan Kaufmann, Amsterdam, Boston, Heidelberg (2013)
59. UserZoom Online Tool. https://www.userzoom.com/card-sorting/. Accessed 14 Sept 2021
60. Whang, M.: Card-sorting usability tests of the WMU libraries' web site. J. Web Librariansh. (2008). https://doi.org/10.1080/19322900802205940
61. Wood, J., Wood, L.: Card sorting: current practices and beyond. J. Usability Stud. **4**(1), 1–6 (2008)

Improving Community Detection Performance in Heterogeneous Music Network by Learning Edge-Type Usefulness Distribution

Zheng Gao[1(✉)], Chun Guo[2], Shutian Ma[3], and Xiaozhong Liu[4]

[1] Indiana University Bloomington, Bloomington, USA
gao27@indiana.edu
[2] Pandora Media LLC, Oakland, USA
cguo@pandora.com
[3] Tencent Holdings Ltd., Shenzhen, China
[4] Worcester Polytechnic Institute, Worcester, USA
xliu14@wpi.edu

Abstract. With music becoming an essential part of daily life, there is an urgent need to develop recommendation systems to assist people targeting better songs with fewer efforts. As the interactions between users and songs naturally construct a complex network, community detection approaches can be applied to reveal users' potential interests on songs by grouping relevant users & songs to the same community. However, as the types of interaction could be heterogeneous, it challenges conventional community detection methods designed originally for homogeneous networks. Although there are existing works on heterogeneous community detection, they are mostly task-driven approaches and not feasible for specific music recommendation. In this paper, we propose a genetic based approach to learn an edge-type usefulness distribution (ETUD) for all edge-types in heterogeneous music networks. ETUD can be regarded as a linear function to project all edges to the same latent space and make them comparable. Therefore a heterogeneous network can be converted to a homogeneous one where those conventional methods are eligible to use. We validate the proposed model on a heterogeneous music network constructed from an online music streaming service. Results show that for conventional methods, ETUD can help to detect communities significantly improving music recommendation accuracy while simultaneously reducing user searching cost.

Keywords: Heterogeneous network analysis · Community detection · Searching cost · Music recommendation

M. Smits (Ed.): iConference 2022, LNCS 13193, pp. 68–78, 2022.
https://doi.org/10.1007/978-3-030-96960-8_5

1 Introduction

According to a new report released by Nielsen Music, on average, Americans now spend more than 32 h a week listening to music[1]. Besides, with the boom of online music streaming services (MSS) in the recent years, user behaviors on MSS (e.g. Pandora and Spotify) become various as well. How to conduct all types of behavior information from MSS to support music recommendation becomes a challenging task. As user behaviors on songs can naturally form a complex heterogeneous network (in Fig. 1), community detection approaches can be a potential solution to solve this recommendation task by grouping relevant users and songs to the same community. Hence, developing more comprehensive and robust community detection models is in urgent need. In this paper, conventional methods refer to methods are originally designed for homogeneous community detection. Although some other works have addressed on heterogeneous networks, they are mostly task-driven approaches and not able to directly apply on musicrecommendation. In this study, in order to build up a bridge for conventional methods to be eligible on heterogeneous networks, we propose a genetic based method to learn the *edge-type usefulness distribution* (ETUD) on heterogeneous networks in an evolutionary manner. Our model can highlight those edge-types more important for music recommendation by assigning higher weights on them. After that, all edges are updated by multiplying related ETUD values on their original weights, which converts a heterogeneous network to a homogeneous one.

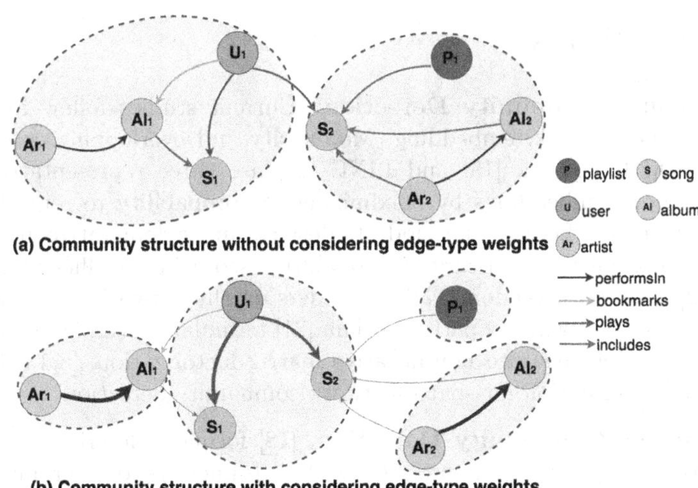

Fig. 1. An example of how ETUD influences the community structure in a heterogeneous music network

[1] https://www.forbes.com/sites/hughmcintyre/2017/11/09/americans-are-spending-more-time-listening-to-music-than-ever-before.

Figure 1 shows an example of how ETUD supports music recommendation on a sample music network from community viewpoint. Figure 1(a) ignores the edge-types and treats the network as a homogeneous one. By leveraging a conventional community detection method (Louvain method [1]), the whole music network is partitioned into two communities. While Fig. 1(b) takes ETUD into account. The thickness of an edge-type refer to its learned ETUD weight. Obviously the *plays* edge-type is more important for music recommendation. After all edge weights are updated by multiplying related ETUD values, four communities are detected by leveraging the same community detection method. Comparing the two community detection results, it is clear to see that involving ETUD can be beneficial to group the user and his/her favored songs to the same community, which supports music recommendation to achieve better accuracy.

The contribution of this paper is threefold:

- First, a genetic based approach is used to learn ETUD on the heterogeneous networks in an evolutionary manner. It converts a heterogeneous network to a homogeneous one to enable conventional community detection methods on heterogeneous networks as well.
- Second, two evaluation tasks are proposed to validate the positive influence of ETUD on heterogeneous networks from searching cost and recommendation accuracy viewpoints.
- Third, extensive experiments applied on a music online streaming service dataset, Xiami Music, validate that our proposed model is feasible for music recommendation in real cases.

2 Related Works

Homogeneous Community Detection. Current studies follow four main trends [6]: random walk, embedding, Modularity and overlapping community. node2vec [10], DeepWalk [15] and LINE [17] are three representative models to learn node embeddings by maximizing the probability to reproduce the network structures. Louvain method [1] designs an agglomerative framework to detect communities with largest Modularity score in an efficient manner. Infomap [2] assumes a random walker wanders on the network, and minimizes the cost to track the walker's path. Bigclam [21] formulates overlapping community detection problems into non-negative matrix factorization. [8,14] leverage cross-domain information for sparse network community detection.

Heterogeneous Community Detection. [18] formally describe the heterogeneous community detection problem with a framework of four integration schemes. [12] aims at overlapping community detection on heterogeneous networks. [4] decomposes the heterogeneous network to multiple simple networks. [20] constructs user profiles from folksonomy systems and use the profiles as auxiliary information for user community detection. [16] proposes to use metapath to control node communities with distinct semantics.

Community-Based Music Recommendation. [5] considers both user behaviors on playlists and music content profile. [3] constructs a hypergraph to model the multi-type objects in a music social community. [11] focus on edge-type selection in the heterogeneous network to retain main semantic meanings and trim the network to a smaller scope. Derived from [7,9], proposes a generic algorithm for music recommendation guided by user information need.

3 Method

In this section, a genetic approach is proposed here to learn the *edge-type usefulness distribution* (ETUD). ETUD is the weights for all edge-types to represent their usefulness towards the network. After each edge's weight is updated by multiplying related ETUD score to its original value according to its edge-type, a heterogeneous network is converted to a homogeneous one. Figure 2 shows the proposed method in detail.

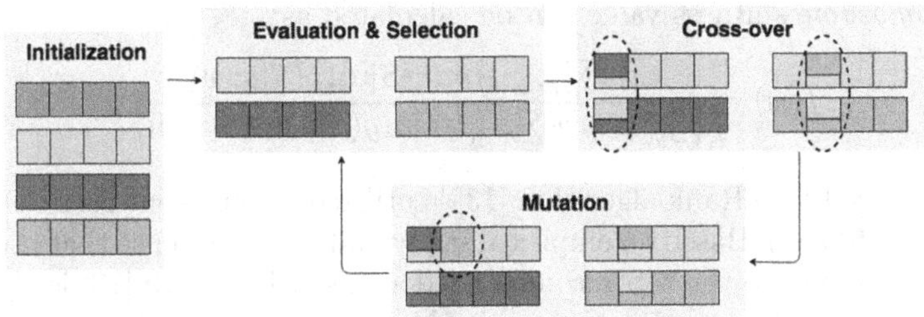

Fig. 2. Genetic approach to learn ETUD in an evolutionary manner

3.1 ETUD Initialization

In our genetic approach, the whole process simulates biological evolution process. We define a *chromosome* to represent a possible ETUD result. A *chromosome* is constructed by a set of *genes*, where each *gene* refers to an edge-type respectively. The value stores in each *gene* represents the usefulness score of a particular edge-type. A *chromosome* is initialized by randomly assigning value $\in [0,1]$ to each of its *gene* in the beginning. In total, P *chromosomes* are randomly initialized for further evolution process.

3.2 ETUD Assessment and Selection

Given P *chromosomes*, a fitness function needs to be set up as a criteria to evaluate each *chromosome*'s performance for music recommendation. The best ETUD should be able to best reproduce users' listening preference. In other words, we should find an ETUD that maximizes the similarity between songs' ranking list generated under this ETUD and user real preference on songs, which is described in Formula 1:

$$\underset{w}{\text{argmax}} \sum_{u \in U} sim(g(S|u), p(S|u; w)) \tag{1}$$

w is the *chromosome* we aim to retrieve, U is the set of all users and S is the set of all songs in the music network. $g(S|u)$ is the real listening preference of user $u \in U$; $p(S|u; w)$ is all songs ranking list we estimated for user u given the ETUD w. Function $sim(\cdot)$ measures the similarity between the two ranking lists. It is hard to leverage stochastic gradient decent on Formula 1 directly as the differential of $p(S|u; w)$ may be too complex to compute. Genetic approach offers an evolution process to solve this challenge instead. As there are in total P *chromosomes* representing possible ETUD results, we can evaluate each *chromosome* and select better ones to bring offspring *chromosomes*. We call a cycle of selecting *chromosomes* and breeding new offspring *chromosomes* as a *generation*. The whole evolution process will keep running until the fittest *chromosome* in each *generation* no longer changes. Derived from Formula 1, In this paper, each *chromosome*'s fitness value can be calculated as:

$$f(w) = \frac{exp(\sum_{u \in U} sim(g(S|u), p(S|u; w))}{\sum_{p \in P} exp(\sum_{u \in U} sim(g(S|u), p(S|u; p))} \tag{2}$$

Personalized PageRank algorithm [13] is utilized to represent user u listening preference $p(S|u; w)$. Based on empirical study and common sense that users may only pay attention to the top recommended songs, NDCG@10 [19] is chosen as the similarity judging function $sim(\cdot, \cdot)$ in this paper. NDCG@10 is an evaluation metric to judge how well the estimated ranking list $p(S|u; w)$ matches the user u's real listening preference $g(S|u)$ and is more sensitive to top ranked results. To represent the fitness score of *chromosome* w, we calculate the similarity scores among all users and normalize it via a Softmax function on all *chromosomes*.

In genetic approach, *chromosomes* with higher fitness score should have higher chance to be preserved for the next-round evolution. Hence, we use bootstrap sampling strategy (random sampling with replicates) to randomly sample P *chromosomes* based on their fitness scores. This sampling strategy has two advantages: First, there are always P *chromosomes* in each generation, which ensures a stable evolution process; Second, *chromosomes* with higher fitness scores are more likely to be preserved, so that the best ETUD result is more likely to be found after running a number of *generations*.

3.3 ETUD Transformation

The initialized & selected *chromosomes* can not fully cover the whole possible ETUD results. Hence, there is a need to search the whole ETUD result space and find out the best one. To achieve this in an efficient manner, two transformation strategies including Cross-over and Mutation are applied. These two strategies help to generate new *chromosomes* from the original selected *chromosomes*, which achieves the *chromosome* evolution.

Specifically, In Cross-over step, all selected *chromosomes* are grouped into pairs first, and the Cross-over transformation will be applied within pairs. Given two *chromosomes* in the same pair, which are denoted as w_1 and w_2. In this step, w_1 and w_2 exchange values stored in partial of their genes to create two offspring *chromosomes*. w_{1k} refers to the edge-type usefulness weight stored in the k_{th} gene of w_1. The whole process is showed as:

$$w_{ij}^* = (\frac{w_{ij}}{w_{1j} + w_{2j}})^{p_j} w_{ij}^{(1-p_j)} \tag{3}$$

$$p_j = \begin{cases} 1, & r_j \geq t_c \\ 0, & r_j < t_c \end{cases} \tag{4}$$

where $i \in \{1, 2\}$ refers to the index of the two newly generated *chromosomes*. w_{ij} is the value of the j_{th} gene in w_i. p_j is an binary indicator to decide whether the cross-over step occurs on the j_{th} gene or not. The value of p_j is controlled by a randomly generated variable $r_j \in [0, 1]$ and a pre-defined threshold $t_c \in [0, 1]$.

Unlike the Cross-over step to generate new offspring *chromosomes* via the interactions between two original *chromosomes*, Mutation step allows a *chromosome* to generate a new offspring *chromosome* within itself. For *chromosome* w_1, instead of exchanging values of genes with another *chromosome* w_2, it exchanges its genes' value with a random variable $\mathcal{X}$ randomly drew from normal distribution $\mathcal{X} \sim \mathcal{N}(0, 1)$. And the gene values of new *chromosome* is still calculated via Formulas 3 and 4 with another pre-defined threshold $t_m \in [0, 1]$.

3.4 ETUD Finalization

The whole evolution process will keep running for *generations* until the best *chromosome* no longer changes for N generations. And the *chromosome* with largest fitness value in the last *generation* will be the returned ETUD.

However, there is still an edge-type dependency issue remained. One example viewed in Fig. 1 is that edge-type *performIn* and edge-type *plays* are independent so that their weights are not comparable. To address this, we define:

Definition 1. Two edge-types are dependent only if they share either same start-node type or same end-node type. And only weights of dependent edge-types are comparable.

Following Definition 1, all edge-types are grouped into several independent sets first (In Fig. 1, the edge-type sets are {*performsIn*, *includes*} and {*plays*, *bookmarks*}). After that, ETUD weights of edge-types in the same set are normalized via the formula:

$$ew_i^* = \frac{ew_i}{\sum_{S(e_i)=S(e_j)} ew_j} \tag{5}$$

e_i refers to the i_{th} edge-type; ew_i refers to the returned ETUD weight of edge-type e_i; $S(e_i)$ is the edge-type set which e_i belongs to. And the normalized ew_i^* is regarded as the final edge-type usefulness weight of e_i.

4 Experiment

4.1 Dataset Description and Parameter Setting

In this paper, the dataset used for music recommendation is from Xiami, one of the largest online music streaming services in China. Based on user behaviors and song profiles, a complex heterogeneous network is constructed. Details of the network are showed in Tables 1 and 2. Besides this network, we also have all users listening history record as ground truth. For each user, all his/her listened songs are labelled as a score $\in \{1, 2, 3, 4\}$, representing the quartile of their play counts belongs to. The listening history of 70% users are randomly sampled used to training our model (used in Sect. 3.2), and the rest 30% users are used for our model validation.

Table 1. Node statistics

Node-type	Count	Node-type	Count	Node-type	Count
Song	54,353	User	38,780	Genre	543
Playlist	47,098	Artist	9,901	Album	17,730

Table 2. Edge statistics

Edge	Name	Count	Edge	Name	Count
user→song	plays	3,991,226	user→playlist	makes	42,775
playlist→song	includes	514,652	album→song	include	40,798
user→artist	plays	238,862	user→artist	comment	36,813
user→song	bookmarks	213,602	artist→album	performsIn	17,457
user→song	comments	136,078	album→genre	categorizedAs	15,174
user→album	bookmarks	89,342	user→playlist	bookmark	9,982
user→album	comments	59,575	artist→genre	categorizedAs	9,726
artist→song	performsIn	57,675	user→playlist	comment	9443

The parameters used in our approach are set based on empirical experiments and previous studies: number of initialized *chromosome* $P = 1000$; Cross-over threshold $t_c = 0.95$ and Mutation threshold $t_m = 0.1$; termination criteria is when the best *chromosome* no longer changes for $\mathbb{N} = 10$ generations.

4.2 Searching Cost with Between-Community Jumping

The first task is to examine whether applying ETUD on heterogeneous networks can reduce the searching cost of retrieving all users' listened songs.

In our music network, each user u will belong to a community after a community detection method is leveraged. When user u looks for songs to listen, there is a searching cost for the user to retrieve all his/her favored songs. We simulate user searching behaviours and define the overall searching cost as:

$$Cost(U_t, S) = \sum_{u \in U_t} \sum_{k=1}^{K} \sum_{s \in C_u^k} \frac{\sum_{s \in C_u^k} \mathbb{I}(s|u)}{\varphi(s|u) \sum_{s \in S} \mathbb{I}(s|u)} \cdot log(\|C_u^{(k-1)}\| \cdot \|C_u^k\|) \quad (6)$$

U_t is the collection of all testing users and S are all songs in the heterogeneous network. There are K communities generated by leveraging conventional methods. As in each community, the number of songs that u listened before can be calculated, all communities are ranked by their contained number of listened songs in the descending order. Therefore C_u^k means the community containing the k_{th} most number of user u's listened songs. $\|C_u^k\|$ is the number of nodes in this community. To make it easier to calculate, we define $\|C_u^0\|= 1$. $\varphi(s|u)$ is the number of times that user u listens song s. $\mathbb{I}(s|u)$ is binary indicator $\in \{0, 1\}$ to judge whether user u listened the song before or not.

This searching cost function depicts how much effort users take to retrieve all their listened songs by jumping between communities. For each user u, the community ranking reveals how user u favors to each community. The user u starts to search from the most favoured community to the least favoured community in a descending sequence until all listened songs are retrieved. Formula 6 defines a searching cost for all testing users jumping between communities. Community sizes of previous community and current community are considered during community jumping as larger community will take users more effort to find the listened songs. The searching cost also has a reciprocal relationship with the number of times users listened on songs because for more favored songs, the searching cost to retrieve them should be less. We calculate communities generated with/without ETUD with six classic conventional community detection algorithms (See Sect. 2 for algorithm description) and compare the searching cost of retrieving the top 5,10,20,50,100 listened songs for all testing users (songs are ranked by the number of listening times). The result is shown in Table 3.

Table 3. Searching cost results comparison

Algorithm	Category	Edge-type	Comm. #	Cost@5	Cost@10	Cost@20	Cost@50	Cost@100
DeepWalk [15]	Embedding	No	100	197.29	420.01	897.37	2309.50	4450.39
		Yes	100	**187.99**	**402.51**	**856.04**	**2054.70**	**4121.64**
LINE [17]	Embedding	No	100	172.03	379.08	811.87	2106.40	4134.17
		Yes	100	**162.29**	**371.29**	**783.70**	**2012.18**	**3922.18**
node2vec [10]	Embedding	No	100	181.84	391.83	849.79	2175.11	4132.87
		Yes	100	**173.60**	**390.29**	**824.02**	**2096.56**	**3984.89**
Louvain [1]	Modularity	No	12	577.40	1275.62	2695.33	6925.05	12845.07
		Yes	38	**533.19**	**1092.83**	**2350.49**	**5963.32**	**10532.66**
Infomap [2]	Random walk	No	3705	850.09	1918.62	4022.01	10372.20	19784.88
		Yes	4507	**682.42**	**1571.91**	**3358.09**	**8494.20**	**15997.72**
BigClam [21]	Overlapping	No	100	11.23	27.80	56.73	131.87	270.42
		Yes	100	**7.91**	**16.68**	**39.36**	**105.74**	**183.10**

Although different algorithms have different-scale searching costs and community number, all community results learned with ETUD require less searching cost than the communities without considering ETUD significantly. It means that learning ETUD via our model on heterogeneous network can reduce users' effort to search their favoured songs.

4.3 Searching Accuracy Within Community

After exploring how well ETUD can help to reduce searching costs, we are also willing to see whether it also benefits music recommendation accuracy within communities. Ideally, the learned ETUD should have positive effect to group users and their favoured songs into the same community. In this task, for each testing user u, we select all songs in the same community as the user, and rank the songs based on their PageRank scores calculated during the training process. NDCG is still the evaluation metric used to evaluate how well the generated PageRank result matches user real listening history. The averaged NDCG score for all testing users is in Table 4. From the result, under all circumstances, NDCG scores with ETUD are significantly higher than scores without ETUD. It infers that by taking ETUD into account, it is more likely to group users and their favoured songs into the same community.

Table 4. Within-community music retrieval accuracy evaluation

Algorithm	Edge-type	NDCG @5	NDCG@10	NDCG@20	NDCG@100
DeepWalk	No	0.6932	0.6974	0.6971	0.5741
	Yes	**0.7529**	**0.7355**	**0.7162**	**0.5992**
LINE	No	0.4883	0.3588	0.2530	0.1055
	Yes	**0.5153**	**0.4141**	**0.3057**	**0.1401**
node2vec	No	0.6995	0.7007	0.6967	0.5796
	Yes	**0.7476**	**0.7349**	**0.7206**	**0.5924**
Louvain	No	0.6764	0.6742	0.6829	0.7168
	Yes	**0.7370**	**0.7366**	**0.7328**	**0.7328**
Infomap	No	0.7020	0.6955	0.6974	0.7264
	Yes	**0.7548**	**0.7430**	**0.7332**	**0.6927**
BigClam	No	0.5963	0.5193	0.4524	0.2626
	Yes	**0.6479**	**0.5793**	**0.5022**	**0.2376**

5 Conclusion

In this paper, we put efforts on how to convert a heterogeneous network to a homogeneous one so that conventional community detection methods can still be eligible to use. It extends the application scope of those conventional methods and endows them more generalizable and robust usage. To achieve this, a genetic based approach is developed to learn the edge-type usefulness distribution (ETUD) on heterogeneous networks. Experiments on a real music dataset show that involving ETUD in heterogeneous community detection is able to facilitate the accuracy of music recommendation with less search cost significantly. In the future, we will explore more sophisticated algorithms such as reinforcement learning methods for ETUD estimation.

References

1. Blondel, V.D., Guillaume, J.L., Lambiotte, R., Lefebvre, E.: Fast unfolding of communities in large networks. J. Stat. Mech: Theory Exp. **2008**(10), P10008 (2008)
2. Bohlin, L., Edler, D., Lancichinetti, A., Rosvall, M.: Community detection and visualization of networks with the map equation framework. In: Ding, Y., Rousseau, R., Wolfram, D. (eds.) Measuring Scholarly Impact, pp. 3–34. Springer, Cham (2014). https://doi.org/10.1007/978-3-319-10377-8_1
3. Bu, J., et al.: Music recommendation by unified hypergraph: combining social media information and music content. In: Proceedings of the 18th ACM international conference on Multimedia, pp. 391–400. ACM (2010)
4. Comar, P.M., Tan, P.-N., Jain, A.K.: Simultaneous classification and community detection on heterogeneous network data. Data Min. Knowl. Disc. **25**(3), 420–449 (2012). https://doi.org/10.1007/s10618-012-0260-3
5. Donaldson, J.: A hybrid social-acoustic recommendation system for popular music. In: Proceedings of the 2007 ACM Conference on Recommender Systems, pp. 187–190. ACM (2007)
6. Gao, Z.: Community detection in graphs. Ph.D. thesis, Indiana University (2020)
7. Gao, Z., Guo, C., Liu, X.: Efficient personalized community detection via genetic evolution. In: Proceedings of the Genetic and Evolutionary Computation Conference, pp. 383–391 (2019)
8. Gao, Z., Li, H., Jiang, Z., Liu, X.: Detecting user community in sparse domain via cross-graph pairwise learning. In: Proceedings of the 43rd International ACM SIGIR Conference on Research and Development in Information Retrieval, pp. 139–148 (2020)
9. Gao, Z., Liu, X.: Personalized community detection in scholarly network. In: iConference 2017 Proceedings, vol. 2 (2017)
10. Grover, A., Leskovec, J.: node2vec: scalable feature learning for networks. In: Proceedings of the 22nd ACM SIGKDD International Conference on Knowledge Discovery and Data Mining, pp. 855–864. ACM (2016)
11. Guo, C.: Feature generation and selection on the heterogeneous graph for music recommendation. In: Proceedings of the Ninth ACM International Conference on Web Search and Data Mining, pp. 715–715. ACM (2016)
12. Huang, M., Zou, G., Zhang, B., Liu, Y., Gu, Y., Jiang, K.: Overlapping community detection in heterogeneous social networks via the user model. Inf. Sci. **432**, 164–184 (2018)
13. Kloumann, I.M., Ugander, J., Kleinberg, J.: Block models and personalized pagerank. Proc. Natl. Acad. Sci. **114**(1), 33–38 (2017)
14. Ma, S., Zhang, C.: Document representation and clustering models for bilingual documents clustering. Proc. Assoc. Inf. Sci. Technol. **54**(1), 499–502 (2017)

15. Perozzi, B., Al-Rfou, R., Skiena, S.: DeepWalk: online learning of social representations. In: Proceedings of the 20th ACM SIGKDD International Conference on Knowledge Discovery and Data Mining, pp. 701–710. ACM (2014)
16. Sun, Y., Norick, B., Han, J., Yan, X., Yu, P.S., Yu, X.: PathSelClus: integrating meta-path selection with user-guided object clustering in heterogeneous information networks. ACM Trans. Knowl. Discov. Data (TKDD) **7**(3), 11 (2013)
17. Tang, J., Qu, M., Wang, M., Zhang, M., Yan, J., Mei, Q.: Line: large-scale information network embedding. In: Proceedings of the 24th International Conference on World Wide Web, pp. 1067–1077. International World Wide Web Conferences Steering Committee (2015)
18. Tang, L., Wang, X., Liu, H.: Community detection via heterogeneous interaction analysis. Data Min. Knowl. Disc. **25**(1), 1–33 (2012)
19. Wang, Y., Wang, L., Li, Y., He, D., Chen, W., Liu, T.Y.: A theoretical analysis of NDCG ranking measures. In: Proceedings of the 26th Annual Conference on Learning Theory (COLT 2013), vol. 8, p. 6. Citeseer (2013)
20. Xie, H., Li, Q., Mao, X., Li, X., Cai, Y., Rao, Y.: Community-aware user profile enrichment in folksonomy. Neural Netw. **58**, 111–121 (2014)
21. Yang, J., Leskovec, J.: Overlapping community detection at scale: a nonnegative matrix factorization approach. In: Proceedings of the Sixth ACM International Conference on Web Search and Data Mining, pp. 587–596. ACM (2013)

Information Literacy, Transition, and Risk in the COVID-19-Environment

Annemaree Lloyd and Alison Hicks(✉)

University College, London (UCL), London WC16BT, UK
{annemaree.lloyd,a.hicks}@ucl.ac.uk

Abstract. This paper examines how people transitioned into newly created pandemic information environments and the ways in which information literacy practices came into view as the SARS-CoV-2 virus took hold in the UK. Employing a qualitative research design, semi-structured interviews were carried out from May 2020-February 2021 with 32 participants, including people who were engaged in new employment, voluntary or caring roles as well as people who had been diagnosed with COVID. Findings demonstrate that transition into new pandemic environments was shaped by an unfolding phase, an intensification phase, and a stable phase, and information literacy emerged as a form of safeguarding as participants mitigated health, financial and wellbeing risks. This paper develops research into the role that information practices play during crisis as well as extending understanding related to the concept of empowerment, which forms a key idea within information literacy discourse. Findings will be useful for librarians and information professionals as well as public health researchers designing health promotion strategies.

Keywords: COVID-19 · Information literacy · Risk · Transition · Avoidance

1 Introduction

The aim of this study is to investigate people's information practices over time as the COVID-19 pandemic played out in the UK throughout 2020 and 2021. During this period, the COVID-19 pandemic led to three periods of government mandated lockdown, including in March-June 2020, October/November 2020, and December-March 2021. Centred on a strict curtailment of face-to-face interaction, restrictions imposed at the time encouraged workers to work from home or to be furloughed under the government scheme and forced schools and universities to move teaching online. Certain groups were additionally classified as "vulnerable" and encouraged to shield in their homes.

As information researchers, we are particularly interested in the way that information literacy practices came into view as people transitioned into pandemic information environments, including taking on new working, caring or voluntary roles. As the pandemic continued, we became further focused on the longer-term implications of functioning in crisis mode as the UK was plunged in and out of local restrictions before returning to national lockdown conditions. From this perspective, we concentrated on how people

M. Smits (Ed.): iConference 2022, LNCS 13193, pp. 79–87, 2022.
https://doi.org/10.1007/978-3-030-96960-8_6

constructed an understanding of risk within the pandemic context as well as how they operationalised information practices to deal with the changing range and volume of information that was being produced across social and technological platforms. These ideas are expressed through the following research question:

- What has informed the UK public's understanding about the COVID-19 pandemic and what information practices and literacies of information came into view during the early days of the pandemic and the subsequent countrywide lockdowns?

Within this framing, information literacy is positioned as a social practice that is enacted in social settings and composed of activities and skills that reference structured and embodied knowledges and ways of knowing relevant to the context [1].

2 Literature Review

2.1 Risk

Risk has typically either been understood through a techno-scientific perspective, as an objective hazard, or through a sociocultural approach, as a concept that is mediated through social and cultural processes [2, 3]. This study adopts a sociocultural perspective, which positions risk as real, but as embedded in a local context [4]. These ideas focus attention on social, corporeal, and epistemic meaning making or how risk is brought into view though "personal embodied experiences, observations and emotional responses, discussions with others and access to expert knowledges" [2, p.45]. To date, the emphasis on techno-scientific approaches to danger means that risk information environments have not been explored in significant detail beyond recognising the role that emotions and trust play within risk societies [e.g., 5]. An exception includes the work of Hicks [6], who studied the information practices of language-learners in a culturally unfamiliar setting. Leading to the production of the grounded theory of mitigating risk, which states that risks produced during language-learners' sojourns overseas catalyse the enactment of information literacy practices that mediate transition within a new setting [6], this localised research points to the important role that information activities play in both constructing and mediating danger.

2.2 COVID-19 Studies

Information use forms a small but important theme within COVID-19 literature to date. Initially focusing on information sources that people employ to adjust to the pandemic [7–10], research has since started to examine the impact of anxiety on information seeking as the pandemic progressed. Within this framing, the amount of COVID-19 information available to people [11], stress [12, 13] and mistrust of the government [14] have been seen to lead to information overload and subsequently, information avoidance. However, studies rarely look beyond the initial stages of the pandemic (March-May 2020), with little research examining the ongoing impact of crisis on information practices. An exception is a report from the British Red Cross [15], which notes how the implementation of local rather than national lockdowns created considerable confusion related to information access and use.

2.3 Crisis Information Studies

Before 2020, studies of the role that information plays during crisis tended to centre on natural hazards, including floods and hurricanes [e.g., 16–18], as well as human disasters such as 9/11 [19]. Typically emphasising the vital role that the community plays in providing emotional and informational support during times of uncertainty [16, 20, 21], these studies have also noted the impact that images [22] and observing environmental cues play in helping people to understand the severity of the situation [22–24]. Trust forms another important subtheme within this literature, with authors exploring these ideas in relation to misinformation [17, 25] and anxiety [16, 26].

3 Methodology

The study employed a qualitative methodology to explore what informed the UK public's understanding about the COVID-19 pandemic. Semi-structured interviews were carried out online from May 2020 through to February 2021 during the UK's three lockdown phases (March-June 2020; October/November 2020; and December-March 2021). The interviews were open-ended but focused on examining transition into and out of each of the lockdown phases, including new furlough, working, caring, or home-schooling roles as well as changing information needs throughout the year. Interviews took place on an end-to-end encrypted video conferencing tool and were audio-recorded and transcribed. Interviews lasted between 30 and 50 min and follow up questions were emailed to participants when necessary.

The study sample comprised 32 participants who were recruited through social media and a snowball sampling method. Participants included keyworkers and people working from home as well as people who had lost their jobs or who were furloughed. Participants also included retirees and people taking on new home-schooling, caring or volunteer roles, as well as people who had previously been diagnosed with COVID. Participants were located throughout the UK and represented a range of ages between 18–80.

Data were coded and analysed by each researcher using the constant comparative technique that is found in constructivist grounded theory methods [27]. Each researcher reviewed and coded the recordings and transcription separately before coming together to discuss the coding over several online sessions. The researchers also undertook a situational analysis [28] to help visualise how participants engaged with information within and throughout the pandemic. Limitations of the study include the relative difficulty recruiting younger participants (18–25) to the research as well as increasing lockdown fatigue, which may have impacted enthusiasm to participate in the project.

4 Findings

Three phases of transition are highlighted as people move into and begin to construct an understanding of the rapidly emerging COVID-19 context, including the evolving conditions and social (re)arrangements that shape their everyday, social, and working lives. Each of these phases references the information activities that help to mediate transition as the pandemic is brought into view and participants start to construct their understanding of risk. These phases are represented in Fig. 1, alongside the study's overarching category of safeguarding, which forms the outcome of information literacy practice during the COVID-19 pandemic. Safeguarding constitutes the agentic information work that participants to understand and then to mitigate the risk established through government, scientific and everyday discourse.

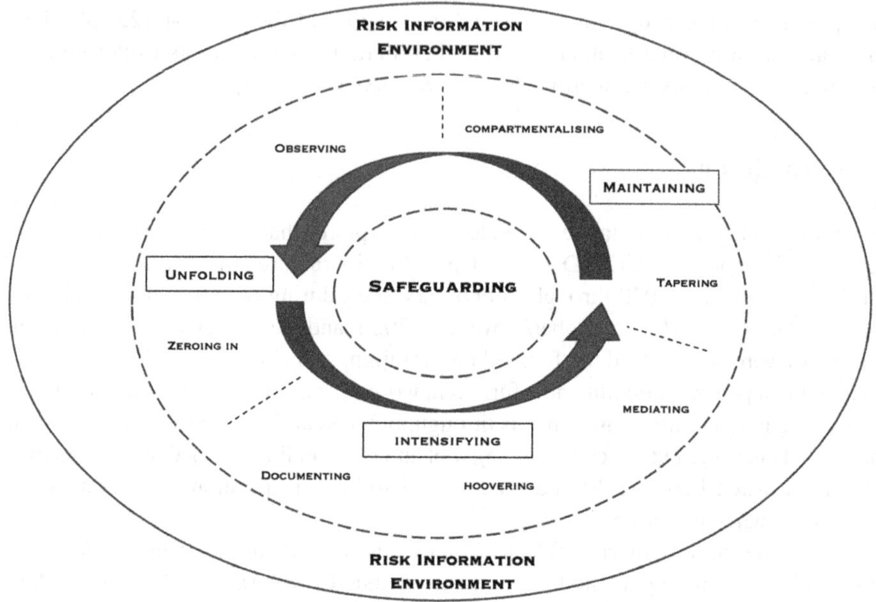

Fig. 1. Information landscape of safeguarding [29]

4.1 Phase One: Unfolding

The COVID-19 information environment begins to unfold within Phase One. During this time, participants' awareness and understanding of the spread of the SARS CoV-2 virus is tinged with disbelief and characterised by exploratory engagement with authoritative information sources, including governmental advice, which is reported via a range of media channels, as well as physical cues. In this stage, which represents an initial engagement with the pandemic theatre, information literacy practice is represented by observing, which refers to a reliance on physical and visual cues to confirm rules that were established through formal governmental and scientific sources, and zeroing in, which refers to the targeting of tried and tested information providers.

4.2 Phase Two: Intensifying

Phase Two is represented by a period of intensification whereby people actively immerse themselves in a wide range of information environments to 'grasp' the pandemic and recognise its implications. Marked by anxiety and stress, this time reflects the growth of new rules and regulations, for instance, the implementation of queuing measures in shops, as well as increased social engagement as people draw upon their social networks to build a more complex understanding of the pandemic. In this stage, information literacy practice is represented by hoovering, which refers to participants' indiscriminate approach to gathering news, mediating, which refers to interpreting information through and with family, friends, and social networks, and documenting, which refers to the creative recording of information about the pandemic, including taking photos and keeping diaries.

4.3 Phase Three: Maintaining

Phase Three emerges as a more stable phase that is represented by a mapped understanding of the information sources and activities that are required to maintain an informed view of the pandemic. During this phase, the ongoing and multilayered complexity of the information environment meant that participants begin to make decisions about the amount of information they require and sources that are trusted. Centring on saturation and the creation of boundaries, information literacy practice during this time is represented by compartmentalising, which refers to avoiding information to reduce the sense of being overwhelmed by a saturated information environment, and tapering off, which refers to the narrowing down of information sources.

4.4 Safeguarding

Transition into the novel pandemic information environment is subsequently characterised in terms of safeguarding, which refers to how participants mitigate the risks of their new setting. As the overarching concept of the study, safeguarding emerges though the information work that participants engage in to firstly, reconcile understanding about the pandemic on social life and secondly, situate themselves intersubjectively in relation to collective knowledge. Emerging as an information practice as people become informed about the changed conditions and arrangements that influence their agency, safeguarding also refers to the ways in which people protect the National Health Service (NHS), which was consistently seen to be at risk of becoming overwhelmed by patient admissions. Safeguarding consequently centres upon the protection of self, family, friends, and institutions and is catalysed by the risks that were produced during the pandemic.

5 Discussion

The findings from this study suggest that during the pandemic, conceptualisations of risk unfolded across three interconnected dimensions to construct the practice of safeguarding, which illustrates how information literacy practice is shaped and enacted. Providing an emerging view of COVID-19 from an information perspective, these ideas draw attention to what comes into view within a pandemic information environment, including transition, information literacy and risk.

5.1 Transition

Transition is brought into view through people's growing understanding of the new conditions and arrangements that shape their everyday social life. Referring to change over time, transition is shaped by sociocultural conditions and focused upon the redefinition of self [30]. From an information perspective, transition is consequently positioned as centred on the reconstruction of information landscapes [1] – that is, participants' awareness of the pandemic changes over time as they engage with and become situated within the unfolding information environment. The concept of transition enables us to make visible how the pandemic information landscape [1] is entered, experienced, and then stabilised as people develop an intersubjective understanding of this new setting.

The feelings of saturation that people experienced as an outcome of the intensifying phase also brings the transitional space between the intensifying and maintenance phases of the pandemic into view.The information avoidance strategies in which people reported engaging within the third maintaining phase, as represented by compartmentalising and tapering off, stood out because they appeared to reference performances of people who are burnt out by the repeated imposition of lockdown measures, particularly when they are referenced against the community reinforcement actions of the unfolding and intensifying stages. Avoidance strategies also became irreconcilably entwined with the idea of resistance as people start to refuse to engage with official government advice. However, we argue that transitional spaces make the emotional demands of the time visible-that is, these actions should be understood as protective measures that people employ to regulate the emotional impact of change rather than being treated as "pathologies" [31]. Grounded in affective judgement, these activities illustrate how transition is facilitated through reflexive processes and agentic performance [32, p.149] as people manage the impact of transformation within their lives.

5.2 Information Literacy

Information literacy, as represented by the practice of safeguarding, is brought into view through the emerging pandemic context, which predetermines practice, agency, and activity. Consisting of three interlinked dimensions, this context is constituted by government briefings and official messaging, which reference the formal political, scientific, medical, and public health risk narratives; corporeal or physical information, which establishes preconditions that enable or constrain agency and performance; and the sharing of information, which creates the collective space through which the pandemic is mediated. From this perspective, information literacy is centred on participation and sensory interaction and reflects the pandemic's legitimised formal discourses.

The important roles that saturation, avoidance and resistance play within the pandemic illustrate how information literacy cannot always be understood affirmatively as a series of proactive and enabling activities. Instead, findings from this study draw attention to the reactive elements of practice, or how people respond to rather than prepare for the conditions of practice. The recognition that information literacy practice is premised upon conditions that purposefully constrain access to information consequently challenges the empowerment narratives that are positioned as a key outcome of information literacy practice [33]. Saturation, avoidance, and resistance also raise questions about how these ideas can be accommodated within educational curricula that typically focus on information literacy's positive narrative.

5.3 Risk

Information activities also bring risk into view, which is positioned in this study as a temporal and spatial enactment that is shaped through the ways in which people access, use and disseminate information. Linked to the negotiation of "meanings, logics, and beliefs" [2, p.44] rather than the acceptance of 'neutral' or objective expertise, these findings also illustrate the important role that affective judgement, including feelings of fear and safety, plays in giving form to danger and hazard. From an information perspective, risk must consequently be understood as shaped through visual, social, corporeal, and epistemic literacies as the pandemic information environments contextualise different forms of knowledge and create discourses that position people within sociocultural frameworks.

6 Conclusion

This yearlong study of how people in the UK coped and lived with the COVID-19 pandemic and its associated lockdowns has provided difficult but unique insight into how information practices emerge within complex and uncertain crisis situations. Findings suggest that risk unfolds across three dimensions to create the practice of safeguarding of self, others, and institutions. Representing information literacy practice within the pandemic situation, safeguarding also helps to demonstrate how information landscapes [1] are entered and stabilised as people transition from pre to pandemic information environments. The extension of our study beyond the initial lockdown period has allowed us to further refine these ideas by examining the idea of transitional space in more detail, including the important role that reactive elements of practice play in safeguarding against intense and accelerated information environments. Implications for this study include the problematisation of empowerment narratives, which play a central role within information literacy discourse. The importance that this study place on the reactive elements of practice, which establish an affirmative/non-affirmative binary, also challenges the labelling of information literacy as holistic. Future research should continue to explore the impact of ongoing crisis upon decision-making as well as to examine concepts of saturation and desensitisation in relation to COVID-19 vaccine hesitancy.

References

1. Lloyd, A.: Information Literacy Landscapes. Chandos Publishing (2010)
2. Lupton, D.: Risk. Routledge, London (2013)
3. Zinn, J.: Introduction: the contribution of sociology to the dicourse on risk and Uncertainty. In: Zinn, J. (ed.) Social Theories of Risk and Uncertainty: An Introduction. New York, John Wiley and Sons (2009)
4. Douglas, M.: Risk and blame: essays in cultural theory. Routledge, London (1992)
5. Choo, C.W.: Seeking and avoiding information in a risky world. Inf. Res. **22**(3) (2017)

6. Hicks, A.: Mitigating risk: mediating transition through the enactment of information literacy practices. J. Document. **75**(5), 1190–1210 (2019)
7. Bray, L., et al.: People play it down and tell me it can't kill people, but I know people are dying each day. children's health literacy relating to a global pandemic (COVID-19); an international cross-sectional study. Plos One, **16**(2) (2021)
8. Lupton, D., Lewis, S.: Learning about COVID-19: a qualitative interview study of Australians' use of information sources. BMC Public Health **21**(1), 1–10 (2021)
9. Savolainen, R.: Sharing experiential information in online discussion: the case of coping with the COVID-19 epidemic. J. Documentation (2021)
10. Sykes, S., Wills, J., Trasolini, A., Wood, K., Frings, D.: eHealth literacy during the COVID-19 pandemic: seeking, sharing, suspicion amongst older and younger UK populations. Health Promotion International (2021)
11. Okan, O., Bollweg, T.M., Berens, E.M., Hurrelmann, K., Bauer, U., Schaeffer, D.: Coronavirus-related health literacy: a cross-sectional study in adults during the COVID-19 infodemic in Germany. Int. J. Environ. Res. Public Health, **17**(15) (2020)
12. Karim, M., Singh, R., Widén, G.: Dealing with the COVID-19 infodemic: understanding young people's emotions and coping mechanisms in Finland and the United States. Nordic J. Library Inf. Stud. **2**(1), 38–57 (2021)
13. Soroya, S.H., Farooq, A., Mahmood, K., Isoaho, J., Zara, S.E.: From information seeking to information avoidance: understanding the health information behavior during a global health crisis. Inf. Process. Manage. **58**(2) (2021)
14. Nielsen R.K., Fletcher, R., Newman, N.: Navigating the 'infodemic': how people in six countries access and rate news and information about coronavirus. Reuters Institute report, Reuters Institute for the Study of Journalism, Oxford. https://reutersinstitute.politics.ox.ac.uk/infodemic-how-people-six-countries-access-and-rate-news-and-information-about-coronavirus. Accessed 6 Aug 2021
15. British Red Cross: The longest year: life under local restrictions. https://www.redcross.org.uk/-/media/documents/about-us/research-publications/emergency-response/the-longest-year-life-under-local-restrictions.pdf. Accessed 6 Aug 2021
16. Lopatovska, I., Smiley, B.: Proposed model of information behaviour in crisis: the case of Hurricane Sandy. Inf. Res. **19**(1) (2013)
17. Pang, N., Karanasios, S., Anwar, M.: Exploring the information worlds of older persons during disasters. J. Am. Soc. Inf. Sci. **71**(6), 619–631 (2020)
18. Rahmi, R., Joho, H., Shirai, T.: An analysis of natural disaster-related information-seeking behavior using temporal stages. J. Am. Soc. Inf. Sci. **70**(7), 715–728 (2019)
19. Fu, L.: The government response to 9/11: communications technology and the media. Library Archival Security **24**(2), 103–118 (2011)
20. Hagar, C.: Crisis information management: communication and technologies. Chandos, Oxford (2011)
21. Shklovski, I., Palen, L., Sutton, J.: Finding community through information and communication technology in disaster response. In: Proceedings of the 2008 ACM Conference on Computer Supported Cooperative Work, pp. 127–136 (2008)
22. Ryan, B.: Establishing information seeking pathways in slow and flash floods. Int. J. Disaster Risk Reduc. **31**, 9–19 (2018)
23. Muhren, W.J., Van de Walle, B.: Sense-making and information management in emergency response. Bull. Am. Soc. Inf. Sci. Technol. **36**(5), 30–33 (2010)
24. Ryan, B.: Information seeking in a flood. Disaster Preven. Manage. Int. J. **22**(3), 229–242 (2013)
25. Starbird, K., Spiro, E.S., Koltai, K.: Misinformation, crisis, and public health—reviewing the literature. Social Science Research Council. https://mediawell.ssrc.org/literature-reviews/misinformation-crisis-and-public-health/versions/v1-0/ (2020)

26. Griffin, R.J., Dunwoody, S., Neuwirth, K.: Proposed model of the relationship of risk information seeking and processing to the development of preventive behaviors. Environ. Res. **80**(2), S230–S245 (1999)
27. Charmaz, K.: Constructing grounded theory. SAGE Publications, London (2014)
28. Clarke, A.: Situational analysis. CA, SAGE Publications, Thousand Oaks (2005)
29. Lloyd, A., Hicks, A.: Contextualising Risk: The unfolding information work and practices of people during the COVID-19 pandemic. J. Documentation **77**(3), 1052–1072 (2021)
30. Meleis, A.I., Sawyer, L.M., Im, E.O., Messias, D.K.H., Schumacher, K.: Experiencing transitions: an emerging middle-range theory. Adv. Nurs. Sci. **23**(1), 12–28 (2000)
31. Bawden, D., Robinson, L.: The dark side of information: overload, anxiety and other paradoxes and pathologies. J. Inf. Sci. **35**(2), 180–191 (2009)
32. Kralik, D.: The quest for ordinariness: transition experienced by midlife women living with chronic illness. J. Adv. Nurs. **39**(2), 146–154 (2002)
33. Hicks, A., Lloyd, A.: Deconstructing information literacy discourse: peeling back the layers in higher education. J. Libr. Inf. Sci. **53**(4), 559–571 (2021)

Intentions to Seek Information About COVID-19 Vaccine Among Young Adults: An Application of the Theory of Planned Behavior

Yue Ming[1], Ying Zhu[1](✉), and Miriam Matteson[2]

[1] College of Communication and Information, Kent State University, Kent, OH 44242, USA
yzhu28@kent.edu

[2] School of Information, Kent State University, Kent, OH 44242, USA

Abstract. Young adults have been one of the lowest vaccinated groups against COVID-19 in the U.S. Since information seeking intention is closely related to individual's behavior intention, this study used expanded theory of planned behavior model to explain COVID-19 vaccine information seeking intention among young adults. Results suggested that attitudes, subjective norms, self-efficacy, perceived susceptibility, and political view were significantly associated with information seeking intention while anticipated regret was not significantly associated with information seeking intention. The overall model contributed a substantive part of variance of information seeking intention ($R^2 = 0.58$). Implications for public health communication strategies and vaccination campaigns were discussed.

Keywords: Information seeking · COVID-19 vaccine · Theory of planned behavior

1 Introduction

According to data from Centers for Disease Control and Prevention (CDC) 40,870,648 cases of COVID-19 and 656,318 deaths in United States have been reported (as of September 13th, 2021) since its first appearance in Washington state back in January, 2020 [1]. Worldwide, there are 225,210,322 cases and 4,638,148 deaths identified as of September 13th, 2021 [2]. Various containment measurements have been implemented by countries all over the world in order to slow the spread of the virus and prevent medical systems from being overwhelmed [3]. Although a small number of countries have the situation under control, most places in the world are still struggling with the virus and related consequences such as long-term illness and unemployment [4]. With the appearance of different variants, especially the delta variant, we are still not out of the woods. As healthcare workers are still trying their best to save lives, it is urgent for the world to have effective treatments and vaccines to ease the tension in order to avoid repeated lockdowns and boost economic recovery.

Vaccination is an effective approach to prevent the transmission of infectious diseases between human beings. Previous successful vaccinations have helped eliminate

M. Smits (Ed.): iConference 2022, LNCS 13193, pp. 88–105, 2022.
https://doi.org/10.1007/978-3-030-96960-8_7

infectious disease and develop herd immunity, such as is the case with small pox and poliomyelitis [5]. From the earliest stage of the pandemic, scientists, public health officials, and political leaders from different countries started working on various vaccines to respond to the SARS-CoV-2. Although a normal vaccine development cycle is about 10–16 years [6], as of September 13th, 2021, of all the COVID-19 vaccines in development, 8 have been approved, 13 have been authorized, and 33 have entered phase three of clinical trial [7]. Especially in the United States, vaccines from Moderna, Pfizer-BioNTech, and Johnson & Johnson have been broadly distributed since early 2021 [8].

A successful vaccination program not only depends on the existence of effective vaccines but also needs collaboration from the public to accept it. In the United States, as of September 13th, 2021, 54% of all ages have been fully vaccinated, while only 49.6% of adults aged 18–24 and 53.8% of adults aged 25–39 are fully vaccinated against COVID-19 [9]. Compared to other age groups, young adults in the U.S. have the lowest rate of COVID-19 vaccination. As the incidence of COVID-19 among young adults has increased significantly during recent months, the low vaccination rate is alarming. Moreover, as rumors, misinformation, and conspiracy theories spread [10], public health practitioners face a big challenge in persuading the public to trust the safety and efficacy of COVID-19 vaccines.

Plenty of studies have investigated people's information seeking behaviors around their intention to receive existing vaccines [11–14]. Studying people's information seeking behaviors of a much-needed vaccine in development can provide additional empirical understanding for vaccination campaigns from a new perspective. Since numerous COVID-19 outbreaks occurred within colleges and universities after students returned to the campus for fall semester 2020, and young adults tend to have low vaccination rates [9], it is important to understand their acceptance rates of a COVID-19 vaccination, and to explore how they collect information about the vaccine.

Therefore, the purpose of this study is to examine the information seeking behavior of college students in United States around COVID-19 vaccines through the lens of the theory of planned behavior. Additional related variables from previous studies such as anticipated regret, perceived susceptibility, and political view will also be examined given the unique political environment within United States. The results will help to enrich the understanding of theory framework, enhance potential COVID-19 vaccination campaigns in practice, and provide empirical evidence for any similar crisis in the future.

2 Literature Review

2.1 Theory of Planned Behavior

The theory of planned behavior (TPB) was first proposed by Ajzen [15] based on the theory of reasoned action (TRA) [16] to examine factors related to behavioral intention. The initial model of TPB suggested that attitudes toward the behavior, subject norms, and perceived behavioral control are associated with behavioral intention.

Attitudes toward the behavior represent an individual's positive or negative attitude regarding actually performing the behavior. Typically, with more positive attitudes toward the behaviors, individuals are more likely to have a stronger intention to perform the behavior. Subject norms represent individuals' evaluation of whether significant others think they need to perform the behavior. Typically, strong subject norms are positively associated with greater intention to perform the behavior. Perceived behavioral control is an individual's perception of the difficulty in performing the behavior. People are less likely to engage in a behavior that they perceive to be difficult to perform. The major difference between TPB and TRA is perceived behavioral control. The TRA uses attitudes and subject norms as the major determinants of behavioral intentions [16]. The TPB expanded the model to include the perceived difficulty thus the model became more comprehensive. Since perceived behavioral control includes the two constructs of self-efficacy and controllability, it is measured separately to identify these two factors' specific influences on behavioral intention [17, 18]. A further variation of the model divided subject norms into descriptive norms (typical behavior patterns) and injunctive norms (individual's perceived prescriptive ways to behave) to more fully reflect how norms influence behavior [17, 18].

Because actions are affected by intentions to act, behavioral intention is valuable for studying various behaviors, especially health behaviors [15]. Numerous studies have validated the TPB in different contexts, such as in weight loss, food safety behavior, seeking mental health services, and vaccinations [19–22]. These studies have provided evidence to support the assumptions of TPB. For instance, subject norms have been found to be positively related to information seeking intention [23], attitudes toward behavior and subject norms have positively predicted HPV vaccination intention [12], and attitudes, the three types of norms, and perceived behavioral control have significantly predicted hand hygiene practices [24].

Since numerous disinformation and misinformation about COVID-19 vaccines have circled on the internet, it is necessary to consider how news regarding side-effects might affect people's information seeking behaviors about COVID-19 vaccines. In addition to examining vaccination intention directly, vaccine information seeking intention is another perspective that has been investigated to help researchers and practitioners understand vaccination behaviors of the public. Although the TPB has not been used as the underlying theoretical framework for these studies, overlaps exist between other frameworks and TPB. The reasoned action approach (RAA), a recent updated model of TPB, has been applied to examine parental information-seeking behavior in childhood vaccinations in Netherland [25]. The risk information seeking and processing (RISP) model was employed to predict intention of seeking information about the influenza vaccine [13]. Attitudes toward vaccine information seeking and subject norms are the common aspects between these models. Both studies found that factors related to attitudes and norms can significantly predict the intention to seek vaccine information under different circumstances.

Additionally, TPB and related models have been used to study the intention of general health information seeking [23]. Attitudes, self-efficacy, and norms are also critical predictors for general health information seeking intent. Therefore, factors from TPB and the additional factors identified below will be examined in this study to understand what affects college students' COVID-19 vaccine information seeking intent.

2.2 Other Related Factors

Since many vaccine related characteristics are unique from general health information, and the COVID-19 pandemic is the most serious pandemic in a century, other factors such as risk, regret, and partisanship should be taken into consideration beyond the traditional behavioral intentions within the TPB.

Anticipated Regret. Since the beginning of the COVID-19 pandemic, many people have experienced various negative emotions regarding to the disease itself, their mental state, the disruption of their daily lives, etc. [26, 27]. Many have also expressed their regrets on various decisions they have made that have caused tragedies [28]. Because of the broad damage the virus has caused, regret may be an important indicator of people's future behaviors.

Anticipated regret (AR), an evaluation for results of future action [23], may affect people's behavioral decision to avoid actual negative emotion. Previous studies have indicated that anticipated regret is significantly associated with actual regret [29]. People who have assessed the behavior beforehand tend to make decisions that they believe will help avoid regret. AR has been studied under different health scenarios such as having junk food and alcohol [30], smoking [31], and HPV vaccination [32]. A meta-analysis from Sandberg and Conner [33] suggested that anticipated regret was a significant direct indicator of behavioral intention, increasing the variance of behavioral intention by around 7% when compared to the original TPB model.

Perceived Susceptibility. Perceived susceptibility, also known as perceived risk, is regularly considered a significant factor affecting information seeking behavior [34]. One popular model which counts perceived susceptibility as an important component is the risk perception attitude (RPA) framework [35, 36]. The RPA model, which is based on extended parallel process model [34], asserts that perceived threat and efficacy are crucial indicators for individuals' intentions of preventive behaviors including health information seeking behaviors. Specifically, individuals with higher levels of perceived threat and efficacy will use health information more than individuals with lower levels of perceived threat and efficacy. In addition to direct influences from perceived threat and efficacy on health information seeking behavior, the interaction between perceived threat and efficacy also significantly impacts health information behaviors [34].

As critical indicators of perceived threat and efficacy, perceived susceptibility and self-efficacy have been frequently measured in research using the RPA model. From the initial research by Rimal [35] which validated the predicted relationship in the context of seeking cardiovascular disease related information, various studies have also applied the model into other contexts, such as skin cancer information seeking [36], HPV vaccination intention [37], information seeking behavior through mobile social media websites [38], diabetes screening promotion [39], and breast cancer information seeking [40].

Since self-efficacy is a common factor within both TPB and RPA, many studies have added perceived susceptibility as an additional variable to the TPB model to test the influence of perceived susceptibility as well. For instance, perceived susceptibility positively affects college students' intention of taking the A/H1N1 vaccine [11] and blood donors' intention to donate blood during an avian influenza outbreak [41]. Chaffee and Roser [42] remarked that although risk is a useful indicator for behavior, it is not easy to clearly capture the concept into health contexts. Extreme high levels of risk producing negative emotions such as fear and anxiety may lead to information avoidance [43, 44]. Therefore, it is necessary to extend the study of perceived susceptibility into COVID-19 context to further examine its impact on vaccine information seeking intention.

Political View. During the COVID-19 pandemic, although overall trust with public health information has grown in the United States, distrust of public health information within the political right still exists [45]. An analysis of Twitter data indicated that politically conservative users are more likely to discuss COVID-19 related misinformation topics (e.g., 5G, deep state, bleach) than liberal users [46]. Public attitudes toward diverse COVID-19 related policies differ by political parties [47]. Specifically, GPS location data from smartphones and survey data suggest Democrats and Republicans have different views about the severity of the outbreak [48, 49]. Moreover, the difference of COVID-19 vaccination rates between red and blue counties is growing [50].

2.3 Vaccine Information

Although numerous evidences show that vaccination is an effective way to enhance public health safety, vaccine hesitancy exists all over the world [51]. Vaccine hesitancy is defined as "A behavior, influenced by a number of factors including issues of confidence (do not trust vaccine or provider), complacency (do not perceive a need for a vaccine, do not value the vaccine), and convenience (access). Vaccine-hesitant individuals are a heterogeneous group who hold varying degrees of indecision about specific vaccines or vaccination in general. Vaccine-hesitant individuals may accept all vaccines but remain concerned about vaccines, some may refuse or delay some vaccines, but accept others; some individuals may refuse all vaccines" [52]. Scholars have studied several vaccine hesitancy related factors including income, education, vaccine specific issues, and social groups [53], suggesting that there are multiple sources of hesitancy. Moreover, vaccine related misinformation has been spread broadly through the internet. The World Health Organization (WHO) has identified misinformation as a major health threat of 2019 [54]. Given the potential harmful effects, vaccine misinformation is a serious issue for researchers and practitioners to tackle.

Online information seeking is a primary way for the public to gather information during past two decades. Zimmerman et al. [55] suggest that websites critical of vaccines have common features such as statements describing adverse reaction from vaccinations, links to other vaccine-critical websites, and claims that civil liberties have been restricted through vaccine mandates. Although previous surveys have indicated that most vaccine-hesitant parents consider medical professionals as the most trusted source to access vaccine information [56, 57], a more polarized online environment and online technologies have developed over the last decade, connecting many fringe anti-vaccination subgroups and distributing online misinformation faster than ever before [58, 59]. A study of social Q&A platforms ("Yahoo! Answers" and a Facebook group) illustrated that both pro-vaccine and anti-vaccine answers were selected by users to be the "best answer" [60]. Moreover, a study from Kortum et al. [61] among high school students in Houston revealed that a high percentage of students using the internet to gain vaccine information left with significant misconceptions about vaccines.

Because vaccination has been widely considered as a key step to ease the COVID-19 global pandemic and bring daily lives back to normal, accurate vaccine information should be available for the public to consult to make health decisions. Unvaccinated people need to seek information to choose an affordable and safe vaccine. Vaccinated people may seek information to persuade other unvaccinated peers to get the vaccine. Vaccine information seeking behavior may well affect individuals' intention to be vaccinated, or also their actual behavior [13]. Just as people's general knowledge about science is related to their risk perception with the MMR vaccine [62], it is important to understand COVID-19 vaccine information seeking behavior and develop better information strategies accordingly.

2.4 Vaccination Behavioral Research

Many studies have applied the TPB model to vaccination behavioral research, such as the HPV vaccine [12, 63] and the A/H1N1 vaccine [11]. Given different contexts and various approaches, the TPB did not fit precisely in each vaccine scenario. Perceived behavioral control's impact on vaccination intentions may vary based on the different diseases that vaccines were developed to protect against. Yet, each study found that attitudes and subject norms significantly affected vaccination intentions among young adults. In addition, the health belief model (HBM) and the TPB have been compared in a vaccination context. The TPB accounted for 39% of the variance in vaccination intention while the HBM accounted for 26% of the variance on vaccination intention [63].

Several studies have examined the intention to receive COVID-19 vaccine based on TPB. Results from Fan et al. [64] suggested that subject norms and perceived behavior control were not significantly related to university students' intention for COVID-19 vaccine in mainland China. On the other hand, [65] reported that a unified model with predictors from HBM and TPB frameworks explained 78% variance of vaccination intention among Israeli adults. Moreover, a representative survey illustrated that all key factors from TPB were significant predictors for COVID-19 vaccination intention in Norway [66].

In summary, because of the uniqueness of COVID-19 vaccines, vaccine information characteristics, and attributes of the current pandemic, it is urgent to understand what factors affect people's intention to seek COVID-19 vaccine information. Moreover, previous studies have mainly focused on either vaccine information seeking intention or general health information seeking intention. The number of studies addressing vaccine information seeking intention is relatively small. It is necessary to extend well-established theoretical frameworks into this new context to gain further understanding about vaccine information seeking intent. Additionally, this research can also provide insights to public health practitioners to consider future vaccine campaign strategies. Therefore, following hypotheses are proposed:

H1: Attitudes will positively associate with COVID-19 vaccine information seeking intention.
H2: Subjective norms will positively associate with COVID-19 vaccine information seeking intention.
H3: Anticipated regret will positively associate with COVID-19 vaccine information seeking intention.
H4: Perceived susceptibility will positively associate with COVID-19 vaccine information seeking intention.
H5: Self-efficacy will negatively associate with COVID-19 vaccine information seeking intention.
H6: Political view will associate with COVID-19 vaccine information seeking intention.

3 Methods

3.1 Sampling and Procedure

After obtaining IRB approval, online questionnaires were distributed via Quatrics through the university's email list to students from a research university in the Midwest United States. The recruiting email included a brief introduction of the purpose of the research and the author's contact information. The survey was available online for about 4 weeks, from mid-March to mid-April, 2021. It generally took participants about 15 min to complete the survey. Students could choose to participant in the online survey voluntarily. A total of 1237 participants started the survey and 1104 responses were collected. Both qualification questions and attention check questions were used to ensure data quality. Participants who did not pass the attention checks were automatically guided to the end of survey and their responses were discarded. A total of 554 valid responses were used for data analysis.

The average age of participants was 21.70, with a range from 18 to 40. About 23.29% of participants were male, 68.95% were female, and 7.76% were self-identified as "Other." There were 84.84% participants who self-reported as "White or Caucasian", 4.33% as "Mixed", 3.61% as "Black or African American", 2.71% as "Hispanic and/or Latinx", 1.81% as "Asian or Asian American", 0.90% as "Other", and 1.81% as "Choose not to Answer."

3.2 Measurements

All of the following measurements are from previous studies which have validated their reliabilities. Items were customized to fit in the context of this study. For detailed items for each key measurement, see Table 1.

Table 1. Measurements for key independent variables

Attitudes Please indicate your agreement with the following items (Strongly Disagree/Disagree/Neutral/Agree/Strongly Agree)
Looking for COVID-19 vaccine information will be beneficial for me
Looking for COVID-19 vaccine information will be painful
Seeking COVID-19 vaccine information will be good for me
Looking for COVID-19 vaccine information is not important for me
Looking for COVID-19 vaccine information will be useful for me
Subjective Norms
Please indicate your agreement with the following items (Strongly Disagree/Disagree/Neutral/Agree/Strongly Agree) My immediate family members think I should look for COVID-19 vaccine information
I want to do what my immediate family members think I should do about looking for COVID-19 vaccine information
My immediate family members would approve of me looking for COVID-19 vaccine information
Most my family members have looked for COVID-19 vaccine information before
My friends think I should look for COVID-19 vaccine information
My friends approve of me looking for COVID-19 vaccine information
My friends have looked for COVID-19 vaccine information before
I want to do what my friends think I should do about looking for COVID-19 vaccine information
Self-Efficacy
Please indicate your agreement with the following items (Strongly Disagree/Disagree/Neutral/Agree/Strongly Agree)
If necessary precautions are taken, I can lower my risk of COVID-19 infection then I may not need to look for COVID-19 vaccine information
If necessary precautions are taken, I do not need to look for COVID-19 vaccine information
Perceived Susceptibility
Please indicate your agreement with the following items (Strongly Disagree/Disagree/Neutral/Agree/Strongly Agree)
I believe that I'm at risk of getting COVID-19
It is likely that I will develop COVID-19 symptoms
It's possible that I'll contract/re-contract COVID-19
Anticipated Regret

(continued)

Table 1. *(continued)*

Attitudes Please indicate your agreement with the following items (Strongly Disagree/Disagree/Neutral/Agree/Strongly Agree)
Please imagine following scenarios and indicate your feelings for each item (Extremely Worried/Very Worried/Neutral/Slightly worried/Not at all worried) (Extremely Regret/Very Regret/Neutral/Slightly Regret/Not at all Regret) (Extremely Tense/Slightly Tense/Neutral/Slightly Relaxed/Extremely Relaxed)
You did not look for information regarding available COVID-19 vaccine then contracted/re-contracted COVID-19
You looked for information regarding available COVID-19 vaccine then contracted/re-contracted COVID-19
Political View
How do you describe your political views? (Liberal/Moderate/Conservative)
Information Seeking Intention
How likely are you to look for information about COVID-19 vaccine in next three months? (Not at all likely/Slightly Likely/Neutral/Very Likely/Extremely Likely)

Attitudes Toward Information Seeking. Attitudes were measured based on Ajzen's [18, 67] TPB questionnaire. A 5-point Likert scale was used by participants to indicate their agreements on each item. There are five items to measure attitudes toward information seeking. Sample questions include "Looking for COVID-19 vaccine information will be beneficial for me" and "Looking for COVID-19 vaccine information will be painful.". After reversing coding for certain items, the measure's reliability was tested as reliable (Cronbach's $\alpha = .82$), therefore the average score from these items was calculated for each individual to indicate their attitudes toward COVID-19 vaccine information seeking. The overall mean score for attitudes is 4.16 (SD = .79).

Subjective Norms. Subjective norms were measured based on Ajzen's [18, 67] TPB questionnaire. A 5-point Likert scale was used by participants to express their agreements on each item. Eight items will be provided to measure subject norms. Sample items include "My immediate family members think I should look for COVID-19 vaccine information" and "I want to do what my immediate family members think I should do about looking for COVID-19 vaccine information." After testing the measure's reliability (Cronbach's $\alpha = .88$), an average score was calculated to represent each individual's subjective norms about COVID-19 vaccine information seeking. The overall mean score for the variable is 3.73 (SD = .83).

Anticipated Regret. Anticipated regret was measured based on three items developed by [68]. Participants were asked to imagine scenarios that they got COVID-19 if 1) they did and 2) did not look for information regarding available vaccines. A 5-point scale from 1 to 5 was used by participants to express their feelings about these two scenarios. Three feeling scales were assessed: worried to not worried, regret to not regret, and tense to relaxed. The differences between each pair of feeling scales for were calculated to form the anticipated regret measurement. After testing the measure's reliability (Cronbach's $\alpha = .88$), an average score of the three differences was used as an indicator of anticipated regret. The overall mean score for the variable is 3.26 (SD = 1.02).

Perceived Susceptibility. Three items were used to measure perceived susceptibility based on So et al. and Witte et al.'s measurements [69, 70]. Three items were used: "I believe that I'm at risk of getting COVID-19," "It is likely that I will develop COVID-19 symptoms," and "It's possible that I'll contract/re-contract COVID-19." A 5-point Likert scale was used by participants to indicate the risk from low to high. After testing the measure's reliability (Cronbach's $\alpha = .82$), an average score of three items was calculated to provide each individual's comprehensive perception of susceptibility regarding COVID-19. The overall mean score for the variable is 3.07 (SD = .90).

Self-efficacy. Perceived self-efficacy was defined as "people's beliefs about their capabilities to exercise control over their own level of functioning and over events that affect their lives" [71]. According to Ajzen [67], a belief-based approach to measuring self-efficacy can reveal insights from a cognitive perspective. Therefore, two items were provided to participants to assess self-efficacy: "If necessary precautions are taken, I can lower my risk of COVID-19 infection then I may not need to look for COVID-19 vaccine information" and "If necessary precautions are taken, I do not need to look for COVID-19 vaccine information." After testing the reliability (Cronbach's $\alpha = .86$), an average score of the two items was calculated to represent the measure for self-efficacy. The overall mean score for the variable is 2.22 (SD = 1.05).

Political View. Participants self-reported their political views by choosing from liberal, moderate, and conservative. Unlike previous variables which are interval variables, this variable is a discrete variable. Among the valid data, 60.47% of participants self-identified their political views as "Liberal", with 29.24% as "Moderate" and 10.29% as "Conservative."

Information Seeking Intention. Information seeking intention is the dependent variable. The measurement was based on the questionnaire from Lu et al. [13]. The single item was "How likely are you to going to look for information about COVID-19 vaccine in next three months?" A 5-point Likert scale was used by participants to indicate their intention to seek information from 1 (not likely at all) to 5 (very likely). The overall mean score for the variable is 3.94 (SD = 1.32).

Control Variables. Regular demographic information, including age, gender, and race were collected to act as control variables in the models for data analysis.

4 Results

The descriptive statistics and correlations for all continuous variables of interest are shown in Table 2. The variance inflation factor (VIF) of each independent variable is reported to rule out possible effects from potential multicollinearity.

Table 2. Descriptive data and correlation among continuous variables (N = 554)

	1	2	3	4	5	6
Attitudes						
Anticipated Regret	.50*					
Subjective Norms	.58*	.45*				
Self-efficacy	−.61*	−.56*	−.53*			
Perceived Susceptibility	.29*	33*	.23*	−.30*		
Information Seeking Intention	.69*	.51*	.55*	−.60*	.34*	
M	4.16	3.26	3.73	2.22	3.07	3.94
SD	.79	1.02	.83	1.05	.90	1.32
Cronbach's Alpha	.82	.88	.88	.86	.82	/

$^{*} p \leq .05$

A multiple linear regression analysis was conducted to test the relationship among information seeking intentions, attitudes, anticipated regret, subjective norms, self-efficacy, perceived susceptibility, and political views after controlling for age, gender and race, see Table 3.

Table 3. Multiple linear regression analysis results

	COVID-19 Vaccine Information Seeking Intention		
	B	SE	VIF
Attitudes	$.63^{***}$	.07	2.07
Anticipated Regret	.07	.05	1.82
Subjective Norms	$.23^{***}$	.06	1.77
Self-efficacy	$-.22^{***}$	.05	1.97
Perceived Susceptibility	$.14^{**}$	.04	1.19
Political View			1.56
Liberal	Reference		
Moderate	$-.29^{**}$	.09	
Conservative	$-.57^{***}$	.14	
F	38.48 (20, 533) ***		
Adj-R2	.58		

(*continued*)

Table 3. (*continued*)

	COVID-19 Vaccine Information Seeking Intention		
	B	SE	VIF
N = 554			

*** $p \leq .001$, ** $p \leq .01$, * $p \leq .05$
Adjusted for gender, age, and race

Results suggest that attitudes, subjective norms, self-efficacy, perceived susceptibility, and political view were significantly related to information seeking intention of COVID-19 vaccine. Specifically, attitudes ($B = .63$, $SE = .07$, $p < .001$) were positively associated with COVID-19 vaccine information seeking intention. Thus, H1 is supported. Similarly, subjective norms ($B = 0.23$, $SE = .06$, $p < .001$) were positively associated with COVID-19 vaccine information seeking intention, supporting H2. H3 hypothesized the association between anticipated regret with COVID-19 vaccine information seeking intention, however; there was not enough evidence to suggest a significant relationship between the variables. Thus, H3 is not supported. Perceived susceptibility was positively associated with COVID-19 vaccine information seeking intention ($B = .14$, $SE = .04$, $p < .01$). Thus, H4 is supported. H5 predicted a negative association between self-efficacy and COVID-19 vaccine information seeking intention, which is also supported ($B = -.22$, $SE = .05$, $p < .001$). Additionally, when compared with individuals identified as liberals, individuals identified as moderates ($B = -.29$, $SE = .09$, $p < .05$) or conservatives ($B = -.57$, $SE = .14$, $p < .01$) had less intention to seek vaccine information. Thus, H6 is supported. Furthermore, the overall model predicted a significant part of changes to COVID-19 vaccine information seeking intention ($R^2 = .58$).

5 Discussion

This study explored how various factors affect young adults' intentions to seek COVID-19 vaccine information based on theory of planned behavior. The study results show that factors including attitudes, subjective norms, perceived susceptibility, self-efficacy, and political views were all significantly related to young adults' COVID-19 vaccine information seeking intention. These results are aligned with previous studies [11, 65] and provide further understanding of the theoretical framework of TPB in the context of COVID-19 pandemic.

One factor in this study that was not significantly associated with the information seeking intention is anticipated regret. This result is different than previous studies on vaccine intention [32, 66]. One possible explanation is that young adults tend to believe that even infected with COVID-19, their health would not be damaged as much as more vulnerable people such as older adults or immune compromised people. Especially with much public awareness eyed more on high-risk groups at the early stages of the pandemic [72], it is possible that participants in this study were less influenced by the idea of potential regret. Young adults may not think vaccination is an urgent issue for them and thus not develop regretful feeling towards not seeking vaccine information. It is also possible that the association between anticipated regret and intention depends on types of intention. As of September 13th, 2021, the vaccination rate among young adults is lower than old adults [9]. However, with the emergence of more damaging COVID variants in recent months, including the delta variant, media reports have changed their reporting about risks among young adults. Future studies should further investigate how new information about the risk of new variants might affect young adults' choices and intention toward the COVID-19 vaccine information seeking.

Practically, this study provides insights on communication regarding COVID-19 vaccine information. Since COVID-19 vaccines are relatively new and some are based on newly emerging technologies, many people have doubts about them and are afraid of potential side effects. Hence, having a positive attitude from within as well as receiving positive messages from the surrounding environment could encourage people to seek more information and understand the benefits from vaccination to make reasonable decisions. Particularly with the return of in-person school and work, universities, colleges, and employers should engage young adults in positive conversation about vaccination and promote accurate, positive, vaccine-related information to them. Moreover, effects from perceived susceptibility and political view indicate the importance of risk message delivery during the pandemic. According to So et al. [70], people tend to seek health information after having been exposed to risk messaging. As the COVID-19 pandemic is unique in many ways compared to previous epidemics, it is more urgent than ever to deliver precise and accurate messages to the public. With the recent announcement of booster shots and the FDA's formal approval of the Pfizer-BioNTech COVID-19 vaccine [73], the constant impact of COVID-19 related risk message delivery can play an important role among young adults' further information seeking behavior. Therefore, health authorities need to explore effective ways to deliver tailored vaccine information to young adults. It is also pivotal to make efforts to increase the public awareness and perception about the severity about infectious diseases. Additionally, considering the role that subject norms played in the vaccine information seeking intention, it is also useful to encourage the public to share reliable vaccine information to their friends and relatives on social media where young adults investigate much time. Lastly, since the efficiency vaccine information communication regarding COVID-19 is likely to have further impacts on future vaccine acceptance for other diseases [65], it is crucial for public health officials to enhance their communication strategies throughout different phases of the current pandemic.

6 Limitations and Future Directions

There are several limitations in this study. First, the survey participants were recruited from the college population, which is a convenient sample that may not be representative. Especially since the majority of survey takers are white people, there is a shortcoming that the results cannot fully represent minority point of views. Second, since the study collected the data through a survey design, only correlational conclusion can be drawn instead of causal conclusion which would be more impactful. Third, because the participation of this study was voluntary, it is possible that the study missed input from other individuals who are hostile to vaccination in general. In the future, researchers could use nationally representative data to examine the relationships in this study more thoroughly. It is also necessary to further explore the association between information seeking and vaccination intention and vaccine decision making. Furthermore, future studies should focus on what kind health information young adults tend to seek and the relationship between information content and decision making.

7 Conclusion

This study illustrated the connection of TPB and young adults' COVID-19 vaccine information seeking intention. Results suggested that various factors contribute to a substantive part of young adults' information seeking intention. In order to approach one of the lowest vaccinated groups [9] more effectively during the ongoing pandemic, it is necessary for health authorities to consider these factors when creating health messages and vaccination campaigns.

References

1. CDC: COVID Data Tracker. https://covid.cdc.gov/covid-data-tracker/#datatracker-home. Accessed 12 Sept 2021
2. Dong, E., Du, H., Gardner, L.: COVID-19 Dashboard by the Center for Systems Science and Engineering (CSSE) at Johns Hopkins University (JHU). https://coronavirus.jhu.edu/map.html%0Ahttps://gisanddata.maps.arcgis.com/apps/opsdashboard/index.html#/bda7594740fd40299423467b48e9ecf6%0Ahttps://www.arcgis.com/apps/opsdashboard/index.html#/bda7594740fd40299423467b48e9ecf6
3. Anderson, R.M., Heesterbeek, H., Klinkenberg, D., Hollingsworth, T.D.: How will country-based mitigation measures influence the course of the COVID-19 epidemic? (2020). https://doi.org/10.1016/S0140-6736(20)30567-5
4. Pierce, M., et al.: Mental health before and during the COVID-19 pandemic: a longitudinal probability sample survey of the UK population. Lancet Psychiatry **7**, 883–892 (2020). https://doi.org/10.1016/S2215-0366(20)30308-4
5. Henderson, D.A.: Countering the posteradication threat of smallpox and polio. Clin. Infect. Dis. **34**, 79–83 (2002). https://doi.org/10.1086/323897
6. Pronker, E.S., Weenen, T.C., Commandeur, H.R., Osterhaus, A.D.M.E., Claassen, H.J.H.M.: The gold industry standard for risk and cost of drug and vaccine development revisited (2011). https://doi.org/10.1016/j.vaccine.2011.06.051
7. Zimmer, C., Corum, J., Wee, S.-L.: Coronavirus Vaccine Tracker. https://www.nytimes.com/interactive/2020/science/coronavirus-vaccine-tracker.html. Accessed 12 Sept 2021
8. CDC: COVID-19 vaccinations in the United States. https://covid.cdc.gov/covid-data-tracker/#vaccinations. Accessed 12 Sept 2021
9. Mayo Clinic: U.S. COVID-19 vaccine tracker: See your state's progress. https://www.mayoclinic.org/coronavirus-covid-19/vaccine-tracker. Accessed 12 Sept 2021
10. Islam, M.S., et al.: COVID-19-Related infodemic and its impact on public health: a global social media analysis. Am. J. Trop. Med. Hyg. **103**, 1621–1629 (2020). https://doi.org/10.4269/ajtmh.20-0812
11. Agarwal, V.: A/H1N1 vaccine intentions in college students: an application of the theory of planned behavior. J. Am. Coll. Health **62**, 416–424 (2014). https://doi.org/10.1080/07448481.2014.917650

12. Catalano, H.P., Knowlden, A.P., Birch, D.A., Leeper, J.D., Paschal, A.M., Usdan, S.L.: Using the theory of planned behavior to predict HPV vaccination intentions of college men. J. Am. Coll. Health **65**, 197–207 (2017). https://doi.org/10.1080/07448481.2016.1269771
13. Lu, H., Winneg, K., Jamieson, K.H., Albarracín, D.: Intentions to seek information about the influenza vaccine: the role of informational subjective norms, anticipated and experienced affect, and information insufficiency among vaccinated and unvaccinated people. Risk Anal. **40**(10), 2040–2056 (2020)
14. Nan, X., Madden, K.: HPV vaccine information in the blogosphere: how positive and negative blogs influence vaccine-related risk perceptions, attitudes, and behavioral intentions. Health Commun. **27**, 829–836 (2012). https://doi.org/10.1080/10410236.2012.661348
15. Ajzen, I.: From intentions to actions: a theory of planned behavior. In: Kuhl, J., Beckmann, J. (eds.) Action Control. SSSSP, pp. 11–39. Springer, Heidelberg (1985). https://doi.org/10.1007/978-3-642-69746-3_2
16. Fishbein, M., Ajzen, I.: Chapter 1. Belief, Attitude, Intention, and Behavior: An Introduction to Theory and Research (1975)
17. Ajzen, I.: Perceived behavioral control, self-efficacy, locus of control, and the theory of planned behavior. J. Appl. Soc. Psychol. **32**, 665–683 (2002). https://doi.org/10.1111/j.1559-1816.2002.tb00236.x
18. Ajzen, I.: Constructing a Theory of Planned Behavior Questionnaire (2006). umass.edu/aizen/pdf/tpb.measurement.pdf
19. Bohon, L.M., Cotter, K.A., Kravitz, R.L., Cello, P.C., Fernandez y Garcia, E.: The theory of planned behavior as it predicts potential intention to seek mental health services for depression among college students. J. Am. Coll. Health **64**, 593–603 (2016). https://doi.org/10.1080/07448481.2016.1207646
20. Lin, N., Roberts, K.R.: Using the theory of planned behavior to predict food safety behavioral intention: a systematic review and meta-analysis. Int. J. Hosp. Manag. **90**, 102612 (2020). https://doi.org/10.1016/j.ijhm.2020.102612
21. Schifter, D.E., Ajzen, I.: Intention, perceived control, and weight loss. An application of the theory of planned behavior. J. Pers. Soc. Psychol. **49**, 843–851 (1985). https://doi.org/10.1037/0022-3514.49.3.843
22. Shi, J., Kim, H.K.: Integrating risk perception attitude framework and the theory of planned behavior to predict mental health promotion behaviors among young adults. Health Commun. **35**, 597–606 (2020). https://doi.org/10.1080/10410236.2019.1573298
23. Ahn, J., Kahlor, L.A.: No regrets when it comes to your health: anticipated regret, subjective norms, information insufficiency and intent to seek health information from multiple sources. Health Commun. **35**, 1295–1302 (2020). https://doi.org/10.1080/10410236.2019.1626535
24. Clayton, D.A., Griffith, C.J.: Efficacy of an extended theory of planned behaviour model for predicting caterers' hand hygiene practices. Int. J. Environ. Health Res. **18**, 83–98 (2008). https://doi.org/10.1080/09603120701358424
25. Harmsen, I.A., Doorman, G.G., Mollema, L., Ruiter, R.A., Kok, G., de Melker, H.E.: Parental information-seeking behaviour in childhood vaccinations. BMC Public Health **13**, 1–10 (2013). https://doi.org/10.1186/1471-2458-13-1219
26. Carstensen, L.L., Shavit, Y.Z., Barnes, J.T.: Age advantages in emotional experience persist even under threat from the COVID-19 pandemic. Psychol. Sci. **31**, 1374–1385 (2020). https://doi.org/10.1177/0956797620967261
27. Xu, C., et al.: Cognitive reappraisal and the association between perceived stress and anxiety symptoms in COVID-19 isolated people. Front. Psychiatry **11**, 858 (2020). https://doi.org/10.3389/fpsyt.2020.00858
28. Godfrey, E.: What COVID-19 Families Hear When Trump Brags About His Strength. https://www.theatlantic.com/politics/archive/2020/10/trumps-covid-19-comments-hurt-victims-families/616715/. Accessed 26 Nov 2020

29. Mellers, B., Schwartz, A., Ritov, I.: Emotion-based choice. J. Exp. Psychol. Gen. **128**, 332–345 (1999). https://doi.org/10.1037/0096-3445.128.3.332
30. Richard, R., van der Pligt, J., de Vries, N.: Anticipated affect and behavioral choice. Basic Appl. Soc. Psychol. **18**, 111–129 (1996). https://doi.org/10.1207/s15324834basp1802_1
31. Conner, M., Sandberg, T., McMillan, B., Higgins, A.: Role of anticipated regret, intentions and intention stability in adolescent smoking initiation. Br. J. Health Psychol. **11**, 85–101 (2006). https://doi.org/10.1348/135910705X40997
32. Cox, D., Sturm, L., Cox, A.D.: Effectiveness of asking anticipated regret in increasing HPV vaccination intention in mothers. Health Psychol. **33**, 1074–1083 (2014). https://doi.org/10.1037/hea0000071
33. Sandberg, T., Conner, M.: Anticipated regret as an additional predictor in the theory of planned behaviour: a meta-analysis. Br. J. Soc. Psychol. **47**, 589–606 (2008). https://doi.org/10.1348/014466607X258704
34. Witte, K.: Putting the fear back into fear appeals: the extended parallel process model. Commun. Monogr. **59**, 329–349 (1992). https://doi.org/10.1080/03637759209376276
35. Rimal, R.N.: Perceived risk and self-efficacy as motivators: understanding individuals' long-term use of health information. J. Commun. **51**, 633–654 (2001). https://doi.org/10.1093/joc/51.4.633
36. Rimal, R.N., Real, K.: Perceived risk and efficacy beliefs as motivators of change: Use of the risk perception attitude (RPA) framework to understand health behaviors. Hum. Commun. Res. **29**(3), 370–399 (2003). https://doi.org/10.1093/hcr/29.3.370
37. Pask, E.B., Rawlins, S.T.: Men's intentions to engage in behaviors to protect against human papillomavirus (HPV): testing the risk perception attitude framework. Health Commun. **31**, 139–149 (2016). https://doi.org/10.1080/10410236.2014.940670
38. Deng, Z., Liu, S.: Understanding consumer health information-seeking behavior from the perspective of the risk perception attitude framework and social support in mobile social media websites. Int. J. Med. Inform. **105**, 98–109 (2017). https://doi.org/10.1016/j.ijmedinf.2017.05.014
39. Rains, S.A., Hingle, M.D., Surdeanu, M., Bell, D., Kobourov, S.: A test of the risk perception attitude framework as a message tailoring strategy to promote diabetes screening. Health Commun. **34**, 672–679 (2019). https://doi.org/10.1080/10410236.2018.1431024
40. Rimal, R.N., Juon, H.S.: Use of the risk perception attitude framework for promoting breast cancer prevention. J. Appl. Soc. Psychol. **40**, 287–310 (2010). https://doi.org/10.1111/j.1559-1816.2009.00574.x
41. Masser, B.M., White, K.M., Hamilton, K., McKimmie, B.M.: An examination of the predictors of blood donors' intentions to donate during two phases of an avian influenza outbreak. Transfusion **51**, 548–557 (2011). https://doi.org/10.1111/j.1537-2995.2010.02887.x
42. Chaffee, S.H., Roser, C.: Involvement and the consistency of knowledge, attitudes, and behaviors. Commun. Res. **13**, 373–399 (1986). https://doi.org/10.1177/009365086013003006
43. Howell, J.L., Shepperd, J.A.: Reducing health-information avoidance through contemplation. Psychol. Sci. **24**, 1696–1703 (2013). https://doi.org/10.1177/0956797613478616
44. Sweeny, K., Melnyk, D., Miller, W., Shepperd, J.A.: Information avoidance: who, what, when, and why. Rev. Gen. Psychol. **14**, 340–353 (2010). https://doi.org/10.1037/a0021288
45. Funk, C., Kennedy, B., Johnson, C.: Trust in Medical Scientists Has Grown in U.S., but Mainly Among Democrats. https://www.pewresearch.org/science/2020/05/21/trust-in-medical-scientists-has-grown-in-u-s-but-mainly-among-democrats/. Accessed 27 Nov 2020
46. Havey, N.F.: Partisan public health: how does political ideology influence support for COVID-19 related misinformation? J. Comput. Soc. Sci. **3**(2), 319–342 (2020). https://doi.org/10.1007/s42001-020-00089-2

47. Bhanot, S.P., Hopkins, D.J.: Partisan polarization and resistance to elite messages: results from survey experiments on social distancing. J. Behav. Public Adm. **3** (2020). https://doi.org/10.30636/jbpa.32.178
48. Allcott, H., Boxell, L., Conway, J., Gentzkow, M., Thaler, M., Yang, D.: Polarization and public health: partisan differences in social distancing during the coronavirus pandemic. J. Public Econ. **191**, 104254 (2020). https://doi.org/10.1016/j.jpubeco.2020.104254
49. Clinton, J., Cohen, J., Lapinski, J., Trussler, M.: Partisan pandemic: how partisanship and public health concerns affect individuals' social distancing during COVID-19. SSRN Electron. J. (2020). https://doi.org/10.2139/ssrn.3633934
50. Kates, J., Tolbert, J., Orgera, K.: The Red/Blue Divide in COVID-19 Vaccination Rates is Growing, https://www.kff.org/policy-watch/the-red-blue-divide-in-covid-19-vaccination-rates-is-growing/. Accessed 12 Sept 2021
51. MacDonald, N.E., et al.: Vaccine hesitancy: definition, scope and determinants. Vaccine **33**, 4161–4164 (2015). https://doi.org/10.1016/j.vaccine.2015.04.036
52. World Health Organization: SAGE working group dealing with vaccine hesitancy. https://www.who.int/immunization/sage/sage_wg_vaccine_hesitancy_apr12/en/. Accessed 27 Nov 2020
53. Larson, H.J., Jarrett, C., Eckersberger, E., Smith, D.M.D., Paterson, P.: Understanding vaccine hesitancy around vaccines and vaccination from a global perspective: a systematic review of published literature, 2007–2012. Vaccine **32**(19), 2150–2159 (2014). https://doi.org/10.1016/j.vaccine.2014.01.081
54. World Health Organization: Ten threats to global health in 2019. https://www.who.int/news-room/spotlight/ten-threats-to-global-health-in-2019. Accessed 08 Dec 2020
55. Zimmerman, R.K., et al.: Vaccine criticism on the world wide web (2005). https://doi.org/10.2196/jmir.7.2.e17
56. Casiday, R., Cresswell, T., Wilson, D., Panter-Brick, C.: A survey of UK parental attitudes to the MMR vaccine and trust in medical authority. Vaccine **24**, 177–184 (2006). https://doi.org/10.1016/j.vaccine.2005.07.063
57. Freed, G.L., Clark, S.J., Butchart, A.T., Singer, D.C., Davis, M.M.: Sources and perceived credibility of vaccine-safety information for parents (2011). https://doi.org/10.1542/peds.2010-1722P
58. Schmidt, A.L., Zollo, F., Scala, A., Betsch, C., Quattrociocchi, W.: Polarization of the vaccination debate on Facebook. Vaccine **36**, 3606–3612 (2018). https://doi.org/10.1016/j.vaccine.2018.05.040
59. Smith, N., Graham, T.: Mapping the anti-vaccination movement on Facebook. Inf. Commun. Soc. **22**, 1310–1327 (2019). https://doi.org/10.1080/1369118X.2017.1418406
60. Sharon, A.J., Yom-Tov, E., Baram-Tsabari, A.: Vaccine information seeking on social Q&A services. Vaccine **38**, 2691–2699 (2020). https://doi.org/10.1016/j.vaccine.2020.02.010
61. Kortum, P., Edwards, C., Richards-Kortum, R.: The impact of inaccurate Internet health information in a secondary school learning environment. J. Med. Internet Res. **10**, e17 (2008). https://doi.org/10.2196/jmir.986
62. Funk, C.: Parents of young children are more 'vaccine hesitant'. https://www.pewresearch.org/fact-tank/2017/02/06/parents-of-young-children-are-more-vaccine-hesitant/. Accessed 27 Nov 2020
63. Gerend, M.A., Shepherd, J.E.: Predicting human papillomavirus vaccine uptake in young adult women: comparing the health belief model and theory of planned behavior. Ann. Behav. Med. **44**, 171–180 (2012). https://doi.org/10.1007/s12160-012-9366-5
64. Fan, C.W., et al.: Extended theory of planned behavior in explaining the intention to COVID-19 vaccination uptake among mainland Chinese university students: an online survey study. Hum. Vaccin. Immunother. (2021). https://doi.org/10.1080/21645515.2021.1933687

65. Shmueli, L.: Predicting intention to receive COVID-19 vaccine among the general population using the health belief model and the theory of planned behavior model. BMC Public Health **21**, 1–13 (2021). https://doi.org/10.1186/s12889-021-10816-7
66. Wolff, K.: COVID-19 vaccination intentions: the theory of planned behavior, optimistic bias, and anticipated regret. Front. Psychol. **12** (2021). https://doi.org/10.3389/fpsyg.2021.648289
67. Ajzen, I.: Constructing a TPB Questionnaire: Conceptual and Methodological Considerations. Time (2002)
68. Richard, R., de Vries, N.K., van der Pligt, J.: Anticipated regret and precautionary sexual behavior. J. Appl. Soc. Psychol. **28**, 1411–1428 (1998). https://doi.org/10.1111/j.1559-1816.1998.tb01684.x
69. Witte, K., Cameron, K.A., McKeon, J.K., Berkowitz, J.M.: Predicting risk behaviors: development and validation of a diagnostic scale. J. Health Commun. **1**, 317–342 (1996). https://doi.org/10.1080/108107396127988
70. So, J., Kuang, K., Cho, H.: Information seeking upon exposure to risk messages: predictors, outcomes, and mediating roles of health information seeking. Commun. Res. **46**, 663–687 (2019). https://doi.org/10.1177/0093650216679536
71. Bandura, A.: Social cognitive theory of self-regulation. Organ. Behav. Hum. Decis. Process. **50**, 248–287 (1991). https://doi.org/10.1016/0749-5978(91)90022-L
72. Abbasi, J.: Younger adults caught in COVID-19 crosshairs as demographics shift. JAMA **324**, 2141 (2020). https://doi.org/10.1001/jama.2020.21913
73. FDA: FDA Approves First COVID-19 Vaccine. https://www.fda.gov/news-events/press-announcements/fda-approves-first-covid-19-vaccine. Accessed 12 Sept 2021

Exploring the Relationship Between Youth Information Behavior, Substance Use, and Substance Use Expectancies: A Pilot Study

Sarah Barriage[1(✉)], Hye Jeong Choi[2], Anne E. Ray[1], Michael L. Hecht[3], Kathryn Greene[4], and Shannon D. Glenn[5]

[1] University of Kentucky, Lexington, KY 40502, USA
sarah.barriage@uky.edu
[2] University of Missouri, Columbia, MO 65203, USA
[3] REAL Prevention LLC, Clifton, NJ 07013, USA
[4] Rutgers, The State University of New Jersey, New Brunswick, NJ 08901, USA
[5] The Pennsylvania State University, State College, PA 16801, USA

Abstract. A substantial body of research has explored the relationship between passive information seeking and youths' beliefs about and use of substances. To date, however, little work has explored other dimensions of youth information behavior (such as active information seeking, information needs, and information use) and substance use. The aim of this study was to pilot the use of an information behavior scale in order to examine the association between youth information behavior and self-reported substance use, as well as use-related expectancies. Youth 12–17 years of age (N = 446) across eight U. S. states completed self-report measures of their information behavior and their use of and expectancies regarding the following: cigarettes; electronic vapor products; chewing tobacco, snuff, dip, or snus; cigars, cigarillos, or little cigars; alcohol; and marijuana. Regression models were conducted to examine the relationship between information behavior, substance use, and substance use expectancies. Results indicated that information behavior was associated with expectancies for tobacco and vaping products, but not for alcohol or marijuana. There was no significant association between information behavior and actual substance use. Results have implications for the development and implementation of both information behavior measures and substance use prevention programs.

Keywords: Information behavior · Substance use prevention · Youth

1 Introduction

Youth substance use continues to be a public health concern in the United States. Sixty-two percent of American 12th graders have consumed alcohol, 44% have used marijuana, 47% have vaped, and 24% have smoked cigarettes at least once in their lifetime [34]. Youth substance abuse is tied to negative outcomes including higher risks of unintentional injury to self and others, sexual violence, suicide attempts, mental health issues, and substance abuse lasting into adulthood [10, 11, 30, 45].

M. Smits (Ed.): iConference 2022, LNCS 13193, pp. 106–122, 2022.
https://doi.org/10.1007/978-3-030-96960-8_8

To address this issue, youth prevention programs have been developed that focus on knowledge, skills, and behaviors predictive of substance use, guided by theory and prior research [25]. For example, existing prevention programs have targeted skills such as social resistance, self-management, communication, and decision making (e.g., [12, 27, 28, 46]. Recently, scholars have examined the role of information in substance use decision processes. For example, media and health literacy scholars concerned with the influence of advertising and other media messages have studied youths' abilities to critically evaluate, analyze, and use information related to alcohol, drugs, and other substances (e.g., [3, 35, 53]).

Although evidence suggests that interventions developed using this approach can have a positive impact on youth substance use [29], this area of research is relatively new. Little is known about youth information behavior (IB) within the context of substances in general, as well as the relationship between youth IB and substance use and use expectancies (the beliefs individuals hold about the positive and negative effects of substance use [6, 38]). Because the basic premise of media and health literacy interventions is that elements of IB drive substance use decisions, research that seeks to elucidate the literacy intervention – IB – outcomes pathway is important to understanding how these approaches work and subsequently moving this area of prevention science forward.

2 Youth Information Behavior and Substance Use

IB has been defined as "the totality of human behavior in relation to sources and channels of information" [65, p. 49], and includes the ways in which "people need, seek, manage, give, and use information in different contexts" [13, p. xix]. While there exist many different theories and models of IB, common among many of these approaches is the understanding that IB is complex and multifaceted, involving cognitive, affective, and behavioral dimensions and an array of actions and activities [44, 49, 65].

Although IB within the context of health is a significant area of inquiry in information science, little research has focused on youth IB in relation to substance use specifically. Existing research has focused on youth engagement with substance-related information. For example, studies have indicated that youth's information needs related to illicit substances include the effects of these substances on users; motivations for using substances; epidemiological data related to substance use; legal issues; guidance on safer substance use; and information related to preventing or ending substance use [1, 40, 48, 58]. Youth seek substance-related information from a variety of online [40, 55] and interpersonal sources [40, 51, 55]. Some young people have expressed confidence in their ability to actively seek information relevant to substances, while others have found information seeking to be difficult [51]. For many young people, seeking substance-related information is an iterative process in which they consult multiple sources of information in order to address a given information need [40, 55]. Youth use substance-related information to facilitate the adoption of harm reduction behaviors [58], and in modifications to their existing knowledge structures [62] and opinions [40] related to substances.

Although some research has examined youth IB as it relates to substance-specific information, there are few inquiries that link IB to actual substance use or theoretical predictors of use (e.g., youth's expectancies about the effects of substances [15, 38,

47, 61]. An exception to this is research examining the relationship between passive information seeking and substance use (for a recent review, see [31]). This work demonstrates that exposure to alcohol-related advertisements and user-generated online content is associated with increased alcohol consumption, future consumption intentions, and positive consumption attitudes [26, 32, 60]. Similar findings have been demonstrated in studies focused on other types of substance-related media exposure and young people's substance use and substance use intentions, such as tobacco [36, 64], e-cigarettes [4, 42, 54], and marijuana [8, 9]. A smaller number of studies have examined the relationship between active information seeking and substance use, demonstrating that actively seeking substance-related information from interpersonal and media sources is positively associated with substance use and substance use intentions (e.g., [39, 43, 66]). The link between IB and expectancies is of particular interest, as this is an important explanatory construct in health behavior theories used to explain substance use (e.g., Theory of Reasoned Action and Planned Behavior, Social Cognitive Theory) [16]. For example, studies show that positive expectancies among youth (i.e., the belief that alcohol will lead to positive effects) are associated with negative alcohol outcomes [61].

However, research has yet to examine the relationship between IB more comprehensively, incorporating constructs such as information needs, both active and passive information seeking, and information use, and youth substance use and use expectancies. Those studies that do address active information seeking use measures focused on frequency of information source use, breadth of information sources consulted, or information source preferences [41]. Missing from these measures are more holistic considerations of youth IB.

3 Current Study

As little is known about the relationship between youth IB and substance use, this study aimed to: 1) pilot test a measure of IB that captures multiple dimensions of youth IB; and 2) examine the association between youth IB and their self-reported substance use, as well as use-related expectancies.

Specifically, a shortened version of Fortier and Burkell's [14] IB scale was pilot tested in this study. The IB scale is a 28-item measure of IB with items related to information needs, information seeking, information use, and information sharing [14]. Originally developed and tested with undergraduate students [14], this scale was shortened to a 9-item version for use in this study due to the comparatively younger age of the participants under study and its use in a larger research project within a community-based setting.

Given the information-rich environment in which today's adolescents are immersed, and the emergence of media literacy in health interventions, this study sought to contribute to IB theory by demonstrating the relationship between dimensions of youths' IB and behavioral outcomes related to substance use, while also informing both the theory and application of prevention science by utilizing an information science perspective. One would expect that youths' IB would influence their expectancies as well as their substance use behaviors. Therefore, this study sought to address the following research question:

RQ: Is IB related to substance use and substance use expectancies?

4 Methods

This study draws from a community-based randomized controlled trial evaluating REAL media, a self-paced online media literacy curriculum for youth focused on substance use prevention. REAL media is designed to decrease substance use in adolescents by increasing awareness of and efficacy in resisting advertising messages. REAL media was developed through multiple iterative stages involving target youth [20, 23, 56, 57], and is based on Youth Message Development, a face-to-face media literacy curriculum designated as evidence-based by the Substance Abuse and Mental Health Services Administration's National Registry of Evidence-based Programs and Practices [2, 3, 21, 24].

The curriculum is based on the Theory of Active Involvement's [19] approach to media literacy and consists of 5 lessons or levels. Level 1 introduces concepts of media reach and cost, as well as media ethics. Level 2 focuses on target audience and persuasion strategies used in advertising. Level 3 identifies arguments or claims used in advertisements including missing information and counter-arguing. Level 4 focuses on attention-getting tactics and major advertising production techniques. In the fifth and final level, youth plan, produce, and share a counter-message (i.e., substance prevention message) targeting their peers.

4.1 Participants

Participants were recruited from 4-H clubs[1] in eight U. S. states (Arizona, Illinois, Louisiana, New Jersey, Ohio, Pennsylvania, Washington, and West Virginia), with three project cohorts launched throughout 2018. Recruitment was initiated at the state level through either local 4-H leaders or a statewide strategy. The project team gave recruitment presentations to county leaders, club leaders, and at state events, and developed a project website and social media presence that were shared widely. When youth demonstrated interest, parental consent forms were distributed and returned directly to research staff. Participants provided assent after research staff obtained parental consent; both parental consent and youth assent were necessary for youth to participate.

The sample consisted of 446 4-H youth members between 12 and 17 years of age (M = 14.83, SD = 1.29) at the time of study pretest. See Table 1 for additional participant demographic information.

[1] In the U. S., 4-H clubs are a network of youth organizations based in land-grant universities and sponsored by the United States Department of Agriculture. The largest youth development organization in the country, 4-H clubs focus on experiential learning, mentoring, and positive youth development in teaching youth leadership and life skills [48]. Prior research has found that 4-H members have patterns of risk behaviors similar to other U.S. youth [35].

Table 1. Participant demographic information

Participant characteristics		*n* (%)
Gender		
	Male	148 (33)
	Female	298 (67)
Race		
	European-American or White	388 (87)
	African-American or Black	20 (4)
	Asian or Pacific Islander	16 (4)
	American Indian or Alaskan Native	5 (1)
	Other/Not identified	17 (4)
Ethnicity		
	Hispanic	31 (7)
	Non-Hispanic	415 (93)
Education		
	Currently attending public school	321 (72)
	Currently attending private school	40 (9)
	Currently being home-schooled	71 (16)
	Other	14 (3)
Have a computer or tablet at home		
	Yes	441 (99)
	No	5 (1)

4.2 Procedure

After assent, youth were randomly assigned to treatment (n = 240, 54%) or delayed use control (n = 206, 46%) conditions, with efforts made to balance condition assignment by participant state, gender, race, and geographic area (i.e., urban/rural). Participants in the treatment group completed the REAL media curriculum after completing the study pre-test, and participants in the delayed use control group were invited to complete the curriculum after completing all study post-tests. REAL media was designed to take approximately 90 min, excluding time spent by youth to design their substance prevention message. Although it was encouraged, not all participating youth completed the program. The attrition rates and consort diagram for the larger study are included in [22]. Study surveys were programmed and distributed via Qualtrics, an online survey tool, and typically took 15–60 min for participants to complete. Participants were given three weeks to complete the surveys on their own time, and research staff sent reminder messages to participants via email and/or text message as needed. The analyses presented here include data from two time periods (pre-test and 3-month post-test). Participants received $10 in compensation after completion of each online survey. Only those participants who completed the pre-test survey were retained in the sample (N = 446). The post-test completion rate was 80% (n = 358).

This study was approved by a university Institutional Review Board and advised by a three-member Data Safety and Monitoring Board.

4.3 Measures

Participants completed self-report measures related to IB, substance use, and substance use expectancies.

Information Behavior. IB was measured at post-test using a subset of nine agree-dis-agree items from Fortier and Burkell's [14] IB scale (see Table 2). The questions in this scale were not specific to substance-related information but rather asked about youths' IB more generally. Although nine items were initially used to measure IB, several items displayed poor internal consistency including all three items from the information seeking subscale and one item from the information needs subscale (alphas by subscale were: information use = .63; information needs = .28; and information seeking = .29). Based on the correlations among items and other psychometrics, a composite variable for IB was created with five items; the final measure consisted of three items from the information use subscale and two items from the information needs subscale. The five items measure an orientation to rule following construct, characterized by actions that have been termed "good information behavior," or, in other words, actions that align with those encouraged by librarians and other information professionals as good practices to employ when seeking and using information, such as questioning the accuracy of information and using criteria to assess information quality ([14], p. 4). Confirmatory factor analysis (CFA) also yielded good fit of this measurement model (x2(5) = 13.68, p = .02, Root Mean Square Error = .07, 90% CI = .03, .12, CFI = .97, TLI = .94). Response categories for all items ranged from 1 (*strongly disagree*) to 7 (*strongly agree*). We averaged these 5 items' response score to make a composite variable, with a higher composite score reflecting higher orientation to rule following (M = 5.40, SD = 0.83, alpha = .67).

Table 2. Information behavior scale subset [14]

Subscale	Item
Information use	I question the accuracy of information.†
	I pay attention to the details about where information comes from.†
	I have criteria that I use to assess the quality of information.†
Information needs	Looking for information comes naturally to me.†
	A lot of information overwhelms me.*
	When I am interested in something, I have lots of questions.†
Information seeking	I prefer using information sources I already know
	I prefer finding information by myself rather than asking for help
	When I have a question, I rely on my friends and family for information

* Reverse-coded item

†Items included in the composite variable.

Substance Use. Youth substance use was measured at post-test with a recall-based dichotomous (yes/no) indicator of whether the respondent reported any of the following in the past three months: cigarette smoking, even one or two puffs; electronic vapor product use, even one or two times; chewing tobacco, snuff, dip, or snus use, even one or two times; cigar, cigarillo, or little cigar use, even one or two puffs; at least one drink of alcohol; and use of marijuana. Items specific to cigarette smoking and use of electronic vapor products were taken from the 2017 National Youth Risk Behavior Survey [5], with parallel items created for all other substances. A composite variable was created by summing all items (*M* = 0.31, *SD* = 0.74, alpha = .59). CFA with these six items supported a one-factor solution ($x^2(9) = 10.27$, p = .33, Root Mean Square Error = .02, 90% CI = .00, .07, CFI = .995, TLI = .992).

Substance Use Expectancies. Both social substance use expectancies and perceived harm expectancies were assessed in this study. Social substance use expectancies for all substances were assessed at post-test with three items per substance, drawn from the Population Assessment of Tobacco and Health (PATH) [63]. Respondents indicated their agreement with these statements for each substance (cigarettes; cigars, cigarillos, or little cigars; electronic vapor products; chewing tobacco, snuff, dip, or snus; alcohol; and marijuana). The three items asked respondents whether using each substance "is enjoyable," "makes it easier to fit in at parties," and "makes people who use the substance 'not attractive'" (reverse coded item). Response categories ranged on a five-point Likert scale from 1 (*strongly disagree*) to 5 (*strongly agree*). Scores were averaged, with higher scores reflecting more positive substance use expectancies. That is, six social expectancy variables for six different substance (smoking cigarettes (*M* = 1.65, *SD* = 0.69, alpha = .51), smoking cigars, cigarillos, or little cigars (*M* = 1.68, *SD* = 0.77 alpha = .65), using electronic vapor products (*M* = 2.17, *SD* = 0.99 alpha = .72), using chewing tobacco, snuff, dip, or snus (*M* = 1.59, *SD* = 0.68 alpha = .54), drinking alcohol (*M* = 2.61, *SD* = 1.07, alpha = .73), and using marijuana (*M* = 2.02, *SD* = 1.01, alpha = .73) were created.

Perceived harm from use of each substance was also measured at pre-test and post-test. An item from the PATH Study [63] specific to cigarette use was used, with parallel items created for all other target substances. Respondents were asked one question per substance to indicate their appraisal of how much people who use the substances harm themselves if they use the target substance on "some days but not every day." Response categories ranged on a four-point Likert scale from 1 (*no harm*) to 4 (*a lot of harm*). Item scores were averaged, with higher scores reflecting greater perceived harm (*M* = 3.22, *SD* = 0.57, alpha = .80).

4.4 Analyses

Prior to examining the relationship between IB and 8 outcomes (overall substance use, cigarette social expectancies, cigar social expectancies, chewing tobacco social expectancies, vaping social expectancies, alcohol social expectancies, marijuana social expectancies, and perceived harm), it was first examined whether IB differed between the treatment and control groups. A t-test indicated no significant difference regarding the IB composite score between control ($n = 187$, $M = 5.43$, $SD = 0.83$) and treatment ($n = 171$, $M = 5.36$, $SD = 0.82$), $t(356) = 0.80$, $p = 0.43$. Thus, the entire sample was included in subsequent analyses. Eight regression models were conducted to examine the relationship between IB and expectancies for each of the six substances, perceived harm, and overall substance use using Mplus. Given the number of regression models, the *p*-value level was adjusted to .01 instead of .05 to avoid an increase in type 1 error. Demographic information (e.g., gender, age) and condition (control = 0 and treatment = 1) were included as covariates in the regression analyses. Because most participants were White, race was dummy-coded (White = 0 and other = 1). One dummy-coded education variable (public school = 1 and other = 0), seven dummy-coded state variables (PA served as the reference group), and lifetime substance use experience (never across any substance = 0 and experience using any substance = 1) were also included at pre-test. In order to control for previous expectancies and use, relevant pre-test versions of each outcome variable were also included as covariates for corresponding outcomes. Previous perceptions including social expectancies across all six different substances (cigarette: $M = 1.59$, $SD = 0.64$, alpha = 0.50; vaping: $M = 2.01$, $SD = 0.89$, alpha = .69; chewing: $M = 1.51$, $SD = 0.62$, alpha = .48; cigar: $M = 1.59$, $SD = 0.67$, alpha = 0.55; alcohol: $M = 2.56$, $SD = 1.01$, alpha = .75; marijuana: $M = 1.91$, $SD = 0.93$, alpha = .70) and as well as perceived harm ($M = 3.24$, $SD = 0.57$, alpha = .81) at pre-test were also controlled for. For example, in the model examining the association between IB and cigarette social expectancies at post-test, cigarette social expectancies at pre-test was included in the model. Eight different regression models were conducted due to concerns about potential multicollinearity (see Table 3), type II error, and the purpose of this study (e.g., association between IB and outcomes by controlling for previous outcomes). Furthermore, given that the regression models are all saturated models (e.g., estimated all relationships), the model fit provides perfect fit indices (e.g., CFI = 1.00) and thus, are not reported. Full information maximum likelihood was employed to handle missing data [17]. Maximum likelihood method was used for outcomes analyses

Table 3. Zero order correlation matrix among key study variables

	1	2	3	4	5	6	7	8
1. IB	–							
2. CE	– 0.23***							
3. VE	– 0.18***	0.64***						
4. CHE	– 0.23***	0.71***	0.48***					
5. CGE	– 0.24***	0.77***	0.59***	0.75***				
6. AE	– 0.10*	0.53***	0.75***	0.37***	0.49***			
7. ME	– 0.10	0.65***	0.75***	0.49***	0.63***	0.68***		
8. PH	0.11*	–0.35***	–0.47***	–0.29***	–0.34***	–0.47***	– 0.47***	
9. 3SU	0.02	0.24***	0.41***	0.09	0.26***	0.41***	0.42***	– 0.28***

Note. 1. IB: information behavior, 2. CE: cigarette expectancy, 3. VE: vaping expectancy, 4. CHE: chewing expectancy, 5. CGE: cigar expectancy, 6. AE: alcohol expectancy, 7. ME: marijuana expectancy, 8. PH: perceived harm, 9. 3SU: 3 month substance use, * < .05, ** < .01, *** < .001

for expectancy and perceived harm and robust maximum likelihood method [7, 67] was used for 3-month substance use at post-test due to the positive skewness of this variable.

5 Results

IB at post-test was negatively related with positive social expectancies on cigarette (b = -–0.12, se = .04, p = .001), vaping (b = - –0.19, se = .05, p < .001), chewing tobacco, (b = - –0.15, se = .04, p < .001), and cigar use (b = - –0.18, se = .04, p < .001). IB was not related with alcohol (b = -–0.09, se = .05, p = .07) and marijuana (b = -0.09, se = .05, p = .06) expectancy variables (see Table 4). Youth who had higher IB scores had lower positive social expectancy scores (i.e., more negative expectancies) regarding tobacco products. There was no significant association between IB and actual substance use as well as the perceived harm variable.

6 Discussion

This study examined the relationship between IB and substance use behaviors and expectancies, pilot testing a shortened version of an existing IB scale. Based on the existing body of research, studies examining additional dimensions of youth IB and substance use are warranted. Results from this study demonstrate that IB is related to drug use expectancies, a powerful predictor of future use [15, 38, 47, 61], but not to self-reported use. Perhaps with a more extended observation of effects, the predicted progression from IB to expectancies to drug use would have emerged.

This study's findings provide support for the relationship between IB and expectancies about use of most substances (and marginally significant effects on expectancies for the others) but not substance use itself nor perceived harm. There are several possible explanations for these findings. It makes sense that the primary effect of IB would be on expectancies, as expectancies are shaped by the information one has. As measured, the rule-following nature of IB involves actions such as questioning the accuracy of information, using criteria to assess information quality, and assessing where information comes from [14]. It is established in the literature that youth have information needs related to substances [1, 40, 48, 58] and use information to modify their existing knowledge and opinions [40, 62]. Thus, it makes sense that expectancies about substances would be related to these actions. If youth look closely and critically at information about substances, they are likely to perceive more negative consequences associated with consumption. Notably, the IB – expectancy association was observed for tobacco-related beliefs and not beliefs about alcohol or marijuana. Perhaps this reflects more consistent messaging and information related to negative aspects of tobacco products relative to other substances. Given the popularity of youth alcohol experimentation as well as the changing legal landscape of marijuana, youth who seek information on alcohol or marijuana may find positive messages that counter any negative information they find.

Table 4. Relationship between social expectancies, perceived harm and information behavior (N = 446)

	Social Expectancies						Perceived Harm	3-Month Substance Use
	Cigarette	Vaping	Chewing	Cigar	Alcohol	Marijuana		
	Est (se)	Est (se)	Est (se)	Est (se)	Est (se)	Est (se)	Est (se)	Est (se)
Information behavior	– 0.12(.04)*	– 0.19(.05)**	– 0.15(.04)**	– 0.18(.04)**	– 0.09(.05)	– 0.09(.05) †	0.04(.03)	– 0.01(.05)
State dummy1	0.02(.12)	– 0.15(.16)	0.17(.13)	0.05(0.13)	– 0.03(.16)	– 0.18(.16)	0.05(.09)	– 0.11(0.16)
State dummy2	0.01(.11)	– 0.14(.14)	– 0.07(.11)	– 0.05(.12)	0.04(.14)	0.01(.14)	– 0.01(.08)	– 0.21(.12)
State dummy3	– 0.01(.10)	– 0.04(.13)	0.06(.11)	0.11(.11)	0.08(.13)	– 0.05(.13)	– 0.11(.08)	– 0.02(.14)
State dummy4	0.14(.18)	– 0.05(.23)	0.21(.19)	0.27(.20)	0.17(.24)	0.15(.23)	0.05(.14)	0.12(.20)
State dummy5	0.30(.40)	0.41(.51)	0.18(.41)	0.40(.43)	0.16(.53)	– 0.06(.51)	– 0.12(.31)	0.38(.37)
State dummy6	– 0.10(.10)	– 0.09(.13)	– 0.03(.10)	0.02(0.11)	– 0.08(.13)	– 0.17(.13)	0.06(.08)	– 0.18(.12)
State dummy7	– 0.14(.13)	– 0.27(.16)	0.01(.13)	0.05(.14)	– 0.07(.17)	– 0.31(.17)	0.06(.10)	– 0.06(.14)
Male (=1, female = 0)	– 0.13(.06)†	– 0.24(.08)*	– 0.08(.07)	– 0.05(.07)	– 0.11(.09)	– 0.15(.08)	0.01(.05)	– 0.06(.07)
Not White (=1, White = 0)	0.06(.10)	– 0.18(.13)	– 0.05(.11)	– 0.24(.11)	– 0.30(.14) †	– 0.07(.14)	– 0.02(.08)	– 0.06(.10)
Public school (=1, others = 0)	– 0.16 (.70) †	0.04(.09)lePara>	– 0.01(.07)	– 0.02(.07)	0.10(.09)	– 0.11(.09)	0.01(.05)	– 0.02(.08)
Treatment (=1 control = 0)	0.10(.06)	0.06(.08)	0.00(.06)	0.07(.07)	– 0.01(.08)	0.02(.08)	0.02(.05)	0.02(.06)
Age	0.01(.02)	0.04(.03)	– 0.01(.03)	0.00(.03)	– 0.01(.03)	0.05(.03)	– 0.01(.02)	0.06(.03) †

(continued)

Table 4. *(continued)*

	Social Expectancies						Perceived Harm	3-Month Substance Use
	Cigarette	Vaping	Chewing	Cigar	Alcohol	Marijuana		
T1 Lifetime substance use (=1, no = 0)	0.11(.07)	0.22(.10) †	0.01(.07)	0.02(.08)	0.18(.10)	0.16(.10)	– 0.05(.06)	0.85(.10)***
T1 Cigarette social expectancies	0.56(.05)**	–	–	–	–	–	–	–
T1 Vaping social expectancies	–	0.67(.05)**	–	–	–	–	–	–
T1 Chewing social expectancies	–	–	0.56(.05)**					
T1 Cigar social expectancies	–	–	–	0.65(0.05)**	–	–	–	–
T1 Alcohol social expectancies	–	–	–	–	0.70(.04)**			
T1 Marijuana social expectancies	–	–	–	–	–	0.69(.05)**	–	–
T1 Perceived harm	–	–	–	–	–	–	0.64(.04)**	
R^2	.39	.50	.33	.42	.54	.52	.45	.34

Note. † $p < .05$, * $p < .01$, ** $p < .001$

6.1 Limitations

Three of the primary limitations of this study were due to constraints on survey length. First, it was not possible to measure IB at pre-test. This meant changes in IB could not be examined, nor could initial IB levels be controlled for. Second, it was not feasible to use the IB scale in its entirety. There are very few measures of IB in existence, and the Fortier and Burkell [14] scale is the only one found that covers multiple dimensions of IB. However, it was too long for the current purpose because this study was conducted among youth in the field where time restrictions do not allow for long, multi-item scales. Although what was believed to be an adequate number of items from each of the dimensions of information seeking, use, and needs were selected for use, contrary to expectations our modifications did not retain the hypothesized dimensionality. To construct a reliable scale, five items that had adequate reliability were chosen for inclusion based on inter-item correlations. This may have influenced the findings. Third, none of the information seeking questions were retained in the five-item composite for IB. As a result, the findings are applicable only to information needs and use, and not information seeking.

Additionally, some of the substance use expectancy scales had relatively low reliability (e.g., smoking cigarettes across two time points). Thus, interpretation should be made with caution. An additional limitation is related to the race/ethnicity of the study population. Because participants were predominantly non-Hispanic white, the findings may not be generalizable to adolescents of other racial/ethnic groups. Finally, any study that relies on self-report data is limited in the claims it can make about behavior. However, although the correlation between self-reported and actual substance use behavior is not perfect, self-reported behavior appears valid for the purposes of comparing outcomes [59]. Others also provide evidence in support of self-reported data, particularly when limited to activities during the past 30 days [18, 33, 52], such as the current focus.

6.2 Future Research

Future research should continue to explore the relationship between youths' IB, substance use, and expectancies. Further development of measures of IB is needed, particularly briefer measures that are better suited for a community-based youth population. Establishing a relationship between IB and these constructs would enable the development of prevention programs that focus on specific aspects of IB related to youth substance use.

Additionally, the lack of findings in this study related to actual substance use indicate the lack of a direct effect of IB on substance use. Given the well-established connection between expectancies and subsequent use of substances [15, 38, 47, 61], it is possible that IB has an indirect effect on use through its association with expectancies that requires a longer observation period. Future longer longitudinal studies are needed to explore expectancies as a mediator between IB and substance use.

From an information science perspective, such work would extend theorization of IB constructs, with a particular focus on information use. The ways in which youth use information related to substances, including the impact that such information has on their behaviors, has received less attention than the information they seek and how they seek it.

Finally, causal direction cannot be clearly established given the cross-sectional nature of these data. Although it makes sense that the IBs measured here would lead to less positive expectancies about substance use, one could argue that youth have negative expectations that might make them more skeptical about positive information about substances. Future research is needed to clarify these issues.

7 Conclusion

This study pilot tested a measure of youth IB in a study examining the relationship between IB and substance use and substance use expectancies. Findings revealed that IB was associated with substance use expectancies but not substance use itself. Expectancies are a more proximal outcome of IB and suggest that longer term follow up may reveal behavioral changes as well. Additionally, there were issues related to the reliability of the shortened IB scale that indicate further work is needed in establishing a quantitative measure of youth IB.

Acknowledgements. The community-based randomized controlled trial on which this manuscript is based received funding from the National Institutes of Health/National Institute of Drug Abuse (grants R41DA039595 and R42DA039595). Co-authors Michael L. Hecht and Kathryn Greene disclose intellectual property interests in the REAL media curriculum.

References

1. Aveyard, H.: Illicit drug use: information-giving strategies requested by students in higher education. Health Educ. J. **58**, 239–248 (1999). https://doi.org/10.1177/0017896999058
2. Banerjee, S.C., Greene, K.: Substance abuse prevention message generation and engaging adolescents in health message planning and/or production of health promotion messages. In: Nussbaum, J.F. (ed.) Oxford Research Encyclopedia of Communication. Oxford University Press, New York (2016). https://doi.org/10.1093/acrefore/9780190228613.013.197
3. Banerjee, S.C., Greene, K., Magsamen-Conrad, K., Elek, E., Hecht, M.L.: Interpersonal communication outcomes of a media literacy alcohol prevention curriculum. Transl. Behav. Med. **5**(4), 425–432 (2015). https://doi.org/10.1007/s13142-015-0329-9
4. Camenga, D., Gutierrez, K.M., Kong, G., Cavallo, D., Simon, P., Krishnan-Sarin, S.: E-cigarette advertising exposure in e-cigarette naïve adolescents and subsequent e-cigarette use: a longitudinal cohort study. Addict. Behav. **81**, 78–83 (2018). https://doi.org/10.1016/j.addbeh.2018.02.008
5. Centers for Disease Control and Prevention: Youth Risk Behavior Survey Questionnaire. https://www.cdc.gov/healthyyouth/data/yrbs/pdf/2017/2017_yrbs_na-tional_hs_questionnaire.pdf (2017)
6. Cooper, M.L., Kuntsche, E., Levitt, A., Barber, L.L., Wolf, S.: Motivational models of substance use: a review of theory and research on motives for using alcohol, marijuana, and tobacco. In: Sher, K.J. (ed.) The Oxford Handbook of Substance use and Substance Use Disorders, vol. 1, pp. 375–421. Oxford University Press, New York (2016)

7. Curran, P.J., West, S.G., Finch, J.F.: The robustness of test statistics to nonnormality and specification error in confirmatory factor analysis. Psychol. Methods **1**, 16–29 (1996). https://doi.org/10.1037/1082-989X.1.1.16
8. Dai, H.: Exposure to advertisements and marijuana use among US adolescents. Prevent. Chronic Dis. **14** (2017). https://doi.org/10.5888/pcd14.170253
9. D'Amico, E.J., Miles, J.N., Tucker, J.S.: Gateway to curiosity: medical marijuana ads and intention and use during middle school. Psychol. Addict. Behav. **29**, 613–619 (2015). https://doi.org/10.1037/adb0000094
10. Degenhardt, L., et al.: The persistence of the association between adolescent cannabis use and common mental disorders into young adulthood. Addiction **108**, 124–133 (2013). https://doi.org/10.1111/j.1360-0443.2012.04015.x
11. Espelage, D.L., Davis, J.P., Basile, K.C., Rostad, W.L., Leemis, R.W.: Alcohol, prescription drug misuse, sexual violence, and dating violence among high school youth. J. Adolescent Health **63**, 601–607 (2018). https://doi.org/10.1016/j.jadohealth.2018.05.024
12. Evans, W., Andrade, E., Goldmeer, S., Smith, M., Snider, J., Girardo, G.: The Living the Example social media substance use prevention program: a pilot evaluation. JMIR Ment. Health, **4** (2017). https://doi.org/10.2196/mental.7839
13. Fisher, K.E., Erdelez, S., McKechnie, L. (E.F.) (eds.): Theories of Information Behavior. Information Today Inc., Medford (2005)
14. Fortier, A., Burkell, J.: Influence of need for cognition and need for cognitive closure on three information behavior orientations. P. Assoc. Inf. Sci. Tech. **51**, 1–8 (2014). https://doi.org/10.1002/meet.2014.14505101066
15. Fromme, K., D'Amico, E.J.: Measuring adolescent alcohol outcome expectancies. Psychol. Addict. Behav. **14**, 206–212 (2000)
16. Glanz, K., Rimer, B.K., Viswanath, K. (eds): Health Behavior: Theory, Research, and Practice (5th ed.). Jossey-Bass, San Francisco (2015)
17. Graham, J.W., Cumsille, P.E., Elek-Fisk, E.: Methods for handling missing data. In: Weiner, I.B. (ed.) Handbook of Psychology. John Wiley & Sons, Hoboken (2003). https://doi.org/10.1002/0471264385.wei0204
18. Graham, J.W., Flay, B.R., Johnson, C.A., Hansen, W.B., Grossman, L.M., Sobel, J.L.: Reliability of self report measures of drug use in prevention research: evaluation of the Project SMART Questionnaire via the test-retest reliability matrix. J. Drug Educ. **14**, 175–193 (1984). https://doi.org/10.2190/CYV0-7DPB-DJFA-EJ5U
19. Greene, K.: The theory of active involvement: processes underlying interventions that engage adolescents in message planning and/or production. Health Commun. **28**, 644–656 (2013). https://doi.org/10.1080/10410236.2012.762824
20. Greene, K., Banerjee, S.C., Ray, A.E., Hecht, M.L.: Active involvement interventions in health and risk messaging. In: Parrott, R.L. (ed.), Oxford Encyclopedia of Health and Risk Message Design and Processing, pp. 1–36. Oxford University Press, New York (2017). https://doi.org/10.1093/acrefore/9780190228613.013.527
21. Greene, K., Catona, D., Elek, E., Magsamen-Conrad, K., Banerjee, S.C., Hecht, M.L.: Improving prevention curricula: lessons learned through formative research on the Youth Message Development Curriculum. J. Health Commun. **21**, 1071–1078 (2016). https://doi.org/10.1080/10810730.2016.1222029
22. Greene, K., Choi, H.J., Glenn, S.D., Ray, A.E., Hecht, M.L.: The role of engagement in effective, digital prevention interventions: the function of engagement in the REAL media substance use prevention curriculum. Prev. Sci. **22**(2), 247–258 (2020). https://doi.org/10.1007/s11121-020-01181-9
23. Greene, K., Ray, A.E., Choi, H.J., Glenn, S.D., Lyons, R.E., Hecht, M.L.: Short term effects of the REAL media e-learning media literacy substance prevention curriculum: an RCT

of adolescents disseminated through a community organization. Drug Alcohol Depen. **214** (2020). https://doi.org/10.1016/j.dru-galcdep.2020.108170
24. Greene, K., et al.: A theory-grounded measure of adolescents' response to a media literacy intervention. J. Media Lit. Educ. **7**, 35–49 (2015)
25. Griffin, K.W., Botvin, G.J.: Evidence-based interventions for preventing substance use disorders in adolescents. Child Adol. Psych. Cl. **19**, 505–526 (2010). https://doi.org/10.1016/j.chc.2010.03.005
26. Gupta, H., Pettigrew, S., Lam, T., Tait, R.J.: A systematic review of the impact of exposure to internet-based alcohol-related content on young people's alcohol use behaviours. Alcohol Alcoholism **51**, 763–771 (2016). https://doi.org/10.1093/al-calc/agw050
27. Haug, S., Paz Castro, R., Wenger, A., Schaub, M.P.: Efficacy of a mobile phone-based life-skills training program for substance use prevention among adolescents: study protocol of a cluster-randomised controlled trial. BMC Public Health **18** (2018). https://doi.org/10.1186/s12889-018-5969-5
28. Hecht, M.L., Graham, J.W., Elek, E.: The drug resistance strategies intervention: program effects on substance use. Health Commun. **20**, 267–276 (2006). https://doi.org/10.1207/s15327027hc2003_6
29. Hindmarsh, C.S., Jones, S.C., Kervin, L.: Effectiveness of alcohol media literacy programmes: a systematic literature review. Health Educ. Res. **30**, 449–465 (2015). https://doi.org/10.1093/her/cyv015
30. Hingson, R.W., Zha, W.: Age of drinking onset, alcohol use disorders, frequent heavy drinking, and unintentionally injuring oneself and others after drinking. Pediatrics **123**, 1477–1484 (2009). https://doi.org/10.1542/peds.2008-2176
31. Jackson, K.M., Janssen, T., Gabrielli, J.: Media/marketing influences on adolescent and young adult substance abuse. Curr. Addict. Report. **5**, 146-157 (2018). https://doi.org/10.1007/s40429-018-0199-6
32. Jernigan, D., Noel, J., Landon, J., Thornton, N., Lobstein, T.: Alcohol marketing and youth alcohol consumption: a systematic review of longitudinal studies published since 2008. Addiction **112**, 7–20 (2017). https://doi.org/10.1111/add.13591
33. Johnston, L.D.: The survey technique in drug abuse assessment. B. Narcotics **41**, 29–39 (1989)
34. Johnston, L.D., Miech, R.A., O'Malley, P.M., Bachman, J.G., Schulenberg, J.E., Patrick, M.E.: Monitoring the Future National Survey Results on Drug Use, 1975–2020: Overview, Key Findings on Adolescent Drug Use. http://monitor-ingthefuture.org/pubs/monographs/mtf-overview2020.pdf (2021)
35. Kupersmidt, J.B., Scull, T.M., Austin, E.W.: Media literacy education for elementary school substance use prevention: study of media detective. Pediatrics **126**, 525–531 (2010). https://doi.org/10.1542/peds.2010-0068
36. Leonardi-Bee, J., Nderi, M., Britton, J.: Smoking in movies and smoking initiation in adolescents: systematic review and meta-analysis. Addiction **111**, 1750–1763 (2016). https://doi.org/10.1111/add.13418
37. Lerner, R.M., Lerner, J.V.: The Positive Development of Youth: Comprehensive Findings From the 4-H Study of Positive Youth Development. http://www.4-h.org/about/youth-development-research/positive-youth-development-study/ (2013)
38. Leventhal, A.M., Schmitz, J.M.: The role of drug use outcome expectancies in substance abuse risk: an interactional-transformational model. Addict. Behav. **31**, 2038–2062 (2006). https://doi.org/10.1016/j.addbeh.2006.02.004
39. Lewis, N., Martinez, L.S.: Information seeking as a predictor of risk behavior: testing a behavior and risk information engagement model (BRIE). J. Health Commun. **25**, 474–483 (2020). https://doi.org/10.1080/10810730.2020.1797247

40. Lewis, N., Martinez, L.S., Agbarya, A., Piatok-Vaisman, T.: Examining patterns and motivations for drug-related information seeking and scanning behavior: a cross-national comparison of American and Israeli college students. Commun. Q. **64**, 145–172 (2016). https://doi.org/10.1080/01463373.2015.1103282
41. Lewis, N., Martinez, L.S., Carmel, O.: Measures of information seeking: a validation study in the context of nonmedical drug use behaviors. Commun. Methods Meas. **11**, 266–288 (2017). https://doi.org/10.1080/19312458.2017.1326021
42. Liu, J., Lochbuehler, K., Yang, Q., Gibson, L.A., Hornik, R.C.: Breadth of media scanning leads to vaping among youth and young adults: evidence of direct and indirect pathways from a national longitudinal survey. J. Health Commun. **25**, 91–104 (2020). https://doi.org/10.1080/10810730.2019.1709925
43. Martinez, L.S., Lewis, N.: A mediation model to explain the effects of information seeking from media and interpersonal sources on young adults' intention to use marijuana. Int. J. Commun.-US **10**, 1809–1832 (2016)
44. Meyer, H.W.J.: Untangling the building blocks: a generic model to explain in-formation behaviour to novice researchers. Inf. Res. **21** (2016). http://infor-mationr.net/ir/21-4/isic/isic1602.html#nah01
45. Miller, J.W., Naimi, T.S., Brewer, R.D., Everett, J.S.: Binge drinking and associated health risk behaviors among high school students. Pediatrics **119**, 6–85 (2007). https://doi.org/10.1542/peds.2006-1517
46. Mogro-Wilson, N.C., Allen, E., Cavallucci, C.: A brief high school prevention program to decrease alcohol usage and change social norms. Soc. Work Res. **41**, 53–62 (2017). https://doi.org/10.1093/swr/svw023
47. Montes, K.S., Witkiewitz, K., Pearson, M.R., Leventhal, A.M.: Alcohol, tobacco, and marijuana expectancies as predictors of substance use initiation in adolescence: a longitudinal examination. Psychol. Addict. Behav. **33**, 26–34 (2019). https://doi.org/10.1037/adb0000422
48. Morton, C.M., Hoefinger, H., Linn-Walton, R., Aikins, R., Falkin, G.P.: What are youth asking about drugs? a report of NIDA Drug Facts Chat Day. J. Drug Educ. **45**, 195–210 (2015). https://doi.org/10.1177/0047237915622084
49. Nahl, D.: A conceptual framework for explaining information behavior. Stud. Media Inf. Lit. Educ. **1**, 1–16 (2001)
50. National 4-H Council: 4-H: Positive Youth Development and Mentoring Organi-zation. https://4-h.org/ (2019)
51. Notley, C., Scaife, V., O'Brien, M., Mceune, R., Biggart, L., Millings, A.: Vulnerable young people and substance-use information-seeking: perceived credibility of different information sources and implications for services. J. Subst. Use **17**, 163–175 (2012). https://doi.org/10.3109/14659891.2010.540297
52. O'Malley, P.M., Bachman, J.G., Johnston, L.D.: Reliability and consistency in self-reports of drug use. Int. J. Addict. **18**, 806–824 (1983). https://doi.org/10.3109/10826088309033049
53. Park, E., Jang, B.G.: Youth substance use prevention using disciplinary literacy strategies: a pilot study. J. Addict. Nurs. **29**(4), 235–243 (2018). https://doi.org/10.1097/JAN.0000000000000253
54. Pokhrel, P., et al.: Social media e-cigarette exposure and e-cigarette expectancies and use among young adults. Addict. Behav. **78**, 51–58 (2018). https://doi.org/10.1016/j.addbeh.2017.10.017
55. Quintero, G., Bundy, H.: "Most of the time you already know": pharmaceutical information assembly by young adults on the internet. Subst. Use Misuse **46**, 898–909 (2011). https://doi.org/10.3109/10826084.2011.570630
56. Ray, A.E., et al.: An e-learning adaptation of an evidence-based media literacy curriculum to prevent youth substance use in community groups: development and feasibility of REAL media. JMIR Form. Res. **3** (2019). https://doi.org/10.2196/12132

57. Ray, A.E., Greene, K., Pristavec, T., Hecht, M.L., Miller-Day, M., Banerjee, S.C.: Exploring indicators of engagement in online learning as applied to adolescent health prevention: a pilot study of REAL media. Educ. Tech. Res. Dev. **68**(6), 3143–3163 (2020). https://doi.org/10.1007/s11423-020-09813-1
58. Seddon, T.: Improving the health of drug-using prisoners: an exploratory study of drug information needs in male young offender institutions. Health Educ. J. **60**, 17–25 (2001). https://doi.org/10.1177/001789690106000103
59. Smith-Donals, L.G., Klitzner, M.D.: Self-reports of youthful drinking and driving: sensitivity analyses of sensitive data. J. Psychoactive Drugs **17**, 179–190 (1985). https://doi.org/10.1080/02791072.1985.10472339
60. Stautz, K., Brown, K.G., King, S.E., Shemilt, I., Marteau, T.M.: Immediate effects of alcohol marketing communications and media portrayals on consumption and cognition: a systematic review and meta-analysis of experimental studies. BMC Public Health **16**, 1–18 (2016). https://doi.org/10.1186/s12889-016-3116-8
61. Stone, A.L., Becker, L.G., Huber, A.M., Catalano, R.F.: Review of risk and protective factors of substance use and problem use in emerging adulthood. Addict. Behav. **37**, 747–775 (2012). https://doi.org/10.1016/j.addbeh.2012.02.014
62. Todd, R.J.: Utilization of heroin information by adolescent girls in Australia: a cognitive analysis. J. Am. Soc. Inform. Sci. **50**, 10–23 (1999). https://doi.org/10.1002/(SICI)1097-4571(1999)50:1%3c10::AID-ASI4%3e3.3.CO;2-2
63. United States Department of Health and Human Services, National Institutes of Health, National Institute on Drug Abuse, Department of Health and Human Services, Food and Drug Administration: Center for Tobacco Products. Population Assessment of Tobacco and Health (PATH) Study Public-Use Files. Inter-university Consortium for Political and Social Research, Ann Arbor (2018)
64. Wellman, R.J., Sugarman, D.B., DiFranza, J.R., Winickoff, J.P.: The extent to which tobacco marketing and tobacco use in films contribute to children's use of tobacco: a meta-analysis. Arch. Pediat. Adol. Med. **160**, 1285–1296 (2006). https://doi.org/10.1001/archpedi.160.12.1285
65. Wilson, T.D.: Human information behaviour. Inf. Sci. **3**, 49–55 (2000)
66. Yang, Q., Liu, J., Lochbuehler, K., Hornik, R.: Does seeking e-cigarette information lead to vaping? evidence from a national longitudinal survey of youth and young adults. Health Commun. **34**, 298–305 (2019). https://doi.org/10.1080/10410236.2017.1407229
67. Yuan, K.H., Bentler, P.M.: Normal theory based test statistics in structural equation modelling. Brit. J. Math. Stat. Psy. **51**, 289–309 (1998). https://doi.org/10.1111/j.2044-8317.1998.tb00682.x

Access to Information Two Years After an ICT4D Project in Bangladesh: New Digital Skills and Traditional Practices

Viviane Frings-Hessami(✉) and Anindita Sarker

Monash University, Caulfield East, VIC, Australia
{Viviane.Hessami,Anindita.Sarker}@monash.edu

Abstract. The continuity of access to information is rarely considered in the design of information and communication technology for development (ICT4D) projects. In this paper, the authors report on the results of a study conducted two years after the end of an ICT4D project which provided 300 Bangladeshi women with smartphones and support services to enable them to access information on agricultural topics. The study shows that although few of the women were still using a smartphone and accessing online information, they still had access to part of the information supplied to them during the project because they had taken the initiative to write it down in notebooks and they had memorised the information they used frequently. However, when they needed to access new information to address new problems, they had to rely on advice from the local agricultural supplies shop. Although the women had developed their literacy skills during the course of the project, and some of them had started new business ventures, most of them did not feel confident enough to select reliable information by themselves and preferred to rely on local "experts". The authors argue that for an ICT4D project to be successful and sustainable, continued access to the information provided during the project and to up-to-date information after the end of the project should be planned for in the design of the project.

Keywords: ICT4D evaluation · Information access · Information preservation · Women · Bangladesh

1 Introduction

Information is increasingly provided in digital form and timely access to information has become essential to perform many economic and social activities. However, the cost of digital technologies and the unreliability of Internet access make it difficult for disadvantaged people living in rural areas in developing countries to access information online. Information and Communication Technology for Development (ICT4D) projects have been designed to attempt to bridge the digital divide by developing systems that give disadvantaged communities access to information and communication technologies (ICTs). However, the continuity of access to information previously accessed is rarely considered in the design of ICT4D projects [1]. Projects focus on providing technologies

M. Smits (Ed.): iConference 2022, LNCS 13193, pp. 123–135, 2022.
https://doi.org/10.1007/978-3-030-96960-8_9

that enable access to information and on supporting the participants with using the technology during the course of the projects, rather than on the information itself. Long-term sustainability has long been recognised as a challenge in ICT4D projects [2–4]. In recent years, many ICT4D projects have shifted from studying community services such as telecentres to the use of mobile phones. While longitudinal studies of telecentres over several years have been conducted [5–7], few researchers have gone back to assess how participants were coping after the end of a project and to evaluate its long-term impact. Moreover, the preservation of information provided to the participants or accessed by the participants themselves during the project is rarely taken into consideration in the design and the evaluation of ICT4D projects. The authors could not find any study that looked at how participants had preserved the information that had been provided to them during an ICT4D project and how their information access practices had evolved after they were no longer provided access to technology. This paper contributes to filling this gap by reporting on interviews with a group of Bangladeshi women two years after the end of an ICT4D project that had provided them with mobile phones and support services for three years.

The Participatory Research and Ownership with Technology, Information and Change (PROTIC) project was a collaborative project between researchers from Monash University in Australia and Oxfam in Bangladesh, which aimed at empowering Bangladeshi women working in agriculture in remote communities through access to information that could help them to improve their agricultural practices. The project provided 300 women in three villages with free smartphones and data packages and developed a series of services to support them, including training programmes and a call centre staffed by agronomists that they could call at any time to ask questions relating to agriculture. In addition, text messages especially designed to meet their agricultural needs and warn them of adverse weather events were sent to them every week. A pilot project was run in 2015, then the selected participants were provided with smartphones and associated support from mid-2016 to mid-2019 [8, 9]. Noticeable improvements were observed during the course of the project in the women's digital skills, in their economic well-being, and in their social status in their communities [9–11]. Thanks to the support provided by PROTIC, the women were able to start cultivating new crops and to set up some small businesses, such as a chicken farm or an animal vaccination service [12, 13], and they became "information hubs" for their communities with whom they shared the information provided to them [14]. In the last year of the project, researchers also observed that in at least one of the villages, Borokoput, in the sub-district of Shyamnagar, in the south of the country, the participants had developed, on their own initiative, documentation practices to preserve the information that they found useful by writing it in notebooks because they had become aware of the fragility of the digital formats in which information had been provided to them [14].

Two years after the end of the PROTIC project, the authors of this paper decided to conduct interviews with a sample of the participants from Borokoput to assess how they were coping without the support provided by PROTIC, what information they still had accessed to and how they were accessing new information they needed. Due to the COVID pandemic and the impossibility to travel to Bangladesh, the interviews had to be conducted over the phone. After a brief discussion of the methodology used by the authors, the paper presents the authors' findings on phone ownership, Internet access, continuing use of the notebooks started during the PROTIC project, and use of other sources of information by the PROTIC women two years after the end of the project. Then, the next section reflects on the new skills acquired by the women, the new ventures they were able to sustain after the end of the project and their return to using traditional ways of accessing information. The paper concludes by highlighting the importance of planning for the preservation of information during and after the end of an ICT4D project and facilitating continuing access to up-to-date information to meet the evolving needs of communities engaging in agriculture in fragile ecosystems.

2 Methodology

This paper is based on data from 11 semi-structured interviews with women from one of the PROTIC villages, Borokoput, located in the Southern sub-district (upazila) of Shyamnagar in the district of Satkhira. The interviews were conducted remotely over the phone by the second author between mid-April and July 2021. The interview questions were prepared by the first author as part of a broader study of information access and preservation practices in rural Bangladesh, and the participants were selected by the second author, who is Bangladeshi and had conducted research for her PhD thesis in the same location two years earlier. At that time, she had asked the participants in her study if they were interested in participating in future research and she had collected the contact details of those who had agreed. A new ethics permission was sought from the authors' university to conduct this research, but her previous contacts in the village greatly facilitated the recruitment of participants and gave her an acute understanding of the context in which the participants lived and worked. The fact that the participants already knew her partly alleviated the limitations of doing interviews over the phone. It made the participants keener to participate in the research and made it easier for the interviewer to establish a rapport with them and to probe them for more detailed stories when their first answer sounded like a standard answer rather than their own story. During the course of the interviews, which had to be spread over three months due to the COVID situation and to time constraints both on the interviewer's and on the participants' sides, the questions were refined based on previous answers in an iterative process. All the interviews were conducted in Bangla and at the day and time that suited the participants. In this paper, the interviewees are referred to by the pseudonyms of PS1-PS11 to preserve their anonymity.

3 Phone Ownership and Access to the Internet

At the end of the PROTIC project, the women had been allowed to keep the smartphones, but by then some of the phones were no longer working, and many stopped working in the following months and proved too costly to repair. Among the women we interviewed, 2 out of 11 were still using the PROTIC phone, 4 were using another smartphone and 5 were using a feature phone with no Internet access. This proportion does not appear to be representative of the number of PROTIC women in the village who are still using their PROTIC phone or have bought another smartphone. Although we have not yet been able to conduct a survey of all the PROTIC women, comments made by the women we interviewed indicate that the vast majority of the PROTIC women are now using feature phones with no Internet connection and only a small number of them are using a smartphone, either the PROTIC one or a newly-acquired one. Comments made by some of the interviewees indicated that buying a new smartphone was not a priority for them. However, we decided that it was important for us to talk with several women who were still using a smartphone in order to understand how they were using their phones to access the Internet and search for information.

One of our first and most important findings is that although women may own a smartphone, their Internet access was very limited because of the cost of data packages. Among the 6 women with a smartphone we interviewed, only one had Internet access all the time. The others could not afford to buy data packages all the time; they bought one when they found a good deal. As a result, they may have Internet access for only one week per month if they bought short-length packages or stay without access for months at a time if they were waiting for a better deal. Among the women who only had a feature phone, only one said that she occasionally used her husband's phone to access the Internet.

The interviewees estimated that around three quarters of the information provided by PROTIC was still useful to them. In particular, they still used the new farming techniques to grow vegetables in saline soil that they had been taught, such as the "tower method" which consists of digging 5.5 feet deep, lining the hole with polythene, then filling it with sand, straw, soil and organic manure (in that order) before planting vegetables. Two women also cited the example of vitamins for plant buds as a PROTIC tip that they still used. However, pests had become resistant to pesticides and new diseases had appeared that required new forms of treatment and therefore new information on how to deal with them. All the women said that they had encountered many new problems for which the solutions suggested by PROTIC were no longer effective. For example, a pesticide spray for mango trees recommended by PROTIC no longer worked and the villagers had not found an effective replacement. In other cases, the dosage of pesticide had to be increased because the insects had become more resistant. Therefore, the women had an acute need to access new information.

4 Access to Information

4.1 Access to Online Information

As a result of having limited access to the Internet, our interviewees did not often use the Internet to look for information to solve agricultural issues. The only woman who had constant access did not use the Internet on her phone to look for agricultural information, but she used it to look for patterns for her tailoring business. Among those who had intermittent access, only one reported using the Internet frequently to look for information related to agriculture or animal husbandry. PS5 said that she often looked for videos about goat-rearing. Having received training on goat vaccination during PROTIC, she had become an expert on goat-rearing in the village and started an animal vaccination service from her home. She said that she often downloaded videos to watch them on her phone and that she kept those that included important information for future reference.

The other women who had occasional Internet access did not often perform Google searches to look for agricultural information because they found it difficult to evaluate the reliability of the information that they could find that way. As PS2 commented, "we used to blindly rely on PROTIC, but we can't trust Google completely". She stressed that if the wrong treatment was applied to cows or goats, the animals could die and that therefore "we cannot really rely on the Google information without consulting with an expert".

Five out of the 6 interviewees who had Internet access used Facebook to keep in touch with friends and relatives and, in some cases, to get agriculture-related information through pages that they had previously liked. The woman who had Internet access but did not use Facebook said that she had problems using the app and that she was waiting for her daughter to help her with it during her next time visit. Two women said that they occasionally used the agricultural app Krishoker Janala (Farmer's Window) which helps farmers to identify plant diseases by looking at pictures (http://krishokerjanala.com/krishokerjanala/home.html), but that this app was not always useful because it was not updated. Among the women who only had a feature phone, only one occasionally used her husband's phone to access the Internet, but it was for searching for job advertisements as she was looking for a job, not for agricultural information. None of the others used a relative's phones to access the Internet.

4.2 Use of Notebooks

Only one of our interviewees still had the text messages sent by PROTIC on her phone. The other woman who still used her PROTIC phone had lost all her text messages when her phone got damaged and was reset. None of the others were able to recover their text messages when their PROTIC phone stopped working. However, most of them still used the text messages and other information they had written in their notebooks during PROTIC and continued to write new information that they found useful. Research conducted during the last year of PROTIC [14] showed that some PROTIC women from Borokoput had started writing down in notebooks the texts of the SMS they received as part of the project after several incidents in which SMS had been lost when phones went for repair. This made them conscious of the fragility of the information provided to them in digital form and they decided to create analogue backups, which they felt would last longer. They also wrote down in the same notebooks information they received from the call centre, such as the names and dosage of medicines, which they thought they might need again later.

Two years later when we conducted our interviews, most women were still using those notebooks. All our interviewees had used a notebook to record information during PROTIC. Two of them had copied all the text messages and information they had been given, while the others had only written what they found particularly relevant to their personal situation. For example, PS5 who had trained in goat vaccination, copied in her notebook all the text messages relating to goats and other domestic animals. All the women we interviewed still had their notebooks, except for two who had lent theirs to a friend or relative; and the majority of them still consulted their notebooks when they wanted to check some information. However, all of them had memorised the information they used regularly and, for that reason, they did not need to check their notebooks very often. Yet, the notebooks could prove very helpful if they wanted to start a new activity that they had not done before. For example, when PS11 recently started raising goats, she looked in her notebook for the text messages relating to taking care of goats, which had not been useful to her when she received them, but which she had carefully written down for future reference.

Moreover, the women continued the practice of writing in a notebook, which had not been something they were accustomed to doing before PROTIC, but was a new skill they had developed during the course of the project [14]. More than half of our interviewees (6 out of 11) said that they wrote it in their notebooks when they discovered new useful information, for example the cure for a new disease or the new dosage for a pesticide. Several of them explained that they did not write all the information they found, but only what had worked for them as they often had to try several remedies before finding one that worked. As PS8 said, "I lost one of my chickens although I applied the medicine suggested by the shopkeeper. So, there is no point in writing that down!".

All the interviewees said that they had memorised the information that they used frequently. This is consistent with traditional practice in Bangladeshi villages where information is usually communicated orally and memorised. In Borokoput, traditional remedies for agricultural problems or cures for health issues are preserved in the memories of elderly people and are not written down. The PROTIC women had memorised the information they were given during the course of the project, in particular the information they used regularly. Therefore, they did not need to check their notebooks frequently. They only did so for specific information (such as medicine dosage) that they had not used for some time. For example, PS8 explained that.

> *I have been using that information for quite a long time. So most of the things that I need are fresh in my memory. But if I am using any medicines or remedies for any plant diseases or for my poultry, I make sure that I follow the instructions exactly. If I am unsure about anything for any reason, then I look in my notebook.*

In particular, they did not write down the farming techniques for which they received detailed instructions during training sessions. In PS7's words: "There is too much information related to that, that's why I did not write it, but at the same time I did not need to as it is well set in my memory". The women felt empowered by the information that they had learnt and memorised. PS9 declared: "I know so many things… That information is in my mind."

4.3 Other Sources of Information

The women also sought information from other PROTIC women in their village who were more experienced in some techniques. Several mentioned that they kept in touch with the other PROTIC women and called them when they encountered a problem. PS11 who recently started rearing goats said that she was taking advice from PROTIC women who were more experienced in goat-rearing. However, the interviewees had lost contact with the PROTIC women who no longer had a phone and did not live close to them.

Neighbours who may be experiencing similar problems were another source of information. Information on which new treatments worked was commonly shared between neighbours and relatives so that others did not have to go through trials and errors to find a solution to the same problem. Interviewees also reported using their feature phones to call relatives who lived far away and had expertise in a particular area. One woman said that she got useful advice from her uncle who was operating a chicken farm in India when she could not get useful information locally.

When they needed advice on a new problem, the women we interviewed commonly asked their husband or another male relative to go to the "medicine shop" which sells agricultural supplies including medicines for animals and pesticides in the nearest bazaar. In accordance with Bangladeshi village customs, women rarely went to the shops themselves. Some of the women were happy with the services that the owners of the medicine shop offered. PS10 commented that during PROTIC, they had to go to the shop anyway to buy the medicine suggested by PROTIC, but that now they were getting both services from the same place: the advice and the product, which she found convenient. However, the products that the shopkeepers suggested did not always work. This may be because they recommended generic treatments. For example, one woman (PS7) explained that the dosage of pesticide recommended by the shopkeeper burnt the leaves of her plants; she then sent her husband again to the shop and the shopkeeper recommended a lower dosage because her plants were younger than he had thought. She commented that he had not asked the size of the plants before prescribing the pesticide whereas the PROTIC call centre operators used to ask all the details. Another woman (PS8) said that she lost one of her chickens when she applied the medicine suggested by the shopkeeper.

A government Agriculture Extension Officer and a Fisheries Officer, as well as a livestock hospital offer free services in Shyamnagar, the sub-district (upazila) town. But, the women did not often go (or send someone) to consult with them because Shyamnagar is too far away from their village. In addition, their advice may be very generic too. PS2 reported that she saw the Livestock Officer at the Upazila Livestock Hospital dispense the same medicine for different problems. The women rarely called the Agriculture Extension Officer because they knew that he was very busy and might not be able to answer their call or to come and assess their problem. In some cases, he was able to solve their problems; in other cases, he came too late. PS5, who specialised in goat rearing and called herself a "doctor of goats", was the only one among our interviewees who used those services regularly. She had developed a good relationship with the Livestock Officer at the Upazila Livestock Hospital and phoned him often when she had questions. Furthermore, she said that she had other doctors' phone numbers that she could call if he was busy.

5 Continuity and Change: New Skills and Return to Traditional Practices

5.1 New Skills and Self-confidence

When asked how well they are managing their agricultural practices two years after the end of the ICT4D project, 3 of our interviewees said that they were doing well, 3 said that they were doing well, but that their situation was harder than before, and 5 said that their situation was very difficult and/or that they felt helpless without PROTIC. However, in the course of the interviews, they all made comments and told stories that enabled us to draw a more nuanced picture of their life after PROTIC. Some women first said that they were doing well, then in responses to other questions, talked about serious problems they had faced due to the unavailability of timely information. Conversely, some women first said that their situation was very difficult without the support that was provided by PROTIC, then told stories that showed that they had adapted relatively well and had been able to access other sources of information. What is clear from all our interviews is that new problems had arisen in the village in the previous two years for which the women and their community had to find new solutions. It is in their assessment of how easy it was for them to find new solutions and how effective these solutions were that they differed. These differences can be related to individual personality traits, such as their level of optimism and their confidence in their own abilities, to personal preferences, and to the severity of the specific problems they encountered.

Some of the women felt that they had become more confident, more knowledgeable and more independent thanks to the digital skills and the technical skills they had acquired during PROTIC. They valued the new agricultural techniques they had learnt, as well as the digital skills that enabled them to use their phones to search for information. PS9 commented that:

> *As a result of my journey with PROTIC, I became more confident taking care of my goats and vegetables. And I know so many things and I don't need to search on the Internet for everything. The information is in my mind!*

She added that she had not yet encountered problems that she could not solve. Other women had acquired skills that led to an income opportunity that was continuing. For example, PS5 who was vaccinating animals and called herself a "doctor of goats" continued to build her expertise through searching information about goats on YouTube and had developed a network of experts whom she could call when she encountered new problems. Even a woman who was finding it hard coping without the support previously provided by PROTIC admitted that PROTIC had changed her life and that what she had learnt from PROTIC "can't be learned anywhere else". And after telling how she went alone for a job interview in a town she did not know and used the Maps app on her phone to find the location, she concluded: "I have become so self-sufficient today thanks to PROTIC!" (PS2).

On the other hand, some of the women felt let down at the end of the project. In PS4's words,

> *We used to feel like we have a guardian who could save us from every possible problem we had regarding plants or our animals, but now we feel helpless without that support. Our plants and domestic animals suffer more and we struggle a lot to save them by managing some remedies on time.*

Some women had to abandon ventures that were no longer profitable (e.g. selling mobile data packages), or stopped cultivating certain crops due to the lack of support. For example, PS6 had started a plant nursery but was not able to keep it going due to the lack of information and support. Some of the women did not feel that they had developed the ability to evaluate information sources found online and to select the most reliable ones or the ones that were applicable to their case. PS2 declared: "Google shows about 14 different medicines for a single problem; we don't understand which of these drugs will be useful, so we can't take any risk!".

Those who felt less confident in their abilities had reverted to the pre-PROTIC practice of relying on the medicine shop in the local bazaar. During the course of the project, the women had been introduced to the Agriculture Extension Officer and to the Fisheries Officer from their sub-district and they came to see them as people they could contact if they had problems. However, they rarely did so because they understood that they were too busy to answer every query and that therefore, it might take too long before they came and assessed their problem if a visit was required. Therefore, they usually resorted to sending someone to the medicine shop in the local bazaar and to buying the medicine or pesticide suggested by the shopkeeper.

The type of phone owned by the women impacts on their ability to access information online and to bypass local intermediaries. Two out of the three women who felt that they were doing well owned a smartphone, whereas three out of the five women who said that their situation was very tough only had a feature phone without access to the Internet. However, this is not the only factor. One woman who only had access to a feature phone felt that she was managing well and did not mind relying on the medicine shop for advice. On the other hand, two of the women who said that their situation was very difficult owned a smartphone although they did not use it much to access information due to the cost of Internet access and to their lack of confidence in their ability to select reliable information.

All the women we interviewed understood that problems should be treated differently depending on their level of severity. Simple problems could be treated by using traditional remedies or the cures suggested by PROTIC if they still worked. However, if the problems were more serious or if those solutions did not work, and they faced the risk of losing their crops or their animals, they understood the need to consult with experts, such as the Agriculture Extension Officer, a vet, or the owner of the medicine shop. Those who were cultivating more land or breeding larger animals, such as cows and goats, would face a bigger loss if they used a wrong treatment due to the higher value of their investment. For example, PS11 who had recently started rearing goats said that "if anything happens to them, I will count a big loss".

Some women had already incurred considerable losses due to the lack of timely information. For example, PS4 lost 80% of her mango trees due to insect infiltration, which affected her whole community. Some of her neighbours talked to the Agriculture Extension Officer and used the remedies that he recommended, but nothing worked.

During PROTIC, the project participants had become sources of information for their community. Their neighbours and relatives came to them when they had questions and if they could not answer them, they could call the PROTIC call centre to ask their questions. They did so readily and, thereby, became informal "information hubs" for their community. Two years after the end of the project, this did not often happen anymore because their friends and neighbours knew that they were no longer receiving information. Still, people sometimes came to them and they helped them if they could, but often they did not know the solution to their problems. Several women commented that they had become more careful in sharing information because they did not want to share something without being sure that it would work. With information provided by PROTIC, they knew that it came from a reliable source and that it had been checked by experts. With information they found themselves online, they could not be so sure. Therefore, they preferred to be cautious and to advise those who came to them to call the Agriculture Extension Officer or visit the medicine shop. However, PS5, who had become an expert in goat-rearing and animal vaccination was still receiving many queries from PROTIC women and other villagers, and was still able to help them. When she did not know the answer, she searched the Internet, called one of the vets that she knew well or some of her relatives who were also experienced in animal husbandry.

5.2 Timeliness and Quality of Information

There were two big issues with the information sources available to the interviewees. The first one was their timeliness. The second one was the quality of the information. The women found it difficult to get timely information due to their distance from potential sources of information in the sub-district town, the cost of travelling there, the limited availability of the Agriculture Extension Officer and the cost of using private services. PS11 commented:

> *PROTIC solutions were timelier and more effective. Whenever needed, I could call them and they helped us... and the medicines they suggested, most of them worked very well... But, now, you know, getting timely support is difficult, and in addition that support is not free and not as effective as PROTIC... Now we sometimes count a loss because we cannot manage timely support.*

PS3 complained that travelling to Shyamnagar to seek the advice of the Agriculture Extension Officer was a "huge waste of time and effort". This was even more so if the suggested remedy did not work. PS2 travelled to the Livestock Hospital in Shyamnagar, but the treatment recommended by the Livestock Officer for her ducks did not work. She then had to travel to the local market and consult a private vet, who charged 150 taka (US$2) for a visit, a considerable amount for her.

One type of information that the women especially missed was the weather-related text messages that were giving them advance warnings and time to prepare for incoming disasters. Nothing had replaced those advanced warnings. Villagers watched the weather forecast on television or read newspapers online. In case of cyclones, public announcements were made over loudspeakers in the village, but these came too late and gave the villagers hardly any time to prepare themselves and their crops and animals.

Moreover, no service available to the women was comparable to the PROTIC call centre which had been providing the PROTIC participants with information that was timely, localised and reliable. The majority of our interviewees said that this was their preferred way to access information. The women who still have Internet access two years later may be able to access information quickly, but they cannot be sure of the quality of the information or of its suitability to their village's agricultural conditions. More reliable information can be obtained from the Agriculture Extension Officer or the Livestock Officer, but it may take too long and come too late. The medicine shop is closer than the free services in the sub-district town centre and more reliable than randomly chosen information found on the Internet, but it is not comparable to the service that used to be provided by the PRODIC call centre which was staffed by agronomists and provided quick information especially developed for their village.

The prominent role played by the local medicine shop as a source of information on agricultural matters exemplifies a return to traditional sources of information in the village. However, at the same time, some of the women have become more confident in their abilities to look for solutions for their problems and have developed literacy skills that help them to evaluate information by themselves. Some may turn to the medicine shop by default as the easiest place or the only place to get information from, but others have made a conscious judgement that it is the best solution in their circumstances.

6 Conclusion: Importance of Continuing Access to Information

The limited number of interviews conducted so far does not allow us to draw general conclusions about the lasting legacy of PROTIC and its impact on the socio-economic status of the women in their community. This will be the subject of further research. We are planning to conduct a survey of all the PROTIC women in Borokoput and to extend our study to the other two villages in the project. However, our interviews have produced rich data on the ways the PROTIC participants are now accessing and using information. The PROTIC women had become dependent on PROTIC for their agricultural information needs, and, since the end of the project, they have had to find by themselves new sources of timely and reliable information. Although few of the interviewees are still using a smartphone and looking for agricultural information online, through PROTIC they developed their knowledge of agricultural techniques adapted to their village's conditions and they still use those techniques. All of them are still able to access at least part of the information that had been provided by PROTIC, not because the project planned for the continuity of access to that information, but because they took themselves the initiative to write it down in notebooks. Moreover, they have memorised and internalised the information they used repeatedly so that they can keep using it without referring back to instructions. Thanks to the PROTIC training and the information provided to them, some of the women have been able to continue successful ventures.

However, the positive achievements that we have noticed do not reduce the need for the continuity of access to information to be taken into consideration from the beginning of an ICT4D project like PROTIC. ICT4D projects should not just focus on providing access to technology. The point of ICTs is to provide access to information and continuing access to information should never be taken for granted in projects that involve disadvantaged communities. In a project that provides free mobile phones and support services for a limited time, it cannot be assumed that the participants will be able to afford the cost of buying a smartphone and Internet access after the end of the project or that they will see that as a priority. Even during the course of PROTIC, the participants had encountered problems to access information when their phones broke down and they lost text messages that they wanted to be able to refer back to. Simple measures could have been taken, such as providing printed copies of the SMS during the course of the project. The need for continuing access to up-to-date information is more difficult to address as it requires a continuous effort. A potential solution could have been to plan for the free call centre service to be replaced by a for-a-fee service at the end of the project. Given that most women clearly preferred that service to other ways of accessing information and that this only requires access to a simple phone, it could have been financially sustainable.

Acknowledgement. The research for this paper was supported by a DECRA Fellowship from the Australian Research Council (DE210100012).

References

1. Anwar, M., Frings-Hessami, V.: Empowering women through access to information: the sustainability of a community informatics project in Bangladesh. In: Sundqvist, A., Berget, G., Nolin, J., Skjerdingstad, K. (eds), Sustainable Digital Communities. ICONFERENCE 2020, LNCS, vol. 12051, pp. 3–14 (2020)
2. Marais, M.: Analysis of the factors affecting the sustainability of ICT4D initiatives. In: ICT for Development: People, Policy and Practice: Proceedings of the IDIA2011, Cape Town, pp. 100–120 (2011)
3. De Zoysa, M.R., Letch, N.: ICT4D project sustainability: an ANT-based analysis. In: Proceedings of the Nineteenth Americas Conference on Information Systems, Chicago, Illinois, 15–17August, pp. 1–10 (2013)
4. Heeks, R.: ICT4D 2.0: the next phase of applying ICT for international development. Computer **41**(6), 26–33 (2008)
5. Best, M.L., Kumar, R.: Sustainability failures of rural telecenters: challenges from the sustainable access in rural India (SARI) project. Inf. Technol. Int. Dev. **4**(4), 31–45 (2008)
6. Burrell, J.: Technology hype vs enduring uses: a longitudinal study of Internet use among early adopters in an African city. First Monday **17**(6) (2012). https://doi.org/10.5210/fm.v17i6.3964
7. Furuholt, B., Saebø, Ø.: The role telecentres play in providing e-government services in rural areas: a longitudinal study of Internet access and e-government services in Tanzania. Electr. J. Inf. Syst. Dev. Countries **84**, 1–14 (2018)
8. Sarrica, M., Denison, T., Stillman, L., Chakraborty, T., Auvi, P.: "What do others think?": an emic approach to participatory action research in Bangladesh. AI & Soc. **34**(3), 495–508 (2019)
9. Stillman, L., Sarrica, M., Anwar, M., Sarker, A., Farinosi, M.: Sociotechnical transformative effects of an ICT project in rural Bangladesh. Am. Behav. Sci. **64**(3), 1871–1888 (2020)
10. Sarker, A.: ICT for women's empowerment in rural Bangladesh, PhD thesis, Monash University, Clayton, Victoria, Australia (2020). https://figshare.com/articles/thesis/ICT_for_Women_s_Empowerment_in_Rural_Bangladesh/14538588
11. Sarker, A., Biswas, M., Stillman, L., Oliver, G., Anwar, M.: "When people come to me for suggestions I feel like an expert": empowering women through smartphones in rural Bangladesh. In: Lechman, E. (ed.) Technology and Women's Empowerment, pp. 181–199. Routledge, London (2021)
12. Jannat, F., Chakraborty, T.R., Aktar, P., Stillman, L.: Evaluating a smartphone phone project in Bangladesh through community monthly meeting reports. In: Stillman, L., Anwar, M. (eds), Proceedings of the 16th CIRN Conference, Prato, Italy, pp. 110–124 (2018)

13. Stillman, L., Sarrica, M., Denison, T., Sarker, A.: After the smartphone has arrived in the village: How practices and proto-practices emerged in an ICT4D project. In: Junio, D.R., Koopman, C. (eds.) Evolving Perspectives on ICTs in Global Souths, 11th International Development Informatics Association Conference, IDIA 2020 CCIS 1236, pp. 81–94. Springer, Cham, Switzerland (2020)
14. Frings-Hessami, V., Sarker, A., Oliver, G., Anwar, M.: Documentation in a community informatics project: the creation and sharing of information by women in Bangladesh. J. Docum. **76**(2), 552–570 (2020)

Understanding and Predicting Characteristics of Test Collections in Information Retrieval

Md. Mustafizur Rahman[1(✉)], Mucahid Kutlu[2], and Matthew Lease[1]

[1] University of Texas at Austin, Austin, USA
{nahid,ml}@utexas.edu
[2] TOBB University of Economics Technology, Ankara, Turkey
m.kutlu@etu.edu.tr

Abstract. Research community evaluations in information retrieval, such as NIST's Text REtrieval Conference (TREC), build reusable test collections by pooling document rankings submitted by many teams. Naturally, the quality of the resulting test collection thus greatly depends on the number of participating teams and the quality of their submitted runs. In this work, we investigate: i) how the number of participants, coupled with other factors, affects the quality of a test collection; and ii) whether the quality of a test collection can be inferred prior to collecting relevance judgments from human assessors. Experiments conducted on six TREC collections illustrate how the number of teams interacts with various other factors to influence the resulting quality of test collections. We also show that the reusability of a test collection can be predicted with high accuracy when the same document collection is used for successive years in an evaluation campaign, as is common in TREC.

Keywords: Evaluation · Test collections · Pooling · Reusability

1 Introduction

Evaluation of information retrieval (IR) systems in the Cranfield paradigm [5] relies on the construction of reusable document *test collections* [12]. A test collection consists of a set of documents to be searched, a set of search *topics* (expressed as user input queries that correspond to underlying user information needs), and judgments of document relevance to different topics. Typically a test collection is constructed by organizing a *shared-task* wherein the organizers (e.g., NIST TREC) provide a document collection and a set of topics developed by experts, then ask the participating teams to submit a ranking of the (predicted) most relevant documents (i.e., *runs*) for each topic. Subsequently, the documents to be judged are selected from the teams' document rankings, canonically via *pooling* [13] the set of top-ranked documents across all team submissions.

In this work, we conduct experiments to shed light on the specific impact that the number of participating teams has on the quality of pooling-based test collections, particularly their *reusability*. We investigate the following two key

M. Smits (Ed.): iConference 2022, LNCS 13193, pp. 136–148, 2022.
https://doi.org/10.1007/978-3-030-96960-8_10

research questions. **RQ-1)** i) how does the number of participants interact with other factors to influence the quality of a test collection? **RQ-2)** Can we predict the quality of a test collection prior to collecting relevance judgments?

For RQ-1, our experiments vary the number of participating teams by down-sampling submissions from past TREC evaluations in order to construct simulated test collections. Then we analyze the interaction between the number of submissions and other factors (e.g., the number of topics, collection size, etc.) on resultant test collection quality. For RQ-2, we develop a model to predict test collection quality using only the number of participants, the number of topics, collection size, and pool depth. We analyze the generalization performance of the prediction model using our designed "Leave-one-test-collection-out" setup.

Experiments conducted over six TREC test collections yield the following findings. Firstly, when we have very few participating teams, increasing the pool depth improves reusability more than increasing the number of topics. Secondly, the size of the document collection and the types of runs play a crucial role when the number of participants is very small. Thirdly, the reusability of a test collection can be predicted with high accuracy when the test collections used for training and testing the model have the same underlying document collection. This means that the results in one year can be used to effectively forecast the quality of the test collections built for the track in following years.

We will share our source code in the final version of the manuscript in order to ensure the reproducibility of our findings.

2 Factors Impacting the Qualities of Test Collections

The quality of a test collection depends on a variety of factors, such as: i) the number of topics; ii) pool depth (assuming pool-based judging); iii) the number of participants; iv) the collection size; and v) the types of runs (e.g., manual runs and automatic runs) and their quality. One might also consider vi) the target evaluation metric (e.g., MAP@1000, NDCG@10) in assessing how well a test collection supports reliable evaluation for a given retrieval task, as measured by a particular metric. Since constructing a test collection is expensive, *reusability* is desirable. Reusability is often measured by how a given run contributing to the pool would have been assessed if excluded from the pool. In this study, we focus on reusability as a key measure of the test collection quality.

While considerable work [8,11,17] has investigated how the quality of a test collection is impacted by the above-mentioned factors, prior studies have not explored how the number of participants interacts with other factors.

Number of Topics. Sparck Jones and Van Rijsbergen [14] suggest that 250 topics can be acceptable, but 1000 topics are needed for reliable evaluation. Voorhees [15] performs an empirical analysis on the TREC6 test collection and shows that system rankings computed based on 5 or 10 topics are relatively unstable, whereas a set of 25 or more topics produces a stable ranking of IR systems. Buckley and Voorhees [2] calculate the error rate of various evaluation measures and find that for reliable evaluation the required number of topics should be at least 25. Webber et al. [18] recommend that a set of 150 topics is required to statistically distinguish the performance of one IR system from other IR systems. Zobel [20] finds that a set of 25 topics can reasonably predict the performance of IR systems on a separate set of 25 topics.

Pool Depth. Prior work has also studied the trade-off between collecting fewer judgments with more topics (i.e., Wide and Shallow (WaS) judging) vs. more judgments with fewer topics (i.e., Narrow and Deep (NaD) judging). Carterette et al. [4] report on TREC Million Query track and conclude that WaS judging produces a more reliable evaluation of IR systems than NaD judging. Kutlu et al. [9] find that NaD judging is preferred to WaS judging if we consider intelligent topic selection or other hidden costs of shallow judging, such as topic creation time and noisier judgments. Voorhees [16] investigates the impact of varying pool depth on the reusability of a test collection.

Run Types. To see how different types of runs (e.g., manual and automatic) impact collection quality, Büttcher et al. [3] adapt the "leave-one-group-out" [20] experiment by removing all unique documents contributed by the manual runs from the pool. The authors find that their setup ranks the runs differently than found in the original TREC 2006 Terabyte task.

Collection Size. Hawking and Robertson [7] study the effect of the document collection size on the Very Large Collection track [6] and observe a higher value of P@20 for runs in the larger collection. Interestingly, they find no change in value between the large and small document collection when the runs are ranked based on MAP.

3 The Impact of Varying the Number of Participants

Our experimental design for analyzing the impact of the number of groups is shown in Algorithm 1. First, we construct the original qrels (Q_o) using runs of all participant groups (G) **[Line 2]**. Then we evaluate all runs using this original qrels (Q_o) in terms of a ranking metric (e.g., MAP@1000 and NDCG@10) and store the ranking of runs in E **[Line 3]**. Next, we change the group number, g, from 1 to $|G|$ with an increment of 1 at each iteration to create test collection with varying number of participants **[Line 5]**. At each iteration, we randomly sample g number of groups ($\hat{G}_i$) from the set of groups G **[Line 7]** and construct the simulated test collection (i.e., qrels) Q_g using only the participants in $\hat{G}_i$ **[Line 8]**. Then, we evaluate all participating runs in set G by using simulated test collection Q_g in terms of a ranking metric (e.g., MAP@1000, NDCG@10, etc.) and store these new ranking of runs in E_g **[Line 9]**. We calculate the performance difference in terms of τ_{ap} [19] and Max Drop [16] (i.e., the maximum drop in a run's rank, between the original ranking of runs E and the ranking of runs obtained via the respective simulated test collection E_g) **[Line 11]**. Note that we calculate average scores across different group samples for a particular parameter setup. In addition, we can also utilize Algorithm 1 to experiments with a varying number of topics and varying pool depth because it takes the set of topics T and pool depth P as inputs.

Algorithm 1: Experimental Design

Input : Set of groups G • Number of samples for groups N • Set of topics T • Pool depth P

Output: E, A set of performance score indexed by group number

$R \leftarrow$ Total number of runs from all groups in G

$Q_o \leftarrow Construct\_Qrels(G, T, P)$ ▷ official qrels

$E \leftarrow Evaluate\_runs(R, Q_o)$ ▷ Evaluate all runs with Q_o

$\hat{E} \leftarrow \emptyset$ ▷ keeps scores of systems with reduced qrels

for *group no* $g \leftarrow 1$ **to** $|G|$ **do**

  for *sample number* $i \leftarrow 1$ **to** N **do**

    $\hat{G}_i \leftarrow$ randomly sample g groups from G

    $Q_g \leftarrow \text{ConstructQrels}(\hat{G}_i, T, P)$

    $E_g \leftarrow Evaluate\_runs(R, Q_g)$ ▷ Evaluate all runs using qrels Q_g

    $\hat{E} \leftarrow \hat{E} \cup E_g$

return *Evaluate_Performance_Difference*$(E, \hat{E})$

3.1 Datasets

We conduct our experiments on six TREC tracks and datasets: the 2013–2014 Web Tracks on ClueWeb12[1], the 2006 Terabyte track on Gov2[2], and the 2004 Robust Retrieval Task (Robust'04), the 1999 TREC-8 *ad hoc* track, the 1998 TREC-7 *ad hoc* track on TIPSTER disks 4–5[3] (excluding the *congressional record*). Table 1 provides statistics about test collections we use. Later tracks have fewer participants than earlier tracks both in terms of the number of groups and the submitted runs. Later tracks also tend to use larger document collections, without commensurate increase in pool depth, leading to an increasing prevalence of relevant documents in judged pools, from ~5% to ~40%.

Table 1. Statistics about the test collections used in this study.

Track	# Groups	# Manual runs	# Auto runs	Pool depth	Collection	# Topics	# Docs	# Judged	%Rel
WT'14	9	4	26	25	ClueWeb12	50	52,343,021	14,432	39.2%
WT'13	13	3	31	10 and 20	ClueWeb12	50	52,343,021	14,474	28.7%
TB'06	20	19	61	50	Gov2	50	25,205,179	31,984	18.4%
Adhoc'99	40	9	62	100	Disks45-CR	50	528,155	86,830	5.4%
Adhoc'98	41	16	68	100	Disks45-CR	50	528,155	80,345	5.8%
Robust'04	14	0	110	100	Disks45-CR	249	528,155	311,410	5.6%

[1] lemurproject.org/clueweb12.

[2] ir.dcs.gla.ac.uk/test_collections/gov2-summary.htm.

[3] trec.nist.gov/data/docs_eng.html.

3.2 Results and Discussion

Impact of Number of Topics. We first consider how the number of topics interacts with the number of groups in relation to test collection quality. To explore this, we study Robust'04 using various subsets of its 249 topics, randomly sampling m topics, with $m \in \{50, 100, 150, 200, 249\}$. Robust'04 topics can be categorized into 5 sets: 301–350 (Adhoc'97), 350–400 (Adhoc'98), 401–450 (Adhoc'99), 601–650 (Robust'03-Hard), and 651–700 (Robust'04). To ensure coverage over the different sets in our sampling, we apply stratified sampling. Algorithm 1 implements our experimental setup for a given topic subset (we vary the topic subset outside of the algorithm). The pool depth is set to 100, and we evaluate MAP@1000 and NDCG@10.

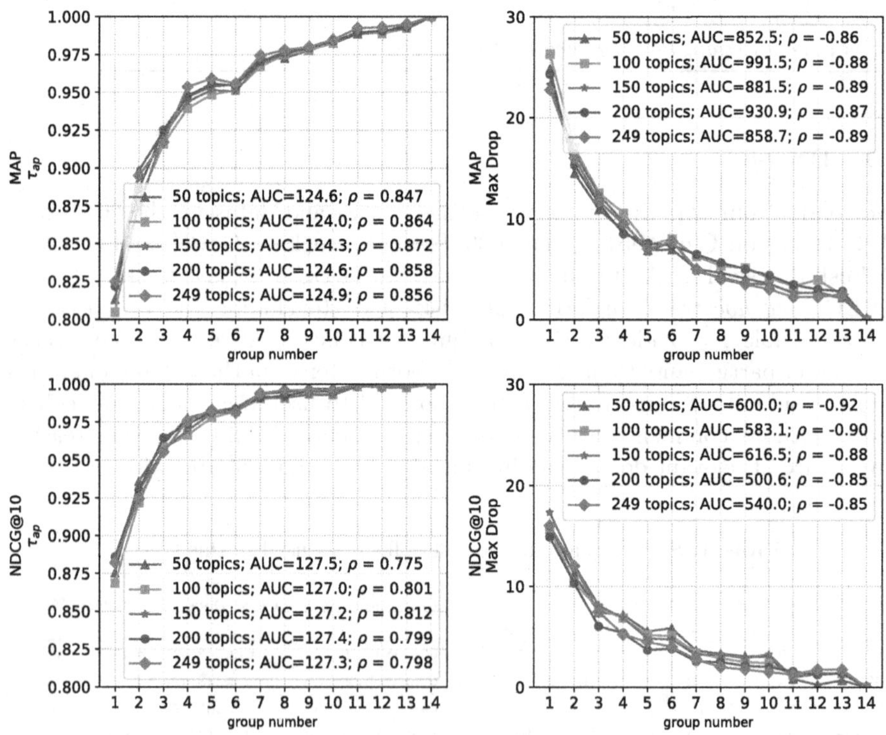

Fig. 1. τ_{ap} (first column), and Max Drop (second column) obtained by simulated test collections with a varying number of topics on the Robust'04 dataset. The x-axis represents the number of groups and the y-axis shows results when runs are ranked using MAP (top row) and NDCG@10 (bottom row).

Figure 1 shows τ_{ap} [19] (larger is better) and Max Drop [16] (smaller is better) on the Robust'04 test collection using all runs. Each line shows an average value of the computed performance metric (e.g., τ_{ap}) across 4 different random samples (i.e., N is set to 4 in Algorithm 1) of groups when m topics are randomly sampled from 249 topics. The first row presents τ_{ap} and Max Drop when the runs are ranked using MAP (i.e., MAP@1000) while the second row reports the same metric when runs are ranked using NDCG@10. We report the Area under the Curve (AUC) for each of the line plots and the Pearson correlation (ρ) between the number of groups and the corresponding performance metrics.

Let us first consider when runs are ranked by MAP (Fig. 1, first row). For τ_{ap} and any number of groups g, we do not see any significant difference in AUC when we down-sample to 50, 100, 150, or 200 topics vs. all 249 topics. Furthermore, we achieve a τ_{ap} correlation of 0.9 using only 3 participating groups, irrespective of the number of topics. We observe the same outcome when using NDCG@10 (Fig. 1, bottom row): there is no significant difference in AUC, and we only need 2 participating groups to achieve a τ_{ap} correlation of 0.9 or above. Since NDCG@10 is far shallower than MAP@1000, it is reasonable to observe that we might need fewer groups to achieve $\tau_{ap} >= 0.9$ using NDCG@10. On the other hand, Max Drop for MAP and NDCG shows a noticeable difference in AUC, when we down-sample topics. We do not see any decreasing pattern in AUC for MAP or NDCG as we increase the number of topics.

In these experiments, we see that for any given number of participating groups, increasing the number of topics does not improve test collection reusability. For both τ_{ap} and Max Drop metrics, this observation holds. However, we should acknowledge the limitations of our experiments. Firstly, since we experiment using only Robust'04 (given its 249 topics), further analysis on other test collections would be needed. Secondly, our experiments only vary the number of topics above 50, so results with more spartan topic sizes might vary. Thirdly, we assume a fixed pool depth of 100. Fourthly, Robust'04 contains only automatic runs; manual runs often find other unique relevant documents. Fifthly, Robust'04 dataset is relatively small compared to a modern collection such as ClueWeb'12 (Table 1). Since larger collections tend to contain more relevant documents, increasing the number of topics for these larger document collections might be more valuable.

Impact of Pool Depth. In the previous experiment, we observe how varying the number of topics interacts with varying the number of participating groups to build a reusable test collection while keeping the pool depth fixed. In this experiment, we also change the pool depth along with the number of topics and the number of groups. The experimental setup for this experiment is the same as discussed in the previous experiment except we vary the pool depth p where p takes values from the set $\{20, 40, 60, 80, 100\}$.

The results for this experiment are reported in Fig. 2. The top row represents results for τ_{ap} whereas the bottom rows present results for Max Drop. The columns of Fig. 2 indicate the number of topics sampled for each of those pool depth variations. Here, we report the results where the runs are ranked using MAP. From the previous experiments, considering the limitations discussed above, we already know that increasing the number of topics does not improve

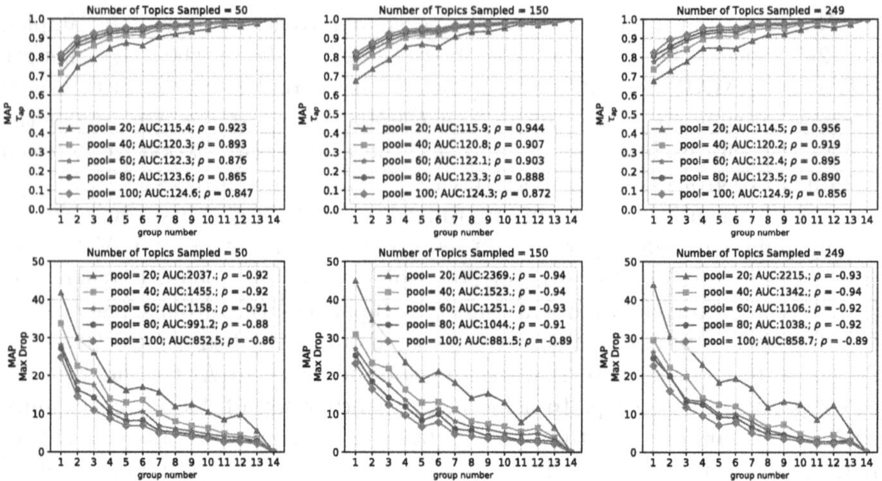

Fig. 2. τ_{ap} (first row), and Max Drop (second row) obtained by simulated test collections with a varying number of topics along with a varying pool depth on the Robust04 dataset. The x-axis represents the number of groups and the y-axis shows results when runs are ranked using MAP.

the reusability of a test collection when the pool depth is 100. This still holds at each varying pool depth reported in Fig. 2.

By observing Fig. 2, we find that for a fixed number of topics, increasing the pool depth improves the AUC in terms of τ_{ap} and lowers the value of AUC in terms of Max Drop, which indicates a better quality test collection. The greatest improvement in AUC happens when we increase the pool depth from 20 to 40 in all topic sets we investigate, suggesting that it has a high return on investment. Based on our results, if we have a large enough evaluation budget, using a pool depth of at least 40 is a reasonable choice.

Another observation from Fig. 2 is how the number of groups interacts with the pool depth. For example, in the plot for 50 topics, when we have a pool depth of only 20, we need at least 7 groups (half of the total number of groups in Robust'04 test collection), to achieve a τ_{ap} correlation of 0.9 or above. However, if the number of participants goes down to 3 groups (one-fifth of the total number of groups in Robust'04 test collection), we need a pool depth of 80 to achieve the same τ_{ap} correlation. This observation holds for all of the other varying numbers of topics sampled in Fig. 2.

Based on the above discussion, we conclude that the number of participants is the most important factor for the quality of test collections. However, if we have few participating groups, rather than increasing the number of topics, we should increase pool depth in order to produce a reusable test collection. This conclusion is also subject to the same limitations discussed in the previous experiment, except for the pool depth.

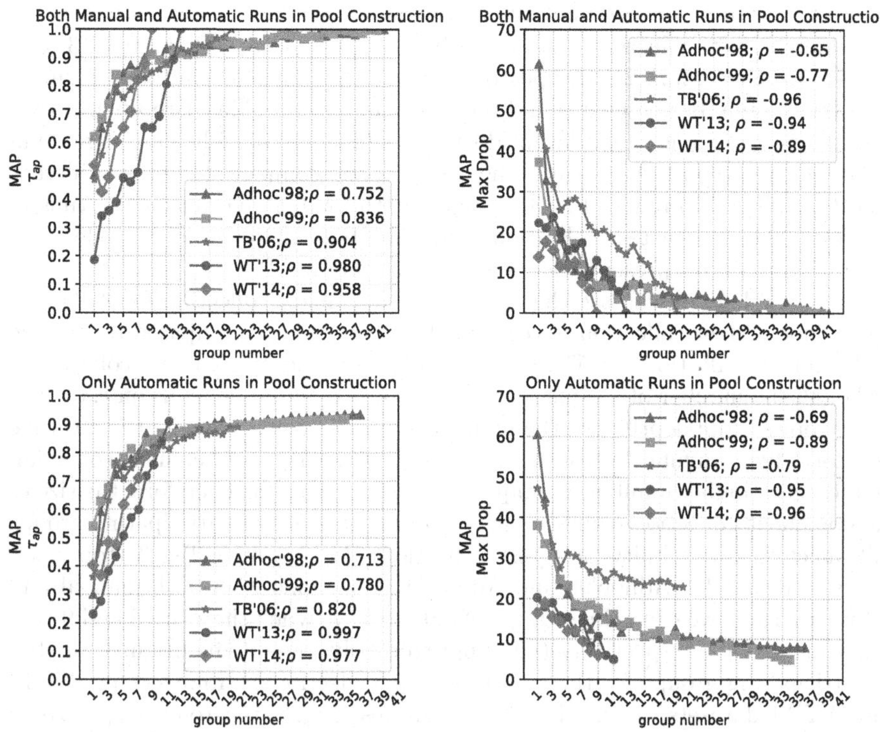

Fig. 3. τ_{ap}, and Max Drop obtained by simulated test collections with a varying number of groups with manual runs (top row) and without manual runs (bottom row) on the five TREC datasets. The x-axis represents the number of groups. Runs are ranked using MAP.

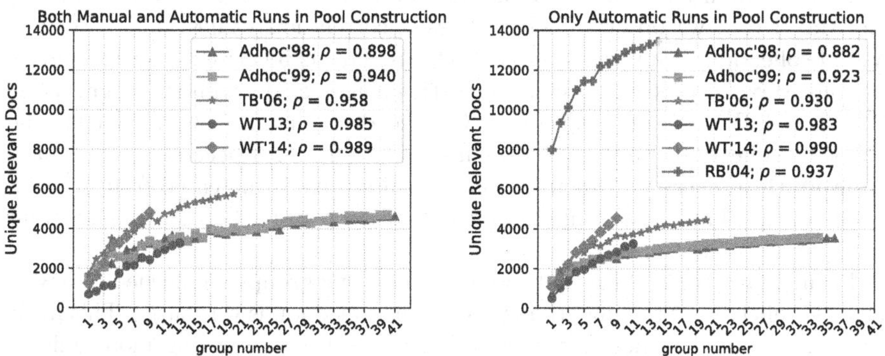

Fig. 4. The number of unique relevant documents obtained by simulated test collections on six different test collections. Left plot does not include Robust'04 (RB'04) dataset as it contains only automatic runs. In the right plot, Robust'04 test collection has a higher number of unique relevant documents because it has 249 topics whereas the other datasets have 50 topics only.

Impact of the Document Collection Size. We conduct experiments on five different test collections, namely Adhoc'99, Adhoc'98, TB'06, WT'13, and WT'14, which contain both types of runs (i.e., manual and automatic runs). We vary the number of groups and report respective τ_{ap}, Max Drop scores (See Fig. 3), and the number of relevant documents (See Fig. 4), following Algorithm 1. We do not report AUC since the AUC is not comparable across different collections. The top row of Fig. 3 considers both manual and automatic runs in the construction of a test collection, while the bottom row only considers the automatic runs. We present results here using only MAP.

From Table 1, we can see that the size of document collection for Adhoc'99 and Adhoc'98 test collection is very small ($\approx$ 0.5 Million) compared to the size of document collection ($\approx$ 52 Million) for WT'13 and WT'14 test collections. Although the number of unique relevant documents found depends on the number of topics, pool depth, and the number of participating groups, it is intuitive that for a fixed number of topics and pool depth, a larger document collection usually has a higher number of unique relevant documents. Therefore, the size of the document collection coupled with a varying number of participating groups will affect the reusability of a test collection. By observing Fig. 3 (top row), we can see that for Adhoc'98 and Adhoc'99 collections with both manual and automatic runs, we can achieve a τ_{ap} of 0.9 or above when there are 8 and 9 participating groups, respectively (i.e., approximately 20% of the original number of participating groups for the respective test collections). However, for WT'13 and WT'14 datasets, we need 12 and 8 groups (Fig. 3, top row), respectively, which is around on average 90% of the original number of participating groups for those respective test collections.

Although there is no acceptable range of values for Max Drop, if we assume that only 90% of the original number of groups participate in WT'13 and WT'14 test collections, the Max Drop lies between 6–10. Regarding Pearson correlation (ρ) scores computed between the number of groups and the corresponding τ_{ap} and Max Drop, we observe higher Pearson correlation values for WT'13 and WT'14 collections than with other collections. This is because τ_{ap} keeps increasing and Max Drop keeps decreasing with an increasing number of groups in WT'13 and WT'14 test collections. On the other hand, both Adhoc'99 and Adhoc'98 collections have low Pearson correlation scores because τ_{ap} increases and Max Drop decreases when the number of groups is increased from 2 to 10. However, after having 10 groups, τ_{ap} and Max Drop scores become almost stable for these two collections.

In summary, we confirm that more participating groups are needed to have a reusable collection if the underlying document collection is very large. This likely stems from runs for these larger document collections returning more unique-relevant documents than runs in other test collections (Fig. 3). Therefore, a run might be highly affected if it does not contribute to the pool. As another hypothesis, the groups participating in the recent shared-tasks are able to develop a more diverse set of IR runs than the groups participated in earlier shared-tasks due to the progress in the field of IR.

However, it should be noted that the finding reported in this experiment has certain limitations. Firstly, all five test collections used in this analysis have only 50 topics. Secondly, for WT'13 and WT'14 collections, the employed pool depth is very shallow (Table 1). A deeper pool depth and a higher number of topics might provide us a different conclusion than the one stated here.

Impact of Manual Runs. In order to see the impact of manual runs on test collection reusability, we remove all manual runs from the simulated test collections and conduct the same experiments as described above. Figure 3, bottom row presents the results for this particular setup. Note from Fig. 4 that the number of unique-relevant documents is reduced noticeably when we do not use any manual run in AdHoc'98, AdHoc'99, and TB'06 test collections, confirming the importance of manual runs providing more unique-relevant documents than automatic runs. We also observe that WT'13 and WT'14 test collections are less affected than other collections in terms of the number of unique relevant documents because there are fewer manual runs in these test collections (See Table 1).

Comparing results between the top and bottom rows of Fig. 3, we find that not having any manual run greatly increases the required number of participating groups to achieve a τ_{ap} correlation of 0.9 or above. For example, for Adhoc'98, and Adhoc'99 collections, we need at least 50% of the original number of participants (Table 3, bottom row) to achieve a τ_{ap} correlation of 0.9 or above which is only 20% (Table 3, top row) when we do include manual runs. For TB'06 and WT'13 collections, we actually need 100% of the original number of participants. Our observations are also similar for Max Drop scores. This suggests that the unique-relevant documents detected by manual runs could not have been detected by any of the automatic runs, thereby affecting the ranking of manual runs during the evaluation.

Ultimately, if we have very few participating groups, it is especially important to have manual runs to develop a reusable test collection. Note that this finding is based on an experiment with 50 topics and a shallow pool depth for the WT'13 and WT'14 test collections.

Table 2. Performance of the multiple linear regression model using Leave-one-test-collection-out setup on five different test collections.

Training set	Testing set	Intersection of document collection between train and test set	MSE τ_{ap}
Adhoc'99, TB'06, WT'13, WT'14	Adhoc'98	Yes	0.005
Adhoc'98, TB'06, WT'13, WT'14	Adhoc'99	Yes	0.003
Adhoc'98, Adhoc'99, WT'13, WT'14	TB'06	No	0.171
Adhoc'98, Adhoc'99, TB'06, WT'14	WT'13	Yes	0.060
Adhoc'98, Adhoc'99, TB'06, WT'13	WT'14	Yes	0.055

4 Predicting the Qualities of Test Collections

We investigate whether it is possible to forecast the quality of a test collection before gathering the ranked lists of participants. Our rationale is that the shared-task organizers can act accordingly based on the predicted quality of a test collection even before spending budget on collecting relevance judgments. In this study, we focus on predicting τ_{AP} as a measure of reusability.

To generate data for our model, we use the same simulated test collections constructed from Algorithm 1 and employ MAP to compute τ_{ap}. We utilize the following features for the prediction model: i) the number of participating groups (G), ii) the number of topics (T), iii) the pool depth (P) and iv) the size of the document collection (C). Then we fit a Multiple Linear Regression model: $\hat{y} = W_0 + W_1 * G + W_2 * T + W_3 * P + W_3 * C$ on the training data to predict τ_{ap}. Here W's are the learned weights for the features of the model. As a performance measure of our prediction model, we report Mean Squared Error (MSE) $= \sum_{i=1}^{n} \frac{(\hat{y_i} - y_i) * (\hat{y_i} - y_i)}{n}$, where y_i, and $\hat{y_i}$ are the predicted and true target value of τ_{ap}, respectively, and n is the total number of data points. A lower value of MSE indicates a better model.

To understand the generalization performance of the prediction model, we employ "*Leave-one-test-collection-out*" (LOTO) strategy. In this LOTO setup, in turn, we hold out one test collection and utilize the remaining test collections from the set of test collections to train the prediction model, and then we test the predictive performance of the trained model on the held-out test collection. For example, in the first row of Table 2, we utilize Adhoc'99, TB'06, WT'13, and WT'14 test collections as training set and Adhoc'98 test collection as testing set for our model. Since Adhoc'98 in the test set shares the same document collection (Table 1) with Adhoc'99 from the train set, the 3rd column of 1st row indicates "Yes". In contrast, TB'06 in the testing set (3rd row) does not share the document collection with any of the test collections utilized in the training set and thus the 3rd column of the 3rd row indicates "No". MSE for predicting τ_{ap} is reported in 4th column of Table 2.

From Table 2, we observe that the model can predict τ_{ap} with a very high accuracy (MSE ≤ 0.06) for all five test collections except for TB'06. This may be because a) runs in Adhoc'98 and Adhoc'99 might be similar due to closeness of two shared-tasks in terms of time, and b) both have the same document collection (Column 3 of Table 2). We can apply the same reasoning for WT'13 and WT'14 test collections.

In summary, our prediction performance improves when we use test collections from the same document collection for both training and testing sets of the model. In practice, our prediction model can be especially useful after its first year as TREC usually continues a track for more than one year. Thus, the results in the first year can be used to forecast the quality of the test collections in the following years for the same track. Test collection construction parameters (i.e., topic set size and pool depth) can be set based on the predictions.

5 Conclusion and Future Work

In this work, we investigate how varying the number of participating groups coupled with other factors in a shared-task affects the reusability of the resulting test collection. Our main findings based on experiments conducted on six TREC test collections are as follows. Firstly, when we have very few participating groups in a shared-task, increasing the pool depth provides a more reusable test collection than increasing the number of topics. Secondly, the size of the document collection and the types of runs play a crucial role when the number of participants is very small. Thirdly, we show that the reusability of a test collection can be predicted with high accuracy when the same document collection is used for successive years in an evaluation campaign, as is commonly done.

There are many possible future directions for this work. For example, our experimental analysis is conducted on pooling-based test collections. However, we plan to extend our work on analyzing test collections constructed using other techniques. For example, the TREC 2017 Common Core track [1] test collection is constructed using a bandit-based technique [10]. In addition, we also plan to address the mentioned limitations of our analysis by using more test collections. Future work might also explore the prediction of test collection quality when the ranked lists of documents are submitted but relevance judgments are not collected yet. This scenario will enable using different features such as the number of unique documents retrieved by groups, rank correlation of ranked lists, and others with more sophisticated machine learning models.

Acknowledgments. We thank the reviewers for their valuable feedback. This research was supported in part by Wipro, the Micron Foundation, and by Good Systems (http://goodsystems.utexas.edu/), a UT Austin Grand Challenge to develop responsible AI technologies. The statements made herein are solely the opinions of the authors and do not reflect the views of the sponsoring agencies.

References

1. Allan, J., Harman, D., Kanoulas, E., Li, D., Van Gysel, C., Voorhees, E.M.: TREC 2017 common core track overview. In: TREC (2017)
2. Buckley, C.: Voorhees: evaluating evaluation measure stability, pp. 33–40 (2000)
3. Büttcher, S., Clarke, C.L., Yeung, P.C., Soboroff, I.: Reliable information retrieval evaluation with incomplete and biased judgements. In: Proceedings of the 30th Annual International ACM SIGIR Conference on Research and Development in Information Retrieval, pp. 63–70. ACM (2007)
4. Carterette, B., Pavlu, V., Kanoulas, E., Aslam, J.A., Allan, J.: Evaluation over thousands of queries. In: Proceedings of the 31st Annual International ACM SIGIR Conference on Research and Development in Information Retrieval - SIGIR 2008, p. 651. ACM Press, Singapore, Singapore (2008)
5. Cleverdon, C.: The cranfield tests on index language devices. In: Aslib Proceedings, vol. 19, pp. 173–194. MCB UP Ltd. (1967)
6. Hawking, D., Craswell, N., Thistlewaite, P.: Overview of TREC-7 very large collection track. NIST Special Publication SP, pp. 93–106 (1998)

7. Hawking, D., Robertson, S.: On collection size and retrieval effectiveness. Inf. Retrieval **6**(1), 99–105 (2003)
8. Kuriyama, K.: Pooling for a large-scale test collection: an analysis of the search results from the first NTCIR workshop, p. 19 (2002)
9. Kutlu, M., Elsayed, T., Lease, M.: Intelligent topic selection for low-cost information retrieval evaluation: A New perspective on deep vs shallow judging. Inf. Process. Manage. **54**(1), 37–59 (2018)
10. Losada, D.E., Parapar, J., Barreiro, A.: Feeling lucky? Multi-armed bandits for ordering judgements in pooling-based evaluation. In: Proceedings of the 31st Annual ACM Symposium on Applied Computing - SAC 2016, pp. 1027–1034. ACM Press, Pisa, Italy (2016)
11. Robertson, S.E., Kanoulas, E.: On per-topic variance in IR evaluation. In: SIGIR 2012, pp. 891–900. Association for Computing Machinery, New York, NY, USA (2012). https://doi.org/10.1145/2348283.2348402
12. Sanderson, M., et al.: Test collection based evaluation of information retrieval systems. Found. Trends® Inf. Retrieval **4**(4), 247–375 (2010)
13. Sparck Jones, K., Van Rijsbergen, C.: Report on the need for and provision of an 'ideal' information retrieval test collection (1975)
14. Sparck Jones, K., Van Rijsbergen, C.J.: Information retrieval test collections. J. Documentation **32**(1), 59–75 (1976)
15. Voorhees, E.M.: Variations in relevance judgments and the measurement of retrieval effectiveness. Inf. Process. Manage. **36**(5), 697–716 (2000)
16. Voorhees, E.M.: On building fair and reusable test collections using bandit techniques. In: Proceedings of the 27th ACM International Conference on Information and Knowledge Management, pp. 407–416, CIKM 2018, ACM, New York, NY, USA (2018)
17. Voorhees, E.M., Samarov, D., Soboroff, I.: Using replicates in information retrieval evaluation. ACM Trans. Inf. Syst. **36**(2), 1–21 (2017). https://doi.org/10.1145/3086701
18. Webber, W., Moffat, A., Zobel, J.: Statistical power in retrieval experimentation. In: Proceeding of the 17th ACM conference on Information and Knowledge Mining - CIKM 2008, p. 571. ACM Press, Napa Valley, California, USA (2008)
19. Yilmaz, E., Aslam, J.A., Robertson, S.: A new rank correlation coefficient for information retrieval. In: Proceedings of the 31st Annual International ACM SIGIR Conference on Research and Development in Information Retrieval, pp. 587–594. ACM (2008)
20. Zobel, J.: How reliable are the results of large-scale information retrieval experiments? In: Proceedings of the 21st Annual International ACM SIGIR Conference on Research and Development in Information Retrieval, pp. 307–314. ACM (1998)

Sentiment and Network Analysis of Twitter Reactions to the U.S. Birthright Citizenship Ban Debate

Adam Worrall[1(✉)], Ana Ndumu[2], and Lynette Hammond Gerido[3]

[1] School of Library and Information Studies, Universitty of Alberta, Edmonton, AB T6G 2G5, Canada
worrall@ualberta.ca

[2] College of Information Studies, University of Maryland College Park, College Park, MD 20742, USA
andumu@umd.edu

[3] School of Public Health, University of Michigan, Ann Arbor, MI 48109-2029, USA
lhgerido@umich.edu

Abstract. This paper explores a case of political speech acts and information behavior on the social media platform Twitter. The researchers explored tweets relating to former U.S. President Trump's October 2018 post on eliminating birthright citizenship with the goal of understanding affect, sentiments, and network patterns among ban supporters and opponents. Over 7,700 relevant tweets were collected and analyzed to characterize and visualize the entire community and its interactions. Knowledge of Twitter users' information behavior concerning the birthright citizenship ban proposal is important to comprehending how online speech acts influence perceptions of social identity and social inclusion.

Keywords: Social informatics · Information behavior · Politics · Immigration · Network analysis · Relational models · United States

1 Introduction

When it comes to real-time, unfiltered, and instinctive political dialogue, Twitter stands out as a preferred platform (Ausserhofer and Maireder 2013; Grover et al. 2019). A defining characteristic of former U.S. President Donald Trump's administration was his visceral Twitter messaging. Politicians had long used Twitter to promote their interests and campaigns. However, in comparison to other recent U.S. presidents, Trump circumvented traditional communication and information mechanisms by turning to Twitter to disseminate his political priorities. After growing tension between Twitter executives and the U.S. president, Twitter eventually suspended his account in the aftermath of the January 6, 2021 insurrection at the U.S. Capitol.

There is an opportunity to investigate Trump's well-known and now bygone use of Twitter as an information phenomenon and, in so doing, add to what is known about social media use and speech acts in the political arena. We focus on how information

M. Smits (Ed.): iConference 2022, LNCS 13193, pp. 149–174, 2022.
https://doi.org/10.1007/978-3-030-96960-8_11

sharing, resource types, and public sentiment relate to social identity. We explore a specific Twitter-based occurrence—Trump's 2018 tweets on birthright citizenship—to test the interplay between information behavior and the ideals of national allegiance, political ideology, and societal belonging.

1.1 Case Study

On October 20, 2018, former U.S. President Donald Trump announced in an interview with Axios Media (Swan and Kight 2018) that he proposed to end birthright citizenship as expressed in the 14th Amendment of the U.S. Constitution (Fig. 1). Subsequent to the Axios interview, former President Trump reiterated through Twitter his administration's intent to end birthright citizenship. His comments were met with immediate public reaction across various media channels, especially on Twitter (Fig. 2). The #birthrightcitizenship case, as we characterize it here in this study, demonstrates the types of speech acts that originate on Twitter and rapidly disseminate into the popular consciousness.

Fig. 1. Sample tweet from Axios Magazine.

Fig. 2. Sample tweet from President Trump.

1.2 Purpose

Twitter is associated with raw, rapid communication. Since posts are limited to 250 words, the platform's forced content brevity is an important part of the Twitter experience. Tweets are thus regarded as speech acts as defined by Austin and Searle speech act theory (Austin 1962; Searle 1969); it suggests that human communication begins not with a sentence or other expression, but rather the performance of language acts stemming from the material world. Information behavior researchers have employed speech act analyses to grasp Facebook debates (Bonnici and Ma 2021), information systems design (Johannesson 1995), archival practice (Henttonen 1994), and more.

We set out to investigate how identity, emotion, and relationships influence speech acts, especially when it comes to proposed immigration policy. What can we learn by looking at the cross between (a) sentiments on birthright citizenship, (b) feelings of joy, trust, fear, sadness, disgust and surprise, and (c) content posting, tagging, and sharing? This study applies network and sentiment analysis to probe how U.S. or American national identity intersects with public opinion on immigration, specifically birthright citizenship.

2 Related Work

Social media shapes the ways in which society understands and responds to political developments. These tools allow the general public to participate in a manner that, until recently, was reserved for high-profile politicians and journalists. Twitter specifically functions as a low-risk, high-agency, and pseudo-anonymous method of civic engagement (Conover et al. 2011). When it comes to the U.S. political spectrum, it is effective in rallying for causes and mobilizing audiences of all backgrounds (Conover et al. 2011;

Hands 2011). Constituents often turn to social media to opine on policy and informally engage with influencers (Tumasjan et al. 2010; Bennett 2012). Leaders themselves use social media to distill messages and promote aims.

Social identity theory (Tajfel et al. 1979) helps us comprehend social media participation as an extension of personal identity. The theory argues that social typing predicts intergroup behaviors through social categorization (e.g., the groups that people belong to), social identification (e.g., how members adopt group characteristics), and social comparison (e.g., ways in which group identity reinforces an in-group and out-group dichotomy). When viewed from this vantage point, Twitter behavior is consistent with social identity and, thus, helps explain political engagement.

The theory informs how immigration-related speech acts arise from ideological conflict around American identity (Byrne and Dixon 2013; Citrin et al. 1990; Schildkraut 2007). It is especially promising for an examination on personal Twitter use and notions of the principles and characteristics of 'Americanness,' which continues to divide the U.S. populace. Partisan social identity has proven to be an important predictor of social media activities. American identity leads some to oppose immigration, as posited by Mangum and Block (2018) who investigated the relationship between American national identity and public opinion on immigration. The prototype or symbolism of what it means to be an American fortifies against those perceived to be un-American. This same social typing and categorization determines boundaries of rightness and wrongness; preferences and aversions; along with sociocultural interpretations of democracy and community. In turn, these boundaries influence modes of expression, as seen in Grover et al.'s (2019) findings that demonstrate pro-immigration tweets contained more language associated with moral foundations of harm, fairness, and loyalty. Anti-immigration tweets corresponded with authority, cognitive rigidity, and negative emotions.

A growing body of research explains the significant role social identity plays in the methods of information sharing and types of shared resources, specifically relating to sentiments toward immigrants. In their work on social identity and communication, Wojcieszak and Garrett (2018) suggest that increasing the salience of national identity can promote affective online polarization toward immigrants. Immigration opponents and proponents displayed significantly different media-sharing behaviors.

Though it is easy to portray political allegiance as haphazard phenomena, there continues to be substantiated links between emotions, political affiliation, and social media use (De Choudhury et al. 2014). Emotions often coalesce political identity, as seen in Glaser and Salovey's (1998) study on how emotional expressions among politicians help to establish a single target of judgment. Sobkowicz and Sobkowicz (2010, 2012) demonstrate the remarkable stability of individual political opinions, even when emotional states fluctuate. Wood (2000) similarly found that highly emotional discussions point to lower chances of actually changing participants' opinions. Examining how immigration speech acts intersect with social identity appears to us to be a viable research goal.

3 Methods

We investigated whether the theory of social identity helps explain immigration-related speech acts, as argued by Segesten and Bossetta (2017) who state that Twitter is often utilized to garner support through calls for action, slogan creation, hashtags, and shared media, regardless of political sentiment. These types of normative information behavior rely on salient groupings and values, it appears. Studying this specific Twitter case from the angles of social categorization, identification, and comparison—as posited by the theory of social identity—can advance knowledge of social media's role in influencing public attitudes toward U.S. immigration policy and social inclusion more broadly. Our study addresses the following research questions:

- RQ1: What are the relationships between Twitter users' social identities and stances on the proposed birthright citizenship ban?
- RQ2: What are the relationships between Twitter users' affect (demonstrated emotions), sentiment (expressed opinions), networks (user associations) and speech acts regarding the proposed birthright citizenship ban?

3.1 Data Collection

We collected messages posted on Twitter between October 31 and November 10, 2018 and identified trending words and phrases. Advanced Twitter search operators allowed for setting data inclusion and exclusion parameters in accordance with a lexicon of the 15 highest trending terms related to the research questions (e.g., "U.S. Constitution," "birthright citizenship," "ban," "14th Amendment"). This rubric resulted in a total of 7,718 usable mined messages. For each message a case was created, which included a de-identified participant ID, tweet text, link shared, number of retweets, as well as participant biographies and personal websites. Sample tweets are included in the discussion section. We maintained the usernames of public figures such as former President Trump and other key political and media leaders; in keeping with Internet research ethics guidelines, other usernames were anonymized (Buchanan 2011).

3.2 Opinion Classification

Next, we established an a priori coding protocol based on content features (e.g., nature of posts; textual indicators of emotion including emoticons, punctuation, and use of offensive language; propensity to share media; and retweet behavior), and contextual features (e.g., self-identified political party affiliation) to manually code a subsample of 415 tweets as either conveying a stance in support or opposition to the proposed birthright citizenship ban. After coding the first 100 messages and establishing an inter-coder reliability score of Cohen's $\kappa = 0.80$ ($p < 0.005$), we then coded the remaining 315 tweets to further investigate opinion patterns. This initial assessment of the two types of corpora was necessary to train a classifier to recognize supportive and opposing opinions via supervised machine learning techniques for natural language processing (NLP) throughout the entire dataset of tweets. Finally, after testing three predictive test classification models in R, the support vector machines (SVM) model demonstrated the best performance with 78.7% accuracy within a 95% confidence interval of 69.7% - 86%. Then the remaining 7,741 cases were analyzed, and incomplete cases were removed from the sample, leaving a remaining sample of 7,718 with stances predicted by the SVM model.

3.3 Sentiment Analysis

To analyze sentiments around the proposed birthright ban, we used the Syuzhet package in R, which combines four sentiment dictionaries within a robust tool for computational sentiment extraction (Jockers and Underwood 2015) and leverages the work of Plutchik (1980) that defines a set of eight emotions conceptualized in a wheel of four pairs with varying degrees of intensity:

- Trust represents confidence and ranges from acceptance to admiration.
- Fear represents anxiety and ranges from timidity to terror.
- Surprise represents consciousness and ranges from uncertainty to amazement.
- Sadness represents comfort and ranges from dislike to loathing.
- Anger represents distress and ranges from annoyance to fury.
- Anticipation represents alertness and ranges from interest to vigilance.
- Joy represents pleasure and ranges from serenity to ecstasy.

The pairs are bipolar such that joy is the opposite of sadness; trust is the opposite of disgust; fear is the opposite of anger; and anticipation is the opposite of surprise.

Opinion Mining and Sentiment Analysis (OMSA) allowed for quantifying associated attitudes, emotions, and affective responses toward President Trump's communications about a hypothetical birthright citizenship ban. OMSA is often used to measure polarity by assessing the amount of positive or negative terms that appear in a tweet. While this approach poses some limitations in interpreting neutrality, it has been recognized for its ability to visualize speech acts within complex social network structures and information flows, specifically Twitter (Himelboim et al. 2017).

3.4 Network Analysis

Finally, we applied network analysis to explore the relationships between users, mentions, and hashtags and, thereby, better understand communities, social comparison, and social identification. The full 7,718 mined messages were analyzed using Gephi software (https://gephi.org/), including examination of key communities within the data using modularity analysis and overlay of the stance of each tweet and average stance for each user and hashtag, as computed from the opinion classification discussed above. The statistics included:

- numbers of nodes (users or hashtags) and edges (tweets) present in each of the top 10 identified communities, and in the network as segmented for each stance (opposing or supporting the ban);
- in-degree (mentions) and out-degree (tweets made) for users and hashtags; and
- measures of network centrality (e.g. betweenness centrality) for users and hashtags.

We used Gephi to create full visualizations of the network and each community, including overlay of stance from the opinion classification and overlay of sentiments from the sentiment analysis. Gephi's OpenOrd algorithm (Martin et al. 2011) allowed us to overlay these visualizations.

4 Results

4.1 Twitter Users by Stance (RQ1)

Regarding actors, the ban-supporting and ban-opposing groups appeared at first glance to be proportionate in that the SVM model predicted slightly fewer ban-supporting (48.7%) than ban-opposing (51.3%) users. However, a Chi-square goodness of fit test determined that the two distributions are not equal (p = 0.02, 95% CI). There were significantly greater numbers of ban opponents than ban supporters (Table 1). By contrast, tweet engagement (retweets and favorites) among ban supporters is nearly double that of ban opponents. Additionally, the number of unique participants in the ban proponents group with more than ten thousand followers is six times greater among ban supporters ($n = 85$) when compared to ban opponents ($n = 14$).

Table 1. Characteristics of groups by stance.

	Support	Oppose
# of Cases	3,756	3,962
# of Retweets	13,661	5,047
# of Favorites	31,547	12,308
Unique Participants	3,384	3,570
Unique Participants with > 1 tweet	262	279
Unique Participants with > 10k followers	85	14

4.2 Twitter Users by Sentiment and Networks (RQ2)

Our second research question explores the links between speech acts, emotions, and relationships among supporters and opponents of the proposed birthright citizenship ban. Results from a Welch Two Sample t-test indicates that there were only two significant differences in sentiment among the groups (Fig. 3). Those who opposed the birthright citizenship ban used speech acts that convey trust more frequently (7,811) than those who support the ban (7,692). Both groups expressed more positive sentiments than negative, with ban opponents (11,503) showing slightly more positivity than ban supporters (11,382).

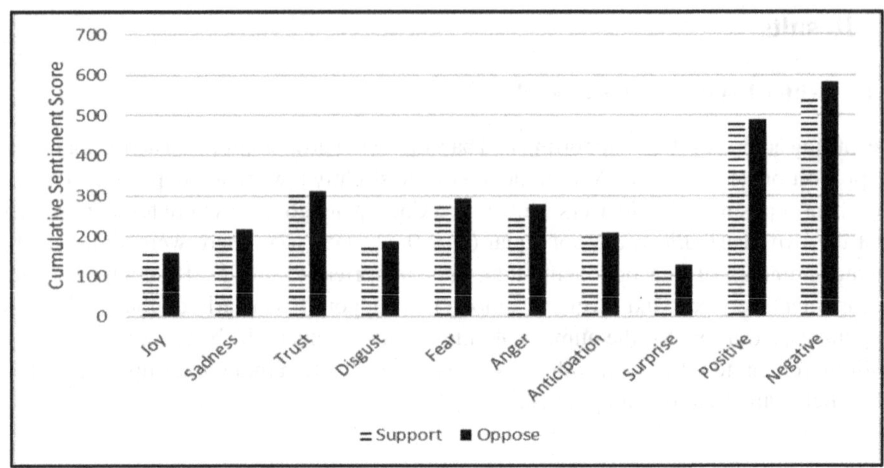

Fig. 3. Comparison of tweet sentiment by stance.

We further explored each emotional dyad to compare the groups by stance. In all cases, the mean emotional sentiment scores did not vary significantly between the groups nor was emotional sentiment a predictor of stance (Table 2).

Table 2. Mean emotional sentiment scores by stance.

	Oppose			Support			Goodness of fit	Independence
	Σ	μ	n	Σ	μ	n	p	p
Joy	3,471	0.88	2,110	3,331	0.89	2,004	0.700	0.558
Sadness	2,802	0.71	1,927	2,779	0.74	1,867	0.100	0.191
Trust	7,811	1.97	3,188	7,692	2.05	3,075	0.050 *	0.182
Disgust	1,954	0.49	1,411	1,925	0.51	1,388	0.300	0.938
Fear	3,789	0.96	2,267	3,717	0.99	2,189	0.788	0.363
Anger	3,408	0.86	2,091	3,222	0.86	2,000	0.900	0.515
Anticipation	3,659	0.92	2,235	3,508	0.93	2,110	0.700	0.364
Surprise	2,592	0.65	1,999	2,474	0.66	1,899	0.800	0.743
Positive	11,503	2.90	3,500	11,382	3.03	3,389	0.010 *	0.155
Negative	6,316	1.59	2,848	6,012	1.60	2,723	0.900	0.796

* Statistically significant, $p < 0.05$

To capture a specific moment in the network activity, we zeroed in on November 8, 2018, or Mid-Term Election Day, and highlighted differences in sentiment by stance (Table 3). Several differences became apparent:

Table 3. Mean emotional sentiment scores by stance on Mid-Term Election Day.

	Oppose			Support			Goodness of fit	Independence
	Σ	μ	n	Σ	μ	n	p	p
Joy	57	0.86	37	57	0.64	41	0.152	0.407
Sadness	57	0.86	38	82	0.92	46	0.733	0.145
Trust	149	2.26	56	140	1.57	61	0.032*	0.281
Disgust	41	0.62	24	56	0.63	40	0.956	0.117
Fear	98	1.49	48	126	1.42	59	0.760	0.691
Anger	71	1.08	39	99	1.11	52	0.852	0.702
Anticipation	80	1.21	48	80	0.90	49	0.080	0.853
Surprise	60	0.91	41	61	0.69	44	0.140	0.652
Positive	219	3.32	60	244	2.74	219	0.206	0.348
Negative	118	1.79	50	171	1.92	63	0.619	0.190

* Statistically significant, $p < 0.05$

- The joy sentiment was higher among ban opponents (Oppose, $\mu = 0.860$; Support, $\mu = 0.640$) (Fig. 4.A).
- The trust sentiment was higher among ban opponents (Oppose, $\mu = 2.260$; Support, $\mu = 1.570$) (Fig. 4.B).
- Anticipation was higher among ban opponents (Oppose, $\mu = 1.210$; Support, $\mu = 1.570$) (Fig. 5.D).
- Surprise was relatively low overall, but was higher among ban opponents (Oppose, $\mu = 0.910$; Support, $\mu = 0.685$) (Fig. 5.D).
- Positivity was higher among ban opponents than ban supporters (Oppose, $\mu = 3.320$; Support, $\mu = 2.740$) (Fig. 6).

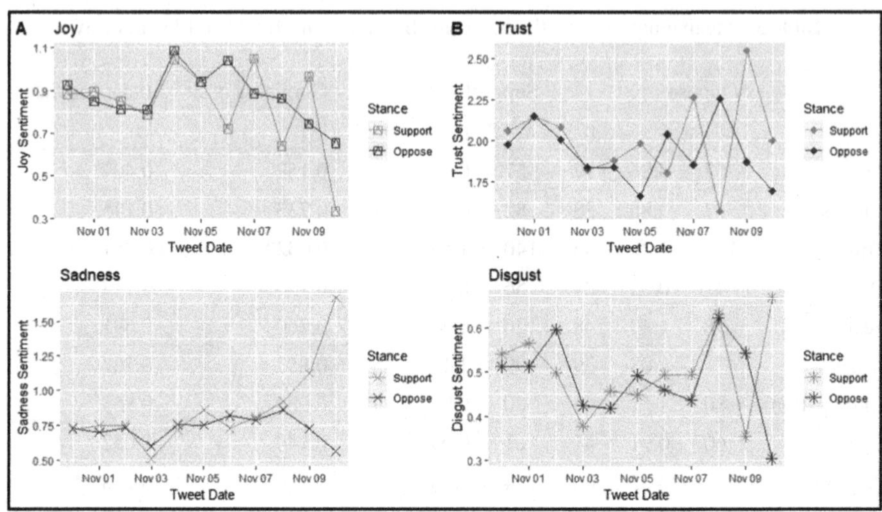

Fig. 4. Comparison of joy, sadness, trust, and disgust sentiment by stance, arranged by dyad.

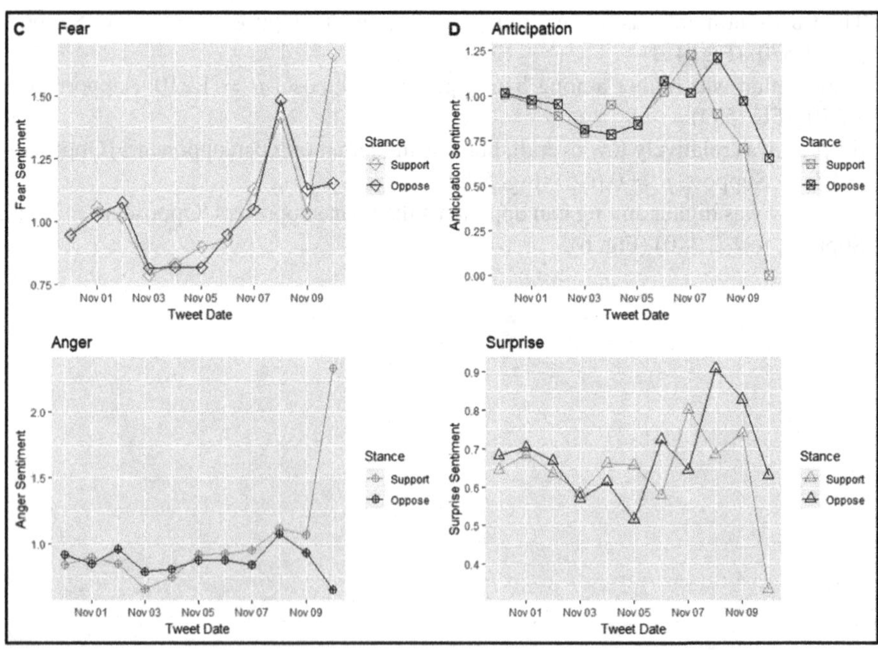

Fig. 5. Comparison of fear, anger, anticipation, and surprise sentiment by stance, arranged by dyad.

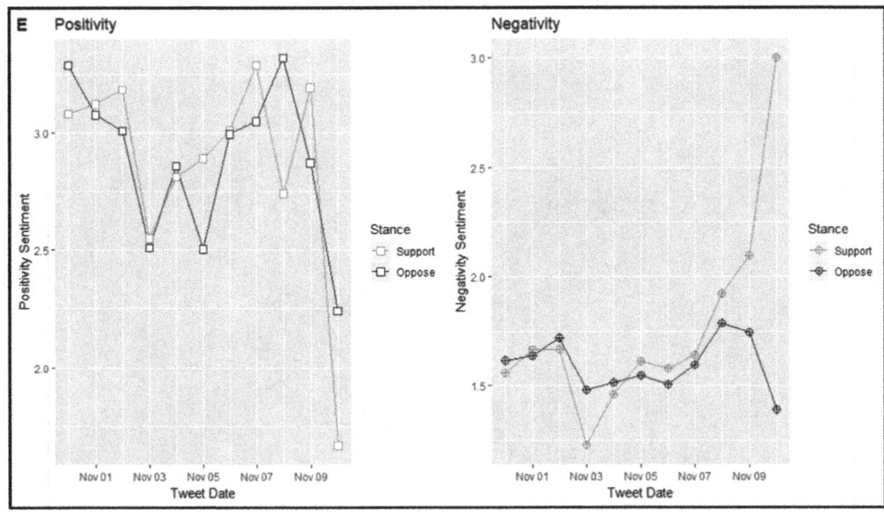

Fig. 6. Comparison of positive and negative sentiments by stance, arranged by dyad.

4.3 Interaction Network

Three visualizations of the full interaction network are shown in Fig. 7, illustrating the network by community. Figures 8 and 9 illustrate the network by stance (proponents in green in Fig. 8, opponents in red in Fig. 9). For users and hashtags, stance is measured by the mean number of tweets made by an account; tweet stance was assigned by the SVM model. Overall, the size of the sub-network of ban proponents was slightly larger at 3,549 users and hashtags, than ban opponents at 3,390 users and hashtags. In terms of information behavior, ban supporters were more likely to mention users and utilize

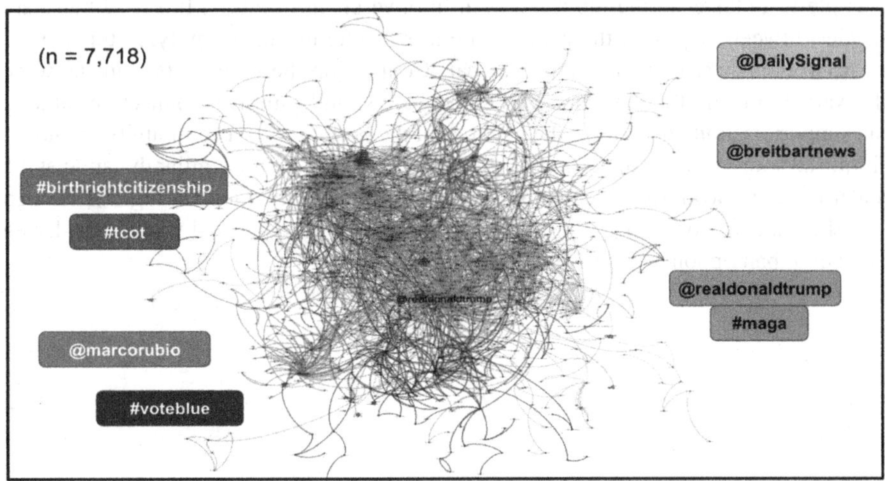

Fig. 7. Full network visualization by community. (Color figure online)

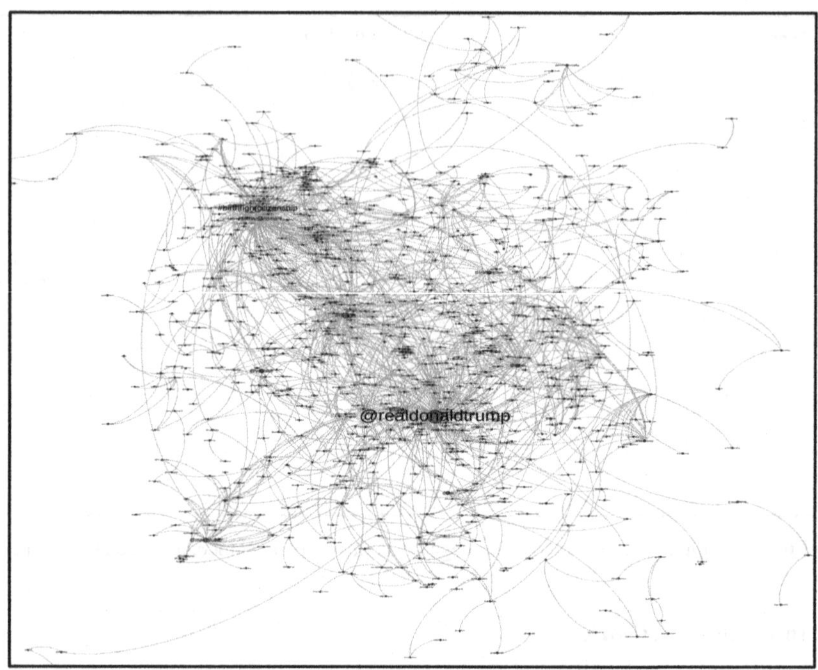

Fig. 8. Network visualization among ban supporters.

hashtags, based on the mean number of mentions (in-degree = 0.2357 for support vs. 0.1245 for oppose) and mean number of tweets (out-degree = 0.4525 for support vs. 0.3426 for oppose). These descriptive statistics suggest the sub-network of ban supporters was more varied in terms of mentions.

Comparisons of Figs. 8 and 9 show some grouping of stances by communities. One example is a cluster in the top right, seen in olive green in Fig. 7. In Fig. 9 these are visible as tweets opposing the ban, but are less visible in Fig. 8, implying this part of the network is more likely to oppose the ban. Connections between parts of the network also vary. For example, as seen in Fig. 8, there are slightly stronger connections among ban supporters along the part of the network in the bottom left - a community including Florida senator @marcorubio (in dark green in Fig. 7). There is a similar dynamic at the center of the network (represented by @realdonaldtrump, in orange in Fig. 7). Though they share a common stance, these connections appear disconnected when considering the overall ban opponents sub-network (see Fig. 9).

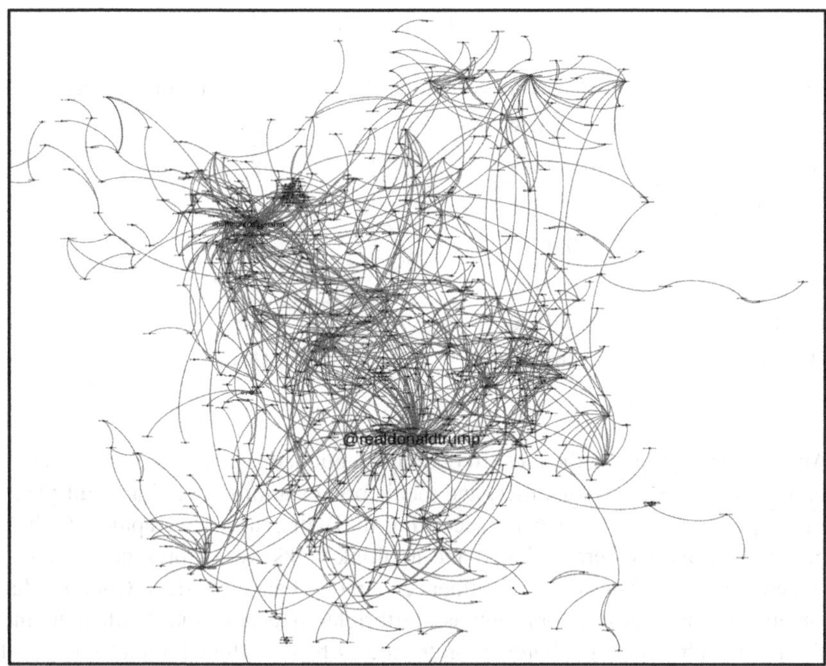

Fig. 9. Network visualization of ban opponents.

4.4 By Stance

When dividing the network into subsets by ban-opposing or ban-supporting stance, the most frequently mentioned accounts contained a mix of ten politicians, think-tanks, media, and opinion leaders. Common hashtags mentioned by this group included #constitution, #birthright, #tcot ("Top Conservatives on Twitter"), #gop (a common abbreviation for the Republican Party), and #blexit (a "Black exit" from the Democratic Party advocated at the time by conservative activists). Table 4 shows a full list including betweenness centrality scores. The presence of #tcot, #blexit, and #gop suggests some interaction and engagement by ban opponents with conservatives and/or Republicans.

Table 4. Ban opponents sub-network – Top hashtags.

Hashtag	Betweenness Centrality	Stance (% of Support)
#constitution	0.002816	47.4%
#tcot	0.002778	44.4%
#blexit	0.002380	34.4%

(*continued*)

Table 4. *(continued)*

Hashtag	Betweenness Centrality	Stance (% of Support)
#gop	0.002049	36.8%
#scotus	0.001525	48.2%
#14thamendment	0.001338	48.5%
#1	0.001119	43.8%
#resist	0.001100	48.1%
#nationalist	0.001070	43.8%
#birthright	0.001030	45.0%

Among ban supporters, the most frequently mentioned accounts are associated with opinion leaders, media personalities, and media organizations, including multiple self-described podcasters and vloggers, according to Twitter user biographies. Only two public political figures were included and no think-tanks were represented, indicative of a heterogeneous sub-network of influencers among ban supporters. Common hashtags included topical descriptors such as #birthrightcitizenship and #14thamendment; the shorter #14a hashtag, an abbreviation for the 14th Amendment often central to discussions of birthright citizenship; and #maga and #americafirst, corresponding with the expected political leanings of those supporting the ban, although #democrats was also frequently used by this group. Based on our interaction network analysis, ban supporters relied on hashtags to a greater extent when compared with ban opponents. See Table 5 for a full list including betweenness centrality scores.

Table 5. Ban supporters sub-network – Top hashtags.

Hashtag	Betweenness Centrality	Stance (% of Support)
#birthrightcitizenship	0.038864	51.9%
#maga	0.027568	52.5%
#14thamendment	0.021321	59.2%
#14a	0.005596	64.3%
#citizenship	0.005115	100.0%
#democrats	0.002831	55.6%
#immigration	0.002251	56.7%
#14th	0.001977	73.3%
#fakenews	0.001943	75.0%
#midterms2018	0.001816	64.3%

4.5 By Community

The top 10 communities within the network were identified through modularity analysis using Gephi and labeled by user mentions or hashtags most central to them. These communities, ranked by size, included:

- @realdonaldtrump
- #birthrightcitizenship
- #voteblue
- @hvonspakovsky (Senior Legal Fellow with the Heritage Foundation think-tank)
- #tcot (Top Conservatives on Twitter)
- @marcorubio (Republican U.S. Senator from Florida)
- @breitbartnews (a right-wing news and opinion site)
- @seanhannity (FOX News opinion host) and @andrewmccarthy (a FOX News contributor and editor at *National Review*)
- #democrats
- @brettschneiderc (writer for *Politico* and *The New York Times*) and @axios (the online news site)

Each community was examined in terms of the number of users and hashtags within the community and its stance on the proposed birthright citizenship ban: opposing, supporting, or neutral. We conducted a similar analysis of the tweets themselves, which are either "oppose" or "support" per the SVM model. As seen in Table 6, these findings convey high polarization between supporters and opponents of the proposed birthright citizenship ban. The communities centered around @hvonspakovsky and @brettschneiderc and @axios are in alignment with the beliefs espoused by these key actors against the ban; both communities are composed mainly of ban opponents.

Notable in the opposite direction are those communities centered around #democrats, #tcot, and @breitbartnews. The hashtag #democrats is used more by ban supporters (65.6% of users and hashtags and 81.8% of tweets classified as supportive), despite the ban opposition expressed by many Democratic politicians. The community centered around conservative media figure @seanhannity and conservative pundit @andrewcmccarthy, as previously seen in the top right of Figs. 7 and 9, features more tweets that oppose the ban than support it (only 45.8% of users and hashtags and 29.6% of tweets being supportive). This pattern is not in line with the views of these two actors.

The use of #democrats by those supporting the ban and interactions around @seanhannity and @andrewcmccarthy by those against the ban is further evidence that each sub-network may be engaging with key figures from the opposing side. Based on Figs. 7, 8, and 9 there is evidence of interaction among Twitter users on either side of the #birthrightcitizenship case. The transcending use of hashtags and mentions among key figures at each ideological end suggests overlap, be that for shared understanding or as co-opting of speech acts used among counterparts.

Table 6. Communities by stance and ranked by overall size.

Community (Centered Around)	Oppose		Support		Neutral	Mean Stance (% of Support)	
	Nodes	Tweets	Nodes	Tweets	Nodes	Nodes	Tweets
@realdonaldtrump	402	409	440	534	378	52.1%	57.1%
#birthrightcitizenship	190	232	202	289	128	50.7%	55.5%
#voteblue	63	73	63	100	58	47.2%	57.8%
@hvonspakovsky	45	85	42	36	35	48.0%	29.8%
#tcot	28	20	42	74	22	61.3%	78.7%
@marcorubio	36	42	34	51	16	50.0%	54.8%
@breitbartnews	26	23	26	47	34	47.4%	67.1%
@seanhannity & @andrewcmccarthy	31	62	27	26	16	45.8%	29.6%
#democrats	15	10	31	45	23	65.6%	81.8%
@brettschneiderc & @axios	11	12	4	5	12	30.6%	29.4%

4.6 Sentiments and the Network

We combined the sentiments with the full network and overlaid them onto visualizations as part of analysis. Data from this overlay is seen in Table 7, which reports the average sentiment score for each of the 10 sentiments for the entire network and the three stance categories (oppose, in red; support, in green; and neutral, in gray). Table 8 reports the average sentiment score for each of the 10 sentiments for the top 10 communities identified above. Hashtags, as non-human nodes, are not given sentiment; scores reflect only human users. The specific communities were more likely to express a given emotion than the entire network as a whole, as seen in the generally higher values in Table 8 versus Table 7. These communities, on the whole, consist of users who are more engaged and emotionally invested users in speech acts regarding the proposed ban.

Key findings that diverge from the full-network averages are highlighted in yellow (high values) and blue (low values) in Table 8. These include the following:

- More joy was expressed in the #voteblue, #tcot, and @marcorubio-centered communities, which may have expressed it due to perceptions their side was "winning" the #birthrightcitizenship argument or (for #tcot and @marcorubio) finding former President Trump's proposal favorable. Less joy was expressed in the #democrats-centered community. Only a few communities expressed sadness, including those centered around @hvonspakovsky, #voteblue, and @axios and @brettschneiderc, likely linked to the ban's potential consequences given all three are more likely to oppose the ban than the full network.
- Trust was relatively high in most communities, but less so in the #democrats-centered community - perhaps, indicative of a lack of trust between the two sides which engaged

Table 7. Sentiment scores in the full network and by stance.

	Full network	Stance: Oppose	Stance: Support	Stance: Neutral
Sample size (*n*)	6,461	3,182	2,992	287
Joy	0.8833	0.8834	0.8773	0.9434
Sadness	0.7079	0.6906	0.7227	0.7451
Trust	1.9920	1.9555	2.0168	2.1369
Disgust	0.5029	0.4922	0.5109	0.5386
Fear	0.9666	0.9509	0.9715	1.0906
Anger	0.8590	0.8662	0.8400	0.9756
Anticipation	0.9399	0.9402	0.9391	0.9458
Surprise	0.6587	0.6570	0.6619	0.6489
Positive	2.9667	2.8941	3.0334	3.0772
Negative	1.5949	1.6017	1.5846	1.6279

around this hashtag. High trust in the small @brettschneiderc and @axios-centered community may or may not imply trust in these sources of news and opinion.

- All communities were more fearful than the full network, but without clear patterns based on ban support or opposition, e.g., both the #tcot and #democrats-centered communities were more fearful than average. This speaks to the cross-stance interaction and engagement referenced above; e.g. those engaging from the opposing side may bring fear to posts and discussions under #tcot.
- High anticipation was seen in the #voteblue and #tcot communities, and low anticipation in the @hvonspakovsky-centered community; in comparison, expressions of surprise were low in most communities and especially among ban supporters and conservatives. Greater surprise in the small @axios and @brettschneiderc-centered community may be due to the topic of birthright citizenship inducing uncertainty, based on Plutchik's (1980) wheel of emotions.
- Negative and positive sentiment was seen across the sample, with the most negativity in the #voteblue community and the most positivity in the conservative, ban-supporting communities around @marcorubio, @seanhannity, and @andrewcmccarthy, possibly relating to favorable perceptions of these central actors.
- Findings for the sentiments of disgust and anger did not vary as significantly across the communities (as seen in their lack of highlighting or emphasis in Table 8).

Table 8. Sentiment scores in each identified community.

	@realdonaldtrump	#birthrightcitizenship	#voteblue	@hvonspakovsky	#tcot
Sample size (n)	563	242	119	89	59
Joy	0.9718	0.9833	1.1650	0.9225	1.1833
Sadness	0.8727	0.6916	1.0003	1.0682	0.6887
Trust	2.2338	2.5862	2.2459	2.3787	2.2243
Disgust	0.6772	0.5206	0.5832	0.7322	0.5353
Fear	1.2359	1.0213	1.1692	1.1315	1.3147
Anger	1.0985	0.8981	1.2986	1.1633	0.9158
Anticipation	1.1207	1.1282	1.2854	0.9273	1.2452
Surprise	0.7079	0.7538	1.0210	0.5206	0.7116
Positive	3.5533	3.7421	3.8429	3.6397	3.6195
Negative	1.9276	1.5199	2.2874	1.9708	2.0085

	@marcorubio	@breitbartnews	@seanhannity & @andrewcmccarthy	#democrats	@brettschniederc & @axios
Sample size (n)	63	61	62	43	16
Joy	1.1230	1.0377	0.9808	0.8663	1.0719
Sadness	0.5939	0.6251	0.7483	0.8779	1.1406
Trust	2.3995	2.3470	2.3178	1.6705	2.7281
Disgust	0.6098	0.5404	0.6838	0.6240	0.5469
Fear	1.0026	1.1055	1.2631	1.3295	1.5719
Anger	0.9220	0.8104	1.2308	0.9496	1.1094
Anticipation	0.9630	1.0377	1.1014	1.0795	1.0875
Surprise	0.5423	0.5899	0.5198	0.9612	1.5469
Positive	4.4405	3.6527	4.6830	2.4922	4.2750
Negative	1.9854	1.6115	2.0440	1.9147	1.9063

5 Discussion

When analyzed from the lens of the social identity theory (Tajfel and Turner 1979), the patterns of information behavior relating to this case of #birthrightcitizenship Twitter speech acts suggest that user identity, emotions, and relationships bolstered social categorization, social identification, and social comparison.

5.1 Social Categorization

Distinct boundaries were drawn around concepts of "the insider" as the native-born and/or versus "the outsider" as the non-native intruder. Ideas of exclusivity and inclusivity determined whether users rejected or accepted the notion of birthright citizenship. These delineations were then expressed through contrasting information sharing and speech acts. Despite nearly proportionate representation among supporting and opposing groups, speech acts among ban supporters demonstrated a feedback loop with nearly double the number of retweets ($n = 13{,}661$) and three times as many favorites ($n = 31{,}547$) than opponents ($n = 5{,}047$ and $n = 12{,}308$, respectively). Network analysis of users further displayed that speech acts among supporters utilized hashtags more frequently. This tagging or sharing of content is indicative of reinforcing communicative behavior, further evidenced by there being six times as many actors with a large number ($>10{,}000$) of followers ($n = 85$) among ban supporters compared with ban opponents ($n = 14$).

The repetitive nature of speech acts sheds light on how sentiment, emotion and immigration views culminate in the types of outcry or protest that are characteristic of political exchanges that, in turn, strengthen group categorization. This dynamic perhaps established a sense of anti-immigration community-building. Based on network details, ban supporters were more prominent in this particular Twitter immigration debate. Highly concentrated and remarkably organized network patterns demonstrate the effect of former President Trump's original tweet, which appeared to coalesce in-group identity or pro-U.S., anti-immigration sameness. It follows, then, that ban supporters comprised the largest communities. These patterns reify Schildkraut's (2007) argument that "Americanism" as a tenant influences public opinion toward immigration. It is also reminiscent of Citrin and Wright's (2009) argument that the pride of being American shapes public preferences regarding how many and what kinds of immigrants should reside in the U.S.

The prominence of ban supporters in the overall network suggests that speech acts revolved around hardline immigration rhetoric. Analysis of summary network statistics display high measures of nodes and degree centrality within the ban supporter subnetwork, which points to greater numbers of mentions and activity among this group. On the other hand, ban opponents garnered around the perceived hypocrisy of altering a U.S. Constitutional tenet. Traditionally, conservative groups reject wavering from or reinterpreting the U.S. Constitution. Ban opponents, therefore, raised concerns regarding the duplicity of suggesting a revision of the 14th Amendment. Ban supporters were more apt to use the hashtag #birthrightcitizenship and share media content that explained what they believed to be the original, constitutional intent of the birthright citizenship, as seen in this tweet:

Great video! Arm yourself with the truth at [link] - search Birthright Citizenship and 14th Amendment for [...]. Hint: The Left likes to leave one phrase out of the #14thAmendment that makes all the difference. Don't be spun! #birthrightcitizenship

Ban opponents responded with hashtags such as #resist (a top 10 hashtag) and #14thamendment. The central focus among the latter group was the idea that positions on reinterpreting the Constitution shifted to suit political purposes, as seen in this tweet:

So let me get this straight. The #Republicans are ok with #Trump changing the #14thamendment because they dislike the #Latinos but refuse to change the 2nd amendment because they love their guns right? Guns more important than people huh? #VoteDem #PleaseVote

5.2 Social Identification

Identity-formation around national origins and ideas of "authentic" American selfhood made up a portion of the information behavior among birthright ban supporters. This cross-section is where actors tended to use insensitive language or slurs such as "anchor baby," "illegals," and "wetback." Expressions of emotion were more clearly delineated and, therefore, provided some evidence of how users self-identified from a political standpoint. Several sentiment patterns—for example, higher levels of joy among ban supporters—point to the possibility that a proposed birthright citizenship ban induces gratification. This same gratification might be associated with perceptions of "winning" the Twitter argument, which, again, reinforces an in-group and out-group binary. In this regard, the findings echo Citrin, Reingold and Green's (1990) pre-social media arguments that normative beliefs of national identity influence the mass public's reactions to the changing ethnic composition of U.S. society.

Each group expressed high levels of fear as seen in mirroring spikes in the fear sentiment. Fear appeared to catalyze both the ban-supporting and ban-opposing groups and was linked to a substantial proportion of network behavior. There may be two plausible explanations: fear of social exclusion drove speech acts among ban opponents. Fear of the threat of intrusion might have similarly mobilized ban supporters. Tangential to this, trust was low and sadness high among opponents, who may have experienced difficulty placing confidence and feeling hopeful in political systems. In the same vein, generally low expressions of surprise among both groups might depict that the #birthrightcitizenship case represents the type of immigration debates that have become normalized in the national arena.

There were also clear parallels between how the two groups referred to themselves and their counterparts; #voteblue or #votedem was utilized by ban opponents to represent the largely liberal affiliation while the same group was pejoratively referred to as simply #democrats by ban supporters. Conversely, #tcot was utilized by ban supporters to describe the predominantly conservative affiliation among its users while #Republicans was applied as a pejorative term by the rival group. Tajfel and Turner (1979) posit that categorization relies on scrutiny of non-members. A method of social identification was thus the use of formal naming of counterparts—or, perhaps, the co-opting of critics' hashtags—along with more informal naming of the self. Sentiments matched up with these distinctions.

5.3 Social Comparison

Tajfel and Turner's (1979) interpretation of social identity suggests that group comparison can also be seen as a predisposition toward self-segregation. Herein, we uncovered unexpected and even counterintuitive results. Despite polarization, overlays of both sentiment and network support that both groups depended on similar language or lexicon. Furthermore, both supporters and opponents exchanged with key figures on opposing sides; actors demonstrated considerable interaction with counterparts, as shown by the full network visualization as well as use of #democrats by ban supporters and, at the same time, tweets directed at, for example, @seanhannity and @andrewcmccarthy by ban opponents. Analysis of the top network bigram and trigrams demonstrated that key figures such as @anncoulter, @donaldtrump, and @marcorubio appeared in both networks. As ban supporters reinforced anti-immigration sentiment, ban opponents directly responded, as is demonstrated by the considerable overlap in language classification. The following retweet is one such example:

> *You are a citizen only because of the 14th Amendment, Marco. You'd have been ineligible to run for president without it. RT @marcorubio: History will remember this as the week liberal politicians & legal "scholars" transformed into constitution originalists ...well at least as it relates to the 14th Amendment.*

In other words, granular data demonstrates echo chambers, but network visualizations along with sentiment overlays depict intercommunication between the groups. Ban supporters, for example, deferred to figureheads and community-vetted resources. Yet, on a grand scale, there was distinct traffic across communities. This trend might depict that, despite extreme political polarization especially around the issue of immigration, differing ideological groups interact with rather than retreat from their critics. Stated differently, affective and philosophical polarization does not equate to communication avoidance, to borrow from Wojcieszak and Garrett (2018). Social identity may influence political polarization among Twitter users, but it does not necessarily result in avoidance of or disengagement from those with contrasting viewpoints.

5.4 Use of Sentiment and Network Analysis

The specific tool used in this study combined four sentiment dictionaries conceptualized as a wheel of four opposite pairs: joy vs. sadness, trust vs. disgust, fear vs. anger, and anticipation vs. surprise. However, these dichotomies were not as precise as might be expected. For example, the #voteblue, @seanhannity and @andrewcmccarthy communities were the most angry, but the @breitbartnews community was the least angry and expressed considerable joy. Users in these groups are expected to display similar information behaviors and political expressions. Nonetheless, we cannot say that there is a uniform propensity toward anger among communities that expressed high degrees of stance polarity in the direction of support of a birthright citizenship ban or conservative political sentiment. Similarly, the data did not support great polarity when it came to the juxtaposed emotions of disgust and trust; degrees of trust and disgust were flat across the network, regardless of stance toward the ban. When it comes to trust, even the highest value in the @hvonspakovsky community is rather low. In a related example, some communities expressed a mixture of binary emotions; for example, the #voteblue community demonstrated substantial levels of both sadness and joy which, according to the wheel of emotions, might suggest that these users approach the #birthrightcitizenship argument with both resolve and discomfort. These varying emotions perhaps tell us that the affective motivations behind political speech acts might not always be fixed as is suggested by Plutchik's (1980) wheel of emotions. As a result, sentiment analysis is a promising but imperfect analytical tool in that users often behave in nonlinear, noncategorical ways.

Similarly, the network analysis revealed relationships among Twitter users can oscillate, which departs from how political polarization and speech acts surrounding immigration are typically understood. We focused on the interaction network among Twitter users' hashtags, keywords, or mentions, as seen previously in studies of news and political events, but findings here showed generally looser ties, greater dispersion, and unclear perimeters than in prior work. Given the deepening political divide in the U.S. and elsewhere, one might expect those for and against the proposed birthright citizenship ban to interact mostly with like-minded users, forming staunchly segregated communities. Modularity analysis and other network analysis tools allowed us to test whether this was actually true. We posit that users' associations and networks can be irregular even where political identification is consistent.

6 Conclusion

This exploratory information behavior study on former President Trump's suggested birthright citizenship ban and subsequent #birthrightcitizenship Twitter speech acts demonstrates that immigration-related speech acts can be at once predictable in terms of rhetoric yet nuanced when it comes to affect and inter-group engagement. The data indicate that there are more similarities than differences regarding Twitter-based speech acts among supporters and opponents of the suggested birthright citizenship ban. Primarily, pro- and anti-immigration communities draw upon the same emotions and sentiments. Findings support that social identity shapes methods of information sharing and types of shared resources, specifically involving sentiments toward U.S immigration policy. Where there were differences, however, the variance was substantial. These differences were seen in the numbers of users, influence of high-profile users, and retweet or media sharing behaviors.

While the theory of social identity as a driver in political social media use holds on a micro level, macro level data unveiled unexpected patterns. The data is perhaps representative of the United States' complex and rapidly evolving political landscape. As a medium for political expression, Twitter is often perceived as a divisive space or an inhibitor to meaningful interaction. Notwithstanding, given the substantial overlap of communities and lexicon, the social media platform may hold potential for constructive communication on any number of issues, including immigration policy. The prominence of political pundits and other opinion leaders within the Twitter network suggests that such a transformation would need to be driven by key actors or immigration policy decision-makers.

Our study's findings uncover the emotional and relational determinants behind complex sociopolitical ideology that are often reduced to salient groupings of conservatives and liberals, nationalists as opposed to globalists, and traditionalists versus progressives. Based on the data, there can, indeed, exist variance in terms of feelings and social conditioning behind political speech acts. The findings support that, though at times imprecise, speech acts and correlative information behavior (i.e., slogan creation, hashtag use, and content sharing) can be linked to expressions of joy, trust, anticipation, trust, fear, anticipation, sadness, disgust, anger, and surprise. This analysis of how users create communities or associations - that is, networks - can advance what is known about social media's role in civic engagement, political ideology, and notions of American social identity. Speech acts are far from random, isolated incidents and instead underscore how public opinions toward immigration are associated with multifaceted emotions, sentiments, and relationships. This study suggests immigration-related speech acts are based on social categories, characteristics, and comparisons; it thus substantiates the propositions presented in Tajfel and Turner's (1979) social identity theory.

There were several limitations to this study. The inability to pinpoint immigrant actors was an area of weakness. Aside from user biographies, there were typically few clues as to immigrant backgrounds. One approach might be to conduct and compare sentiment and network analysis within another social media platform such as Reddit or Quora. We hope to highlight characteristics of immigrant information behavior and center these communities in future social informatics work.

References

Abbasi, A., Chen, H., Thoms, S., Fu, T.: Affect analysis of web forums and blogs using correlation ensembles. IEEE Trans. Knowl. Data Eng. **20**(9), 1168–1180 (2008)

Agarwal, A.: Tweet archiver – G Suite Marketplace. https://gsuite.google.com/marketplace/app/tweet_archiver/976886281542?pann=cwsdp&hl=en-US. Accessed 25 Apr 2020

Allyn, B.: Stung by Twitter, Trump signs executive order to weaken social media companies. NPR News (2020). https://www.npr.org/2020/05/28/863932758/stung-by-twitter-trump-signs-executive-order-to-weaken-social-media-companies. Accessed 12 Sep 2021

Arnaboldi, V., Passarella, A., Conti, M., Dunbar, R.: Structure of ego-alter relationships of politicians in Twitter. J. Comput.-Medicated Commun. **22**(5), 231–247 (2017)

Ausserhofer, J., Maireder, A.: National politics on Twitter: structures and topics of a networked public sphere. Inf. Commun. Soc. **16**(3), 291–314 (2013)

Austin, J.L.: How to Do Things with Words. Oxford University Press, Oxford, UK (1962)

Bennett, L.: Transformations through Twitter: the England riots, television viewership and negotiations of power through media convergence. Participations Int. J. Audience Reception Stud. **9**(2), 511–525 (2012)

Block, P.: Community: the structure of belonging. Berrett-Koehler, Oakland, CA (2018)

Blondel, V.D., Guillaume, J.-L., Lambiotte, R., Lefebvre, E.: Fast unfolding of communities in large networks. J. Stat. Mech: Theory Exp. **10**, P10008 (2008)

Bonnici, L., Ma, J.: What are they saying? a speech act analysis of a vaccination information debate on Facebook. Canadian J. Inf. Library Sci. **44**(1), 19–37 (2021)

Borge-Holthoefer, J., Magdy, W., Darwish, K., Weber, I.: Content and network dynamics behind Egyptian political polarization on Twitter. In: Proceedings of the 18th ACM Conference on Computer Supported Cooperative Work and Social Computing (CSCW 2015), pp. 700–711. ACM, New York, NY (2015)

Bruns, A., Burgess, J.: Researching news discussion on Twitter: new methodologies. J. Stud. **13**(5), 801–814 (2012)

Buchanan, E.A.: Internet research ethics: past, present, and future. In: Consalvo, M., Ess, C. (eds.) The Handbook of Internet Studies, pp. 83–108. Blackwell, New York, NY (2011)

Byrne, J., Dixon, G.C.: Reevaluating American attitudes toward immigrants in the twenty-first century: the role of a multicreedal national identity. Politics Policy **41**(1), 83–116 (2013)

Citrin, J., Reingold, B., Green, D.P.: American identity and the politics of ethnic change. J. Politics **52**(4), 1124–1154 (1990)

Citrin, J., Wright, M.: Defining the circle of we: American identity and immigration policy. Forum **7**(3) (2009)

Conover, M.D., Gonçalves, B., Ratkiewicz, J., Flammini, A., Menczer, F.: Predicting the political alignment of Twitter users. In: Proceedings of 2011 IEEE Third International Conference on Privacy, Security, Risk, and Trust and 2011 IEEE Third International Conference on Social Computing, pp. 192–199. IEEE, Piscataway, NJ (2011)

De Choudhury, M., Monroy-Hernandez, A., Mack, G.: Narco emotions: affect and desensitization in social media during the Mexican drug war. In: Proceedings of the 32nd annual ACM conference on Human Factors in Computing Systems (CHI 2014), pp. 3563–3572. ACM, New York, NY (2014)

Dowdskin, E.: Twitter's decision to label Trump's tweets was two years in the making. Washington Post, 29 May 2020. https://www.washingtonpost.com/technology/2020/05/29/inside-twitter-trump-label/. Accessed 29 May 2020

Glaser, J., Salovey, P.: Affect in electoral politics. Pers. Soc. Psychol. Rev. **2**(3), 156–172 (1998)

Gounari, P.: Authoritariamism, discourse and social media: trump as the 'American agitator.' In: Morelock, J. (ed.) Critical Theory and Authoritarian Populism, pp. 207–227. University of Westminster Press, London, UK (2018)

Grover, P., Kar, A., Yogesh, D., Janssen, M.: Polarization and acculturation in US Election 2016 outcomes: can Twitter analytics predict changes in voting preferences? Technol. Forecast. Soc. Chang. **145**, 438–460 (2019)

Hands, J.: @ is for Activism: Dissent, Resistance, and Rebellion in a Digital Culture. Pluto Press, New York, NY (2011)

Henttonen, P.: Looking at archival concepts and practice in the light of speech act theory. Archival Multiverse **57**, 328–344 (1994)

Himelboim, I., Smith, M.A., Rainie, L., Schneiderman, B., Espina, C.: Classifying Twitter topic-networks using social media analysis. Soc. Media and Soc. **3**(1), 2056305117691545 (2017)

Himelboim, I., Sweetser, K.D., Tinkham, S.F., Cameron, K., Danelo, M., West, K.: Valence-based homophily on Twitter: network analysis of emotions and political talk in the 2012 presidential election. New Media Soc. **18**(7), 1382–1400 (2016)

Hogan, J., Haltinner, K.: Floods, invaders, and parasites: immigration threat narratives and right-wing populism in the USA, UK, and Australia. J. Intercult. Stud. **36**(5), 520–542 (2015)

Johannesson, P.: Representation and communication: a speech act based approach to information systems design. Inf. Syst. **20**(4), 291–303 (1995)

Jockers, M.L., Underwood, T.: Text-mining the humanities. In: Schreibman, S., Siemens, R., Unsworth, J. (eds.) A New Companion to Digital Humanities, pp. 291–206. Wiley, New York, NY (2015)

Kries, R.: The "tweet politics" of President Trump. J. Lang. Politics **16**(4), 607–618 (2017)
Khonsari, K.K., Nayeri, Z.A., Fathalian, A., Fathalian, L.: Social network analysis of Iran's Green movement opposition groups using Twitter. In: 2010 IEEE international conference on Advances in Social Networks Analysis and Mining, pp. 414–415. IEEE, Piscataway, NJ (2010)
Li, H., Dombrowski, L, Brady, E.: Working toward empowering a community: How immigrant-focused nonprofit organizations use Twitter during political conflicts. In: Proceedings of the 2018 ACM conference on supporting groupwork (GROUP 2018), pp. 335–346. ACM, New York, NY (2018)
Martin, S.W., Brown, M., Klavans, R., Boyack, K.W.: OpenOrd: an open-source toolbox for large graph layout. In: Wong, P.C., et al. (eds.) Visualization and Data Analysis 2011, vol. 7868 (IS&T/SPIE Electronic Imaging). International Society for Optics and Photonics, New York, NY (2011)
Mendes, A.E.: Digital demagogue: the critical candidacy of Donald. J. Trump. J. Contemporary Rhetoric **6**(3/4), 62–73 (2016)
Ott, B.L.: The age of Twitter: Donald J. Trump and the politics of debasement. Critical Stud. Media Commun. **34**(1), 59–68 (2017)
Plutchik, R.: A general psychoevolutionary theory of emotion. In: Plutchik, R., Kellerman, H. (eds.) Theories of Emotion, pp. 3–33. Academic Press, New York, NY (1980)
Piryani, R., Madhavi, D., Singh, V.K.: Analytical mapping of opinion mining and sentiment analysis research during 2000–2015. Inf. Process. Manage. **53**(1), 122–150 (2017)
Restad, H.E.: What makes America great? Donald Trump, national identity, and US foreign policy. Global Affairs **6**(1), 21–36 (2020)
Robertson, L., Farley, R., Rieder, R.: Trump tweets flagged by Twitter for misinformation. FactCheck.org (2020), https://www.factcheck.org/2020/11/trump-tweets-flagged-by-twitter-for-misinformation/. Accessed 12 Sep 2021
Schildkraut, D.J.: Defining American identity in the twenty-first century: how much "there" is there? J. Politics **69**(3), 597–615 (2007)
Searle, J.R.: Speech Acts: An Essay in the Philosophy of Language. Cambridge University Press, Cambridge, UK (1969)
Segesten, A., Bossetta, M.: A typology of political participation online: how citizens used Twitter to mobilize during the 2015 British general elections. Inf. Commun. Soc. **20**(11), 1625–1643 (2017)
Sobkowicz, P., Sobkowicz, A.: Dynamics of hate-based Internet user networks. Eur. Phys. J. **73**(4), 633–643 (2010)
Sobkowicz, P., Sobkowicz, A.: Properties of social network in an Internet political discussion forum. Adv. Complex Syst. **15**(6), 1250062 (2012)
Swan, J., Kight, S.W.: Exclusive: trump targeting birthright citizenship with executive order. Axios on HBO (2018), https://www.axios.com/trump-birthright-citizenship-executive-order-0cf4285a-16c6-48f2-a933-bd71fd72ea82.html. Accessed 18 Oct 2019
Tajfel, H., Turner, J.C.: An integrative theory of intergroup conflict. In: Hatch, M.J., Schultz, M. (eds.) Organizational Identity: A Reader, pp. 56–65. Oxford University Press, Oxford, UK (1979)
Tremayne, M.: Anatomy of protest in the digital era: a network analysis of Twitter and Occupy Wall Street. Soc. Mov. Stud. **13**(1), 110–126 (2014)
Trump, D.J.: Donald Trump August 2019 Ohio political rally speech: Transcript, https://www.rev.com/blog/donald-trump-ohio-rally-speech-transcript-full-transcript-of-august-1-2019-rally-in-cincinnati. Accessed 13 Sep 2019
Tumasjan, A., Sprenger, T.O., Sandner, P.G., Welpe, I.M.: Predicting elections with Twitter: What 140 characters reveal about political sentiment. In: Fourth international AAAI conference on Weblogs and Social Media (ICWSM 2010), pp. 178–185. AAAI Press, Palo Alto, CA (2010)

Varnali, K., Gorgulu, V.: A social influence perspective on expressive political participation in Twitter: the case of #OccupyGezi. Inf. Commun. Soc. **18**(1), 1–16 (2015)

Wood, W.: Attitude change: persuasion and social influence. Annu. Rev. Psychol. **51**, 539–570 (2000)

Wojcieszak, M., Garrett, R.K.: Social identity, selective exposure, and affective polarization: how priming national identity shapes attitudes toward immigrants via news selection. Hum. Commun. Res. **44**(3), 247–273 (2018)

Understanding Information and Communication Opportunities and Challenges for Rural Women Through the Sustainable Livelihood Framework

Monisha Biswas(✉), Misita Anwar, Larry Stillman, and Gillian Oliver

Faculty of Information Technology, Monash University, Melbourne, Australia
{monisha.biswas,misita.anwar,larry.stillman,
gillian.oliver}@monash.edu

Abstract. The inclusion of marginalized women remains a challenging issue in ICT-based development interventions. Rural poor, particularly women in Bangladesh, may not realize information-related benefits from digital technologies. This is due to multifaceted challenges such as poverty, inequality, inadequate infrastructure, lack of information and education, and restraining social factors like patriarchy. Using the SLF [5, 10], smartphone applications' impact on rural Bangladeshi women farmers' lives was examined in this study. We found that smartphone access acted as a vehicle to improving information access and communication opportunities, reducing rural women's vulnerabilities, thus improving livelihoods, facilitating better access to agricultural extension services and local markets, and promoting women's agency [22]. Using the SLF lens, our insight offers designing insight to understand barriers to information and communication opportunities for rural women in developing contexts.

Keywords: Mobile phone · ICT4D · Information access · Women's agency · SLF

1 Introduction

The concept of Information and Communication Technology for Development (ICT4D) has been a focus of debate because of its broad coverage and significant intensity of impact in the international development process [15–17]. More recently, attention has shifted to such issues as social inclusion, sustainable development and the impact of ICT4D to match the changing international development context [12, 17, 36].

The use of mobile technology, particularly by rural women in development contexts, has also emerged as a much-discussed research topic in the ICT4D literature [7, 14]. However, despite the rapid growth of mobile technologies, scholars have argued that systemic poverty, inequality, and the exclusion of marginalized women's issues in the post-2015 development agenda continue to remain significant in understanding complex development dynamics [7, 14–17, 36].

While this socio-technical change has been occurring, the Sustainable Livelihood Framework (SLF) has been widely applied in development interventions by leading international Non-Governmental Organizations (NGOs) such as the Cooperative for Assistance and Relief Everywhere (CARE) and Oxfam [33]. The SLF is relevant because

M. Smits (Ed.): iConference 2022, LNCS 13193, pp. 175–191, 2022.
https://doi.org/10.1007/978-3-030-96960-8_12

it helps to address the linkages between contextual vulnerability, societal structure, institutional processes, livelihood strategies, and outcomes for marginalized communities. In Bangladesh, the SLF has been used by international, national and local NGOs, government institutions, UN agencies, and other bilateral donors. Thus, because of the increasing importance of ICTs, there is scope to theorize further the ICT4D interventions concepts for strategic policy advocacy and sustained impact.

The paper examines the case of a group of marginalized rural women farmers and maize micro-entrepreneurs from Bangladesh and explains the role of smartphone applications as an empowering communication and information vehicle. Findings highlight structural changes brought about by smartphones to rural women's communication and information practices and their relationship to the livelihood elements of the SLF. This empirical research in Bangladesh provides insights for designing similar ICT4D projects in other developing contexts.

The paper begins by discussing the related literature. This is followed by an explanation of the core elements and relevance of the SLF as a conceptual model. The subsequent section outlines the research methodology and describes the comprehensive data collection and analysis process. The following sections present the findings, discussion, and provide future research suggestions. Finally, the paper concludes by highlighting the relevance of SLF in understanding the importance of information and communication opportunities and challenges for rural women's empowerment.

2 Related Literature

2.1 Mobile Phone and Women's Agency in Emerging Economies

Given the current rapid growth of mobile technology, ICT4D research needs to address the relationship of ICTs to complex multidimensional issues in international development [14, 16]. Furthermore, because of their relatively low cost, portability, and simplicity, mobile-based technology and mobile phones have become prominent tools for information and communication compared to other ICT devices, such as desktops and laptops [17, 36].

Accordingly, multidisciplinary research incorporating insights from sociology and ICT is conducted to understand the ICT4D change process, mainly in developing contexts in Africa and Asia, focusing on mobile phone-based development interventions [21, 26].

Understanding ICT4D intervention trends in developing country contexts are essential [14, 17, 30]. However, many developing countries struggle because of gaps in policy and practical challenges relating to rural communities' uptake [7, 29]. For example, rural women in Bangladesh still face issues with availability and access to smartphones due to cultural and other factors [2]. Therefore, a deeper understanding of relationships between rural women's communication and information processes that occur via mobile phones in women's cultural and related contexts helps develop strategies to minimize the digital divide, and promote inclusive, sustainable development agendas.

Several studies have shown a positive correlation between ICT4D interventions (including mobile technology, e-inclusion, enterprise growth) and women's empowerment in promoting their agencies [4, 19, 21, 26, 34]. For example, researchers have noted a positive correlation between mobile phones and improvement in income level, housing conditions, living standards, awareness about health, agriculture and an overall improvement in rural women's lives in Bangladesh [31, 35]. For example, mobile phones can improve the living standards of rural women because there is a direct connection of mobile phone use in managing information flow, financial transaction processes, and better financial inclusion, such as 'bKash' mobile banking services in Bangladesh [20]. Similar studies of 'M-Pesa' in Kenya show the relevance of mobile money transfers for financial inclusion and business growth [25, 26].

However, only a few studies have analyzed the correlation between mobile phone applications, availability of information, growth of micro-enterprises [1, 4, 23], and the results vary from one to another. For example, a survey in Uganda shows how mobile phone usage can facilitate a positive change in the entrepreneurial ability of women by increasing their ability to handle emergencies, reducing transactional and trading costs, and minimizing risk factors [23]. However, at the same time, the survey indicates that a mobile phone may increase the domestic care work burden, and it may even increase domestic violence in some cases. Furthermore, there is no standard definition of micro-enterprise, and the numbers of employees may vary depending on the size and nature of the enterprise [9].

Research also shows that mobile phones can strengthen social capital in addition to business networks [1, 3, 7]. For example, research in Indonesia suggests that mobile phones provide the means to enhance social capital and resources for business activities; hence, they are counted as crucial resource capabilities for women entrepreneurs [1]. However, previous research also observed the blurred boundary between the business and personal use of mobile phones [8]. For example, rural women in Bangladesh use mobile phones for economic activities and maintain family relationships with improved social interaction [2].

Similarly, researchers have noted a gender dimension to women's access to mobile phones that reduces expected benefits [7, 11, 34]. Compared to men, women have less opportunity to use mobile phones because of social norms. Though mobile phones were considered a means to improve livelihood opportunities for women micro-entrepreneurs, in places like India, such a technological intervention could not address the broader social divisions within a society [6]. This body of research shows that while women's use of mobile phones is enhancing women's livelihoods and wellbeing, there remain structural, cultural, personal safety and labour inequality issues that limit opportunity for women.

2.2 SLF and International Development

Since 1990, the SLF has become a widely used development approach in Africa, Asia, South America, Central and Eastern Europe adopted by international development agencies and NGOs such as Oxfam, CARE, the UK's Department for International Development (DFID) and the United Nations Development Program (UNDP) [33]. The SLF approach was initiated by Robert Chambers [5], a leading development researcher and theorist. He advocated for the SLF as a practical development model for the 21st century and defined the concept by adapting the World Commission on Environment and Development panel definition. The major elements of this framework include contextual analysis focusing on vulnerability, shocks, seasonality, different types of assets, such as physical, social, natural; the role of different institutions and stakeholders, such as governments and markets; livelihood strategies and outcomes.

The definition of livelihood in the framework is as follows [5, p. 6]:

A livelihood comprises the capabilities, assets (stores, resources, claims and access) and activities required for a means of living: a livelihood is sustainable which can cope with and recover from stress and shocks, maintain or enhance its capabilities and assets, and provide sustainable livelihood opportunities for the next generation; and which contributes net benefits to other livelihoods at the local and global levels and in the short and long term.

As a generic development program design tool developed before the ICT4D trend in international development, the SLF did not pay sufficient attention to broader macro-economic and political issues relevant to ICT4D interventions [10, 27]. Furthermore, a limitation of the current form of SLF is its lack of theoretical alignment with any development or socio-technical theory [33]. Consequently, there is room for academic researchers to apply this model for ICT4D research and theory development [10, 33] and offer practical design direction to development practitioners [27, 33].

3 SLF as a Conceptual Model

This paper offers critical insights into the significance of various social factors (communication and information culture and practice, power, class, gender and social capital) in designing socio-technical projects focusing on women's empowerment and other mobile-based development interventions in Bangladesh.

As discussed above, previous research suggested an improved scope for theoretical development of the SLF approach to use it as a tool to understand the role of ICT in reducing the vulnerability of rural poor to social and economic challenges [10, 33]. Researchers also emphasized the importance of in-depth empirical analysis to make the SLF a more robust tool.

We applied the SLF as a conceptual model to review the nature of vulnerabilities faced by rural women, their connection with social and economic structures, gender relationships within family and society to understand the role of smartphones in promoting women's agency.

As shown in Fig. 1 below, the main elements of the SLF are: a) Vulnerabilities, b) Assets, c) Societal Structures and Processes, d) Livelihood Strategies, e) Livelihood Outcomes [18, p. 41]. These elements are briefly explained here:

- Vulnerabilities: contextual vulnerability refers to the external factors that may affect people's livelihood and wellbeing. These may include natural disasters (e.g. flood and cyclone), trends (e.g. migration, financial crisis, COVID-19) or seasonality (e.g. food price hike).
- Assets: five types of assets are identified, namely financial capital, physical capital, social capital, human capital, and natural capital. Remittances, wages, mobile banking, micro-finance savings and credit are examples of financial capital. Physical capital may include housing or infrastructure, information and communication technology

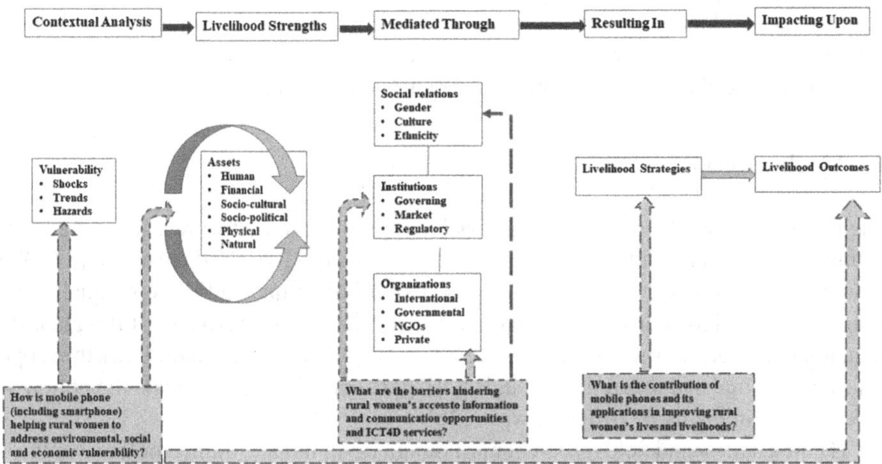

Fig. 1. Sustainable Livelihood Framework Adapted from Duncombe [10, p. 84]:

and tools, energy and transport. Social capital may include relationships within the community, collective effort and networking. Education, knowledge and skills, and health are examples of human capital. Land, water and aquatic resources, forests, wildlife are examples of natural capital.

- Structures: For example, different institutions and organizations from the public, private and NGO sectors, legal and financial mechanisms.
- Social Processes: processes include decision making and gendered social, cultural norms.
- Livelihood Strategies: livelihood strategies refer to both long term and short-term strategies. These may include forming a micro-enterprise group and networking with extension service providers.
- Livelihood Outcomes: livelihood outcomes refer to better wellbeing. This can be associated with more income, improved food security, better access to information and technology.

This conceptual model invites us to analyze and understand different aspects of a societal change process. Therefore, we considered the elements of SLF while examining the role of smartphone application-led interventions in rural Bangladesh. As a result, as shown in Fig. 1, three questions were addressed.

- How are smartphones helping rural women to address environmental, social and economic vulnerability? This question aids in understanding vulnerability in contexts, rural women's capabilities, livelihood strategies and outcomes.
- What is the contribution of smartphones and their applications in improving rural women's lives and livelihoods? This question relates to understanding livelihood assets and livelihood strategies.

- What barriers hinder rural women's access to information and communication opportunities and ICT4D services? This question explores social relations and social structures and the role of different institutions and stakeholders.

4 Methodology

The research adopted a qualitative approach within the interpretive research paradigm, noting the importance of the interpretive case study method in ICT4D research [37]. We followed the exploratory case study method exploring unique and in-depth qualitative insights [28, 37] based on empirical data collected from the northern part of Bangladesh. A qualitative interpretive case study is relevant to ICT4D research as it provides the scope to test conceptual and theoretical models [28], generate nuance, and tackle the notion of development in distinctly different ways [36].

The first author and field researcher is a Bangladeshi female, trained in social anthropology in Bangladesh and advanced ICT research methods from Monash University. Because of her experience in NGO management and fieldwork with village communities, she understands rural development and the national policy contexts in Bangladesh. During the data collection and analysis, she was conscious of unequal gender and patriarchal perception, hierarchy and power structure that exists within rural communities and between the communities and outsiders. She built rapport through informal communication before engaging in the formal data collection process. Language and basic understanding of local culture enabled her to ask follow-up questions to develop meaningful insights from interviews and focus group discussions. Considering possible effects on relationships between the researcher and research participants and noting the influence of the local NGOs and openness to overall information-sharing behaviour in the community, she compared and verified responses from different categories of research participants and used her field observation notes. Other authors with different national backgrounds contributed outsiders' perspectives to data interpretation and thematic analysis [32]. The research received ethics approval from the Monash University research committee, and informed consent from local communities was obtained.

4.1 Research Participants

Participants were rural farmers, maize producers involved in the PROTIC[1] project, and local service providers in Nilphamari Upazilla[2] (located in the northern sandy island region and identified as one of the most poverty prone and geographically vulnerable areas of Bangladesh [31]). A total of 100 marginalized rural women farmers received smartphones, online and phone information services and training through PolliSree (a local NGO) as part of PROTIC. The action research project was implemented by Monash University in conjunction with Oxfam, an international NGO. Some women also acted as maize entrepreneurs with financial and mobile application skills, collecting maize from farmers and selling them to maize wholesalers in the local market.

1 Participatory Research and Ownership with Technology, Information and Change (PROTIC) is an ICT4D action research project.

2 An Upazilla refers to a lower level administrative unit in Bangladesh.

Research participants were selected using the purposive sampling technique, following a set of criteria developed by the first author and modified in consultation with PolliSree (which had trusted relationships with the rural women and local service providers).

The main selection criteria were leadership quality, living conditions, knowledge of mobile application use in agricultural production, and entrepreneurial activities. Data collection started with focus group discussions with rural women farmers, entrepreneurs, and their husbands. Then, based on the field researcher's observations, the most articulate and successful rural women were approached for in-depth interviews to understand the local situation better. Finally, local service provider participants were identified based on their roles, availability, knowledge and relationships with rural producers and entrepreneurs.

Table 1. Research participants

Data Collection Techniques/ Participant Category	Interview	Focus Group 1	Focus Group 2
Women farmers and entrepreneurs	7	8	8
Local service providers	15	–	–
Women entrepreneurs' husbands	–	3	–
Total research participants	**22**	**11**	**8**

Table 1 shows that in total 22 research participants took part in semi-structured in-depth interviews while 19 participated in two focus group discussions. Three women farmers interviewed also took part in the focus groups. Three male farmers were included in one focus group with their wives supporting maize production and involved in the collective maize microenterprise ventures to learn their perspectives. In addition, 15 local service providers (including agriculture extension service providers, ICT4D service providers, NGO workers and maize wholesalers from the local market) were interviewed as part of the maize farming ecosystems at the village level. Comparison of responses from women farmers and entrepreneurs, particularly on vulnerability, livelihood strategy and outcomes while using smartphones provided more nuanced insight.

4.2 Data Collection and Analysis

Three types of data collection techniques were used: a) in-depth semi-structured interviews, b) focus groups, and c) field observations. The first author of this paper conducted a field visit in the northern part of Bangladesh from April to September 2019 to collect empirical data. The Otter and Voice Recorder apps on smartphones were used to record the interview and focus group data. Special attention was given to observe: seasonality in agricultural production; daily agricultural activities performed by rural men and women farmers; household roles played by rural women; women's relationship and status within family, community, market and local power structures. Before and after conducting individual interviews, interpersonal communication amongst women farmers with their family members, including husband and in-laws, was observed to better understand family dynamics and power relations.

Interview questions for the semi-structured interviews and checklists for focus groups with the rural female, male farmers and entrepreneurs were translated to Bangla to ensure comprehensible communication and high-quality data collection. During the key informant interviews, research participants responded to the following topics:

- type of mobile device and its applications used in daily life;
- changes in life observed after started using smartphones;
- the types of information and purpose of communication, e.g. interpersonal communication with family and relative, information and learning exchange related communication with social network and community, business communication with seller and buyers;
- challenges faced in using a phone;

While finalizing the questionnaire and checklist, the field researcher had several informal discussions with the local NGO staff to identify the correct terms to use those respondents would understand which would address the essential research concepts. Later meanings of such terms were co-created with research participants during data collection. For example, the concept of women's empowerment (*'narir khamatyan'* in Bangla) meant 'women's power', and 'ICT4D' meant 'advancement (*'unnyan'* in Bangla) with smartphones' in this research context. This initiative created a lively environment leading to a meaningful dialogue between the field researcher and research participants.

NVivo 12 plus was used as a data analysis tool to open data coding at the first phase and thematic coding during the second phase. Additional memos were developed at the data analysis stage to interpret data collected from the fieldwork.

5 Findings

We found that smartphones (including smartphones and its applications) acted as a communication and information enabler that increased women's agency [22]. The smartphone was used to reduce vulnerability related to a disaster, improve livelihood outcomes, and connect women with the local market and local service providers. Overall, it helped to improve women's status. We have organized the findings into three thematic areas illustrating these points.

5.1 Mobile Phone as a Channel for Communication, Information and Consequently a Livelihood Asset and Strategy

The first notable and overarching findings show how access to mobile phones (including smartphones) improved women's wellbeing, including economic, personal, and social elements. Next, this section reports how smartphones were regarded as livelihood assets, and the use of mobile applications became a part of rural women's livelihood strategies.

The majority of the research participants acknowledged the positive impact of mobile technologies in rural women farmers' lives and livelihoods. The women farmers reported that ownership of smartphones made them feel confident, which acted as a gateway to knowledge and subsequent action. Through training provided by the local NGO, they learnt how to use smartphones to look for the relevant information they needed in their day to day life. A woman expressed her confidence with joy:

> *"I know how to use the Google search option and download apps from Google Play!"* R (age 34), farmer

We also found that the rural women groups were not homogenous, and they were using different types of mobile phones and technologies. During a focus group discussion, a woman said:

> *"Some of us have 'button phones'[mobile phones with basic features], and some have 'touch phones' [smartphones] like me."* F (age 31), farmer

Despite the difference in mobile device and technology level, all reported mobile phones as valuable assets.

We noted during a focus group discussion that most rural women mentioned using 10–12 types of standard features on their smartphones despite not having a formal education. They said:

> *"We use many apps, such as Google, Opera Mini, and ShareIt, and so on various [mobile] apps."* focus group 2 participant

Another participant from the other focus group mentioned that smartphones and their applications are associated with their livelihood strategies. She said:

> *"We use [smart]phones for different purposes including agricultural production, communicating with others, and using Facebook. We use different features and apps, such as camera, clock, calendar, calculator, mobile apps for agriculture and education."* focus group 1 participant

From the interviews, it was apparent that the use of smartphones was not limited to essential activities but also for what is often regarded as complementary use, such as entertainment and memory capture. For example:

> *"First of all, we use phones to communicate with others. We also use it for entertainment - we listen to music and songs, watch dramas, capture photos and watch those. We watch cooking shows on YouTube and learn new recipes."* F (age 31), farmer

We found that rural women valued their increased day-to-day interpersonal interactions with family members above other types of communication. During the focus groups and interviews, most women farmers also emphasized their sense of improved connections with family and relatives in neighbouring villages. This was explicit in the case of the husband or other close family members who went to any city within Bangladesh or outside of the country primarily for work purposes. Several women reported that in such cases, they felt connected because of regular communication over smartphones. This positive emotion of being connected is reflected here:

> *"My cousin lives abroad. I can communicate with him through the Imo [mobile app]."* S (age 26), farmer

5.2 Vulnerabilities and Coping Mechanisms with Information Opportunity

We found that rural women entrepreneurs faced multidimensional vulnerabilities and shocks regularly. Natural disasters such as floods and river erosions were challenging their lives and livelihoods. Moreover, uncertain market prices such as sudden price fall or unpredicted illness or death of family members impacted their micro-enterprise operation.

A positive correlation was observed between receiving up-to-date information from the call centre via smartphones; becoming aware of implications of disasters such as flood, or extreme weather information, such as heavy rainfall or fog; getting prepared to take appropriate actions to nurture their agricultural production, and sharing updated knowledge with neighbours and extended family members in the locality.

a) Disaster Preparedness

We observed that smartphone access allowed rural women to address their information and communication needs when traditional cultural boundaries limit physical mobility. For example, some women farmers were exceptionally skilled in learning and sharing disaster preparedness information and became role models in their community while successfully saving their crops or livestock. As a result, others started to depend on them for updated information and followed their agricultural practice for better production. For example, one of the woman farmers explained that several neighbours approached her for information:

> *"Each day, at least ten people come to me to get service. Most of them want to know about the weather update and solve agriculture production-related problems."* F, (age 34), farmer

b) Increased Access to Information and Agricultural Extension Services

Women farmers explained that after receiving smartphones and training, they became aware of the government's available support and services, consequently regularly visiting the local Digital Centre to obtain those services. They checked information from the 'citizen charter' (individual entitlements from the government) and other mobile apps using smartphones. One of the respondents explained the categories of services they access:

> *"We go to the Union Digital Centre [lower level local setup to provide public digital service] on several occasions. For example, to obtain a birth certificate, to collect paper for land disputes, to take passport size photos for passport and visa, to get welfare benefits for widows and elderly people."* F (age 31), maize entrepreneur

We found that smartphones helped them track allocation status to their community and created easy access to those with accurate information. Rural women said that this experience contributed to improving their confidence level. The quote below illustrates one woman, but other women farmers shared the same experience:

"Now I feel confident! I often make phone calls to the 'Union Parishad' [lower level local administrative unit to provide public extension service] members asking for updates on the local safety net [public welfare program] allocated to our village." P (age 26), farmer

Women farmers said that smartphones had saved their time and money to access public extension services for information or arrange visits to their agricultural fields and livestock. Some of them could never do it in the past or depended on male family members to do this for them. In addition, smartphones provided a means for women to navigate the social barrier of communication with male public officials.

c) Access to the Local Market

Both male and female entrepreneurs involved in the maize enterprise considered that smartphones saved time and money. For example, while checking the market price with the retailers and wholesalers, they could compare the prices offered. In addition, smartphones helped them contact other farmers in the locality for maize collection instead of meeting them in person. Smartphones also saved their time and money by fixing appropriate times to collect and deliver bulk maize stock to the wholesalers. However, both categories of research participants mentioned that neither the wholesalers nor the farmers had any negotiation power over the big national companies, the leading player in the maize value chain.

5.3 Barriers Hindering Women's Access to Information, Communication Opportunities and ICT4D Services

We found that rural women faced various kinds of institutional and patriarchal social barriers utilizing their livelihood strategies, such as bureaucracy, uneven societal power structure, and patriarchal mindset. For example, we noted a strong negative gendered perception of women's physical capabilities shared by maize women farmers and wholesalers, as essential tasks involved physical strength, i.e. carrying heavy weights and handling the bulk transfer of production.

One of the maize wholesalers said that often, women would ask their husbands to arrange the maize transportation and delivery. He explained that women's direct communication with people outside their relatives and family was not encouraged.

Thus, because maize wholesalers were male, direct communication between male wholesalers and male farmers instead of female farmers was more acceptable to conform to the social and cultural norms in a patriarchal society. He also mentioned circumstances when women who are not married or widows, in the absence of a male member in the family, communicate with them directly. He said:

"We collect maize directly from the producers. I have regular contacts with 120 maize farmers; most of them are men. Some four-five women are either widowed

or divorced. They work on their own as farmers. Otherwise, women mostly help their husbands in farming. Women do not come here to collect money or fertilizer." A, (age 45), maize wholesaler

In addition, most maize delivery and business transactions were conducted in the evening when women were not supposed to travel, as explained by another maize wholesaler:

"Women cannot work as maize suppliers for us. The delivery of maize and the payment transaction takes place in the evening or night. Women cannot travel at that time, but their husbands can do that. Men are in charge of managing maize collection from small farmers and dealing with financial transactions." K (age 60), maize wholesaler

The rural women micro-entrepreneurs considered smartphones and their applications helpful in addressing the challenge of social constraints on mobility by creating an alternative mechanism of networking with the market and financial institutions. Most research participants noted the overall positive impact of smartphones, which directly contributed to increased networking, improved livelihood outcomes and better social acceptance within society. For example, a young woman entrepreneur mentioned how she balanced the social norms, maintained contact with the local market and managed personal debt. She said:

"I do not need to go to the market to sell my product. This [smart]phone is helping me to communicate with the market, staying at home and earning more. I feel thrilled when I can return money to my father-in-law, which we borrowed a few years back." P (age 26), farmer

6 Discussion

Our discussion is organized in three thematic areas in the following subsections to expand our findings and indicate possible implications.

6.1 Understanding the Communication and Information Affordances via Smartphones as Livelihood Assets and Strategies

We found that the SLF is useful for examining the role of smartphones in reducing vulnerability, connecting rural women with local economic and power structures, institutions and processes. As a result, their vulnerability to environmental and social causes is reduced. Similar findings were also advocated by Duncombe [10].

We found that smartphones and phone applications are acting as significant factors helping to diversify rural women's livelihoods, such as agricultural production and maize enterprise development. Smartphones acted as a vehicle for information access, leading to crucial decisions, such as getting prepared for floods, extreme heat, or heavy rainfalls to preserve their agricultural production. This observation relates to Gigler's [12] concept of 'informational capabilities' concerning ICT use. He explained, "... 'informational capabilities' refers to the combination between a person's existing livelihood resources in terms of information (informational capital) and his/her agency (ability) to strengthen these assets and to use them in such a way that the use of information can help a person to transform his/her options in life in order to achieve the 'beings' and 'doings' a person would like to achieve." [12, p. 8].

The model allows for systematic tracing of the livelihood outcomes resulting from the use of mobile technologies. It shows, for example, how human assets, enhanced by mobile use, are empowering women in navigating through and, to some extent, transforming structures and processes within the village level.

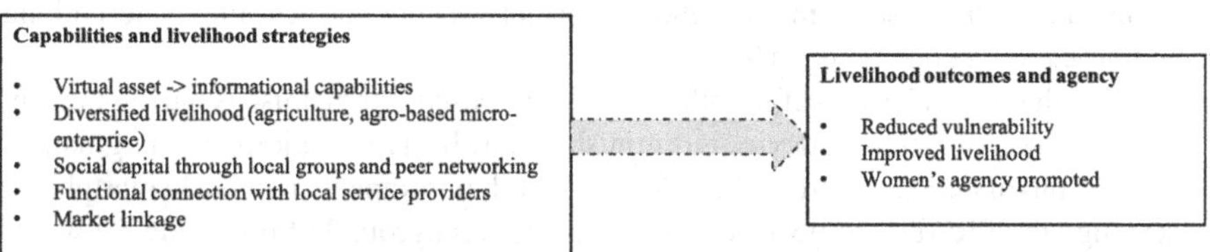

Fig. 2. Information access via smartphones leads to livelihood outcomes & women's agency

According to the SLF model (Fig. 1), smartphones can be considered a physical asset. However, considering the affordability and significance of mobile technologies in rural women's lives and livelihood, we propose to add another category of asset, namely 'virtual asset' referring to rural women's expertise on mobile applications use and its relationships to the concept of 'informational capabilities' [12]. These capabilities and strategies materialize through women's capacity to appropriate the virtual asset, i.e. information afforded by the use of mobile applications. Given the significance of mobile technologies as a virtual force in the developing world, this is a substantial chance for the assets contained in the proposed SLF model.

6.2 Livelihood Strategy, Outcomes and Agency of Rural Women

Our findings show that increased information access and knowledge about smartphone apps helped many rural women make informed decisions, provide better access to available public agricultural services, and establish market relationships. The research showed how access to communication and information played an essential role in promoting women's agency for individual achievements, within families, and collectively in their communities.

We found that women's interaction with the virtual asset and capability provided by the communications power of smartphones, and their apps in particular, resulted in a 'material agency' [24] and influenced the change process in the rural society in the Bangladesh context. Women were able to use smartphones to achieve livelihood outcomes by increasing their knowledge, through market access, public agricultural extension, and financial services, and opening up avenues for informed decision making. Consequently, women's agency and smartphone affordances lead to their informational capabilities and improved livelihood outcomes as explained in Fig. 2.

These preliminary results show the potential of this framework in enabling a richer analysis using the SLF as outlined in Sect. 3.

6.3 Information Access Issues for Women

Based on the findings, the following observations on issues relating to women's access to information can be identified:

a. During the data collection process, rural women referred to some factors hindering their smartphone access. These included patriarchal social and cultural norms, which constrained their use of mobile phones for networking and learning. International empirical data confirm this issue.
b. Although the gender gap of mobile and mobile-based internet use is narrowing, and the price of a smartphone device is diminishing day by day, a majority of marginalized rural women cannot afford to buy one. Research participants received smartphones through the PROTIC project, which formed the background of this study. However, they could still not afford to buy or repair the device at the end of the project.
c. Poor infrastructure, e.g. inadequate electricity supply and internet connectivity, create obstacles to using smartphones and the internet. In addition, research participants mentioned that they have to travel to the local market to get their mobile charged and pay fees for that.

These observations are confirmed by international empirical data that women still face challenges, namely lack of literacy and digital literacy, the cost of mobile handset particularly in case of a smartphone, the cost of internet use and the disapproval of families for mobile and internet use by women [13, p. 49]. Thus, while an ICT4D intervention project may initiate rural women empowerment by providing access to information and other services, barriers still exist, from social barriers to ICT infrastructure and cost issues hindering their access to opportunities, which will affect their livelihood outcomes [31].

7 Limitations and Future Work

This paper emphasized understanding the enabling contribution of mobile phones and their applications in improving marginalized women farmers' livelihood outcomes. Of course, we recognize that our insights are based upon a small group of people chosen for an ICT4D project. However, it captured perspectives of rural communities, which provided valuable lessons in different designs and applications of such projects [31]. We modified the SLF model by conceptualising smartphones as both physical and virtual assets with women's agency in a particular context and validated its relevance. While based on qualitative data, this model can be tested further in other rural developing contexts to gather insight for inclusive digital development for women and other excluded groups [10]. This analysis can be a reference point to help other academic researchers to develop a theory-based understanding of the underlying issue in addressing ICT impact in other vulnerable contexts.

8 Conclusion

The SLF and reflective research can be applied as a valuable lens to look deeper into the gaps and underlying causal relationships of ICT4D interventions. We demonstrated the relevance of the SLF model to explain vulnerability, livelihoods strategy, and outcomes for rural women in Bangladesh.

As an example, the paper shows how smartphones and their applications can be vehicles for communication and information, which enable the women farmers to reduce vulnerability related to disasters, increase livelihood outcomes, connect them with the local market and local service providers, and improve their overall wellbeing. Our findings draw attention to the importance of understanding challenges rural women farmers face in digital development due to economic and social structural barriers, such as inadequate infrastructure and patriarchy. Furthermore, it demonstrates the significance of smartphones in affecting interrelated empowerment dimensions of rural women's wellbeing, livelihood and identity.

This empirical insight will likely be transferable to similar resource-constrained and vulnerable community contexts. Moreover, this insight can assist international development stakeholders, such as governments, NGOs and ICT4D implementing institutions, to make strategic decisions to design and implement mobile phone-based development interventions.

References

1. Anwar, M., Johanson, G.: Mobile phones, family and personal relationships: the case of Indonesian micro-entrepreneurs. Soc. Inform. Socinfo **2012**(7710), 216–231 (2012)
2. Ashraf, M., Grunfeld, H., Harris, R., Alam, N., Ferdousi, S., Malik, B.T.: An explorative study of ICT for developmental impact in rural areas of Bangladesh. Media Asia **38**(1), 22–31 (2011). https://doi.org/10.1080/01296612.2011.11726888
3. Bacishoga, K.B., Hooper, V.A., Johnston, K.A.: The role of mobile phones in the development of social capital among refugees in South Africa. Electron. J. Inf. Syst. Dev. Countries **72**(1), 1–21 (2016)
4. Burrell, J., Oreglia, E.: The myth of market price information: mobile phones and the application of economic knowledge in ICTD. Econ. Soc. **44**(2), 271–292 (2015). https://doi.org/10.1080/03085147.2015.1013742
5. Chambers, R., Conway, G.: Sustainable rural livelihoods: practical concepts for the 21st century. IDS Discussion Paper, **296**, 1–29 (1991). ISBN0903715589
6. Chew, H.E., Levy, M.R., Ilavarasan, P.V.: The limited impact of ICTs on microenterprise growth: a study of businesses owned by women in Urban India. Inf. Technol. Int. Dev. **7**(4), 1–16 (2011). http://itidjournal.org/itid/article/view/788
7. Donner, J.: Research approaches to mobile use in the developing world: a review of the literature. Inf. Soc. **24**(3), 140–159 (2008)
8. Donner, J.: Blurring livelihoods and lives: the social uses of mobile phones and socioeconomic development. Innov. Technol. Governance, Global. **4**(1), 91–101 (2009)
9. Donovan, K., Donner, J.: A note on the availability (and importance) of pre-paid mobile data in Africa. In: Proceedings of the 2nd International Conference on M4D: Mobile Communication Technology for Development (2010)

10. Duncombe, R.: Using the livelihoods framework to analyze ICT applications for poverty reduction through microenterprise. Inf. Technol. Int. Dev. **3**(3), 81–100 (2006). https://doi.org/10.1162/itid.2007.3.3.81
11. Duncombe, R., Heeks, R.: Information, ICTs and small enterprise: findings from Botswana. Dev. Inform. (1999). https://doi.org/10.1016/0736-5853(84)90003-0
12. Gigler, B.S.: Informational capabilities-the missing link for the impact of ICT on development. Available at SSRN 2191594 (2011)
13. GSMA Intelligence. Connected Women the Mobile Gender Gap Report 2020 (2020). https://www.gsma.com/mobilefordevelopment/wp-content/uploads/2020/05/GSMA-The-Mobile-Gender-Gap-Report-2020.pdf
14. Heeks, R.: ICT4D 3.0? Part 1—The components of an emerging "digital-for-development" paradigm. Electron. J. Inf. Syst. Dev. Countries **86**(3), e12124 (2020). https://doi.org/10.1002/isd2.12124
15. Heeks, R.: Development 2.0. Commun. ACM, **53**(4), 22 (2010a). https://doi.org/10.1145/1721654.1721665
16. Heeks, R.: Where next for ICTs and international development? (2010b). https://doi.org/10.1007/978-90-313-8458-7_10
17. Heeks, R.: ICT4D. Academe (2014). https://doi.org/10.1002/jid
18. Heeks, R., Molla, A.: Compendium on Impact Assessment of ICT-for- Development Projects (2009)
19. Hoque, D.S.M.S., Mahiuddin, K., Alam, S.M.S.: E-Governance: a way forward to digital Bangladesh. SSRN (2015). https://doi.org/10.2139/ssrn.2279312
20. Islam, M.K., Slack, F.: Women in rural Bangladesh: empowered by access to mobile phones. In: Proceedings of the 9th International Conference on Theory and Practice of Electronic Governance (2016). https://doi.org/10.1145/2910019.2910074
21. Islam, M.M., Habes, E.M., Alam, M.M.: The usage and social capital of mobile phones and their effect on the performance of microenterprise: an empirical study. Technol. Forecast. Soc. Change **132**, 156–164 (2018). https://doi.org/10.1016/j.techfore.2018.01.029
22. Kabeer, N.: Resources, agency, achievements: reflections on the measurement of women's empowerment. Dev. Chang. **30**(3), 435–464 (1999)
23. Komunte, M.: Usage of mobile technology in women entrepreneurs: a case study of Uganda. African J. Inf. Syst. **7**(3), 3 (2015)
24. Leonardi, P.M.: Theoretical foundations for the study of sociomateriality. Inf. Organ. **23**(2), 59–76 (2013). https://doi.org/10.1016/j.infoandorg.2013.02.002
25. Lyytinen, T.: Preliminary insights to the role of the private sector in developing mobile services for low-income segment: case M-Pesa and Ovi life tools. In: Proceedings of the 2nd International Conference on M4D (2010)
26. Mbogo, M.: The impact of mobile payments on the success and growth of micro-business: the case of M-Pesa in Kenya. J. Lang. Technol. Entrepreneurship Africa, **2**(1), 182–203 (2010). https://doi.org/10.4314/jolte.v2i1.51998
27. Parkinson, S., Ramirez, R.: Using a sustainable livelihoods approach to assess the impact of ICTs in development. J. Community Inform. (2006). https://doi.org/10.1006/phrs.1999.0613
28. Ponelis, S.R.: Using interpretive qualitative case studies for exploratory research in doctoral studies: a case of Information Systems research in small and medium enterprises. Int. J. Doctoral Stud. **10**, 535–550 (2015). http://ijds.org/Volume10/IJDSv10p535-550Ponelis0624.pdf
29. Porter, G., et al.: Mobile phones, gender, and female empowerment in sub-Saharan Africa: studies with African youth. Inf. Technol. Dev. **26**(1), 180–193 (2020)
30. Rotondi, V., Kashyap, R., Pesando, L.M., Spinelli, S., Billari, F.C.: Leveraging mobile phones to attain sustainable development. Proc. Natl. Acad. Sci. **117**(24), 13413–13420 (2020)

31. Sarker, A., Biswas, M., Anwar, M., Stillman, L., Oliver, G.: When people come to me for suggestions, I feel like an expert" Empowering women through smartphones in rural Bangladesh. In: Lechman, E.: Technology and Women's Empowerment, 1st ed., pp. 181–99. London, Routledge (2021). https://doi.org/10.4324/9781003045946
32. Sarrica, M., Denison, T., Stillman, L., Chakraborty, T., Auvi, P.: "What do others think?" an emic approach to participatory action research in Bangladesh. AI & Soc. **34**(3), 495–508 (2017). https://doi.org/10.1007/s00146-017-0765-9
33. Small, L.-A.: The sustainable rural livelihoods approach: a critical review. Canadian J. Dev. Stud. / Revue Canadienne d'études Du Développement. (2011). https://doi.org/10.1080/02255189.2007.9669186
34. Tacchi, J., Kitner, K.R., Crawford, K.: Meaningful mobility: gender, development and mobile phones. Fem. Media Stud. **12**(4), 528–537 (2012)
35. Uddin, M.J.: Microcredit and building social capital in rural Bangladesh - drawing the uneasy link. Contemporary South Asia, **22**(2), 143–156 (2014). https://doi.org/10.1080/09584935.2014.899979
36. Walsham, G.: ICT4D research: reflections on history and future agenda. Inf. Technol. Dev. **23**(1), 18–41 (2017). https://doi.org/10.1080/02681102.201
37. Yin, R.: Case Study Research and Applications: Design and Methods (Sixth ed.) (2018)

Communities and Media

You Are What You Tweet: Profiling Users by Past Tweets to Improve Hate Speech Detection

Prateek Chaudhry(✉) and Matthew Lease

University of Texas at Austin, Austin, USA
ml@utexas.edu

Abstract. Hate speech detection research has predominantly focused on purely content-based methods, without exploiting other contextual data. We briefly critique pros and cons of this task formulation. We then investigate profiling users by their past utterances as an informative prior to better predict whether new utterances constitute hate speech. To evaluate this, we augment three Twitter hate speech datasets with additional timeline data, then embed this additional context into a strong baseline model. Promising results suggest merit for further investigation.

Keywords: Hate speech · Classification · Modeling · Profiles · Twitter

1 Introduction

Online hate speech is a vast and continually growing problem [10,12,13,18]. The detection task is most commonly framed as purely content-based: each utterance is classified without any additional context. However, history often repeats itself, and "A user who is known to write hate speech messages may do so again" [18]. Facebook researchers have also recently noted that "a user or group that has posted violating content in the past may be prone to do so more often in the future" [10]. This suggests that modeling of user priors may be highly informative and complementary to purely content-based detection models. We return to discussion of ethical considerations in Sect. 7.

To investigate user profiling, we augment three Twitter hate speech datasets [1,5,20] with additional recent *timeline* Tweets by each author, then embed this additional context into a strong baseline model [2] that was later further refined [1]. Results show strong improvement on one dataset, little benefit on another, and fairly consistent improvement on a third. Overall, results across experimental conditions and metrics suggest user modeling merits further work, though analysis is complicated by differences in annotation schemes and processes, as well as Twitter API limitations and data sharing policies.

2 Related Work

While most hate speech detection models have been content-oriented and non-contextual, there are notable exceptions. After Hovy [11] showed modeling value

M. Smits (Ed.): iConference 2022, LNCS 13193, pp. 195–203, 2022.
https://doi.org/10.1007/978-3-030-96960-8_13

of demographics for classification tasks, Waseem and Hovy [20] applied this to hate speech, inferring gender (by name) and location (by timezone) to classify hate speech with modest benefit: only gender raised hate detection accuracy, and it was statistically significant only when both gender and location were used. A challenge with demographics is that they are sensitive and often not widely available, if captured at all by the platform.

Rather than classify hateful utterances, other work has sought to classify hateful users. Assuming "birds of a feather flock together", *community detection* [8] has sought to identify hater communities. Ribeiro et al. [17] and Mathew et al. [14] analyze Twitter's retweet graph to detect users likely to spread hateful content. Mishra et al. [15] is the only work we are aware of to profile hateful users, via the follower graph, and then use these profiles to improve hate speech detection over baseline models.

Some hate speech datasets are heavily dominated by a few prolific haters. In Waseem and Hovy [20], all racist-labeled tweets came from 9 users. In fact, Arango et al. [1] note that a single user generates 96% of all racist tweets, while another user produces 44% of all sexist tweets. Arango et al. aptly critique that benchmarking on such highly skewed datasets risks overfitting a few individuals rather than learning a broadly applicable model. Similar concerns have been voiced about over-fitting idiosyncrasies of a few annotators [9]. We agree that datasets should have many diverse examples of the phenomena being modeled (i.e., hate speech examples from many users). However, dataset composition is orthogonal to model design: how can we best model historical context in prediction and fairly evaluate vs. context-free models?

Some past studies (cf., [20,21]) have partitioned train/test data by utterance (i.e., by tweet), rather than by user. The consequence of such experimental design is that any model trained and tested in this manner can be expected to make better predictions on users found in both train and test splits. However, we should not confuse desirable user modeling with questionable experimental design in which user history is only captured haphazardly by whichever users happen to have some tweets in the training data, and the ratio of that user-specific history vs. training tweets from other users. Such a scheme does not reflect intentional design or controlled evaluation of user modeling.

An intuitive language-based approach is to model each user by a "document" of their past utterances. Such historical data is certainly available to social media companies, and often publicly via API or crawling. The closest work we are aware of on content-based modeling of haters is by Dadvar et al. [4], though they only considered the user's past number of obscene words as a modeling feature.

3 Datasets

We adopt the same three datasets studied by Arango et al. [1]; see statistics in Table 1. As is common in other problem domains, each hate speech dataset has various limitations; by evaluating across several datasets, we test across varying data conditions.

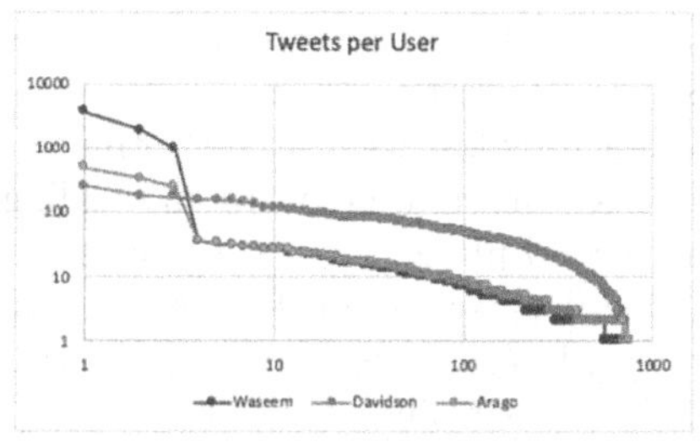

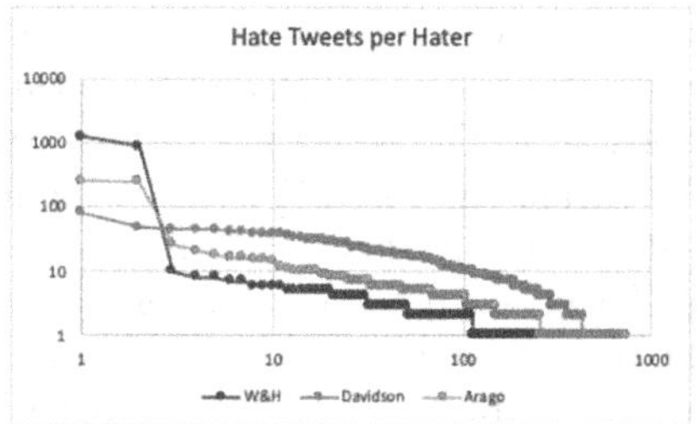

Fig. 1. Log-log distribution of tweets per user (top) and hate tweets per user for users producing 1 or more hate tweets (bottom), for all three datasets. The y-axis indicates the number of tweets while the x-axis simply enumerates users in descending order of activity.

Waseem and Hovy [20] (W&H) label 16K tweets for 3 classes: Racism, Sexism and Neither. After author labeling, tweets labeled as hate speech were reviewed by a 25-year old female "studying gender studies and a nonactivist feminist". Agreement between author and reviewer was $\kappa = 0.84$, with 85% of disagreements on sexist labels, and 98% of these changed to neither. Tweet IDs and labels were shared, with tweets obtained via the Twitter API. Since tweets and user accounts are often deleted, 15K tweets are found in [1]. We find 10K tweets (and only 6 racist ones) over 1,458 users.

Davidson et al. [5] crowd-label 25K tweets for 3 classes: Hate, Offensive and Neither. Majority voting over 3 or more workers was used for label aggregation. 200 tweets were discarded with no majority over the 3 classes. For hate, only 5% were labeled by 2/3 and only 1.3% by 3/3. Most were labeled offensive (76% at 2/3, 53% at 3/3) and the rest non-offensive (16.6% at 2/3, 11.8% at 3/3). We find 18K tweets (~75%) from 741 users.

Arango et al. [1] identify three issues: 1) W&H has few haters; 2) those haters are prolific; and 3) train/test splits by utterance mean the same hater often appears in both train and test splits. To address this, they 1) add to W&H all hate-labeled tweets from DAVIDSON; 2) restrict to at most 250 tweets per user per class; and 3) perform train/test split by user rather than by utterance. Their fused dataset had 7K tweets, collapsing labels to simple binary hate vs. non-hate. We find 5.4K over 1746 users.

Figure 1 shows the distribution of tweets per user across datasets. For all users who produce 1 or more hate tweet (W&H: 443 users, Davidson: 566, Arango: 734), we also plot the number of hate tweets from each such "hater".

4 Profiling Users by Past Tweets

As a strong baseline, we adopt Badjatiya et al. [2]'s 2-phase model, using [1]'s corrected version in which word embeddings are derived only from training data. An LSTM classifier is first trained to predict the label. Each word is converted to a dense vector representation using a word embedding matrix initialized with pretrained GloVe embeddings [16]. The final vector from the LSTM is followed by a fully connected layer and a softmax or sigmoid layer for obtaining prediction probability. The network is trained with cross entropy loss with Adam optimizer. Once training of LSTM is done, the first layer is extracted, i.e. word embedding matrix fine tuned on the training set. In the second phase, a tweet is converted to a fixed sized vector by averaging the embedding vectors of its tokens using the trained embeddings from the previous phase. Representing the tweet by this vector, a Gradient Boosted Decision Tree (GBDT) is trained for classification.

Given a tweet ID, we use the Twitter API to retrieve the author's *timeline*[1]: their latest 20 tweets. This size of 20 reflects an API maximum, but it would be interesting in future work to model longer histories. Given this history, we augment existing public datasets (Sect. 3) with these timelines. W&H includes tweet IDs, and Davidson kindly shared their tweet IDs with us upon request. In practice, timeline tweets should precede tweets being classified; here we use existing datasets. By augmenting existing datasets, we can assess the relative benefit with and without user profiling on hate speech datasets that are already familiar to the research community.

We utilize these user profiles in (Arango et al. [1]'s corrected version of) [2]'s model as follows. Given a tweet, the author's timeline is averaged using the same trained word embedding used for tweet representation. Following this, both tweet representation and timeline representation are concatenated and used to train the GBDT classifier. In general, a history-informed prior of the user ought to complement any content-based model of the tweet alone. We expect future work will continue to benefit from exploiting such a prior-informed modeling architecture, irrespective of the specific model.

5 Experimental Setup

We build on Badjatiya et al. [2]'s and Arango et al. [1]'s shared source code. We use 10-fold cross validation with default hyperparameters for [2]'s model. The LSTM word embeddings are initialized with 200 dimensional pretrained GloVe embeddings, and the size of the LSTM representation is 200. We also add dropout of 0.25 and 0.5 after the word embedding layer and the LSTM, respectively. We train the LSTM based architecture for 10 epochs, and then train the GBDT using the final word embeddings.

With nearly all racism tweets in W&H deleted, we train it as a binary classifier: sexism vs. none. For DAVIDSON, we train a ternary classifier over its three classes. ARANGO fuses W&H and DAVIDSON label sets by collapsing classes into simple binary classification of hate vs. non-hate.

Tweet deletions make comparison to prior published results more difficult, with only 2/3 of W&H and 3/4 of DAVIDSON datasets still available, and nearly all W&H racist tweets deleted. Arango et al. [1] note that partitioning train/test by tweet, as in past studies, results in prolific tweeters appearing in both splits.

[1] https://developer.twitter.com/en/docs/tweets/timelines/.

Table 1. Baseline vs. timeline accuracy across datasets and train/test partitions: by tweet or user. For each (dataset, split, metric) tuple, we bold the higher accuracy between baseline vs. timeline.

				Split by tweet						Split by user					
				Baseline			With timeline			Baseline			With timeline		
Dataset	Label	Tweets	Found	P	R	F1	P	R	F1	P	R	F1	P	R	F1
W&H	Racism	1,851	6	-	-	-	-	-	-	-	-	-	-	-	-
	Sexism	2,988	2,777	76.8	65.6	70.7	**83.7**	**80.2**	**81.9**	59.2	33.2	37.8	**63.7**	**35.4**	**40.8**
	Neither	10,110	7,320	87.7	92.4	89.9	**92.6**	**94.1**	**93.3**	82.2	91.4	84.3	**82.6**	**93.9**	**86.5**
	Micro Avg			85.1	85.1	85.1	**90.3**	**90.3**	**90.3**	76.0	76.0	76.0	**79.3**	**79.3**	**79.3**
	Macro Avg	14,949	10,103	82.2	79.0	80.3	**88.2**	**87.2**	**87.6**	70.7	62.3	61.1	**73.1**	**64.6**	**63.6**
DAVID-SON	Hate	1,430	1,118	55.4	24.3	33.6	**56.4**	**24.7**	**34.1**	**53.6**	**22.1**	**31.0**	52.2	21.5	30.3
	Offensive	19,190	13,931	**91.3**	95.9	93.5	91.2	95.9	93.5	91.2	**95.9**	**93.5**	91.2	95.8	93.4
	Neither	4,163	2,978	**83.8**	**81.5**	**82.7**	83.7	81.1	82.3	**82.8**	**81.3**	**82.0**	82.7	81.2	81.9
	Micro Avg			**89.1**	**89.1**	**89.1**	89.0	89.0	89.0	**88.9**	**88.9**	**88.9**	88.8	88.8	88.8
	Macro Avg	24,783	18,027	76.8	**67.3**	69.9	**77.1**	67.2	**70.0**	**75.9**	**66.4**	**68.8**	75.3	66.2	68.6
ARANGO	Hate	2,920	1,988	81.0	72.4	76.4	**85.2**	**75.2**	**79.8**	**80.7**	63.1	68.5	79.6	**65.7**	**69.8**
	None	4,086	3,481	85.1	90.3	87.6	**86.7**	**92.5**	**89.5**	81.5	**87.9**	**82.8**	**82.6**	86.1	82.3
	Micro Avg			83.8	83.8	83.8	**86.1**	**86.1**	**86.1**	79.8	79.8	79.8	**80.1**	**80.1**	**80.1**
	Macro Avg	7,006	5,469	83.1	81.3	82.0	**86.0**	**83.8**	**84.6**	81.1	75.5	75.7	81.1	**75.9**	**76.1**

The risk this poses is potentially overfitting to particular users. Instead, they argue for splitting train/test by user. To be as comprehensive as possible, we report results both ways for completeness.

6 Results

Table 1 compares model performance with and without user timeline history across the three datasets and the two train/test data partitions: by tweet vs. by user. With regard to testing baseline vs. timeline results, splitting by user is cleaner because for any users appearing in the test data, there are no tweets from that user in the training set.

Results show strong improvement on W&H but little change on DAVIDSON. We do see split-by-tweet shows modest improvement for DAVIDSON on the Hate category, but not on other categories or for split-by-user. Between W&H and DAVIDSON extremes, we see more modest but fairly consistent improvement on Arango et al.'s dataset, which fuses W&H and DAVIDSON by adding to W&H all hate-labeled tweets from DAVIDSON and down-sampling to at most 250 tweets per user per class to reduce skew. Consistent with Arango et al. [1], we see much higher results on W&H and their fused dataset when splitting by tweet rather than by user (Arango et al. do not report on DAVIDSON).

Given the difference in model performance across the datasets, what explains this? Table 1 and Fig. 1 show important differences in data scale and distribution across different datasets. The classes being annotated also differ, as does the method of annotation: W&H uses traditional annotators while DAVIDSON relies on crowd annotators. Such differences highlight several dimensions of ongoing

Table 2. Detection accuracy on user subgroups, based on amount of Twitter timeline available per user (0–20 most recent tweets). Train/test partition of data is by tweet unless noted otherwise.

			Baseline			With timeline		
Dataset	Size Timeline	Tweets	P	R	F	P	R	F
W&H	0–5	58	**78.2**	**74.1**	**75.8**	68.8	67.4	68.0
	6–10	18	47.1	47.1	47.1	**75.0**	**97.1**	**81.8**
	11–15	34	**60.0**	**54.7**	**53.0**	50.5	50.2	46.0
	16–20	9,991	82.2	79.0	80.4	**88.3**	**87.4**	**87.9**
DAVIDSON	0–5	4,943	**76.6**	**66.6**	**69.6**	76.3	66.4	69.4
	6–10	22	96.5	72.2	80.4	NAN	0	NAN
	11–15	287	**66.0**	**58.8**	**61.5**	58.5	54.0	55.8
	16–20	12,775	76.9	67.5	70.1	**77.2**	**67.6**	**70.3**
ARANGO	0–5	59	**76.5**	**75.4**	**75.9**	70.0	70.0	70.0
	6–10	20	**100.0**	**100.0**	**100.0**	97.2	83.3	88.6
	11–15	49	**81.2**	**80.3**	**79.5**	77.0	76.2	75.4
	16–20	5,341	83.0	81.3	82.0	**86.1**	**84.0**	**84.9**
ARANGO	0–5	59	81.9	77.8	79.4	**85.3**	**78.9**	**81.3**
(split by user)	6–10	20	97.2	**83.3**	88.6	97.2	83.2	88.6
	11–15	49	84.9	80.8	79.2	84.9	80.8	79.2
	16–20	5,341	**78.3**	76.1	76.9	78.2	**77.1**	**77.6**

debate in hate speech research surrounding differing approaches to annotation categories and processes [3,7,19].

We also conducted a further analysis to assess whether the amount of timeline history per user varied significantly across datasets. Results appear in Table 2, where we bin users by the count of timeline tweets found: 0–5, 6–10, 11–15, or 16–20. We see that the vast majority of users have 16–20 past timeline tweets, and for this category we see consistent improvement across datasets and train/test split conditions, driving scores.

Crucially, however, on DAVIDSON we see nearly 5K tweets (~28%) from users with only 0–5 timeline tweets available, where we expect small to no improvement from timelines due to lack of history. This holds across datasets when splitting by tweet, including DAVIDSON, which indeed drives down overall results on this dataset. When splitting by user on ARANGO, we do see increased accuracy even with 0–5 timeline tweets, though the sample size is quite small to draw conclusions.

Further limited qualitative analysis helped give us a sense of examples where profiling a user created an informative prior for correctly classifying tweets that might have been missed otherwise. We explored most prolific tweeters in W&H for evidence of sexist timeline tweets. As an example, one user made a possibly sexist tweet *".@USER1 @USER2 when was she good? i confuse her and ten other women, which is why their pay is lower btw. supply vs. demand."* which was easier to predict by their earlier timeline tweet *"#FeminismIsAwful"*. Use of the timeline correctly predicts the 'sexist' label, and increases overall detection accuracy for this user from 53% to 87%.

7 Ethical Considerations

While user modeling is common in personalized ranking and recommendation systems (e.g., Google or Netflix), some users may wish to opt-out, and GDPR allows "the right to be forgotten". User modeling to prevent fraud and abuse, while equally common in commercial systems, may raise different sorts of ethical and legal questions. We know that social media platforms already do monitor user accounts for terms of service violations, suspending accounts demonstrating repeated abusive behaviors [10]. Given the vast scale and expense of commercial content moderation, and extensive user histories available, platforms cannot afford to ignore such a strong predictive signal.

However, what challenges may arise? Would a reformed hater have difficulty overcoming his/her past profile a model had learned? One idea would be to decay weight assigned to past tweets by age, or to completely restrict history to a recent window (e.g., our current timeline of past 20 tweets). In fact, the opposite problem is significant on platforms today: a bad actor who is suspended often circumvents this by creating a new account, with a cycle of continuing abusive behaviors by re-entrant bad actors.

8 Conclusion

Producers of hate speech are often repeat offenders, yet we know of no prior work explicitly profiling users by their past tweets to improve hate speech detection accuracy. We collect Twitter timeline data toward this end to augment existing hate speech datasets. Results on several datasets, metrics, and experimental settings are encouraging, but confounds remain. Future work might explore better modeling (e.g., via BERT [6]), collecting more user history, and combining with other profiling approaches [15]. Other approaches may explore adding other features extracted from user twitter timeline, such as hate speech tweet frequency, number of hate speech retweets, etc.

Acknowledgments. We thank the reviewers for their valuable feedback, and the many talented workers who provided the hate speech annotations that enable research on it. This research was supported in part by Wipro, the Micron Foundation, and by Good Systems (http://goodsystems.utexas.edu/), a UT Austin Grand Challenge to develop responsible AI technologies. The statements made herein are solely the opinions of the authors and do not reflect the views of the sponsoring agencies.

References

1. Arango, A., Pérez, J., Poblete, B.: Hate speech detection is not as easy as you may think: a closer look at model validation. In: Proceedings of the 42nd International ACM SIGIR Conference on Research and Development in Information Retrieval, pp. 45–54 (2019). https://github.com/aymeam/User_distribution_experiments
2. Badjatiya, P., Gupta, S., Gupta, M., Varma, V.: Deep learning for hate speech detection in tweets. In: Proceedings of the 26th International Conference on World Wide Web Companion, pp. 759–760 (2017). https://github.com/pinkeshbadjatiya/twitter-hatespeech
3. Balayn, A., Bozzon, A.: Designing evaluations of machine learning models for subjective inference: the case of sentence toxicity. arXiv preprint arXiv:1911.02471 (2019)
4. Dadvar, M., Trieschnigg, D., Ordelman, R., de Jong, F.: Improving cyberbullying detection with user context. In: Serdyukov, P., et al. (eds.) ECIR 2013. LNCS, vol. 7814, pp. 693–696. Springer, Heidelberg (2013). https://doi.org/10.1007/978-3-642-36973-5_62
5. Davidson, T., Warmsley, D., Macy, M., Weber, I.: Automated hate speech detection and the problem of offensive language. In: Eleventh International AAAI Conference on Web and Social Media (2017). https://github.com/t-davidson/hate-speech-and-offensive-language
6. Devlin, J., Chang, M.W., Lee, K., Toutanova, K.: Bert: pre-training of deep bidirectional transformers for language understanding. arXiv preprint arXiv:1810.04805 (2018)
7. Fortuna, P., Soler, J., Wanner, L.: Toxic, hateful, offensive or abusive? what are we really classifying? an empirical analysis of hate speech datasets. In: Proceedings of the 12th Language Resources and Evaluation Conference, pp. 6786–6794 (2020)
8. Fortunato, S.: Community detection in graphs. Phys. Rep. **486**(3–5), 75–174 (2010)
9. Geva, M., Goldberg, Y., Berant, J.: Are we modeling the task or the annotator? an investigation of annotator bias in natural language understanding datasets. In: Proceedings of the 2019 Conference on Empirical Methods in Natural Language Processing and the 9th International Joint Conference on Natural Language Processing (EMNLP-IJCNLP), pp. 1161–1166 (2019)
10. Halevy, A., et al.: Preserving integrity in online social networks. arXiv preprint arXiv:2009.10311 (2020)
11. Hovy, D.: Demographic factors improve classification performance. In: Proceedings of the 53rd Annual Meeting of the Association for Computational Linguistics and the 7th International Joint Conference on Natural Language Processing (vol. 1: Long papers), pp. 752–762 (2015)
12. Jurgens, D., Chandrasekharan, E., Hemphill, L.: A just and comprehensive strategy for using NLP to address online abuse. arXiv preprint arXiv:1906.01738 (2019)
13. MacAvaney, S., Yao, H.R., Yang, E., Russell, K., Goharian, N., Frieder, O.: Hate speech detection: challenges and solutions. PloS One **14**(8), e0221152 (2019)
14. Mathew, B., Dutt, R., Goyal, P., Mukherjee, A.: Spread of hate speech in online social media. In: Proceedings of the 10th ACM Conference on Web Science, pp. 173–182 (2019)
15. Mishra, P., Del Tredici, M., Yannakoudakis, H., Shutova, E.: Author profiling for abuse detection. In: Proceedings of the 27th International Conference on Computational Linguistics, pp. 1088–1098 (2018)

16. Pennington, J., Socher, R., Manning, C.D.: Glove: global vectors for word representation. In: Empirical Methods in Natural Language Processing (EMNLP), pp. 1532–1543 (2014). http://www.aclweb.org/anthology/D14-1162
17. Ribeiro, M.H., Calais, P.H., Santos, Y.A., Almeida, V.A., Meira Jr., W.: Characterizing and detecting hateful users on twitter. In: Twelfth International AAAI Conference on Web and Social Media (2018)
18. Schmidt, A., Wiegand, M.: A survey on hate speech detection using natural language processing. In: Proceedings of the Fifth International Workshop on Natural Language Processing for Social Media, pp. 1–10 (2017)
19. Waseem, Z.: Are you a racist or am i seeing things? annotator influence on hate speech detection on twitter. In: Proceedings of the First Workshop on NLP and Computational Social Science, pp. 138–142 (2016)
20. Waseem, Z., Hovy, D.: Hateful symbols or hateful people? predictive features for hate speech detection on twitter. In: Proceedings of the NAACL Student Research Workshop, pp. 88–93 (2016). https://github.com/zeerakw/hatespeech
21. Xiang, G., Fan, B., Wang, L., Hong, J., Rose, C.: Detecting offensive tweets via topical feature discovery over a large scale twitter corpus. In: Proceedings of the 21st ACM International Conference on Information and Knowledge Management, pp. 1980–1984 (2012)

A Digital Bridge: Increasing Digital Access to Low-Income Job Seekers and the Role of Community Organizations

Yvette Iribe Ramirez(✉) and Stacey Wedlake

Information School, University of Washington, Seattle, WA, USA
yiribe@uw.edu

Abstract. With the onset of the COVID-19 pandemic in the Spring of 2020, much of work and professional life shifted to virtual environments. For many with existing and reliable access to digital devices, the internet, and digital literacy skills, this sudden shift was a minor adjustment. However, for many others the shift to online work life highlighted the disparities in access to reliable technology and exacerbated the existing digital divide among vulnerable populations. In response to this change, the City of Seattle, and the Seattle Jobs Initiative (SJI) launched the Digital Bridge (DB) program, a pilot program aimed at providing reliable internet access and digital devices to current job seekers working with SJI. Through the DB program, we see needs beyond initial access to technology and the internet, and the role that community organizations play in providing assistance. This paper aims to explore two key components: 1) lessons learned from the Digital Bridge project, and 2) organizational relationships and the impacts on program implementation.

Keywords: Digital access · Digital divide · Digital literacy · Employment

1 Introduction

As the COVID-19 pandemic forced lockdowns and limited in-person interaction and services at the start of Spring 2020, much of our work and professional life switched to online environments, as well as much of our personal and social lives. However, for many this switch, although inconvenient, wasn't a completely new concept as telecommuting had been possible for many employees before the start of the pandemic. This necessary change was also made less burdensome for workers who already had existing reliable internet access, access to digital devices like computers, tablets, and phones, as well as the skills and practice to navigate and mostly digital work environment. However, for many workers and job seekers, this change highlighted the disparities in access to internet services and digital devices, especially for those from vulnerable populations. Not only that, but the switch to remote work exacerbated the existing digital divide.

In response to the change, the City of Seattle, and Seattle Jobs Initiatives (SJI), a nonprofit focused workforce development and job training, partnered with Comcast to design and implement the Digital Bridge (DB) program. The primary goal of DB was

M. Smits (Ed.): iConference 2022, LNCS 13193, pp. 204–210, 2022.
https://doi.org/10.1007/978-3-030-96960-8_14

to provide job seekers, in this case current clients of SJI, with the digital tools necessary to continue their skills training and job searches throughout the pandemic. The program was designed to "prioritize its resources for low-income earning individuals, and BIPOC individuals who lack an internet connection and access to the technology and digital skills necessary to obtain gainful employment in our economy." (Braxton 2020) Beyond the program design, a unique aspect of Digital Bridge was the collaborative effort of multiple organizations and city departments, including Goodwill, Interconnections, the City of Seattle's Office of Economic Development and Seattle Information Technology, and the University of Washington's Technology and Social Change Group. This paper aims to focus on the key lessons learned from the Digital Bridge project assessment and implementation, as well as understanding organizational relationships that directly influence the project's implementation and sustainability.

2 Background

Digital Bridge demonstrates another example of community need beyond initial access. Access to technology and the internet is important, especially for communities with reduced resources and during a global pandemic in which professional and personal interactions have migrated to an online environment. However, many participants needed additional support that was often difficult to obtain and maintain. Gonzalez describes the concept of technology maintenance, which accounts for the experience of technology users after initial access to technology resources has been established. Gonzalez states,

> "Technology maintenance predicts that, 'as the poor increasingly have initial in-home and public access to technology, the digital divide will begin to center on differences in the ability to maintain that access' (Gonzales 2014; Gonzales, Ems and Suri 2014)...Previously applied only to barriers to cell phone access, technology maintenance would also suggest that Internet access in low-income communities must be continuously maintained, often at substantial ongoing economic and social cost"(Gonzales 2016)

To that end, another important aspect of technology maintenance is the ongoing burden that access to reliable internet and tech resources places on low-income communities. The cost of maintaining services at home, or accessing community resources, like the internet at public libraries, each presents an additional hurdle for tech use. Once initial access has been established and users become accustomed to accessing and using digital resources for daily tasks, it becomes increasingly an issue of inequality to experience disconnection from the internet. (Gonzales 2016) This burden is of course heightened by the COVID-19 pandemic that has impacted employment, income, and access to public services, like libraries.

Information and communication technologies function as a tool that aids the facilitation of development, rather than as a solution. (Mthoko and Khene 2018) That is, that ICT interventions, like the Digital Bridge program, have a greater chance of success when the focus is placed on relationships and community capacity building. ICT initiatives are prone to failure when the only emphasis is on the technology, i.e., to get devices to participants without assessment and support for need. (Heeks 2005; Mthoko and Khene 2018).

3 Digital Bridge Overview

The Digital Bridge project is a collaboration between the City of Seattle's Office of Economic Development and Seattle Jobs Initiative, a nonprofit organization offering employment services and support for job seekers. As a direct response to services and processes moving to an online, remote form, the primary goal of this partnership was to connect job seekers with internet access and laptop computers to assist them in reentering the workplace and providing stable access to technology. We wanted to understand aspects of the project through two research questions, first, "*How have the participants' employment and technology learning goals changed since the pandemic?*" and second, "*What types of support do new device owners need to use technology to look for and prepare for employment?*".

We set out to answer these questions through interviews, as well as understanding day-to-day uses of technology through voicemail diaries. With help from SJI, we were able to recruit study participants from the pool of 197 clients who had received either internet services, or laptops. Recruitment was difficult, a sign that illustrates the complexities of conducting research during a pandemic, in an online environment, with a population that is already experiencing precarity. However, we were able to recruit 15 participants, asking them to submit voicemail diaries for 7 consecutive days, followed by an interview. Participants received varying levels of compensation for their time in the form of a Visa gift card depending on how many voicemails they left and whether or not they ultimately participated in an interview.

Voicemail diaries as a data collection tool, required participants to call in to a designated phone number used solely for the voicemail feature. Participants were asked to call every day, for seven consecutive days and answer questions about their daily technology use and successes and challenges they had while using their technologies. After completing the voicemail diaries, we scheduled a one-hour interview with participants that encompassed five areas: 1) Employment Goals 2) Internet Access 3) Technology Use 4) Support and 5) Voicemail Diary Follow-Up. Having time to ask participants questions about their voicemails gave us an opportunity to dive deeper into the experiences they had throughout the week and explore some of the issues or successes they experienced with their technology. We adapted this method from Palen & Salzman, who used diary studies to understand participant experience in realistic conditions. Given the remote nature of research during a pandemic, voicemail diaries served as a way to capture the daily experiences Digital Bridge participants were having with their devices and internet.

To understand the process of technology distribution and support behind the scenes, we asked case managers working on the project to leave audio diaries for one work week and participate in a focus group. Case managers are the primary source of support for clients as SJI, helping participants through enrollment, training, job seeking, and job placement. During the role of Digital Bridge, case managers were also the point of contact for receiving equipment, and oftentimes, offering technical support and impromptu digital skills training. (Carson et al. 2021; Wedlake et al. 2021).

Participants had an existing relationship with SJI, meaning they are participating in services and programming offered by SJI and have an established relationship with a case manager. In order to qualify to receive assistance from SJI, clients have an income that falls below the federal poverty line, in some cases participants do not have an income, are experiencing homelessness, or living in subsidized housing.

Because of SJI's collaboration with the Congolese Immigration Network and PIE the Digital Bridge program was able to work with immigrant and refugee communities. Seventy-three percent of the participants were Black/African American, with a large percentage of these being recent Congolese immigrants. Seventy-two percent of participants are between 25 and 54 and thus are more likely to have family and caretaking responsibilities than workers newly entering the workforce and senior workers. (Carson et al. 2021).

3.1 Key Findings

The primary lessons we learned from the Digital bridge program, are 1) it is essential to provide low-income job seekers with reliable computer and internet access if recovering from this pandemic is to be inclusive and actively determined to shrink digital inequalities. 2) Recognizing that access to digital resources is not enough, communities need ongoing technical support and digital skills training and capacity building. 3) Using refurbished computers requires that the program also increase support when it comes to troubleshooting and repairing devices, as well providing support that can distinguish between equipment failure and user error. 4) Community organizations are in a particularly important situation to effectively provide access and support to increasing access to digital resources for BIPOC, immigrant, and refugee communities. However, they are also limited in resources, funding, and staffing that requires reinforcement and robust financial investment that will help organizations increase their reach and collaboration with communities. 5) Finally, it is essential that employees that work directly with job seekers, have access to quality digital skills training that can prepare them to assist digital novices. In this case, case managers at SJI needed additional training to be able to both do their existing duties, and provide job related support, like accessing job skills training, job bulletins and applications, and navigating programs like Zoom for interviews. (Carson et al. 2021).

4 Organizational Relationships

While answering our primary research questions during the project, we became interested in how the relationships between the organizations impacted and influenced project implementation. The partnerships within the Digital Bridge structure adds complexity in the development and implementation of the program, each participating organization is invested in the success of the program and the ability to provide assistance during a time that has impacted employment, especially for communities that are already marginalized by other social factors. Organizational structures and relationships are nuanced, some organizations are providing funding, others are providing equipment and support, and others are facilitating connections between clients and the services that the program is providing. However, the forward-facing role - the day-to-day aspect of the program, and perhaps the hardest to implement successfully, becomes the responsibility of one organization, in this case SJI, whose case managers already have established responsibilities and duties outside of the Digital Bridge program. Supporting organizations don't offer capacity building aside from tech support whose goal is to troubleshoot, rather than teaching a culture of repair, i.e., teaching skills to encourage people to troubleshoot their own devices, rather it acts more like a help desk.

The complexity of these organizational relationships expanded the program's reach but also increased the administrative burden on SJI. See the Table below for an overview of the organizations involved in Digital Bridge. (Braxton 2020; Carson et al. 2021).

Organization	Role in DB
Seattle Jobs Initiative	Organization responsible for project implementation. SJI had an existing funding relationship with OED and partnership with the six nonprofit implementation organizations. SJI's Executive Director had worked briefly with UW iSchool researcher Wedlake immediately before DB began. SJI had not previously worked with Seattle IT or Interconnection
City of Seattle Department of Economic Development (OED)	OED was the main funder of the program, contributing $50,000 for evaluation and operational support. OED and SJI had an existing contract prior to DB. OED also connected SJI to one of the nonprofit partners
City of Seattle Department of Information Technology (Seattle IT)	Seattle IT's digital equity team provided the project evaluation framework. Additionally, they leveraged existing connections and partnerships with Interconnection and local ISPs as sources of technologies for participants. Comcast also provided a grant to pay for 12 months of internet access for all participants
University of Washington Information School (UW iSchool)	UW iSchool collected qualitative data for the project evaluation. UW iSchool had not worked previously with SJI but had relationships with OED and Seattle IT
Interconnection	Computer refurbisher and mobile hotspot supplier. Seattle IT had an existing partnership with Interconnection. SJI had not previously worked with Interconnection
Six nonprofit implementation partner organizations	SJI had previous relationships with five of the six nonprofit partners. Each nonprofit had its own group of participants that received technology from DB. Each participant received employment services and support from one of the seven (including SJI) organizations

The different organizations implemented their own processes and working with program participants also impacted their experience getting technology help. For some participants, their case managers were an extension of their personal networks as a resource for getting technology assistance:

> "If I need help using my computer, I can call one friend, Jose. I can ask him, what can I do, or I can call [my case manager], I can ask what can I do." - Isabel

Different organizations had different structures with how participants interact and receive assistance from their case managers. At organizations like SJI, the relationship is more hands-on with regular interactions built into the program. During these check-ins, case managers would ask about any problems they had using technologies. Other participants were also involved in online job training and received even more one-on-one help to facilitate successful class participation.

At other organizations, the case manager and participant relationship were more hands-off, and participants wanted for more support:

> I got the laptop and they told me that someone would be contacting me...That didn't happen as I got it, a time wasn't set up right away. I think it was like two or three weeks after I received if. It would have been good if I were able to sign up more quickly for initial orientation and assessments regarding the program...I think it would probably help ...Maybe more frequent, like maybe a weekly email from the program about how I'm doing or if I have any questions. – John

Part of the determination of how participants' experience receiving the technology depended upon what organization they happened to be receiving services from. Oftentimes, this was a good thing – two organizations focused on serving immigrants and refugees. These organizations had staff that came from the communities that they were serving and could offer assistance in participants' primary languages. However, other times, from what the participants shared, they needed more help than what the organization was set up to provide.

5 Conclusion

While information and communication technologies are tools that can facilitate development, including in a major U.S. city like Seattle, they can also widen gaps in inequality that low-income, BIPOC, immigrant, and refugee communities already face. Without ongoing and committed support for ICT interventions like Digital Bridge, these communities will continue to experience the digital divide, which in the current climate is detrimental to economic recovery. However, what we have also learned is that the concept of technology maintenance is equally, if not more important than simply providing initial access to technology and the internet. Aside from support to initiate and implement an ICT initiative like Digital Bridge, there needs to be commitment to provide ongoing support to communities so that they may not experience continued access to technology as a burden. Finally, we have learned that collaborative relationships between community-based organizations are vital and require clearly defined roles, and commitment, both funding and in person-to-person services and support. Community organizations are primed to engage and support their communities, and they provide vital support during an unprecedented time, so it's equally important that they receive support by way of financial support, and skills training so that they can provide quality assistance to their clients. ICT initiatives like Digital Bridge will be an essential component to economic recovery and civil life as we continue to grapple with the effects of COVID-19. It is important that we recognize that relationships, capacity building, and committed support are key components of success beyond initial access to technology and the internet.

References

Braxton, K.: City of Seattle and Comcast Invest $100,000 to Address Digital Equity, 20 July 2020. https://web.archive.org/web/20210410104951/https://bottomline.seattle.gov/2020/07/20/city-of-seattle-and-comcast-invest-100000-to-address-digital-equity/

Carson, K., Wedlake, S., Houghton, M., Keyes, D., Iribe Ramirez, Y.: Digital bridge: providing digital access to low-income job seekers during the COVID-19 pandemic. Seattle Jobs Initiative, City of Seattle (2021)

Gonzales, A.: The contemporary US digital divide: from initial access to technology maintenance. Inf. Commun. Soc. **19**(2), 234–248 (2016)

Heeks, R.: Foundations of ICTs in development: the information chain. eDevelopment Brief. **3**(1), 1–2 (2005)

Mthoko, H., Khene, C.: Building theory in ICT4D evaluation: a comprehensive approach to assessing outcome and impact. Inf. Technol. Dev. **24**(1), 138–164 (2018)

Palen, L., Salzman, M.: Voice-mail diary studies for naturalistic data capture under mobile conditions. In: Proceedings of the 2002 ACM Conference on Computer Supported Cooperative Work, pp. 87–95 (2002)

Wedlake, S., Iribe Ramirez, Y., Carson, K., Jowaisas, C., Keyes, D., Houghton, M.: Policy implications from a pandemic broadband adoption program for low-income job seekers. Technology and Social Change Group (TASCHA), University of Washington Information School (2021). http://hdl.handle.net/1773/48134

Using Local Community to Ease Long Haul Uncertainty During the COVID-19 Pandemic

Jeongwon Jo[1(✉)], Tiffany Knearem[1], Chun-hua Tsai[2], and John M. Carroll[1]

[1] Pennsylvania State University, University Park, PA, USA
{jzj5543,tak54,jmc56}@psu.edu

[2] University of Nebraska at Omaha, Omaha, USA
chunhuatsai@unomaha.edu

Abstract. The COVID-19 pandemic ushered in an era of unprecedented hardship worldwide, bringing uncertainty to new levels as people's routines were disrupted and what was once considered normal was called into question. Citizens initiated online local communities to support information-seeking amidst the pandemic. In this paper, we explore what types of information were sought and how people engaged in uncertainty reduction with others in their area during the initial phase of COVID-19. We conducted content analysis on a pandemic-relief online local community. We found that people leveraged local networks to get updates about timely situations in local areas, clear confusion around local COVID-19 regulations, and seek confirmation on emerging social norms. However, there existed inaccurate information exchange about regulations and conflicting opinions on social norms. We provide design suggestions to increase the potentials of uncertainty management through online local communities.

Keywords: Crisis informatics · Disaster communication · Information seeking

1 Introduction

Uncertainty surges during disasters due to their unpredictable outbreaks and consequences [1]. A highly contagious virus, COVID-19, has caused waves of uncertainty for over a year in over 200 countries at the time of this writing [2]. At the onset of the pandemic, appropriate testing for the disease was short in supply, known symptoms and aftereffects of the disease were changing frequently, and a vaccine had not yet been created [3]. People did not have a clear answer about when the pandemic will end, which led to over-purchasing and panic buying behaviors [4]. Other than the virus itself, new policies and interventions to respond to the pandemic were unfamiliar to citizens. Policies and preventive measures for COVID-19 varied from place to place and were in a semi-constant

M. Smits (Ed.): iConference 2022, LNCS 13193, pp. 211–227, 2022.
https://doi.org/10.1007/978-3-030-96960-8_15

state of flux as new data became available. The pandemic changed every aspect of everyday life and created multiple layers of confusion about the world.

People are often uncomfortable with unpredictable and unknown situations and will actively engage in information-seeking behaviors to alleviate uncertainty [5]. Knowing the types of information people sought in previous disasters can guide what information should be appropriately distributed in future crises, potentially enhancing uncertainty management. However, less is known about information demands amidst an epidemic crisis compared to other disaster scenarios due to its infrequency [6,7]. Moreover, due to the long-lasting characteristic of the pandemic, uncertainties varied over time.

Due to social distancing measures mandated during the pandemic, people relied on social media to fulfill information needs [8], which makes it a valuable source to explore the information people sought and associated uncertainties. A body of research in crisis informatics emphasized the value of connecting with people nearby through online communities during crises because those in affected areas can provide precise and locale-specific information in real-time [14–17]. Although COVID-19 was a global disaster, each local community was affected differently (e.g., mask inventory status or severity of panic buying), which suggests that there are benefits in timeliness and accuracy to turning to an online community tied to one's geographic area to seek information from people who live nearby.

In this study, we aimed to investigate information-seeking behaviors through the lens of the local geographic community, focusing on the initial phase of the pandemic (i.e., first six month) when people were still adjusting to new situations. The following research question guided our study: *What types of local-specific information were sought in local communities at the initial phase of COVID-19?* We performed a qualitative content analysis on posts that asked for information and associated comments in a local pandemic-relief Facebook group that focused on a city in Texas, United States. Our analysis surfaced that people sought information relating to assessing health risks of visiting local areas, inventory status, local pandemic-related regulations, and seeking confirmation around new social norms. COVID-19 is likely not the only pandemic that humanity will face in the near-term future, therefore we suggest implications for designing systems that can augment the benefits of seeking information in local-focused online communities during epidemic crises.

Our contributions to crisis informatics are three-fold: First, we discover local-specific information demands that exist amidst an epidemic crisis. Second, we examined how online local communities responded to information requests. Third, we proposed design implications for improving online local epidemic-relief communities for information exchange.

2 Related Work: Online Local Communities for Uncertainty Management Amidst Crises

The development of Information and Communications Technology (ICT) has elevated the capabilities of citizens to participate in disaster communication.

Email listservs, community websites, microblogs, and social media provided a place for citizens to gather and provide support when displaced due to hazards virtually. One of their ways to provide support was to actively disseminate text, photo, and video-based information as citizen journalists [11].

Research to date in crisis informatics has emphasized the unique role physical proximity plays in disaster communication. Individuals in impacted areas favored social media posts from others nearby due to their real-time updates and accuracy [12]. People sometimes relied more heavily on informal news sources generated by locals than national news media because people in impacted areas were already familiar with local geographies and were able to generate up-to-date situational information [14–17]. For instance, in the aftermath of the Boston Marathon Bombings in 2013, people considered photos uploaded on Twitter by people near the impacted area more reliable and accurate than what was reported by major news media [18].

However, information demands differ by disaster types because each of them creates distinct situations [6,20]. For instance, during a wildfire outbreak, citizens wanted to know impacted local areas and evacuation places through local community websites [19], while they asked for a list of victims and missing persons after a mass shooting outbreak on Facebook groups [13]. Understanding information people seek in a specific disaster situation is essential to provide appropriate information and effectively manage public uncertainties.

Compared to other common disasters (e.g., hurricanes, floods), local information citizens seek during an epidemic outbreak is underinvestigated due to its infrequency. The few studies that explored information sharing on social media during epidemics mostly analyzed posts from official disaster organizations [21,22]. The only study that examined local information provided on online forums amidst the Zika outbreak mainly focused on information demands to make a rational decision on traveling rather than everyday life [7]. Moreover, COVID-19 was unprecedentedly long and expansive to this generation, forcing people to look for information not sought in previous epidemics. To discover what public uncertainties existed in these uncertain times of the global pandemic and how locals can help manage them, we directly examined information citizens asked others nearby in a pandemic-relief online local community.

3 Methodology

After the pandemic outbreak, people created online groups to exchange support with others nearby. A Facebook group dedicated to different counties or cities was the most widely-used platform to connect with local community members in the United States [23]. Previous research noted that participation in disaster communities declined as situations stabilized [19], so Facebook groups targeted in areas with high COVID-19 transmission over a long time were of interest. Therefore, the following criteria were used to select a local pandemic-relief Facebook group to study: (1) covers a local area with consistently high severity of COVID-19 cases; (2) open to anyone to join, view, and post; and (3) high group activity (e.g., average posts per day, the number of members).

The selected group satisfied all selection criteria, 'Local Community Support for COVID-19 Relief in Austin'[1] was focused on Austin, Texas. By the end of the data collection window, the group had around 4,500 members, with 11 posts uploaded per day on average. As we were interested in information-seeking behaviors at the beginning of the pandemic, we retrieved all posts uploaded within the first seven months of the pandemic: between the start of the group, March 14, 2020 and October 25, 2020. We collected 2,120 posts in total.

Members of the group uploaded a wide variety of posts, including recommendations for local places, advice on personal situations, local news articles, aid requests and offers, and virtual events. We were interested in posts that asked for information, advice, or suggestions to explore underlying uncertainties the poster had. One research team member read all the collected posts and categorized each post based on whether the poster was asking for information or something else to filter out irrelevant posts (e.g., asking for emotional or instrumental support). To meet the criteria for *asking information*, the post needed to contain one of the following phrases (or variations thereof): *"Does anyone have suggestions...", "Does anyone know...", "Where/how can I...", "Looking for recommendations/advice/suggestions...", "How do you...", "How are people...", "Has anyone...", or "...Any ideas/suggestions/recommendations?"*. In total, we identified 256 posts to be information-seeking posts.

In the next step, we coded the 256 posts based on the type of information the poster sought using the constant comparative analysis approach for data analysis [24]. One research team member initially performed descriptive open coding using Nvivo. After the initial coding process, the research team of four had a series of meetings and collectively read and discussed the posts and associated comments to validate identified codes. The final coding scheme encompassed multiple codes, but we only selected those that directly matched the focus of this study: what COVID-19-related local information was sought in a local-based disaster-relief group. We discarded codes associated with information requests irrelevant to COVID-19 (e.g., *general home maintenance, suggestions for products*), not local-specific (e.g., *COVID-19 symptoms and testing, COVID-19 prevention strategies*), or information that could be obtained from official national agencies (e.g., *Nationwide COVID-19 regulations*). The remaining codes included *Recommendations for safe and stocked local places, Local COVID-19 regulations*, and *Reasonable social behaviors*, which will be presented in the following section.

4 Findings

We discovered three pandemic-related locally relevant information types people asked: (1) up-to-date situations in local regions and recommendations on safe places; (2) confusion due to the absence of rules and emerging official regulations; (3) other's confirmation on social behaviors and routines. Because the pandemic

[1] pseudonym for anonymity.

situation and guidelines were frequently evolving, we provided specific dates when each post or comment was uploaded for better understanding.

4.1 Recommendations for Safe and Stocked Local Places

We present findings related to perceived high risks of catching the virus, which raised uncertainties on which places are safe to visit, and during which hours. Moreover, panic buying ensued in the early stage of the pandemic, and people wondered which hours were best to get certain items at local stores. Because the community was targeted to a specific region, other members provided locale-specific (hyperlocal) and up-to-date (hypertemporal) information.

Hyperlocal Information. People wanted to be assured that the places they were visiting were low-risk of COVID-19 with fewer people or proper safety measures. For example, a poster had to take precautions due to pre-existing health conditions and asked what preventive measures were being done at a specific grocery store. The poster received very detailed information from other members:

> ***Comment:*** *The one downtown does a pretty good job [...] They limit volume of customers, wipe down carts, offer disposable gloves and sanitizer, and the staff wears masks. They space out lines to check out and have a plexi shield between cashier and shopper. They don't let people bring reusable bags in from home* (May 31, 2020)

Because personal health conditions were disclosed in that post, the poster also received adjusted recommendations: *"If you are a senior or immune-system-compromised you can shop an hour before the regular hours"* (May 31, 2020).

Some wanted recommendations of local stores that took proper preventive measures. One user asked for a hair salon that was doing a good job of disinfecting. Others suggested local salons, sharing personal experience on their disinfection measures:

> ***Comment 1:*** *My stylist came to my home and cut my hair on the back patio. We both wore masks [...] I felt very safe outside.*
> ***Comment 2:*** `Business A` *in downtown did an amazing job. You can't walk in, [they] let you in, then you sanitize, they take your temp, everyone has masks on, and anything anyone touches (employee or guest) was sanitized immediately.*
> (July 16, 2020)

Similarly, people were unsure which places to visit because large crowds can increase the risk of infection, and many places were temporarily closed due to the pandemic. For instance, a user with health concerns who was new to the area wanted to know which places were less-crowded. Group members oriented the poster to safe local places:

> ***Comment***: *Bike the Walnut Creek Trail on a weekday. It runs from Govalle Park all the way out to Manor. Usually empty, plus you'll be biking by anyone outdoors, so very low risk.* (June 20, 2020)

Hypertemporal Information. Many posts asked about the inventory status at local stores or where they could get a specific item such as toilet paper or masks. These posts were common in the initial phase of the COVID-19 outbreak in Texas, in March and April, when panicked people stock-piled household goods, food, and PPE [31].

For those posts asking about inventory status, some people commented with photos of shelves at stores to give posters a sense of the situation. Sometimes, others told posters which local stores to go with a reference to the specific time or date that they visited:

> ***Comment 1***: *Dollar Tree, yesterday. They were small containers but they had quite a few.*
> ***Comment 2***: *Target @ [this location] had some tubes of Lysol wipes in stock a few hours ago.*
> ***Comment 3***: *Was able to get a pack of Clorox wipes at Costco on Saturday by being there at opening time*
> ***Comment 4***: *Just saw a lot at the cashier counter at the H-E-B gas station at [this location]*
> (all July 17, 2020)

Besides inventory status, knowing up-to-date busy hours was important for people who wanted to avoid a large crowd at stores. Also, some stores limited the number of customers inside to reduce the risk of infection, which resulted in long line-ups. Some asked about other's experiences at particular grocery stores, such as crowd levels. People provided a specific day of the week or time they visited when narrating their experience because store situations changed by day and time. These are exemplary comments from different posts asking about when they should visit stores to avoid crowdedness:

> ***Comment 1***: *I went early last Friday and it was very quiet.* (May 31, 2020)
> ***Comment 2***: *I recommend to go during the week and early afternoon in order to avoid any lines [...] I've actually gone a few times on Sundays and it wasn't even that bad though.* (May 31, 2020)
> ***Comment 3***: *Go in the morning at like 8am.. I went at 7am the other day, right when they opened. No line.. but there were more people [...] when I left at 8.* (April 18, 2020)
> ***Comment 4***: *I went about an hour and a half before closing Wednesday and it was fine* (April 18, 2020)

During COVID-19, people were unsure of safe places to visit, such as places taking proper preventive measures or less crowded outdoors. They were also unsure when to visit local stores to find specific items or avoid a large crowd. Online local community members provided local-specific and timely information, being in the same neighborhood.

4.2 Uncertainty About Local COVID-19 Regulations

Citizens had to follow up with frequent changes in orders that differed by state and county and differed from day to day, which added another layer of uncertainty. They had to keep up with what the correct measure was, depending on place and time.

People were unfamiliar with emerging COVID-19-related regulations. One user was unsure if any official agency was accepting reports against a local business where staff was not wearing a facial mask. Other members specifically guided her to official routes she could report them through. However, there was one member who complained that suggested penalties were not applicable in a county close to Austin:

> ***Comment 1:*** *It's up to a $2,000 fine in Austin for not wearing a mask. Call 311!*
> ***Comment 2:*** *[a link to the 'Report a Hazard Form' on a county government website]*
> ***Comment 3:*** *Note that really only works within the city limits of Austin. If you report one in [this county] the police don't care and will not take action.*
> (uploaded between July 9-10, 2020)

Comment 3 implies that Austin practically imposed, or at least had official penalties against people not abiding by mask mandate. In contrast, a county near Austin might not have executed such penalties or did not even have one. In either case, different situations by the county could increase uncertainty.

There was also a case where a poster asked about the COVID-19 policies in Texas in general. People referred to the situation in Austin because the Facebook group focused on Austin, Texas. However, the poster restated that she wanted policies in another county close to Austin, which turned out to have different orders:

> ***Poster:*** *Will someone please share the official guidance for Texas on high-risk people? My 83-year old mother with asthma decided it was a good idea to go to church this weekend. [...] If she won't listen to me, perhaps she will listen to official guidance.*
> ***Commenter:*** *High risk people should not be in groups greater than 10 [...] [a link to the Austin government website]*
> ***Poster:*** *She is in El Paso.*
> ***Commenter:*** *Ok, it appears to be better there than here. They are at the lowest level [...] and churches are 50% capacity.*
> (uploaded between September 21-22, 2020)

Their conversation implies how different situations were by county, which led to distinct orders. It implies that it can be better to set up an online local community on the county level, where everyone has a common ground that they are all stating to the same locality. It could make the communication process more effective and increase the likelihood of getting the right information.

In Texas, the state governor altered COVID-19 regulations several times, constantly mandating or lifting face-covering policies depending on the situation. This added another confusion about the situation. Under a post where a group member asked how to deal with local stores not having their staffs wear a mask, contrasting responses were left, which reflected their confusion with frequently changing orders:

> ***Commenter 1:*** *I believe it's not being mandated. I don't know what reporting our concerns would really do.*
> ***Commenter 2:*** *Austin is masks in public and in all businesses as of Tuesday*
> ***Commenter 3:*** *it is re-mandated now.*
> ***Commenter 1:*** *Oh, GOOD! Should have never been lifted.*
> (June 20, 2020)

In that post, three other members mentioned a date when mask mandate begins, but they all referred to different dates:

> ***Commenter 1:*** *It's not required until Tuesday.* [which is 22nd]
> ***Commenter 2:*** *Starting the 25th they will be required to wear them.*
> ***Commenter 3:*** *23rd, not 25th*
> (June 19, 2020)

We discovered that different counties had differing rules, which increased uncertainty and emphasized the importance of setting up an online local community on a narrower level by county. Frequently changing regulations sometimes led to the diffusion of misinformation within the community, and people who kept an eye on them corrected it.

4.3 Seeking Confirmation on Social Behaviors

Due to the lack of specific mandates and inexperience in living in the pandemic era, what social behaviors were considered rational depended on personal beliefs and values and how people around them behaved. Reasonable behaviors were socially defined, and the local-based online community was a channel to confirm surrounding social expectations.

There was uncertainty about whether wearing a mask had now become a general social behavior. For instance, a poster asked others if one can directly ask house cleaners to wear a mask:

> *We are moving. We will have the house professionally cleaned the day after the furniture arrives. 1) Is it ok to ask the house cleaners to wear masks? 2) Is it ok to move in the day they clean or should we wait a day or two to be on the safe side?*
> (July 6, 2020)

People assured the poster that wearing a mask was now regarded as a social norm: *"Yes it's ok to ask them to wear masks, they should be anyway given the mandate"* (July 6, 2020). Some shared their similar recent experience to convey more assurance: *"It's absolutely okay to ask, we just moved as well and our moving company were already planning on wearing masks"* (July 6, 2020).

The second question in the post above was related to proper COVID-19 preventive measures when moving-in, which was usually unavailable in official guidelines, which focused on addressing daily activities. In this Facebook group, the poster was able to get confirmation and suggestions from others who already had experienced house-moving during the pandemic:

> *We have had maid service at our home [...] I'd wait at least a day or two before moving in after they clean [and] open some windows and move right in after they clean.* (July 6, 2020)

Similarly, there was a hairdresser who wanted to get other's thoughts on whether or not it was acceptable to book customers selectively, which was also not explicitly addressed in official guidelines. She asked if it was irrational to turn away some customers who might be high at risk of transmitting the virus:

> *Asking in earnest As a hairdresser, am I being unreasonable by turning away clients who work with many other people? [...] I feel that by only accepting clients who are sheltering in place, I'm not exposing client A to all of client B's coworkers. I believe that by accepting public-facing, clients, I'd be exponentially increasing the risk of my salon becoming a vector for covid.* (July 8, 2020)

Before the pandemic, refusing to provide service to certain people was considered unethical. However, because it was risky to interact with others during the pandemic, others assured the poster that the safety should be prioritized: *"It is your right to screen in any way you choose. It is ultimately your health, the health of your clients and your liability"* (July 8, 2020). Some users appreciated the poster for being socially responsible. However, other comments pointed out potential flaws in her approach:

> ***Comment 1:*** *The fallacy of it all is at end of day those clients aren't catching it from other clients directly. You're the common variable. So unless you take yourself out of the equation, the risk will continue to be quite high, regardless if you asked if they've been sheltering in place. You have no way of knowing if they're lying about it.* (July 8, 2020)
> ***Comment 2:*** *I know so many people who will claim they're being safe but aren't really.* (July 16, 2020)

There was also a comment which pointed out possible discrimination embedded in this protocol:

> *Are you saying you won't do all the people on the front line? Like grocery workers? What about immune compromised? [...] There's a fine line for some form of discrimination here.* (July 16, 2020)

People had contrasting reactions to the post because one prioritized the safety of the hairdresser and customers, while others recognized that some people could not shelter at home due to their classification as essential workers. Both approaches were rational.

In another example, a poster also received two contrasting but reasonable opinions. As it had not been long since wearing a mask became the "new normal", people were unsure in which situations it was mandatory to wear a mask and when not wearing one was excusable. One poster was skeptical about not wearing a mask when biking or running outside and asked others for help deciding what to do. In the comments, people discussed whether or not wearing a mask should be mandatory when working out:

> ***Commenter 1:*** *If you click on the link [to official guidelines] and scroll down you will find the requirements. I assume that while running you could be restricted from breathing if you wear it..*
> ***Commenter 2:*** *That is not an exception. I see almost no-one wearing them while out running and biking and it makes me cringe... the whole point is to keep your breath and the droplets in it from getting out into the air, and the people exercising are likely putting out far more of this [...]*
> ***Commenter 3:*** *It is an exception - [(a link to a news article)].*
> ***Commenter 2:*** *not sure why the article interprets the actual county announcement and guidelines that way [...] I still think they're all being inconsiderate.*
> ***Commenter 3:*** *But in my neighborhood - people walking and running are mostly 20 to hundreds of feet apart. I would not expect they should wear a mask. If you have allergies or any underlying condition, impeding your breathing could be serious.*
> (between April 18 and 19, 2020)

Commenter 1 and 3 insisted that masks were not mandated when exercising outside and provided links to an official guideline and a news article. Commenter 3 reminded others of a few exceptional cases where wearing a mask while exercising could be life-threatening. In contrast, Commenter 2 emphasized that not wearing a mask while exercising could put others around them at risk. Although the official guideline that Commenter 1 posted did not explicitly specify mask mandates during exercise, the news article from Commenter 3 said that exercise activities were not part of the mask mandate. The vagueness of the official guidelines raised questions about the appropriateness of exercising without a mask.

People also conflicted on the right to know about someone's positive COVID-19 status. Although many felt that notifying their contacts that they tested positive was a social obligation, it was not easy for them to tell others that they might have infected them with a potentially life-threatening disease. People wondered to whom and when they should tell others about the possible infection. In the following example, a poster described a situation and asked whether people whom they contacted should be notified of the potential risk:

> *A staff member at a pre-school facility had family in their home last week and the family members tested positive for Covid-19 within 3 days of returning home [...] Do coworkers, auxiliary staff, students, etc need to be quarantined? Should parents of students be notified of the staff member's exposure to the virus [...] ?* (October 19, 2020)

Some suggested that the poster did not need to tell others of the possible risk in this case, such as:

> ***Comment 1:*** *No they generally wouldn't be notified unless the person that works there is positive. [...] I'm almost certain APH would not ask you to notify anyone until the staff directly involved has a positive test. It is not confirmed without that.*
> ***Comment 2:*** *Contact Austin Public Health. They can help you. I have a licensed preschool in my home and I've been told to direct these types of questions to their offices [...] I'm pretty sure notifications only go out when symptoms of infectious disease are present or if there is a positive test result*
> (both October 19, 2020)

They made their assertions by referring to the existing regulations, health agencies, or relevant personal experience. However, there were conflicting comments which argued that the poster should notify parents and students of the situation. For example, one comment emphasized the right to know about possible risks:

> *Our company states that if symptom free, just monitor and isolate the sick one. I was a total turd when a sick person was in my work [...] I was mad because I wanted to know so I could test if needed.* (October 19, 2020)

Due to the altered world, people sought others' opinions on their behaviors or decisions, which used to be their routines pre-COVID-19. Local members responded with diverse opinions, which sometimes did not reach a consensus. Heated discussions ignited when people responded with different but rational viewpoints.

5 Discussion

In this section, we discuss each of three uncertainties that lingered amidst the initial phase of the pandemic that led to information seeking: (1) uncertainty on where and when to visit local places; (2) uncertainty on confusing regulations; (3) uncertainty on reasonable social behaviors. We state how local members alleviated or added uncertainties and suggested design implications that can better online local pandemic-support community for uncertainty management.

5.1 Hyperlocal and Hypertemporal Information Requests During the Pandemic

The types of hyperlocal and hypertemporal information people seek after common disasters have been well-investigated [19,32,33], but information needs amidst an epidemic crisis are yet unknown due to its infrequency. In this study, we fill this gap by discovering what hyperlocal and hypertemporal information people asked in the online local community during COVID-19 when it was one of the few channels to retrieve information due to lockdowns and stay-at-home orders. Unlike other disaster situations, risks associated with each location have not been stable amidst the pandemic. For instance, places considered safe at one point may not be in a few hours if a large crowd gathers. Thereby, demands for situational updates during an epidemic crisis turned out to be highly frequent. In the Facebook group we analyzed, people asked about: disinfection measures taken at a local store; less crowded outdoors; recent inventory status; less busy hours at stores.

We have seen that group members provided highly contextual and up-to-date local knowledge, which extends the findings of prior research that emphasized the value of geographically focused online communities during disasters [14,19,25]. For example, they shared which local areas were safe to visit, what time local stores got crowded each day, and which hard-to-find items can be found at what time at which stores. Local knowledge they shared was highly relevant to everyday life and to residents, which national news media for a wider audience was not able to provide [15–17]. Although COVID-19 was a global pandemic, detailed local-specific information was still crucial as the severity of the pandemic differed by locality.

However, posts requesting local information and comments were mixed with other posts, which could quickly be buried in the Facebook group timeline, and the process of getting such information was question-and-answer-based; someone had to upload a post to ask for such information; otherwise, the information was not available to anyone. A crowdsourced geo-tagging feature can facilitate information exchange about less crowded outdoors, recent inventory status, less busy hours, and disinfection measures taken at local stores. For instance, users can enable automatic location-sharing on their phones or manually mark which local area they visit. Highly crowded areas can be colored in red, moderate in orange, and less in green. Users can add inventory tags or photos of shelves at local stores with timestamps for items that are hard to find during epidemic crises. Regarding disinfection measures taken at local stores, users may check on one or more boxes that indicate safety protocols, like sanitized carts and baskets or limits in the number of customers.

5.2 Confusing COVID-19 Regulations

How COVID-19 regulations were passed down from state and local governments in the U.S. escalated citizens' confusion; emerging laws were different not only by state but also by county. Adding to that, citizens had to follow up with frequently changing regulations. Frequent regulatory changes resulted in the accidental sharing of incorrect information. Although some members provided accurate rule-related information with reference to local government websites, others shared inaccurate information (e.g., wrong dates for mask mandates). Such incorrect information worsened uncertainty rather than alleviation.

In the Facebook group we observed, some members actively corrected inaccurate information in the comments. This echoes findings from previous research where members of online groups voluntarily corrected inaccurate information shared by others [18,35]. Behaviors of correcting inaccurate information were valuable in the community we observed, as inaccurate information on safety regulations can lead to inappropriate health-protective behaviors (e.g., not wearing facial masks). However, citizens can be overloaded following up with quickly changing local COVID-19 policies and keeping an eye on possible accidental sharing of inaccurate information in the community to fix it.

Disaster relief communities should plan effective strategies to communicate new local regulation updates during a crisis. The findings suggest that setting up online disaster relief groups on a county basis instead of state-level can help reduce dissemination of inaccurate information around policies in the U.S. They can also consider the cooperation with local governments to effectively inform citizens of changing policies. Online platforms widely used for disaster relief like Facebook tend to have a large user pool and are likely to be more frequently visited than government websites, which can effectuate communication of policy updates. During the pandemic crisis, most states imposed multiple phases of regulations on social gatherings and local businesses based on the severity of COVID-19 [36]. A banner that specifies a phase of regulation can be incorporated into a platform for disaster relief. With the banner having different colors representing distinct phases, the level of policy strictness and correct policies can be disseminated under control.

5.3 Collective Sense-Making Under Uncertainty

Unfamiliar situations make people question daily routines [19], and they often seek other's opinions to predict possible outcomes of certain behaviors before they act [37]. We discovered a similar pattern in the local pandemic-relief group. There were no detailed official guidelines on how to handle life events which occur seldomly (e.g., moving house), and ambiguous gray areas in the guidelines triggered different interpretations and risk assessments from various people. People were uncertain about their behavioral choices and were unsure if their perceptions of ongoing situations were on the same page with others. They asked others' thoughts on their reasoning to make sense of the situation collectively. However, this collective sense-making process was not always smooth with conflicting opinions which is in line with previous studies [16,38,39]; some confirmed that they were reasonable, while others pointed out how their reasoning could be troublesome. While the conflicting opinions could be logical on all sides, they did not completely resolve uncertainties.

Conflicting opinions were dispersed throughout unstructured comments on the original post, making it harder to come up with conclusions on rational behavior. Moreover, when people face opinions that conflict with their beliefs, they easily feel cognitive dissonance, which can lead to ignoring conflicting opinions, and halting their assessment of them [40]. However, stubbornly rejecting opinions can pose a risk to one's health amidst an epidemic crisis. Nudging people to hold a dialogue with others and outlining the pros and cons of two different viewpoints are essential for collective sense-making [41].

To help people cope with cognitive dissonance, we suggest including a venue for public deliberation in online platforms for disaster relief. Public deliberation is a way to bring in diverse opinions, compare the pros and cons of possible decisions, and come up with new solutions [42]. The concept has been applied to politics or urban planning [43–45], but its usage can be extended to disaster management. Common public deliberation systems involve a pro and a con list, and this feature can be used to make the collective reasoning process more visible and structured. Under each confirmation seeking request, those who agree with the poster can leave their rationale on the pro list, while those who disagree can post their arguments on the con list. Positives and negatives associated with two different behavioral choices can become apparent, which can help the poster conveniently weigh confirmations and denials of their behavioral choice in order to make a decision in their best interest.

Limitations. In this study, we investigated one local Facebook pandemic-relief group to understand locally relevant information requests in the initial phase of the pandemic when people have not yet adapted to new situations. Our key focus was an in-depth understanding of certain information demands amidst an epidemic crisis and how local-focused online communities can fulfill them rather than obtaining broad trends. The Facebook group was focused on Austin, Texas, in the U.S., which had a relatively high number of infections in the first six months of COVID-19. Future studies can observe other communities based on different areas or analyze posts uploaded in a different timeframe of the pandemic to see if other information demands exist.

6 Conclusion

COVID-19 disrupted social functioning, which prompted people to engage in online local communities to understand the confusing world. To decipher how peer-to-peer interactions alleviate uncertainty during this long-lasting crisis, we observed information-seeking behavior in a local Facebook group for disaster relief. Uncertainty arose around frequent updates on local places, the ever-changing and confusing local regulations, and emerging social norms. Mitigating uncertainty during epidemics through online local communities could be better enabled with crowdsourced geo-tagging maps, increased visibility around regulatory updates, and opportunities to engage in public deliberation. When the next pandemic will occur is unknown, but we believe that leveraging local online communities will help citizens adapt.

References

1. Longstaff, P.H.: Security, resilience, and communication in unpredictable environments such as terrorism, natural disasters, and complex technology. Center for Information Policy Research, Harvard University (2005)
2. WHO coronavirus disease (COVID-19) dashboard. https://covid19.who.int/. Accessed 12 Sept 2021
3. Wu, Y.C., Chen, C.S., Chan, Y.J.: The outbreak of COVID-19: an overview. J. Chin. Med. Assoc. **83**(3), 217 (2020)
4. Arafat, S.Y., Kar, S.K., Marthoenis, M., Sharma, P., Apu, E.H., Kabir, R.: Psychological underpinning of panic buying during pandemic (COVID-19). In: Psychiatry research, pp. 113061. Psychiatry research (2020)
5. Berger, C.R., Calabrese, R.J.: Some explorations in initial interaction and beyond: toward a developmental theory of interpersonal communication. Human Commun. Res. **1**(2), 99–112 (1974)
6. Olteanu, A., Vieweg, S., Castillo, C.: What to expect when the unexpected happens: social media communications across crises. In: Proceedings of the 18th ACM Conference on Computer Supported Cooperative Work and Social Computing, pp. 994–1009. ACM (2015)
7. Gui, X., Kou, Y., Pine, K. H., Chen, Y.: Managing uncertainty: using social media for risk assessment during a public health crisis. In: Proceedings of the 2017 CHI Conference on Human Factors in Computing Systems, pp. 4520–4533. ACM (2017)
8. Pine, K. H., Lee, M., Whitman, S. A., Chen, Y., Henne, K.: Making sense of risk information amidst uncertainty: individuals' perceived risks associated with the COVID-19 pandemic. In: Proceedings of the 2021 CHI Conference on Human Factors in Computing Systems, pp. 1–15. ACM (2021)
9. Jaeger, P.T., Shneiderman, B., Fleischmann, K.R., Preece, J., Qu, Y., Wu, P.F.: Community response grids: E-government, social networks, and effective emergency management. Telecommun. Policy **31**(10–11), 592–604 (2007)
10. Palen, L., Hughes, A.L.: Social media in disaster communication. In: Rodriguez, H., Donner, W., Trainor, J. (eds.) Handbook of Disaster Research. Handbooks of Sociology and Social Research. Springer, Cham (2018). https://doi.org/10.1007/978-3-319-63254-4_24
11. Gillmor, D.: We the media: the rise of citizen journalists. Nation. Civic Rev. **93**(3), 58–63 (2004)
12. Kogan, M., Palen, L., Anderson, K.M.: Think local, retweet global: retweeting by the geographically-vulnerable during Hurricane Sandy. In: Proceedings of the 18th ACM Conference on Computer Supported Cooperative Work and Social Computing, pp. 981–993. ACM (2015)
13. Vieweg, S., Palen, L., Liu, S.B., Hughes, A.L., Sutton, J.N.: Collective intelligence in disaster: examination of the phenomenon in the aftermath of the 2007 Virginia Tech shooting. University of Colorado Boulder, CO (2008)
14. Sutton, J.N., Palen, L., Shklovski, I.: Backchannels on the front lines: emergency uses of social media in the 2007 Southern California Wildfires (2008)
15. Starbird, K., Palen, L.: Pass it on?: retweeting in mass emergency. In: ISCRAM (2010)
16. Heverin, T., Zach, L.: Use of microblogging for collective sense-making during violent crises: a study of three campus shootings. J. Am. Soc. Inf. Sci. Technol. **63**(1), 34–47 (2012)

17. Hagar, C: The information and social needs of Cumbrian farmers during the UK 2001 foot and mouth disease outbreak and the role of information and communication technologies. The socio-cultural impact of foot and mouth disease in the UK in (2001)
18. Huang, Y.L., Starbird, K., Orand, M., Stanek, S.A., Pedersen, H.T.: Connected through crisis: emotional proximity and the spread of misinformation online. In: Proceedings of the 18th ACM Conference on Computer Supported Cooperative Work and Social Computing, pp. 969–980. ACM (2015)
19. Shklovski, I., Palen, L., Sutton, J.: Finding community through information and communication technology in disaster response. In: Proceedings of the 2008 ACM Conference on Computer Supported Cooperative Work, pp. 127–136. ACM (2008)
20. Fraustino, J.D., Liu, B., Jin, Y.: Social media use during disasters: a review of the knowledge base and gaps (2012)
21. Guidry, J.P., Jin, Y., Orr, C.A., Messner, M., Meganck, S.: Ebola on Instagram and Twitter: how health organizations address the health crisis in their social media engagement. Public Relations Rev. **43**(3), 477–486 (2017)
22. Lwin, M.O., Lu, J., Sheldenkar, A., Schulz, P.J.: Strategic uses of Facebook in Zika outbreak communication: implications for the crisis and emergency risk communication model. Int. J. Environ. Res. Public Health **15**(9), 1974 (2018)
23. Knearem, T., Jo, J., Tsai, C.H., Carroll, J. M.: Making space for support: an exploratory analysis of pandemic-response mutual aid platforms. In: C&T'21: Proceedings of the 10th International Conference on Communities and Technologies-Wicked Problems in the Age of Tech, pp. 38–43. ACM (2021)
24. Charmaz, K.: Constructing grounded theory: a practical guide through qualitative analysis. sage (2006)
25. Carroll, M.S., Cohn, P.J., Seesholtz, D.N., Higgins, L.L.: Fire as a galvanizing and fragmenting influence on communities: the case of the Rodeo-Chediski fire. Soc. Nat. Resour. **18**(4), 301–320 (2005)
26. Eshghi, K., Larson, R.C.: Disasters: lessons from the past 105 years. Disaster Preven. Manage. Int. J. (2008)
27. Ludvigson, S.C., Ma, S., Ng, S.: COVID-19 and the macroeconomic effects of costly disasters (No. w26987). National Bureau Econ. Res. (2020)
28. Van Damme, W., et al.: The COVID-19 pandemic: diverse contexts; different epidemics-how and why?. BMJ Global Health **5**(7), e003098 (2020)
29. Olalekan, A., Iwalokun, B., Akinloye, O.M., Popoola, O., Samuel, T.A., Akinloye, O.: COVID-19 rapid diagnostic test could contain transmission in low-and middle-income countries. African J. Lab. Med. **9**(1), 1–8 (2020)
30. Trends in Number of COVID-19 Cases and Deaths in the US Reported to CDC, by State/Territory, https://covid.cdc.gov/covid-data-tracker/trendsdailytrendscases. Accessed 12 Sept 2021
31. Nicola, M., et al.: The socio-economic implications of the coronavirus pandemic (COVID-19): a review. Int. J. Surg. (London, England) **78**, 185–193 (2020)
32. Shklovski, I., Burke, M., Kiesler, S., Kraut, R.: Technology adoption and use in the aftermath of Hurricane Katrina in New Orleans. Am. Behav. Sci. **53**(8), 1228–1246 (2010)
33. Qu, Y., Huang, C., Zhang, P., Zhang, J.: Microblogging after a major disaster in China: a case study of the 2010 Yushu earthquake. In: Proceedings of the ACM 2011 conference on Computer supported cooperative work, pp. 25–34. ACM (2011)
34. Williams, S. N., Armitage, C. J., Tampe, T., Dienes, K.: Public perceptions of non-adherence to COVID-19 measures by self and others in the United Kingdom. MedRxiv (2020)

35. Starbird, K., Spiro, E., Edwards, I., Zhou, K., Maddock, J., Narasimhan, S.: Could this be true? I think so! Expressed uncertainty in online rumoring. In: Proceedings of the 2016 CHI Conference on Human Factors in Computing Systems, pp. 360–371. ACM (2016)
36. Courtemanche, C., Garuccio, J., Le, A., Pinkston, J., Yelowitz, A.: Strong social distancing measures in the United States reduced the COVID-19 growth rate: study evaluates the impact of social distancing measures on the growth rate of confirmed COVID-19 cases across the United States. Health Affairs **39**(7), 1237–1246 (2020)
37. Berger, C.R.: Beyond initial interaction: uncertainty, understanding, and the development of interpersonal relationships. Lang. Soc. Psychol. **6**, 122–144 (1979)
38. Bordia, P., DiFonzo, N.: Problem solving in social interactions on the Internet: rumor as social cognition. Soc. Psychol. Quart. **67**(1), 33–49 (2004)
39. Shibutani, T.: Improvised news: a sociological study of rumor. Ardent Media (1966)
40. Festinger, L.: A theory of cognitive dissonance, vol. 2. Stanford University Press (1957)
41. Muhren, W., Eede, G.V.D., Walle, B.V.D.: Sensemaking and implications for information systems design: findings from the Democratic Republic of Congo's ongoing crisis. Inf. Technol. Develop. **14**(3), 197–212 (2008)
42. Gastil, J.: Political communication and deliberation. Sage (2008)
43. Kriplean, T., Morgan, J., Freelon, D., Borning, A., Bennett, L.: Supporting reflective public thought with considerit. In: Proceedings of the ACM 2012 conference on Computer Supported Cooperative Work, pp. 265–274. ACM (2012)
44. Semaan, B., Faucett, H., Robertson, S.P., Maruyama, M., Douglas, S.: Designing political deliberation environments to support interactions in the public sphere. In: Proceedings of the 33rd Annual ACM Conference on Human Factors in Computing Systems, pp. 3167–3176. ACM (2015)
45. Borning, A., Friedman, B., Davis, J., Lin, P.: Informing public deliberation: value sensitive design of indicators for a large-scale urban simulation. In: Gellersen, H., Schmidt, K., Beaudouin-Lafon, M., Mackay, W. (eds.) Springer, Dordrecht (2005). https://doi.org/10.1007/1-4020-4023-7_23

Perceiving Libraries in a Making Context: Voices of Arts and Crafts Hobbyists

Lo Lee(✉) and Melissa G. Ocepek

University of Illinois Urbana-Champaign, Champaign, IL 61820, USA
{lolee2,mgocepek}@illinois.edu

Abstract. The burgeoning popularity attained by the maker culture has enlivened the library environment regarding its approach to engaging patrons. Despite the extensive makerspace literature, little is written on making from the hobbyist perspective, particularly beyond youth. To tackle inquiry about the potential relation between libraries and hobbyism as a form of leisure, we recruited 25 arts and crafts hobbyists and conducted a qualitative project. Combining diary studies and individual interviews, we aim to explore the perception making hobbyists have of libraries. Grounded upon the empirical data, we found that hobbyist participants mostly considered libraries a resource provider whose informative provision could go beyond traditional forms of print and digital collections. We also identified the value of librarianship to bolster inclusion in a making context to involve people of all ages, demonstrating the underlying need to reconsider the current support of libraries to the making activity. This is especially true in unexpected situations, like when physical library access is discouraged during the pandemic.

Keywords: Making · Arts and crafts · Library · Hobby

1 Introduction

The role of libraries has evolved throughout history. In the past, libraries acted as a place of information acquisition that provided physical and intellectual access to ideas and sources [1]. Following the power of the Web, the relationship between libraries and patrons is changed with the influence of the maker movement [2, 3]. Originated in Europe in the last century, the maker movement is broadly defined as "participation in the creative production of physical and digital artifacts in people's day-to-day lives" [4, 5]. Its belief in the human agency in passive consumption asserts the importance of creating, which is suggested to be inherent in our bodies [6]. Since the first public library makerspace was established in New York in 2011, the maker movement has prompted more and more library makerspaces in the U.S. that span academic, school, and other types of libraries [7, 8]. To epitomize the maker spirit, libraries extend their traditional services to spotlight the making practice, developing programs to give access to material and equipment usually unavailable at home like 3D printing, laser, and vinyl cutting, to name a few [9, 10]. From the social aspect, library makerspaces offer people a venue to learn and have fun while connecting and communicating with others, implying

M. Smits (Ed.): iConference 2022, LNCS 13193, pp. 228–242, 2022.
https://doi.org/10.1007/978-3-030-96960-8_16

the support of libraries to address caring and emotional needs of communities [11]. Indeed, the image of libraries has been transformed with the acceptance of the maker culture. Libraries are no longer a quiet place to consume information but a stimulating environment to explore, play, design, build, and tinker with material, leading patrons to become "active productive users of information, artifacts, and knowledge" [3, 12–14].

The discussion on library makerspaces is considerable in Information Science. However, it is rare to see the making activity as a leisure pursuit is discussed in the library setting. Moreover, although the maker culture shares the value of the arts and crafts movement to regard making as activism against mass production, the former is still more featured with modern technology than traditional crafts in the press [15, 16]. Herein, we see making as the activity encompassing various media beyond electronics. Based on the idea of serious leisure in which hobbyism is considered a form of leisure [17], we are prompted to ask our research question: how does the making community, explicitly speaking, adult arts and crafts hobbyists, perceive libraries in a making context? The rest of this paper comprises a literature review on how the maker culture and leisure, respectively, are manifested and perpetuated in the library setting. Next, we report methods used to conduct this qualitative research. After presenting the findings and discussion, we conclude to demonstrate the value of making from the hobbyist perspective and how librarianship may employ it to encourage creative practice.

2 Literature Review

Compared with the earlier period when the maker movement just emerged in the U.S., there is increasing scholarly work on making in the library setting. These include, for example, multiple makerspace case studies, empirical research on learning in making, conceptual work on making drawing upon existing frameworks, and others [18–21]. All such work is significant to illustrate that libraries take up the maker movement to facilitate learning, production, and warrant inclusion and equity [22, 23]. Nevertheless, the power of making as a leisure pursuit, which is experiencing a surge during the pandemic, in the library environment is still under investigated [24]. This limitation can result in our lack of understanding of making regarding its potential to engage patrons beyond youth. In this section, we first introduce how the maker culture is sustained in libraries. We then switch our attention to the role of leisure in the library setting.

2.1 Reconsidering Libraries in the Maker Culture

The maker culture has brought about a profound change to libraries. In previous literature, learning is one of the major subjects permeating academic discourse on library makerspaces [14]. Participating in making programs, people try unfamiliar tools, learn new skills, adapt current knowledge to different domains, communicate, and cooperate with others to solve problems [25]. To facilitate making, librarians carry out roles beyond information specialists and serve as experts and educators, expanding the meaning of librarianship [26]. In addition to working with peers and librarians, patrons get a chance to make with professional artists to produce something innovative in library makerspaces, as found in the Bubbler's Artist-in-Residence programs [5, 27]. Mann [28] reported that the information literacy skills could also be trained as patrons participated in makerspace programs. All these benefits show that the maker culture has invigorated libraries to grow as a social hub to involve and engage more individuals to explore possibilities that may not exist before.

Making is considered an activity for everyone, as suggested by Dougherty [6]. Nonetheless, this vision is often hard to achieve because of how making is branded in the popular media [29]. In reality, a call for making seems to highlight what is made, usually by middle-class white men, and how these products make these people unique, neglecting the value of everyday making as those traditionally done by women [30, 31]. A stream of literature on makerspace equity, diversity, and inclusion thus exists. For instance, Ratto [32] articulated the critical making practice to combine critical thinking and material production in the joint conversation where different views are discussed. Looking at young people, Moorefield-Lang and Kitzie [33] posited that library makerspaces could be a safe place for LGBTQ youth to express their identities and challenge stereotypes. Making programs can also enhance library accessibility to involve youth from different backgrounds by implementing "making the body" activities where people make something with physical activity [34].

2.2 Applying Leisure Pursuit to Library Services

The discussion of leisure is not rare in our field, yet typically not directly addressed in the library setting. One prominent framework to understand leisure pursuit is the Serious Leisure Perspective (SLP) that covers three forms of leisure: serious leisure, casual leisure, and project-based leisure [35]. Serious leisure is the most complex leisure activity due to its systematic pursuit. A substantial amount of time and effort is involved in serious leisure to acquire knowledge and experience in amateur, hobbyist, and volunteer work. Casual leisure, however, is oriented more with hedonism, providing people with immediate pleasure with no training required. Project-based leisure is a relatively short-term pursuit with reasonably complicated content. Although it is occasional or even a one-shot activity, project-based leisure has to be carefully planned and often requires some extent of skills and knowledge. The SLP is characterized by its intrinsic character, explaining that people engage in leisure not because they are coerced to do so but because they want to. Stebbins [36] posited that the SLP could be well bridged to Library and Information Science due to its information heavy nature. This trend can be found in the information behavior literature where growing research on hobbyists is conducted, such as knitters and readers reading for pleasure [37, 38].

Although the SLP is informative to map out the leisure landscape, its application in the library context is scant. A few exceptions include the recent work of Mansourian and Bannister [39] and VanScoy and colleagues [40]. Mansourian and Bannister [39] advised public libraries to engage more with serious leisure groups to enhance their services. The scholars specified five legitimate reasons, including the benefits of strengthening social ties, making the library more welcoming, building communities of interest, encouraging new lifestyles, and developing library collections and events. Mansourian [41] further upheld this concept in another research, noting that the advantages gained from supporting serious leisure would circle back to enrich library services. In the work of VanScoy and colleagues [40], they discovered the patchy distribution of programs in leisure forms after analyzing a two-week sample of adult, leisure-related programs in four North American public libraries. Casual leisure was adopted more than serious and project-based leisure, with the most identified programs falling into active and passive entertainment (e.g., "Adult Coloring;" "Thursday Film Series"). There was also an uneven distribution of programs in hobby types under serious leisure, with most cases belonging to liberal arts pursuits (e.g., "book discussion groups"). The scholars argued that using the SLP as a tool for library programming is appropriate for librarians and information professionals to evaluate, inventory, and arrange leisure-related programs.

Drawing upon prior research, we recognize the impact of maker culture in the library setting and the potential to incorporate the leisure perspective in library programming. However, as the literature revealed, the discussion on making, including its benefit and possibility, widely focused on youth and missed capturing adult hobbyists who were "among very good friends of public libraries" [41]. Accordingly, we intend to fill this gap by probing how arts and crafts hobbyists perceive libraries in a making context to see how libraries can better facilitate creative practice.

3 Methods

This research is part of a bigger project on making and information behavior. Herein, to investigate participants' first-hand experiences in a natural setting, we conducted a naturalistic inquiry with minimum investigator intervention [42]. Applying purposeful and snowball sampling, we recruited arts and crafts hobbyists using personal contacts, social media, and a university newsletter system. All eligible participants were over 18 years old, self-identified as arts and crafts hobbyists, and planned to begin a project soon. The definition of arts and crafts is comprehensive to acknowledge various forms of making. The current study comprised two phases: a diary study for Phase I and an individual semi-structured interview for Phase II. Before diary studies, we held initial briefing sessions to explain research procedures and obtained oral informed consent. An information sheet and a diary template were also provided. In diary studies, participants were requested to document the making process for two weeks adopting visual techniques of their choosing like drawing, photographing, and even audio journaling. They were asked to make an entry and respond to the six open-ended questions each time they progressed on their projects. The reason for setting this tentative two-week period was to give participants a flexible use of their time, and there was no restriction on how long they should spend on their projects each day. As shown in Fig. 1 in Appendix, we phrased questions in the diaries to emphasize the processual dimension of making. Since the initial project is larger in scope to map information behavior in a making context, we do not narrow questions into specific information sources, such as libraries, in drafting the template. Although we offered people a template to use, they were allowed to customize the layout as long as they addressed the six inquiries. Regarding ethical concerns, with the protocol approved by the IRB to protect privacy and confidentiality, we asked participants to avoid photographing others not involved in this research. We paid close attention to removing any identifiable information as amassing data.

After Phase I, we invited people to join individual interviews, conducted virtually, for Phase II. The interviews ran 50 min on average and were designed to dig deeper into participants' diaries, making projects, and their experiences with arts and crafts. We audio-recorded each interview upon agreement and transcribed it for later analysis. We assigned pseudonyms to participants employing the random name generator [43] based on the U.S. census data delineated by gender, as shown in Table 1. A total of 25 participants were involved, among which two participants, Nicole and Una, only joined diary sessions due to the scheduling issue. We still included their diary data for analysis. Participants were compensated with $20 Amazon e-gift cards at the end of their participation.

Regarding data analysis, we applied a mix of analysis techniques to grapple with textual and visual data gathered in this research. In the current study, we focus on the textual data. To analyze the interview transcripts, we generally followed steps of reflexive thematic analysis [44]. Using the qualitative data analysis software Atlas.ti, we first went through the interview transcripts to generate initial codes. Next, we reread the data to consolidate codes to identify potential themes. As candidate themes were recognized, we refined and named the themes to produce the deliverable. Memos were created throughout this process to record any random thought that may serve as a critical point for later interpretation.

4 Findings

We found five primary themes after analyzing data collected from 25 hobbyist participants. Each theme and relevant examples are introduced below.

4.1 Print and Digital Collections

The top identified theme of the perception participants had of libraries is the resources they offered, mentioned 16 times. When engaging in making, participants found that it would be beneficial if libraries could allocate more online and offline resources for them to access. Print resources are favored more than digital resources, with 11 and 5 mentions, respectively. For example, Doris described her habit of using library collections as a critical information source for arts and crafts projects.

> Doris: I've gone to the library before, for instance, when I made the covers for the pillows on my sofa. I went to the librarian and got a few different sewing books for tips on how to do that correctly, like how to make the corners correctly and other stuff like that. I still will look at print media, and I don't know if that is a function more of, you know, at my age, or that my mom used to do that. I would go with my mom to the library all the time. So, that is still just a resource that I would initially think of in addition to looking online.

In a like manner, Ivette expressed her thoughts of utilizing library collections to learn about photography. While majoring in physics and pursuing this career path, Ivette mentioned that she expects to have more time to dig deeper into video shooting as a hobby after graduation. In doing so, Ivette believes libraries would be a great place to visit to borrow books on relevant subjects.

Table 1. Participants and their making projects.

Participant	Project titles	Type(s) of projects
Anne	My Future	Painting
Betty	Ski Chalet Stained Class	Stained glass
Connie	Bill and Pete Digital Sculpture	Digital sculpture
Doris	Highbrow Lunch Satchel	Leatherwork
Emiko	The Lantern Festival Series; The White Day Series	Polymer clay
Fannie	Let's Stay Home Quilt; Red Bear's Friend; Photo Embroidery	Quilting, crocheting, embroidery
Gloria	Baby Quilt	Quilting
Hazel	Dining Room Table	Woodwork
Ivette	A Letter to Spring, from Winter	Video making
Joyce	Couch Pillows; Baby Blanket (with a Teddy Bear)	Sewing, crocheting
Kimberly	Bottle Cap Wall Piece; Beach Glass Windchime	Metalwork, glasswork
Lynne	We Can - Artivism for a Gender Equality of UNWOMEN	Papercraft
Martha	Puppet for Promotional Video	Animation
Nicole	Blooming Ball, No-Glue Re-Do	Papercraft
Oliver	Bougainvillea Bonsai	Bonsai
Phyllis	Disney Castle Glass	Stained glass
Quincy	Everyday Photography	Photography
Ruby	Living Room Table	Woodwork
Sammy	Pottery Earrings; Flower and Leaf Rubbing Series	Pottery
Taylor	The Expanse - Rocinante	Papercraft
Una	Sliceform Monster Village	Papercraft
Violet	Knitted Shawl	Knitting
Willie	Boba Fett-ish Helmet	Papercraft
Yoko	Splash	Watercolor
Zoey	Mushroom Love in Pink and Blue; Amanita Mushrooms; Succulent Love	Lampwork

> Ivette: I think libraries sometimes have books about photography. In the future, if I have some time and also the motivation, I may spend some time reading about it. I understand this is a really serious and professional career for those who are making very nice films, but for me, I'm not trained to do so. So, if I want to be self-trained, I can go to the libraries and find some resources to see how they deal with the lines or the scenes and all the other things.

For digital resources, participants found them useful in terms of their quick and convenient access. However, as shown in Zoey's case, some participants indicated the lack of collections on specific arts and crafts types in libraries.

> Zoey: I actually haven't seen any interesting glasswork resource in any library. [...] It should probably be a specific crafts-oriented online library for me to get a look at, then it should have some interesting-looking material. I think there are only a couple of books on lampwork here [in the studio], but the US-based authors tend to be really stingy with their knowledge in books, like there are 20 projects in the books, but they're all the same.

Other digital resources that participants deemed essential are online courses. Hobbyist participants, especially those novices, regarded online courses as a notable learning material by which they could see instructors make something in front of their eyes. Although many online courses are available on the Internet, they usually cost money that not every person is able to afford them. To this end, participants thought libraries, characterized by their role of granting free access to information, would be an ideal venue to obtain this material [5]. Yoko, a watercolor hobbyist new to this domain, mentioned she preferred to watch and followed what was shown on the screen while practicing.

> Yoko: For me, it's much easier to learn watercolor with online resources than from books, like checking out library books. Books gave me insights and some basics of watercolor, like the color theory and different techniques, before I began the activity. But online courses are used during the activities. They're helpful for me to keep track of my performance when following through with the courses.

Still, for more experienced arts and crafts hobbyists, technical services as a resource provided by libraries meet their needs better than online courses. For instance, Connie already had sufficient knowledge of digital sculpture when working on her project. As a college student relying heavily on the campus lab space, Connie explained she spent a long time setting up her workspace at home since the pandemic hit. She stated that it would be good if libraries could expand their technological access to cover specific software tutorials: "It'd be great if some resources in the library teach the technical stuff, those related to specific software. Now, those can only be found on YouTube or from the professors and are not available in the library."

4.2 Workshops

The second top identified theme, similar to online courses in terms of its resource provision, is workshops organized by libraries, mentioned 13 times. Participants thought it would be interesting to see more arts and crafts workshops hosted in libraries, particularly workshops beyond textile crafts. Ruby mentioned the issue of whether woodwork could fit library programming: "I think a lot of people when they go to the library, they think more to go for feminine crafts, knitting, cooking, or whatever. I'm not sure if woodworking would be something that people would think of." Here, what Ruby pointed out reflects an ongoing conversation on "'what counts' as making or tinkering," where scholars are concerned by how making is advertised can pose a risk of overlooking voices absent in the public discourse [31]. Apart from the woodwork, Taylor considered libraries a proper venue to promote papercraft as a hobby. He depicted that papercraft programs in libraries did not have to be too complicated but focused on the fun aspect by showing something easy to do.

> Taylor: The library can go buy a stack of card stock paper and print out some basic shapes, like hearts for Valentine's Day or how to make a certain kind of flower. It probably wouldn't be anything too complex because you'd want to be able to get most of it done in one sitting, but it could be really interesting to introduce people to that kind of craft in the library. You could have sets of the tools that you need in order to get started on that, and that could be really basic. It could be like one pair of scissors, one fresh hobby blade, a cutting mat, and a ruler, and that would be most of what a person would need to assemble a basic model.

Anne also described the inviting vibe conveyed in craft workshops. Though not directly related to her making project in this research, Anne recalled her previous experience volunteering in a library knitting night where the local library engaged the community in the intergenerational making: "So many people from the town came. They would go in the children's section where there was so much space, tables, chairs, and they would do a knitting program together. [...] It's really nice!".

Following the conversation on library programming, a few participants, in fact, signaled their willingness to help libraries run workshops. This finding is mostly found in cases where participants have vast experiences and sound knowledge of a particular type of arts and crafts. For example, Lynne expressed that she would love to teach or hold workshops in libraries. The participant said, "I've thought lately about teaching this [papercraft] when I'm better. A library would be a great place to teach and learn this. [...] It could also be a meeting point for artists." Likely, Kimberly told the researcher that she was just looking online to see if the local library allowed her to run workshops.

> Kimberly: I love libraries! I would go through their art sections, art history, different artists, and pull books, [...] showing students how to take something and dissect it and use it for inspiration. [...] I was actually looking at teaching some courses here because they do workshops, especially for teens, and they have a maker lab. I think there's a really good way for artists to work with the libraries.

4.3 Tools

The third theme recognized is tools and equipment available in libraries, mentioned seven times. This theme is relevant to the second, again, in terms of its resource provision. When libraries host workshops, they usually offer free tools and equipment for patrons to use.

Ruby depicted that it would be convenient if libraries could lend expensive woodwork tools to people to work on projects.

> Ruby: I know some libraries have more than books that they lend. It would be cool if a library has tools that they could lend to community members cuz that's a big expense to get into woodworking as a craft. You could easily spend thousands of dollars on tools and still not have every tool you need for any given project.

Gloria discussed a similar notion and described a tool library located in her town. She said that borrowing tools from this kind of special library is nice, especially "if it's a tool that you don't need for every single project."

> Gloria: In my area, there is a tool library. My husband and I are kind of handy around the house, and we fix things ourselves, like we built a fence last year or things like that. There is a tool library where you can go and take classes on how to use certain tools and then check them out and use them for your home project. It's not affiliated with our public library system, but it works in a similar way.

4.4 Social Interactions

The fourth theme recognized is the interactive aspect of libraries, found in three cases. This theme looks at libraries mainly from the social lens and illustrates how participants perceived libraries based on their role as a social hub. Fannie, a competent craft hobbyist doing a project on photo transferring, gave a detailed explanation about what she expected to see from her local library. Her illustration is based on her positive experience of doing craft projects in a clubhouse in town.

> Fannie: I love libraries, but I wish they were more social. I'm a writer, and I often go to libraries to sit and be quiet and do the writing. There's research material on hand right away, but I long for libraries to be like, Town Square, that's what I long for. [...] Not that there isn't a quiet space, but there's also this big space where people can have a cup of coffee and meet new people and work on projects. That's why when I was describing that D.I.Y. place to you, there was a bar, and then they had their own little kits. I want that to be attached to my library. I don't need the food, and I don't need the alcohol or any of that. What I need is a space where other people are creating things because then if you didn't know how to do something, the library is right there for you to look it up. […] Wouldn't it be great if I could check out the time of someone who does photo transfers in the library space and have them teach me how to do photo transfers properly?

Another participant that well addresses the social aspect of libraries is Oliver. Oliver is the only participant who explicitly underscored the importance of librarianship, sharing that he missed librarians a lot since he could no longer visit the library in person. This case displays that the practice of librarianship is fundamental to hobbyists' making activities, even during the pandemic when librarians have worked hard to shift their services online [19].

Oliver: Basically, I've heard loads of things about how you can check out books digitally and manage catalogs digitally, and it's cool! But one of the things I miss about going physically to the library is the librarians. They were always quite great at pointing me out in the correct direction or helping me with my research. I can find a book all right, and I can get it, but I haven't been able to replace their help. So, I'm guessing some sort of ask-a-librarian thing might be useful.

4.5 Dedicated Environments

The last theme recognized is physical spaces available in libraries, also found in three cases. The space described in this theme is not exactly the same as makerspaces that offer various tools and equipment. What people referred to here, instead, are empty spaces for rent. A few participants affirmed the benefit of renting a room or an area in libraries to conduct projects that took up huge spaces. Anne expressed that her university library provided a service to book the room to do personal work, which she found useful.

Anne: In my physical library at my university, they have a lot of open spaces with chairs and a lot of empty rooms where you can do anything that you want. You can rent out a little room, and it just has a desk, chairs, and a whiteboard. I think those could be good for students. Maybe they're artists, but they don't have any space in their dorm rooms to do the paintings or arts and crafts. So, I think using those [open] rooms would just be the best way.

Fannie adopted a similar perspective, saying that it would be nice if she could rent out a space, with the added bonus of tools, to focus on her projects. Fannie is a library lover and frequented the place before the pandemic.

Fannie: Libraries are everything. When I realized that you could do a heat transfer by tiny heat transfer machines, the first thing I did was look at my local library to see if they had one that I could check out. They didn't, sadly, because [if they did] that would have been fantastic. What I always thought in the back of my head is that wouldn't it be lovely if all libraries had a workspace where people could check out time in the workspace. I'm complaining because I don't have a solid or big enough table to cut out fabrics. It would be great if I could rent an hour of space somewhere where there was a big, large solid table, and I could cut out all the fabric that I had to cut out, or that there was a serger that was set up and you could go and rent an hour of serger time and do all the serging you need to do. [...]

What Fannie described here, along with her portrayal of libraries as Town Square, shown earlier, lies across the themes of the interactive aspect of libraries and their tool and spatial availability. Her depiction signifies that making is multifaceted, which is implied in the literature about discursive constructions of library makerspaces [5, 14].

5 Discussion

In this section, we interpret and elaborate on our findings to reply to our research question: how do adult arts and crafts hobbyists perceive libraries in a making context? Grounded on our empirical data of 25 participants, we found that most participants considered libraries a resource provider when asked about what role libraries served in the making process. First, print and digital information resources for making are deemed the most helpful. In particular, the higher number of mentions of print collections reveals that hobbyists do not completely switch to digital information sources to fulfill information needs despite their instant access. This finding concurs with the research of Prigoda and McKenzie [37] and Ross [38], whose hobbyist participants approved the informative aspect of libraries on intellectual access. Nevertheless, this does not mean that hobbyists care less about digital resources. Instead, their expectations of digital resources are also high, encompassing those they suggest conducive to creative making, including online courses, software, and tutorials. Here, rather than considering them as properties coming along with makerspace programming [3], we interpret these resources as crucial information that libraries can consider supplying even when there is no physical makerspace involved in their environments.

Second, similar to a resource provider yet in a different lens, participants regarded libraries as a place offering free workshops, tools, and spaces to attend, use, and rent out. Based on prior work, this practice is manifested chiefly through establishing makerspaces following the maker movement philosophy. A few participants of this research described the makerspaces in their local libraries, whereas most of them did not cover this point. We think this is because participants are aware that those spaces are typically designed for youth, not adults. One participant, Kimberly, made this point clear, saying, "They [the library] do have a makerspace, a small one, and it's for teenagers. I haven't really explored that yet. I don't know if they would let me come in and use it or not." Library makerspaces, with untiring effort made by librarians, are acknowledged to bring libraries "to engage more patrons, to attract more people to the library to learn new things, to welcome everyone with or without experience" [14]. Therefore, our result shows the need to somewhat rebrand library makerspaces to make adult hobbyists not feel excluded to enhance inclusion as a core library mission.

Speaking of workshops as part of library programming, we find it interesting that participants conveyed enthusiasm for organizing making workshops in libraries. From their perspective, the process of hosting craft workshops per se is a fantastic learning opportunity. This is also an approach to diversifying library making programs to show items beyond technology and ensure people interested in different arts and crafts have a voice in making [18, 31]. In this situation, arts and crafts hobbyists become a practical human source that librarians can turn to beyond reviewing relevant literature when brainstorming craft programs [40]. This finding reflects the social role of libraries in connecting the public with hobbyists, which extends the idea of Bubbler's Artist-in-Residence programs where professional artists are involved [5, 27].

Regarding the theme dealing with the interactive aspect of libraries, our finding confirms the role of libraries as a social hub from hobbyists' perspectives, showing that most hobbyist participants have close relationships with libraries [41]. As the participant, Fannie, noted, while the making activity can be done individually, making with others is usually more fun, and libraries are an ideal venue to do so. We continue the conversation to cover the unexpected situation when patrons have limited physical access to the library space and when face-to-face communications are discouraged. In this context, other than appreciating the significance of librarianship in the making activity where librarians are a vital source, we stress the necessity to reconsider our current understanding of the library support to making [13, 26]. In addition to constructing the environment to facilitate making, we suggest it is worthwhile to reexamine how libraries can maximize their value to highlight the social aspect of making, especially during the pandemic [11].

6 Conclusion

The maker culture has enlivened the library environment by bringing the pleasure and fun of the making activity to the fore. The meaning of librarianship is also reflected and broadened by the mission of this movement. Previous literature offered remarkable insight into how libraries may facilitate making by providing technological access while, in the meantime, encouraging equity, diversity, and inclusion. Still, the making activity as a leisure pursuit with growing popularity has not yet been deeply examined regarding its relation to libraries from the hobbyist perspective. Consequently, we conducted a qualitative project comprising diary studies and individual interviews with 25 arts and crafts hobbyists to probe their perceptions of libraries. The findings show that libraries are typically seen as a resource provider to allocate resources beyond print and digital collections but include creative material like workshops, tools, and spaces. Plus, the results capture the interactive facet of libraries in a making context, demonstrating the value of librarianship to establish a space for creators of all ages to engage people in the same community. Grounded upon voices besides youth, these findings expand our current knowledge of the support of libraries to making during the pandemic when physical access to libraries is restrained. From a theoretical perspective, the current study is part of a bigger project on making and information behavior. Accordingly, the results contribute to the literature on information acquisition and use by articulating how the SLP serves as a key instrument to reflect libraries as a fertile source addressing hobbyists' diverse information needs.

One limitation of this research is the sample size of our participants. Although we recruited 25 participants who undertook distinct projects, there was an uneven distribution of arts and crafts types spanning physical and digital. The varied nature of arts and crafts can initiate fruitful discussions, but more focused work, such as concentrating on one making category or sole media, can provide a new lens. As a result, we encourage future researchers to consider this a potential path to explore making, seeing how different arts and crafts may shape librarianship and library service design. Heading in this probable direction, we expect to extend the current study by translating the findings into practical implementation. In future research, we attempt to conceive implications for practice to support making, particularly intergenerational making, as an all-age activity in libraries to embrace inclusion and equity. We are curious to see how the integration of hobbyism may inform and empower library programming and staff training to bring making closer to the public. It is worth further capturing the voices of hobbyists to appreciate diversity and reconsider leisure as a holistic view to promote making in pursuit of creative endeavor in a modern library context.

Appendix

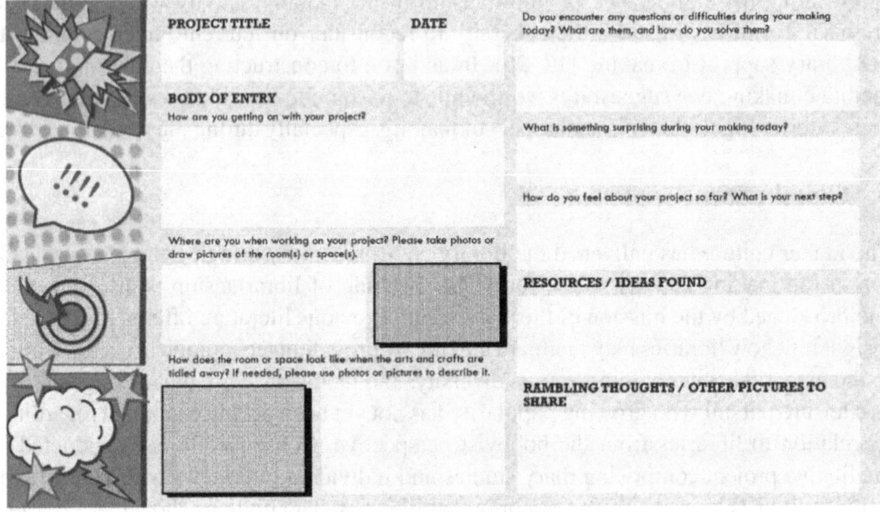
PROJECT TITLE

DATE

BODY OF ENTRY

How are you getting on with your project?

Where are you when working on your project? Please take photos or draw pictures of the room(s) or space(s).

How does the room or space look like when the arts and crafts are tidied away? If needed, please use photos or pictures to describe it.

Do you encounter any questions or difficulties during your making today? What are them, and how do you solve them?

What is something surprising during your making today?

How do you feel about your project so far? What is your next step?

RESOURCES / IDEAS FOUND

RAMBLING THOUGHTS / OTHER PICTURES TO SHARE

Fig. 1. Diary template

References

1. Kuhlthau, C.C.: Kuhlthau's model of information seeking. In: Fisher, K.E., Erdelez, S., McKechnie, L. (eds.) Theories of Information Behavior, pp. 230–234. American Society for Information Science and Technology, Medford (2004)
2. Anderson, C.: Makers: The New Industrial Revolution. Crown, UK (2012)
3. Moorefield-Lang, H.: Change in the making: makerspaces and the ever-changing landscape of libraries. TechTrends **59**(3), 107–112 (2015)
4. Davies, S.R.: Hackerspaces: Making the Maker Movement. Polity Press, Malden (2017)
5. Lakind, A., Willett, R., Halverson, E.R.: Democratizing the maker movement: a case study of one public library system's makerspace program. Ref. User Serv. Q. **58**(4), 234–245 (2019)
6. Dougherty, D.: Free to Make: How the Maker Movement is Changing Our Schools, Our Jobs, and Our Minds. North Atlantic Books, Berkeley (2016)
7. Irie, N.R., Hsu, Y.-C., Ching, Y.-H.: Makerspaces in diverse places: a comparative analysis of distinctive national discourses surrounding the maker movement and education in four countries. TechTrends **63**(4), 397–407 (2019)
8. Moorefield-Lang, H., Dubnjakovic, A.: Factors influencing intention to introduce accessibility in makerspace planning and implementation. School Libr. Worldwide **26**(2), 14–26 (2020)
9. Abram, S.: Makerspaces in libraries, education, and beyond. Internet@Schools **20**(2), 18–20 (2013). https://teamhughmanatee.files.wordpress.com/2013/04/abrammakerspaces-in-libraries-education-and-beyond.pdf. Accessed 7 Sept 2021
10. Cirell, A.M., Kellam, N., Boklage, A., Coley, B.: Reimagining the thirdspace through the makerspace. In: Melo, M., Nichols, J.T. (eds.) Remaking the Library Makerspace: Critical Theories, Reflections, and Practices, pp. 47–82. Library Juice Press, Sacramento (2020)

11. Fourie, I., Meyer, A.: What to make of makerspaces: tools and DIY only or is there an interconnected information resources space? Libr. Hi Tech **33**(4), 519–525 (2015)
12. Bruns, A.: Blogs, Wikipedia, Second Life, and Beyond: From Production to Produsage. Peter Lang, New York (2008)
13. Bowler, L.: Creativity through "maker" experiences and design thinking in the education of librarians. Knowl. Quest **42**(5), 58–61 (2014)
14. Willett, R.: Making, makers, and makerspaces: a discourse analysis of professional journal articles and blog posts about makerspaces in public libraries. Libr. Q. **86**(3), 313–329 (2016)
15. Bender, S.: Electronics meets textiles: sewing the way to powerful new ideas about technology. In: Peppler, K., Halverson, E.R., Kafai, Y.B. (eds.) Makeology: Makers as Learners, pp. 125–144. Routledge, New York (2016)
16. Levine, F., Heimerl, C.: Handmade Nation: The Rise of DIY, Art, Craft, and Design. Princeton Architectural Press, New York (2008)
17. Stebbins, R.A.: New Directions in the Theory and Research of Serious Leisure. Edwin Mellen Press, Lewiston (2001)
18. Beavers, K., Cady, J.E., Jiang, A., McCoy, L.: Establishing a maker culture beyond the makerspace. Libr. Hi Tech **37**(2), 219–232 (2019)
19. Kim, S.H., Choi, G.W., Jung, Y.J.: Design principles for transforming making programs into online settings at public libraries. Inf. Learn. Sci. **121**(7/8), 619–630 (2020)
20. Meyer, A., Fourie, I.: Thematic analysis of the value of Kuhlthau's work for the investigation of information behaviour in creative workspaces in academic libraries. In: Proceedings of ISIC, the Information Behaviour Conference, Zadar, Croatia, 20–23 September 2016. Inf. Res. **22**(1), paper isic 1626 (2017). InformationR.net/ir/22-1/isic/isic1626.html. Accessed 8 Sept 2021
21. Slatter, D., Howard, Z.: A place to make, hack, and learn: makerspaces in Australian public libraries. Austr. Libr. J. **62**(4), 272–284 (2013)
22. Koh, K., Abbas, J., Willett, R.: Makerspaces in libraries. In: Lee, V.R., Philips, A.L. (eds.) Reconceptualizing Libraries: Perspectives from the Information and Learning Sciences, pp. 17–36. Routledge, New York (2018)
23. Melo, M., Nichols, J.T.: Centering voices from the margins: unsettling the exceptionalist lore of makerspaces. In: Melo, M., Nichols, J.T. (eds.) Remaking the Library Makerspace: Critical Theories, Reflections, and Practices, pp. 1–7. Library Juice Press, Sacramento (2020)
24. Machemer, T.: Arts and crafts are experiencing surge in popularity amid COVID-19. Smithsonian Magazine (2020). http://smithsonianmag.com/smart-news/people-are-getting-crafty-while-they-stay-home-180974811/. Accessed 30 Aug 2021
25. Sheridan, K., Halverson, E.R., Litts, B., Brahms, L., Jacobs-Priebe, L., Owens, T.: Learning in the making: a comparative case study of three makerspaces. Harv. Educ. Rev. **84**(4), 505–531 (2014)
26. Williams, R.D., Willett, R.: Makerspaces and boundary work: the role of librarians as educators in public library makerspaces. J. Librariansh. Inf. Sci. **51**(3), 801–813 (2019)
27. Halverson, E., Lakind, A., Willett, R.: The Bubbler as systemwide makerspace: a design case of how making became a core service of the public libraries. Int. J. Des. Learn. **8**(1), 57–68 (2017)
28. Mann, L.: Making a place for makerspaces in information literacy. Ref. User Serv. Q. **58**(2), 82–86 (2018)
29. Martin, L., Dixon, C., Betser, S.: Iterative design toward equity: youth repertoires of practice in a high school maker space. Equity Excellence Educ. **51**(1), 36–47 (2018)
30. Chachra, D.: Why I am not a maker. The Atlantic (2015). http://theatlantic.com/technology/archive/2015/01/why-i-am-not-a-maker/384767/. Accessed 31 Aug 2021
31. Vossoughi, S., Hooper, P.K., Escude, M.: Making through the lens of culture and power: toward transformative visions for educational equity. Harv. Educ. Rev. **86**(2), 206–232 (2016)

32. Ratto, M.: Critical making: conceptual and material studies in technology and social life. Inf. Soc. **27**(4), 252–260 (2011)
33. Moorefield-Lang, H., Kitzie, V.: Makerspaces for all: Serving LGBTQ makers in school libraries. Knowl. Quest **47**(1), 46–50 (2018)
34. Lenstra, N., Moorefield-Lang, H.: Making the body: physical activity in makerspaces. In: Melo, M., Nichols, J.T. (eds.) Remaking the Library Makerspace: Critical Theories, Reflections, and Practices, pp. 101–114. Library Juice Press, Sacramento (2020)
35. Stebbins, R.A.: The Serious Leisure Perspective: A Synthesis. Palgrave Macmillan, Switzerland (2020). https://doi.org/10.1007/978-3-030-48036-3
36. Stebbins, R.A.: Leisure and its relationship to library and information science: bridging the gap. Libr. Trends **57**(4), 618–631 (2009)
37. Prigoda, E., McKenzie, P.J.: Purls of wisdom: a collectivist study of human information behaviour in a public library knitting group. J. Doc. **63**(1), 90–114 (2007)
38. Ross, C.S.: Finding without seeking: the information encounter in the context of reading for pleasure. Inf. Process. Manag. **35**(6), 783–799 (1999)
39. Mansourian, Y., Bannister, M.: Five benefits of serious leisure for a public library. Incite **40**(5/6), 32–33 (2019)
40. VanScoy, A., Thomson, L., Hartel, J.: Applying theory in practice: the serious leisure perspective and public library programming. Libr. Inf. Sci. Res. **42**(3), 101034 (2020)
41. Mansourian, Y.: Information activities in serious leisure as a catalyst for self-actualisation and social engagement. J. Doc. **77**(4), 887–905 (2021)
42. Patton, M.: Qualitative Research & Evaluation Methods: Integrating Theory and Practice, 4th edn. SAGE Publications, Thousand Oaks (2015)
43. Random Name Generator. random-name-generator.info. Accessed 10 Sept 2021
44. Braun, V., Clarke, V., Hayfield, N., Terry, G.: Thematic analysis. In: Liamputtong, P. (ed.) Handbook of Research Methods in Health Social Sciences, pp. 843–860. Springer, Singapore (2019)

Flames of Justice in a Virtual Garden: An Analysis of a Digital Campaign on Twitter Surrounding the Death of an Indian Celebrity

Subhasree Sengupta(✉) and Jasmina Tacheva

Syracuse University, Syracuse, NY, USA
{susengup,ztacheva}@syr.edu

Abstract. Social media particularly Twitter has emerged as a powerful medium for expression and discussion for a wide range of topics. Through the use of hashtags, a powerful and popular affordance of Twitter, several online campaigns aimed at raising awareness and consciousness towards various issues of civic and social justice, have emerged. Although prior scholarship has investigated forms of rhetoric and impacts of such narrative movements on Twitter, an important consideration is to understand the structural forms that such narratives take depending on context and regional culture wherein the movement originates, rendering each campaign unique in its collective identity and objective. To this end, this study embarks on a mixed-methods analysis of 27,265 tweets related to calls of action and social justice in the aftermath of the death of a popular Indian movie star. The analysis reveals a diverse spectrum of themes ranging from expressions of loss and grief to astute critiques of the major institutions of power. Parallel but powerful themes also demonstrated attempts to nurture and embolden the campaign. Temporal trends provide insights into the collective orientation and gradual development of a community focus among campaign participants. The ultimate aim of this analysis is to provide insights into how such channels of discourse should be designed to create and nurture a medium for freedom of expression and foster safe spaces for civic engagement.

Keywords: Social justice · Community norms · Civic engagement · Twitter · Content analysis

1 Introduction

The rise of ubiquitous computing and information and communication technology (ICT) has been associated with both the empowerment of individuals and communities as well as with problematic developments related to data privacy and societal divides. Specifically, the proliferation of social media platforms (SMPs) has been credited with enabling everyday Internet users to participate in the democratic processes of their communities by taking part in open public

M. Smits (Ed.): iConference 2022, LNCS 13193, pp. 243–258, 2022.
https://doi.org/10.1007/978-3-030-96960-8_17

debates about contentious social issues online [32]. It has even been associated with inspiring digital movements that have subsequently taken on an on-the-ground form and helped topple oppressive regimes as in the case of the Arab Spring, referred to by some as a "Twitter Revolution" [54]. Outside the political realm, SMPs often serve as conduits for creating and maintaining informal online communities centered on a wide variety of social activities such as advice-seeking [52] social support, especially in healthcare contexts [36], and fandom groups [16], among others. At the same time, the large swaths of user-generated data SMPs have helped generate have also created opportunities for its indiscriminate use by online marketers, technology companies, governments, and rogue players resulting in troublesome practices such as the contentious spread of misinformation [50], the propagation of toxic and offensive content [15], addictive Internet usage [34] and the growth of social and political polarization [22].

Understanding this complex multi-layered dynamic requires a critical sociotechnical theoretical lens which, due to its focus on both structures and agents, can adequately capture both the promise of SMPs as tools for liberation, and their societal cost [19]. While a critical sociotechnical view of social media can provide a roadmap for understanding the macro-state view of the intentions that drive social groups to use such online spaces, a direct engagement with the ensuing discourse within such groups can benefit from a more granular analysis of the emerging communication patterns to further understand how such initiatives as organized and sustained in such online collectives [25]. Genre system analysis is one such perspective which seeks to explain the organizing structure of social interaction [57]. Such a classification mechanism is particularly salient in the context of digital campaigns due to the need to understand how such online movements generate a sense of collective affinity and shared sentiment, which ultimately is essential for such campaigns to succeed and survive [41,42]. In extant literature, the macro- and micro-state of social media interactions have often been explored separately which obstructs the process of constructing an adequate knowledge framework about the use of social media in civic discourse. To address this gap in the literature, this paper aims to integrate the two theoretical approaches of critical sociotechnical theory and genre system analysis in the context of an online social movement on Twitter spurred by the sudden death of Indian actor Sushant Singh Rajput (SSR) on June 14th, 2020 [1]. The motivation for studying the genre system emerging in the online movement sparked by the sudden death of Sushant Singh Rajput is two-fold. First, this tragic event represents an important case study on the confluence of public grief surrounding a celebrity's death and social movement building which can help elucidate crucial theoretical aspects that spark and shape social movements, especially in the digital context. Second, no less important, is the unique relationship between Rajput's death and the mobilization of a robust grassroots campaign for social justice stemming not just from the pedestal of unstinted love and admiration of the Indian public actors like him have traditionally enjoyed but also from the discontentment with the Indian systems of power the subsequent investigation (and lack thereof) galvanized. Thus, this case acted as the catalyst for a digital campaign, first of its kind in certain ways, that gave the Indian public the ability to mourn a much loved celebrity but also a way to express the need for reform in the system and a critical interrogation of power. It is this unique blend of theoretical and social justice-oriented motivations that inspires this investigation. The key research questions this study seeks to elucidate are the following:

RQ1: What themes emerge throughout the lifecycle of the digital campaign?

RQ2: What are the constitutive characteristics of each theme with regards to the common goal of seeking justice?

RQ3: How are the emerging themes being governed and organized by campaign participants to aid the social movement?

Answering these research questions using the dual lens of critical sociotechnical research and genre system analysis can contribute to the theoretical and methodological aspects of information science research on the topic of online social movement development in several important ways. First, it offers an actionable template for the analysis of digital campaign discourse both at the macro-level of institutional structures, the micro-level of semantic meaning and the interplay of the macro and the micro. Second, the choice of a case study - the death of a celebrity - extends the repertoire of social movement contexts to include the confluence of fandom groups and political activism. Third, the non-Western geographic positioning of the campaign under consideration highlights important regional nuances which serve to critique the homogenizing idea that since people everywhere use SMPs, they use them in the same way regardless of ethnicity, race, caste, class, gender, sexuality, or ability.

The remainder of the paper is organized as follows: In Sect. 2, we delineate the dual theoretical lens this study adopts which combines critical sociotechnical theory with genre system analysis. Section 3 summarizes the methods used for data collection and analysis. The results of the study are presented in Sect. 4 and discussed in depth in Sect. 5. Section 6 concludes the paper and offers avenues for future research.

2 Theoretical Motivation and Related Work

Our analysis of digital campaign discourse is informed by the intersection of two theoretical perspectives: critical sociotechnical theory [19] and genre system analysis [57]. The former is particularly useful for conceptualizing the conditions responsible for the emergence of online social movements, while the latter focuses on the communicative structure of the interactions between digital campaign actors. It is important to note that while the two perspectives are functionally different and operate at different levels of analysis, both share motivations with the social scientific research framework advanced by structuration theory [20]. According to this theory, the complex links between actors in the information environment and social action in general, cannot fully be accounted for unless we take into consideration the dynamic interconnections of meaning, norms, and values, along with the co-constituting relationship between structures, such as political, cultural, and educational institutions, and individual agents.

2.1 Social Media and Online Communities: A Critical Sociotechnical View

In the context of social media, the structurationist interplay between structures, in the face of technical and digital infrastructures, market capital, and political and cultural power, and agents, or Internet users, has been powerfully captured by the critical materialist and sociotechnical view advanced by Fuchs (2014) which centers the social aspect of social media platforms by defining online sociality as consisting of three primary dimensions: cognition - the individual engagement with written and visual information online, communication - interactions with other Internet users, and cooperation, or participation in online communities [19]. Spaces like the Internet, and SMPs in particular, by virtue of giving their users the opportunity to gather and actively negotiate key aspects of social life and act in concert, take on the role of a public sphere in the sense of an arena for civic and political action [3,19]. The public sphere afforded by SMPs thus becomes the digital milieu for people to organize around specific interests as social groups with socioeconomic, sociopolitical, and sociocultural dimensions that are always already situated in a specific discourse of power and concrete material conditions [19].

Within the SMP public sphere ecosystem, the role of online communities in reshaping social movement activism has seen a steady growth in scholarly investigations [47] due to the ability of SMPs to transmit information in near-real time via bidirectional communication channels as opposed to traditional media's unidirectional information stream [59] and the efficacy of these new communication platforms in mobilizing large groups of followers united by a common social or political goal [35]. SMPs' impact on the nature and lifecycle of social movements has been so profound that some scholars refer to social movements in the era of Web 2.0 as Social Movement 2.0 to highlight the recent convergence of the Internet and activism [18]. In this complex virtual landscape, the predominant view in the extant literature tends to categorize online social movements as emergent, often spontaneous, informal communities which are less rigid and norm-bound than their on-the-ground counterparts but precisely because of the lack of a formal structure, may risk dissipating without having met their original goals [53]. This motivates the importance of investigating factors that affect the sustenance of such movements [27]. Prior work in this regard, highlights the concept of narrative agency, which indicates how the structure of such narrative movements may be contextual and depend on several intersecting social and cultural factors thus rendering each social movement unique in its narrative form [56]. This warrants the need and importance to understand the key conversational norms and practices that drive online movements, the theoretical motivation for which is as described in the next section.

2.2 Organizing an Online Movement Communicatively Through Genre Systems

A common way of monitoring the health of an online community is by assessing the level of engagement exhibited by its participants [45]. This form of community participation exploration tends to focus on measurable tokens of engagement such as the volume, frequency, and valence of posts o the intensity of social contacts among community members represented by comments or likes [44]. Assessing the conversational dynamics of a social group provides another promising approach to taking the pulse of an online community by investigating the underlying semantic or narrative structures present in community discourse. Long-standing research in social psychology and computational linguistics has found consistent evidence of the relationship between personal narratives and the way they are expressed in textual artifacts on the one hand, and authors' attitudes, emotions, and values on the other [40]. The importance of analyzing narratives to uncover underlying themes is demonstrated by the large scholarly interest in thematic analysis and other related qualitative techniques [8].

In the context of online communication in particular, genre analysis has been effective in determining what types of user-generated content in the form of web documents exist on the Internet and how they interact with each other [21]. Grounded in both rhetoric and linguistics, genre theory commonly defines a genre as a class of communicative events with a shared set of communicative purposes [51]. This communicative paradigm of social interaction allows for a more nuanced understanding of latent categories such as identity, affect, and cognition [12]. Since different genres rarely operate in a vacuum, the theory of genre systems has been advanced to account for the complexity of genre interactions, especially in online communication [57]. An example of a genre system is for instance the sequence of the following genres: a job ad, job letter and resume, invitation to an interview, the interview itself, and a job offer (or rejection), which map onto the hiring process [58]. Analysing genre systems is important because the interdependent genres that comprise them serve as organizing structures within a community which demarcate the norms, purpose, content, participants, form, time, and place of communicative interaction [57]. While genre system theory has been widely used to characterize emergent themes of discourse that guide social interactions in deliberate and routine online communities [2], it has not yet been applied to the analysis of emergent online social movements. By combining it with a critical sociotechnical perspective of social media, we seek to extend the theory of online social movements through both a materialist and narrative-based approach to the co-constitutive interplay between genre systems shaping the norms of a digital campaign for justice and the participants in the campaign in turn shaping the genre systems present in the community.

3 Methods

To understand how the narrative campaign emerges and is sustained, the goal was to explore the textual conversation traces related to the hashtag *#JusticeForSushantSinghRajput* from Twitter to understand the themes or genres of conversational practice that arise. To achieve this aim, we followed a three step analysis framework (Fig. 1), post data collection. Each of these iteratively build on each other and help to scale and bring rigor to the analysis [17]. These steps are described below.

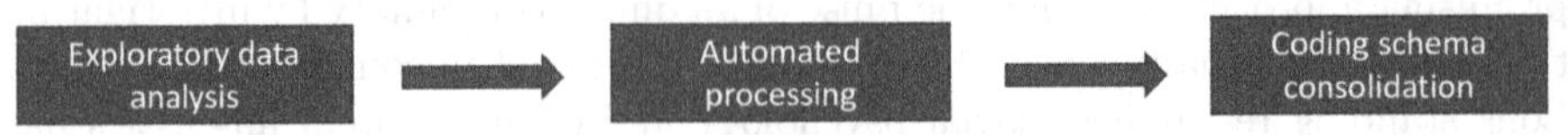

Fig. 1. Three part analysis pipeline

3.1 Data Collection

Data was collected using the latest version of the Twitter API[1], and spans the seven-month period between June and December, 2020. This time period was chosen to align with the time after the death of SSR (on 14th June, 2020). Inspired by the scholarship on genre systems, that highlight how communication norms develop and sustain through repeated and routinized use [57], we also collected a sample of data points from June to August, 2021 to gain an understanding of the evolution and recent trends of the campaign. In light of the large amount of tweets generated during this time frame, which is beyond the scope of the present investigation, we used a random sampling technique by selecting tweets from every fifth day of the month to account for possible tweet variation in day of the week or time of day. The theoretical and empirical robustness of this sampling strategy for topical analysis of Twitter content has been validated by prior research which show that it tends to outperform other widely-used sampling techniques such as constructed sampling [26,31]. The goal was to have a sample of approximately 3000 tweets per month, over the ten-month span for which the data was collected. Further descriptive details about this corpus are in Table 1.

Table 1. Descriptive statistics for final corpus

Statistic	Value
Number of tweets	27265
Number of unique users	2825
Earliest creation date	6/14/2020
Latest creation date	8/19/2021
Average like count	7.12
Average retweet count	3.52

[1] https://developer.twitter.com/en/docs/twitter-api/early-access.

3.2 Analysis Pipeline

Exploratory Data Analysis: The goal of the first phase of the analysis pipeline was to gain an initial understanding of the type and number of diverse topics comprising the narrative structure observed. Rooted in grounded theory, a thematic coding approach was used to derive the initial set of exploratory themes [9], from a random sample of 150 tweets from the corpus. This initial schema was developed and validated by both the authors and yielded a set of six distinct themes.

Automated Processing: This second stage of the analysis was primarily motivated by scaling the exploration to the entire corpus collected and also to investigate any additional insights regarding the thematic categorization obtained in the previous step. To extract these categories computationally, we used Topic modeling, which is an unsupervised machine learning algorithm that uses the semantic and syntactic properties of the data to infer latent themes [7]. The non-negative matrix factorization (NMF) approach was used to apply topic modeling since prior research has found it to be more robust, especially for sparse datasets [38]. Additional preprocessing steps such as stop word removal and normalization of the document term matrix were also carried out to consolidate the analysis.

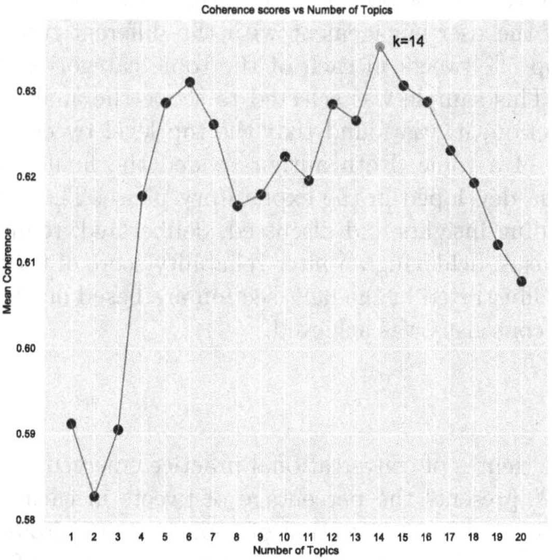

Fig. 2. Coherence scores for the entire corpus

A challenge with implementing topic models is initializing the model with the number of topics to be generated. To overcome this issue, we created an end-to-end analysis approach by augmenting topic modeling with topic coherence [5]. Topic coherence is the concept of calculating a coherence value for a particular topic model to quantitatively evaluate how well the topic clusters capture the semantic properties of the data [37]. To compute coherence scores, Word2Vec which is a popular and robust model to compute similarity scores between word pairs, was used [33]. To implement this augmented approach, first, topic models were generated for a range of topics and then the coherence score for each topic model was calculated, finally the topic model that had the highest topic coherence score in this set was chosen for subsequent analysis [38]. Figure 2 illustrates this process. While the best performing model appears to be the one with 14 topics, for the current analysis we chose to use the model with *6* topics, as the coherence scores are very close to the model with 14 topics and this also aligns with the number of themes found in the exploratory phase. All models were developed in python using the Scikit-learn [39] and Gensim libraries [43].

Coding Schema Consolidation: The final step of the analysis included pruning the results obtained in the automated processing step. While the automated analysis is helpful to categorize the data, it is important to attach contextual meaning to these themes, which was the chief aim of this step. Further, the goal was to refine and finalize the themes and insights about the categories as deduced from the previous stages of the analysis. To infer the topic labels, the following steps were followed. First the data was sorted according to a metric (which as computed as the sum of the like count, reply count, quote count and retweet count for each data point). This metric was chosen to get a holistic understanding of the user engagement with the different topical themes. Subsequently, the top 5% tweets in each of the topic categories were selected for final inspection. This sample was selected to scope the analysis and also since on manual inspection, it was found that the top level tweets best capture the semantic nuance of a topic. Both authors coded the final data sample using the coding schema developed in the exploratory phase. The authors frequently compared the coding insights and discussed, deliberated, refined the results to arrive at a consensus, achieving an inter-reliability score of 0.72 [6]. The results as described and illustrated in the next section are based on the final set of 971 tweets for which consensus was achieved.

4 Results

Six key themes or genres of conversational practice emerged as the result of our analysis. Figure 3, presents the percentage of tweets in each category). These themes encompass a wide cross-section of topics ranging from active demands for fairness and retribution to expressions of grief and a sense of mourning for the the late actor. In this mixture of topics, some were more focused on developing a sense of community among those participating in the digital campaign, whereas some were focused on empowering the campaign by sharing resources, information and updates as to how the matter was being handled by the institutions of justice. These themes are as described below.

Motivation and Solidarity: This was the most prominent theme of the digital movement and represented a sense of togetherness and drive to empower, encourage and support those who were a part of the campaign. An example tweet was- *"Victory is always possible for the person who refuses to stop fighting. SSRians will not give up the fight for #JusticeForSushantSinghRajput"*. Many of these conversations depicted a keen sense of camaradarie and fellow feeling, aimed at emboldening the campaign. An example tweet that captured this sentiment was - *"SSRians Bonded For Justice, would keep raising voice until #JusticeForSushantSinghRajput is served."* Many tweets in this category also bore an element of spiritualism and were often tinged with a deep sense of piety. An example tweet in this regard was: *"May this Christmas Santa will fill SSRians with hope and as a gift will bring justice for Sushant Singh Rajput"*. This highlights how religion and political sentiment often intertwine and affect the conversational focus of socio-political campaigns in India even in the digital context [24].

Disillusionment with the System: This was another important and powerful theme that emerged. These posts were centered on expressing anger, disgust and condemned the way the case was being handled and investigated by Indian authorities. An example tweet was - *"How could police say that he committed suicide immediately? They gave their statements without inquiries and post mortem reports. They said whatever they was paid for!!"* Few of the tweets in this category also captured a sense of dejection and questioned the basic foundation of morality and integrity of the major institutions of power in India [4]. An example tweet in this regard was: *"SSR life is perfect example of how this world treats good people"*. Aligned with the theme of dejection, some tweets were also aimed at the scruples of those associated with the entertainment industry and were questioning their sense of responsibility towards the public. An example tweet that relays this sentiment was: *"Shame on Gutterwood! For never having the guts or the spine to speak up for Sushant. For normalizing murders in your midst. For being completely devoid of any kind of basic human emotion like empathy."*. Thus, this theme formed the heart of the narrative campaign and provided the scaffolding to help sustain the movement.

Parasocial Attachment: This theme helped to consolidate the movement and posts in this category were aimed at expressing grief, attachment and a sense of loss when reminiscing about the late actor. Akin to prior studies on celebrity death and public mourning in such cases on social media, these tweets depict a strong sense of affinity and emotional connection with the departed soul [10]. An example tweet in this category was: *"I hope from over the clouds wherever you are you are proud to call us your SSRians. There is not a single second you do not cross my mind. #JusticeForSushantSinghRajput"*. In certain cases, it was also observed that this theme was intertwined with the themes of motivation and solidarity and disillusionment with the system. An example tweet that highlights this overlap was: *"Memories of certain people don't let us get rid of them with time, rather it invigorates the sprouting vessel which contains their good acts. Let's celebrate the reminiscence of his golden days"*. Thus, this highlights that these tweets were pivotal in helping campaigners find a common cause and purpose to participate in this campaign and so played a vital role in sustaining the movement.

Protecting the Campaign: Aimed at preserving the momentum and focus of the campaign, tweets related to this category discussed strategies to grow and further consolidate the movement. In that regard, tweets provided additional insights, references and sources to highlight the progress or updates regarding the case. Many of the tweets also urged campaigners to continue contributing and sharing resources in order to nurture and grow the campaign. An example tweet in this category was: *"We are preparing for an online meeting, in which it is mandatory for all SSRians to be there, and then we will discuss further strategy regarding this movement, please stay connected."*.

Appreciation of Contribution: Essential to sustain any digital campaign, is rewarding and acknowledging the contributions of those participating, which was the key aim of tweets in this category. An example tweet in this regard was *"A big round of applause to each of my fellow warrior here who put their Heart and Soul today. We all Did it again and We will till #JusticeForSushantSinghRajput has been Served."*

Raising Awareness Towards on the Ground Protests: These tweets were aimed at raising awareness towards the way in which on-the-ground protests were being organized and coordinated regarding the case. This theme highlights how the digital campaign can help to generate support and spread information regarding how protests in the offline context were being held. This shows the power of the digital medium to help generate a larger sense of consciousness and provide a boost the campaign's goal and objective beyond the digital context. An example tweet in this regard was : *"Let us give more priority to ground protests and appreciate People joining the protest"*.

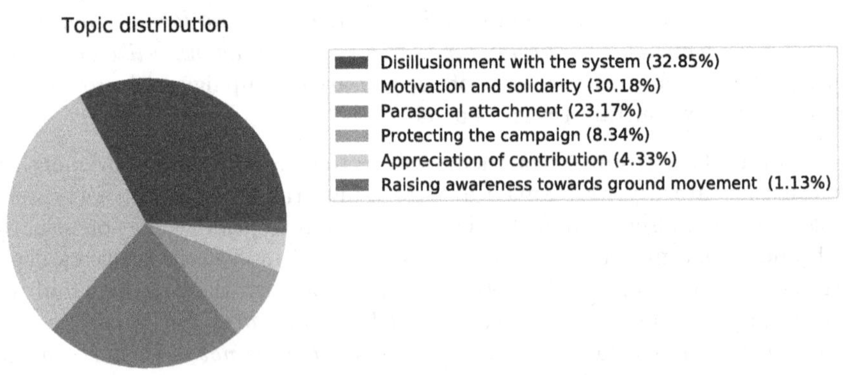

Fig. 3. Tweet distribution across each topic

5 Discussion

The above themes help to elaborate on different conversation norms that define the narrative structure of a digital campaign for justice. Thus, through the repeated use and proliferation of these themes or genres, we get an understanding of how this digital campaign creates its own collective identity, a sense of shared responsibility and purpose which is driven and sustained by the narrative practices that emerge [41]. To further illustrate this point, we present the month-wise distribution of tweets across the six themes in Fig. 4.

This diagram helps to discern how the narrative structure and the collective sentiment associated with this campaign evolves and grows over the time period we investigated. Prominently visible is the growth in the theme of "Motivation and Solidarity." This theme steadily grows between June and December, 2020 and appears to be one of the main drivers of conversation in 2021. This shift likely aligns with the needs of the campaign and could be influenced by the growing sense of community among participants, thereby highlighting how community is shaped through the development of common streams of sentiment and purpose [42]. For example, as illustrated in this tweet *"I am always here for Sushant till my last. My message is for demotivated Warriors to stay and not leave this campaign."*, in 2021, many of the conversations were oriented towards encouraging participants, so that they would continue their association with the campaign and not lose hope, given the delay in the justice they desired and expected. Similar resonating sentiments can also be observed for the tweets associated with the category of "Protecting the campaign,". In 2021, the number of tweets seem to have increased in comparison with the earlier stages, which again signifies the importance of ensuring that the campaign sustains. In contrast, the initial phases of the movement, seem to be driven mainly by the theme of "Disillusionment with the system," which is probably motivated by the need to create ground for the campaign and appeal to the authorities to take action. These help to explicate the structure trends and growing sense of affinity and common purpose among campaign participants [41].

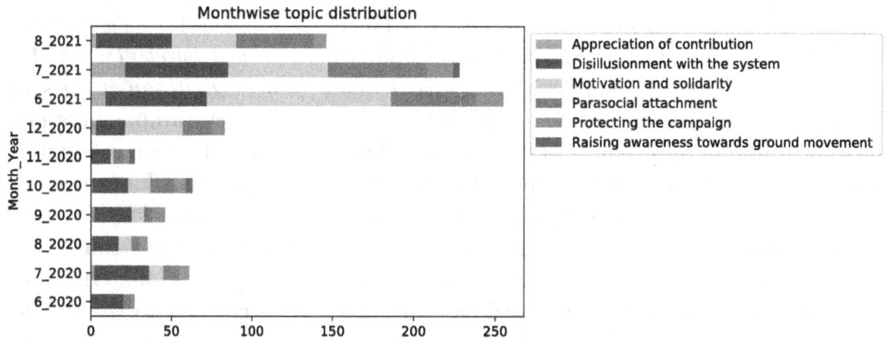

Fig. 4. Month-wise tweet distribution across each topic

Community building can be key to ensuring the success and sustenance of a digital campaign [23]. Community building can be important not only to boost the campaign but also to protect the objectives of the campaign. For example, in the following tweet, *"Guys, we have enough to handle already, please do not use defamatory Hashtags against anyone, it will only impact the movement and get SSRian accounts Suspended."*, we see how participants were setting norms for participation and were essentially urging all those involved to support and maintain a proper decorum when contributing to the campaign, reflecting the values and community moderation practices that shape up in such informal, self-organizing, contexts [49]. Key to building community is a sense of attachment and commitment to the community [44], this is best demonstrated by the increasing number of tweets associated with the category "Appreciation of contribution." These trends and gradual formation of a community perspective are also indicative of the creation and maintenance of social capital in such digital forums [55], which can also play a crucial role in empowering and can help to grow the digital campaign [60]. Akin to the notion of bonding capital, the themes of "motivation and solidarity," and "appreciation of contribution" highlight rapport-building and a sense of togetherness being fostered among those participating in the campaign which further strengthens over time [14]. Similarly, akin to the notion of bridging capital, the themes of "protecting the campaign" and "disillusionment with the campaign and raising awareness towards ground protests" highlight practices of knowledge sharing, raising concern and awareness, which help to spread and grow the campaign [14]. Recent scholarship has also highlighted a middle ground in social capital creation, which maintains both a knowledge- and information-sharing perspective and a community outlook [48]. In line with this perspective, the theme of "protecting the campaign" highlights a need to bring cohesiveness and drive to the community associated with the campaign, while also ensuring the information and knowledge being spread adheres to the norms of the community.

The social capital created is primarily driven by the affordances of the digital medium. Affordances can play a pivotal role in the way a digital campaign is organized and performed via a virtual channel like Twitter [28]. Certain tweets in our corpus also indicated the role of the virtual medium plays in controlling the campaign through its various affordances. For example: *"Twitter you are a disappointment! This has been one trouble-some pinned tweet! Twitter has been playing it up for long now, all those I know who liked it say it goes off overnight.Today it stands at 302."*. Such tweets highlight how campaigners perceive the different affordances of the medium that affect content recommendation and regulation and thus may impact the success of a campaign. Affordances can play a key role in the way people participate and disclose information [11]. Particularly, content presentation algorithms and moderation practices can be the key drivers controlling the narrative structure of such campaigns [46]. Our analysis highlights how cultural and regional anecdotes are etc.hed onto the themes that drive participation in such digital campaigns for justice and thus can provide insights into how such channels should be designed and maintained to afford extended participation from a global perspective [13]. Finally, the affordances of such platforms can be key to the creation of a safe space that allows free and equitable discussion and deliberation on a wide variety of ideas and thus can be vital for the sustenance of digital campaigns [29]. Fleshing out the emergent genre system of a digital campaign for justice as the one spurred by the death of Sushant Singh Rajput is pivotal not just for understanding the mechanism of campaign development but also for ensuring social media platforms function as inclusive spaces for civic engagement [30] which nurture and help grow the movement for justice rather than deepen division and domination.

6 Conclusion and Future Work

To conclude, the goal of our exploration was to investigate how a narrative campaign regarding the death of an Indian movie star emerges and strengthens through the mediation of Twitter. Using a detailed mixed methods analysis, our key contribution is to highlight a six themed genre system that forms the key conversational foundation for the digital campaign inspected. This genre system view provides a deep insight into the practices, norms and goals of the campaign explored using a sample data set constructed across a ten month time span. The creation of this genre system also helps to highlight the role of community development which strengthens over time and helps to build social capital to sustain the movement, which is another contribution of this research. The aim of such a discourse-centric analysis is to provide key ways in which the design and governance of virtual channels (such as Twitter) can be considered to support and scaffold narrative movements in a global context.

Future work in this regard, will include primarily scaling the analysis using supervised learning models with the coding schema developed as part of this exploration. Such an extension will help to further validate and refine the observations as presented here. Secondly, quantitative and qualitative approaches will be used to understand trends in participation and contribution through a social network perspective, glimpses of which can be gleaned from the discourse patterns as presented in this analysis.

References

1. Akbar, S.Z., Sharma, A., Negi, H., Panda, A., Pal, J.: Anatomy of a rumour: social media and the suicide of sushant singh rajput. arXiv preprint arXiv:2009.11744 (2020)
2. Alasmari, H., Zavalina, O.L.: Examination of the content of covid-19-related tweets during the march-april 2020 pandemic peak (2021)
3. Arendt, H.: The human condition (dt. udt vita activa, 1960) (1958)
4. Axford, B., Gulmez, D.B., Gulmez, S.B.: Introduction: rethinking ideology and protests in the age of globalization-bridging divides. In: Rethinking Ideology in the Age of Global Discontent, pp. 1–6. Routledge (2017)
5. Belford, M., Mac Namee, B., Greene, D.: Stability of topic modeling via matrix factorization. Expert Syst. Appl. **91**, 159–169 (2018)

6. Belotto, M.J.: Data analysis methods for qualitative research: managing the challenges of coding, interrater reliability, and thematic analysis. Qual. Report **23**(11) (2018)
7. Blei, D.M.: Probabilistic topic models. Commun. ACM **55**(4), 77–84 (2012)
8. Braun, V., Clarke, V.: Using thematic analysis in psychology. Qual. Res. Psychol. **3**(2), 77–101 (2006)
9. Chapman, A., Hadfield, M., Chapman, C.: Qualitative research in healthcare: an introduction to grounded theory using thematic analysis. J. Royal College Physic. Edinburgh **45**(3), 201–205 (2015)
10. Cohen, E.L., Hoffner, C.: Finding meaning in a celebrity's death: the relationship between parasocial attachment, grief, and sharing educational health information related to robin williams on social network sites. Comput. Human Behav. **65**, 643–650 (2016)
11. De Choudhury, M., De, S.: Mental health discourse on reddit: self-disclosure, social support, and anonymity. In: Eighth International AAAI Conference on Weblogs and Social Media (2014)
12. Devitt, A.J.: Genre performances: John swales' genre analysis and rhetorical-linguistic genre studies. J. English Acad. Purposes **19**, 44–51 (2015)
13. Dosono, B., Semaan, B.: Decolonizing tactics as collective resilience: identity work of aapi communities on reddit. Proceed. ACM Human Comput. Interact. **4**(CSCW1), 1–20 (2020)
14. Ellison, N.B., Steinfield, C., Lampe, C.: The benefits of facebook "friends:" social capital and college students' use of online social network sites. J. Comput. Mediated Commun. **12**(4), 1143–1168 (2007)
15. Fichman, P., Brill, R.: The impact of question type and topic on misinformation and trolling on yahoo! answers. In: Toeppe, K., Yan, H., Chu, S.K.W. (eds.) Diversity, Divergence, Dialogue. iConference 2021. LNCS, vol. 12646. Springer, Cham (2021). https://doi.org/10.1007/978-3-030-71305-8_10
16. Fiesler, C., Morrison, S., Shapiro, R.B., Bruckman, A.S.: Growing their own: legitimate peripheral participation for computational learning in an online fandom community. In: Proceedings of the 2017 ACM Conference on Computer Supported Cooperative Work and Social Computing, pp. 1375–1386 (2017)
17. Forman, J., Damschroder, L.: Qualitative content analysis. In: Empirical methods for bioethics: A primer. Emerald Group Publishing Limited (2007)
18. Foust, C.R., Hoyt, K.D.: Social movement 2.0: integrating and assessing scholarship on social media and movement. Rev. Commun. **18**(1), 37–55 (2018)
19. Fuchs, C.: Social media and the public sphere. tripleC: communication, capitalism and critique. Open Access J. Global Sustain. Inf. Soc. **12**(1), 57–101 (2014)
20. Giddens, A.: The constitution of society: outline of the theory of structuration. Univ. California Press, **349** (1984)
21. Herring, S.C., Scheidt, L.A., Bonus, S., Wright, E.: Bridging the gap: a genre analysis of weblogs. In: Proceedings of the 37th Annual Hawaii International Conference on System Sciences, 2004, pp. 11. IEEE (2004)
22. Ho, S.M., Kao, D., Li, W., Lai, C.J., Chiu-Huang, M.J.: On the left side, there's nothing right. On the right side, there's nothing left: polarization of political opinion by news media. In: Sundqvist, A., Berget, G., Nolin, J., Skjerdingstad, K. (eds.) Sustainable Digital Communities. iConference 2020. LNCS, vol. 12051. Springer, Cham (2020). https://doi.org/10.1007/978-3-030-43687-2_16
23. Jackson, S.J., Bailey, M., Foucault Welles, B.: # girlslikeus: trans advocacy and community building online. New Media Soc. **20**(5), 1868–1888 (2018)

24. Jaffrelot, C.: Religion, caste, and politics in India. Primus Books (2010)
25. Karami, A., Shaw, G.: An exploratory study of (#) exercise in the twittersphere. In: iConference 2019 Proceedings (2019)
26. Kim, H., Jang, S.M., Kim, S.H., Wan, A.: Evaluating sampling methods for content analysis of twitter data. Soc. Media+ Soc. **4**(2), 2056305118772836 (2018)
27. Kusuma, K.S.: Media, technology and protest: an indian experience. Language India **18**(7) (2018)
28. Lee, F.L., Liang, H., Cheng, E.W., Tang, G.K., Yuen, S.: Affordances, movement dynamics, and a centralized digital communication platform in a networked movement. Inf. Commun. Soc. 1–18 (2021)
29. Lucero, L.: Safe spaces in online places: social media and lgbtq youth. Multicult. Educ. Rev. **9**(2), 117–128 (2017)
30. Mainsah, H., Morrison, A.: Social media, design and civic engagement by youth: a cultural view. In: Proceedings of the 12th Participatory Design Conference: Research Papers, vol. 1, pp. 1–9 (2012)
31. Marvi, S., et al.: Covid needles in social media haystacks: identifying cross-language and longitudinal changes in pandemic-related discussion topics
32. Mernissi, F.: Islam and democracy: fear of the modern world with new introduction. Basic books (2009)
33. Mikolov, T., Sutskever, I., Chen, K., Corrado, G.S., Dean, J.: Distributed representations of words and phrases and their compositionality. In: Advances in neural information processing systems, pp. 3111–3119 (2013)
34. Müller, K.W., Dreier, M., Beutel, M.E., Duven, E., Giralt, S., Wölfling, K.: A hidden type of internet addiction? intense and addictive use of social networking sites in adolescents. Comput. Human Behav. **55**, 172–177 (2016)
35. Nahon, K., Hemsley, J., Mason, R.M., Walker, S., Eckert, J.: Information flows in events of political unrest (2013)
36. Neal, L., Oakley, K., Lindgaard, G., Kaufman, D., Leimeister, J.M., Selker, T.: Online health communities. In: CHI'07 Extended Abstracts on Human Factors in Computing Systems, pp. 2129–2132 (2007)
37. Newman, D., Lau, J.H., Grieser, K., Baldwin, T.: Automatic evaluation of topic coherence. In: Human Language Technologies: The 2010 Annual Conference of the North American Chapter of the Association for Computational Linguistics, pp. 100–108 (2010)
38. O'callaghan, D., Greene, D., Carthy, J., Cunningham, P.: An analysis of the coherence of descriptors in topic modeling. Expert Syst. Appl. **42**(13), 5645–5657 (2015)
39. Pedregosa, F., et al.: Scikit-learn: machine learning in python. J. Mach. Learn. Res. **12**, 2825–2830 (2011)
40. Pennebaker, J.W.: Writing about emotional experiences as a therapeutic process. Psychol. Sci. **8**(3), 162–166 (1997)
41. Pierre, J.: Putting the "Move" in social movements: assessing the role of Kama Muta in online activism. In: Taylor, N., Christian-Lamb, C., Martin, M., Nardi, B. (eds.) Information in Contemporary Society. iConference 2019. LNCS, vol. 11420. Springer, Cham (2019). https://doi.org/10.1007/978-3-030-15742-5_35
42. Rathnayake, C., Caliandro, A.: Repurposing sentiment analysis for social research scopes: an inquiry into emotion expression within affective publics on twitter during the covid-19 emergency. Diversity Divergence Dialogue **12645**, 396 (2021)
43. Řehřek, R., Sojka, P., et al.: Gensim-statistical semantics in python. Genism. Org (2011)

44. Ren, Y., Harper, F.M., Drenner, S., Terveen, L., Kiesler, S., Riedl, J., Kraut, R.E.: Building member attachment in online communities: applying theories of group identity and interpersonal bonds. MIS Quarter. 841–864 (2012)
45. Ren, Y., Harper, F.M., Drenner, S., Terveen, L., Kiesler, S., Riedl, J., Kraut, R.E.: Increasing attachment to online communities: designing from theory. MIS Quarter. **36**(3), 841–864 (2012)
46. Schmitt, J.B., Rieger, D., Rutkowski, O., Ernst, J.: Counter-messages as prevention or promotion of extremism?! the potential role of youtube: recommendation algorithms. J. Commun. **68**(4), 780–808 (2018)
47. Selander, L., Jarvenpaa, S.L.: Digital action repertoires and transforming a social movement organization. MIS Quarter. **40**(2), 331–352 (2016)
48. Sengupta, S.: A tale of two virtual communities: a comparative analysis of culture and discourse in two online programming communities. In: Proceedings of the 54th Hawaii International Conference on System Sciences, p. 34 (2021)
49. Seraj, M.: We create, we connect, we respect, therefore we are: intellectual, social, and cultural value in online communities. J. Interact. Marketing **26**(4), 209–222 (2012)
50. Starbird, K., Maddock, J., Orand, M., Achterman, P., Mason, R.M.: Rumors, false flags, and digital vigilantes: misinformation on twitter after the 2013 boston marathon bombing. In: IConference 2014 Proceedings (2014)
51. Swales, J.: Genre analysis: english in academic and research settings. Cambridge University Press (1990)
52. Tomprou, M., Dabbish, L., Kraut, R.E., Liu, F.: Career mentoring in online communities: seeking and receiving advice from an online community. In: Proceedings of the 2019 CHI Conference on Human Factors in Computing Systems, pp. 1–12 (2019)
53. Tufekci, Z.: Twitter and tear gas. Yale University Press (2017)
54. Tufekci, Z., Wilson, C.: Social media and the decision to participate in political protest: observations from tahrir square. J. Commun. **62**(2), 363–379 (2012)
55. Wellman, B., Haase, A.Q., Witte, J., Hampton, K.: Does the internet increase, decrease, or supplement social capital? social networks, participation, and community commitment. Am. Behav. Scien. **45**(3), 436–455 (2001)
56. Yang, G.: Narrative agency in hashtag activism: the case of# blacklivesmatter. Media Commun. **4**(4), 13 (2016)
57. Yates, J., Orlikowski, W.: Genre systems: structuring interaction through communicative norms. J. Business Commun. (1973) **39**(1), 13–35 (2002)
58. Yates, J., Orlikowski, W.J., Rennecker, J.: Collaborative genres for collaboration: genre systems in digital media. In: Proceedings of the Thirtieth Hawaii International Conference on System Sciences. vol. 6, pp. 50–59. IEEE (1997)
59. Zade, H., Shah, K., Rangarajan, V., Kshirsagar, P., Imran, M., Starbird, K.: From situational awareness to actionability: towards improving the utility of social media data for crisis response. Proceed. ACM Human Comput. Interact. **2**(CSCW), 1–18 (2018)
60. Gil de Zúñiga, H., Jung, N., Valenzuela, S.: Social media use for news and individuals' social capital, civic engagement and political participation. J. Comput. Mediated Commun. **17**(3), 319–336 (2012)

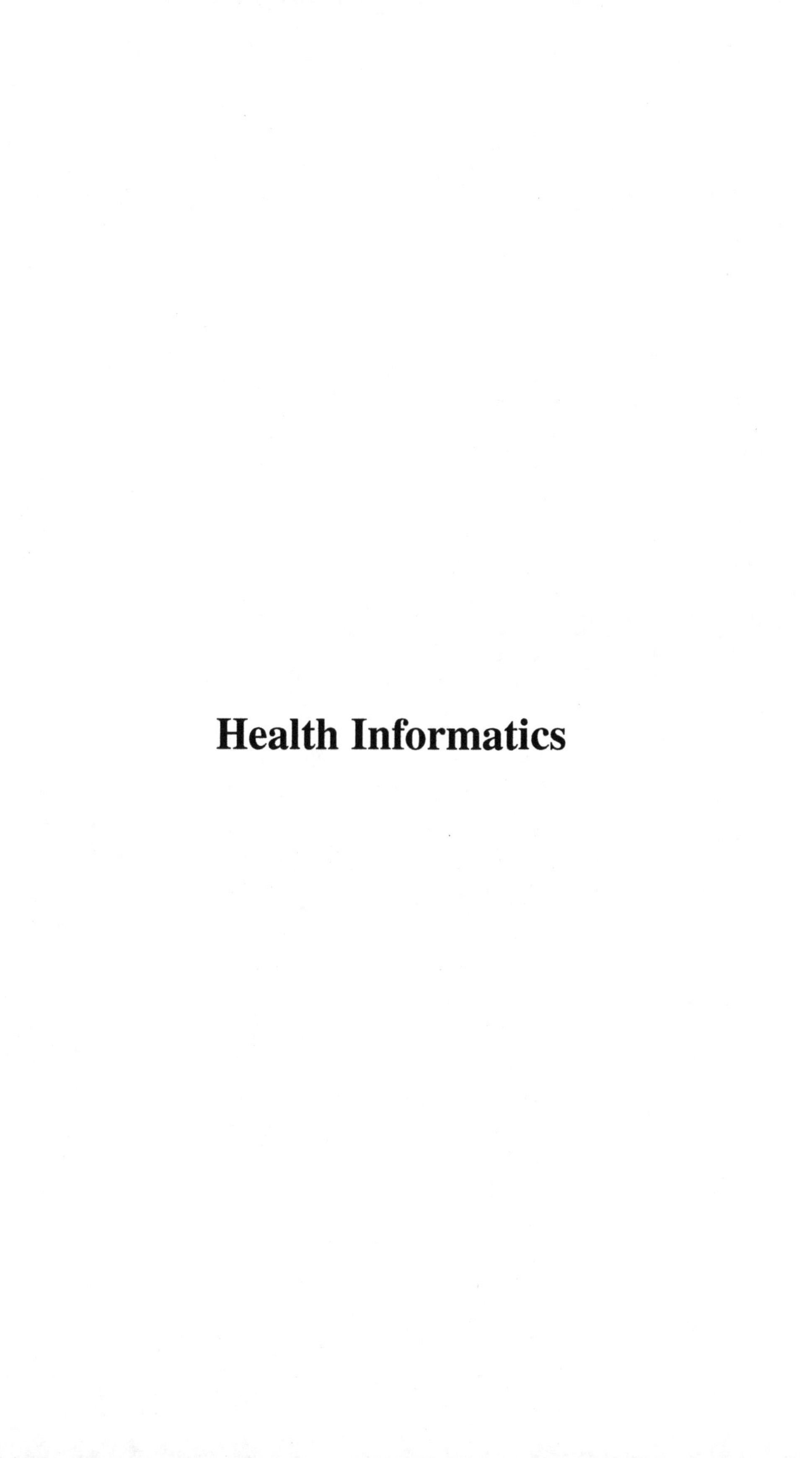

Health Informatics

Advice Giving in Medical Research Literature

Yingya Li and Bei Yu(✉)

School of Information Studies, Syracuse University, Syracuse, NY 13244, USA
{yli48,byu}@syr.edu

Abstract. Evidence-based health advice, i.e., clinical or policy recommendations, contributes greatly to guiding medical practice and public health policies. However, whether to give health advice, especially based on individual study results, is a controversial issue: on the one hand, such advice may lack a comprehensive review of all evidence and alternative practices; on the other hand, researchers have been encouraged to translate research findings to actionable practice. To date, limited attention has been given to understanding how and where health researchers give advice in their publications, which could be critical for assessing the quality of health advice in medical literature. In this study, we conducted a content analysis of all 4,866 sentences in the abstract and discussion sections in 100 individual study papers (both randomized controlled trials and observational studies), labeling each sentence as either "strong advice", "weak advice", or "no advice". We found that most authors gave advice in individual studies, but they rarely gave advice in abstract only. The common practice is either to give advice in discussion sections only, or in both abstracts and discussions. When giving advice in both sections, authors tended to give weak and non-specific advice in abstracts, while using more sentences in the discussion sections to give strong and more specific advice, adding conditions required for the recommendations. The result suggests that most researchers support giving advice in individual studies, but they are generally cautious in giving advice in abstracts.

Keywords: Health advice · Medical research literature · Content analysis

1 Introduction

Evidence-based health advice contributes greatly to guiding medical practice and public health policies. However, the science community has not reached a consensus on whether to give health advice based on individual study results. Some researchers are concerned about the quality of health advice based on individual study results. They argued that a single research publication may lack sufficient information for all evidence or a full review of alternative practices [1]. Specifically, medical experts have noted a great number of clinical or policy recommendations derived from research publications could not be fully justified by study designs and results [2–6]. For example, Prasad et al. [3] manually examined the conclusions of 298 observational studies in leading medical journals and found about more than half of the studies contained recommendations for a medical practice; however, only a small percentage of the studies call for Randomized Controlled Trials (RCTs) to validate the recommendations.

M. Smits (Ed.): iConference 2022, LNCS 13193, pp. 261–272, 2022.
https://doi.org/10.1007/978-3-030-96960-8_18

On the contrary, supporters of "actionable research" encourage more efficient and effective science evidence into practice [7]. From their perspective, if researchers themselves do not discuss the practical implications of their studies, other information stakeholders such as journalists or social media users might overinterpret the study results during the science communication process. For instance, Sumner et al. [8] found 40% of press releases created health advice that did not exist in the original research papers. Haneef et al. [9] found that about 20% of health news stories in Google News contain health advice that could not be supported by the original study conclusions. The overinterpreted health advice could spread and evolve further when picked up by social media.

Besides the question of whether to give health advice based on individual study results, medical researchers also face the question of where to give health advice. Researchers can choose to give advice in the abstract sections, or in the discussion sections after presenting the study results, or both. Due to the length limit, abstracts offer very little room for giving detailed advice. At the same time, they are usually accessible to the public, and thus can have a broad audience. In comparison, discussions, as a part of full-text articles, are often behind pay walls, although they allow for more room to discuss the implications [23]. Prior studies have found that the location of advice could affect its reach and impact. For example, clinicians would be more likely to read the full text or rate a treatment as beneficial if the abstracts have discussed its significance (e.g., giving weak recommendation) [22]. However, giving advice in abstracts can be problematic due to the limited space and thus the lack of a thorough discussion of the context. The quality of health advice in abstracts is also questionable - prior studies have found that more than 80% of studies assessing medical interventions had misrepresentations of research findings in abstracts, such as claiming exaggerated significance and inadequate recommendations for practice in certain clinical areas [5, 6, 21].

Although prior studies have raised concerns over the advice-giving behaviors among medical researchers, in-depth investigations are lacking, leaving many questions unanswered. For example, what is the majority opinion on advice-giving in individual studies, to give advice or not? Do researchers prefer to give advice in abstracts or in discussions? If recommendations were given in both sections, are they semantically equivalent, or does one version tend to be stronger than the other?

To answer these research questions, we conducted a manual content analysis. We sampled 100 medical research papers with various study designs, and manually annotated each sentence in the abstracts and discussion sections as either containing health advice or not. Then for the advice-giving sentences, we further annotated whether the recommendations are strong or weak. We then aggregated the sentence-level annotations into section levels and compared researchers' advice-giving behavior in abstracts and discussions. More specifically, we compared 1) the numbers of papers that gave advice and those that did not; 2) the strength of advice made in abstracts vs. discussion sections.

2 Related Work

Establishing advice based on research evidence is not a trivial task. The potential overinterpretation of study results has led to both arguments for and against the value of giving health advice based on studies in guiding health decisions. Researchers have found a large proportion of health advice was misrepresented, as such advice frequently represents logical leaps that lead to possible misinterpretation of study findings [2, 3]. Meanwhile, scientists may also have the tendency to rely on their "wishful thinking" rather than scientific evidence to draw research conclusions [34]. The process of inferring recommendations from research evidence requires cognitive and scientific reasoning. However, scientists can be "motivated reasoners" highly influenced by their hopes and emotions when evaluating evidence [37]. Although quite a few instructions and frameworks have been proposed to help scientists formulate evidence-based guidelines and recommendations for clinical practice [e.g., 36, 37, 39], clinical recommendations were commonly found to have clarity problems. The fact that advice can be given in more than one place also causes the inconsistency problem. A content analysis on systematic reviews of therapeutic interventions found a large proportion of health advice in abstracts was not only overclaimed but also inconsistent with the advice given in discussions, where researchers would have more room to explain their advice in more details [39].

To label and compare the health advice made in abstracts and discussion sections in medical literature, we need to identify whether a sentence contains advice and how strong it is. From language perspective, advice is a form of imperative utterance that can convey a speaker's wishes or suggestions of an action [24]. Imperative language is also part of an illocutionary act which is one of the essential units of human linguistic communication [25]. The strength of advice is normally realized by language indicators, such as hedges [26–28], modalities [29, 30], and evidentials [32].

To identify whether a sentence contains advice, we consulted linguistic theories to define an advice-giving sentence as one that contains imperative statements or attempts of illocutionary act. According to Austin [25], an illocutionary act can be captured when someone delivers a finding, gives or commits a decision in favor of or against a certain course of an action, presents or explains views, and express reactions to other people's behavior and attitudes. Searle [14] further categorized illocutionary acts into five categories, including representatives, directives, commissives, expressives, and declarations. Among these categories, directives indicate the attempts that a speaker would like the hearer to do something. Such attempts can be very modest when an invitation or suggestion is offered, or they can be very fierce when the speaker insists the hearer do a certain act.

Linguistic cues such as hedges, modalities, and evidentials in imperative statements are important indicators to distinguish weak advice from strong advice. Lakoff [26] defined hedges as "words whose meaning implicitly involves fuzziness – words whose job is to make things fuzzier or less fuzzy" (p.195). Hedges can express tentativeness and possibility, or strength writers withhold to their statements, and for qualifying authors' confidence in the truth of a proposition [26, 27]. Modality is an expression of individuals' subjective attitudes and opinions [29]. The term traditionally associated with strength and speculation in language is epistemic modality [30]. Strength can also be reflected by evidentials that reveal a degree of information reliability. By a narrow definition, evidentials express the evidence a person has for making factual claims [32]. In a broader definition, evidentials involve various attitudes toward knowledge and their functions are more than marking the evidence in the claim. They can evaluate the degree of reliability of knowledge; specify the mode of knowledge; and mark the contrast between knowledge and expectation.

With the purpose to measure the status of health advice in the science and scholarly communication process, previous studies normally formulated the task as a binary classification problem to distinguish statements with or without advice [3]. To capture the advice type with more granularity, Read et al. [17] categorized advice in clinical practice guidelines into *"strong"*, *"moderate"*, and *"weak"* by the level of confidence of the advice giver. Similarly, Sumner et al. [8] categorized health advice into four levels: *"no advice", "implicit advice", "explicit advice, but not to the reader or general public", and "explicit advice to the reader or general public"*. In comparison, explicit advice is a direct recommendation for changes. Implicit advice hints for changes without a direct recommendation and it can show different linguistic patterns. Overall, the definition of *"explicit/implicit"* advice is aligned well with the *"strong/weak"* classification, with both distinguishing the strength of advice.

Drawing on the health advice definitions in past studies, we focused on the occurrence and strength of health advice. Occurrence indicates whether statements contain imperative statements or not; while strength shows how strong the advice is. We applied the "strong/weak" classification and we categorized sentences in research articles as *"no advice"*, *"weak advice"*, or *"strong advice"* in this study.

3 Method

In this section, we first introduce the process of data collection for health advice analysis (Sect. 3.1). Then we discuss the annotation process (Sect. 3.2) and the analysis process applied in this study (Sect. 3.3).

3.1 Data Collection

To the best of our knowledge, no prior dataset is available for measuring the occurrence and strength of health advice in medical research literature, we then collected a sample of medical research publications that contain both abstracts and discussion sections in full text. We chose PubMed Central as the source. PubMed Central is the open-access subset of PubMed database which has more than 27 million citations for health and biomedical literature from Medline, life science journals, and online books. In addition to the abstracts and rich metadata such as study designs provided by PubMed, PubMed Central also provides full-text content of a portion of PubMed-indexed publications.

In evidence-based medicine, different study designs may lead to different levels of evidence towards medical decision-making [18]. In general, RCTs are the strongest design for clinical interventions [33]. An RCT randomly assigns individuals into experiment and control groups, and compares treatment effects between groups [12]. In comparison, observational studies are conducted in earlier-stage research or when RCTs are unethical for a research problem. Cross-sectional, case-control, retrospective, and prospective studies are four common types of observational studies with an increasing strength in study design [15]. Therefore, we applied a stratified sampling approach to select research papers from different study designs. From PubMed Central, we sampled RCTs and 4 types of observational studies using their MeSH terms (i.e. "Randomized Controlled Trials", "Cross-Sectional Studies", "Case-Control Studies", "Retrospective Studies", and "Prospective Studies"). Overall, we sampled 100 papers in total, 20 papers from each type of the five study designs.

After downloading all the XML files from PubMed Central, we extracted the abstract section and the discussion section from each paper. The abstract section has a unique XML tag, and thus easy to identify. The discussions may appear in sections with various headers (e.g., "discussions", "discussion and conclusion", "conclusion", "conclusions" etc.). We compiled a list of discussion section headers and used it to locate all discussion sections. We then used the Stanford CoreNLP tool to split the abstracts and discussion sections into sentences. In the end, a total of 4,866 sentences (934 from abstracts and 3932 from discussions) were extracted from the 100 medical research papers for analysis.

3.2 Health Advice Annotation

To compare health advice in abstracts and discussions, we first labeled if a sentence contains advice – imperative statements as discussed in the literature review section. If a sentence does not contain an imperative statement, it will be annotated as *"no advice"*. For sentences that contain advice, we relied on the linguistic cues such as hedges, modalities, and evidentials to distinguish *"weak advice"* from *"strong advice"*. Table 1 shows the annotation schema and *"no advice"*, *"weak advice"*, and *"strong advice"* examples. The linguistic cues for weak and strong advice were underlined in the sentence examples. Sometimes, a sentence could be an imperative statement (as shown in e.g., 3 in Table 1), however, it is a suggestion for follow-up studies but not health-related behavior changes. For these imperative statements, we would label them as "no advice".

To test the validity of the annotation schema, we randomly sampled 100 sentences for inter-coder agreement checking. Two annotators labeled the sentences based on the linguistic cues for imperative statement and claim strength. The Cohen's Kappa agreement [19] value was .86, suggesting our annotation schema reached almost perfect inter-coder agreement [20]. The disagreed cases in the annotation were later resolved by the two annotators through discussion. After inter-coder agreement checking, three annotators with academic backgrounds in clinical psychology, linguistics, and information management were trained to annotate the sentences in abstracts and discussions in sampled research articles. All the team members discussed the unsure cases after the individual annotation process and reached an agreement on the annotations.

Table 1. Advice and non-advice sentences in medical research literature.

Category	Definition	Sentence
No advice	No imperative statement is in the sentence. The sentence describes study background, methods, results, or limitations. In some cases, the sentence may give suggestions for future study, however, no recommendation is made for health-related behavior	1. The ARR is associated with chronic kidney disease (CKD), renal artery stenosis, renin adenoma. (PMC: 4525911) 2. We retrospectively analyzed data from 65 patients. (PMC: 3426471) 3. Future research in this area needs to use more rigorous methods and more diverse and representative participants. (PMC: 7387868)
Weak advice	The sentence contains cues for an imperative statement. Linguistic cues such as hedging words, modalities are in the sentence, which hints or gives implicit recommendation that either behavior or health-related practice needs changing	4. Therefore, due to the cost, possible side effects, and the limited saving of homologous blood, intraoperative antifibrinolytic therapy may not be indicated in routine cardiac surgery. (PMC: 325258) 5. Hypericum extract, with its favorable tolerability profile, could be an interesting option for long-term prophylaxis. (PMC: 6878444)
Strong advice	The sentence contains cues for an imperative statement. It gives straightforward recommendations for actionable practice and policy changes. No hedging word or modality is in the sentence to lower the strength	6. Hysterectomy should be performed at least 4 weeks after conization. (PMC: 6302663) 7. We recommend gas calibration of the CDI before use in the period before in-vivo calibration. (PMC: 21848172)

3.3 Health Advice Aggregation and Comparison

For our analysis, we aggregated the sentence-level labeling result (as described in Sect. 3.2) to the section level, using the rule that a section contains health advice if at least one abstract or conclusion/discussion sentence does. Besides, if both *"weak"* and *"strong"* recommendations were found, we then took the stronger one namely *"strong advice"* and assigned it to the section. Based on the section-level labels, we were able to count the number of advice-giving articles and to analyze the practice of giving health advice.

To compare the health advice made in abstracts and discussion sections, we further categorized each paper into four groups. Group 1 (the "advice-in-neither-section" group) includes articles that did not give advice in either abstracts or discussion sections; group 2 (the "advice-in-abstract-only" group) includes articles that only give advice in abstracts; group 3 (the "advice-in-discussion-only" group) includes articles that only give advice in discussion sections; group 4 (the "advice-in-both-sections" group is for articles that give advice in both abstracts and discussion sections. By comparing the numbers of articles in each group, we would be able to answer the first two research questions (1) whether advice-giving in individual studies is a common practice in medical publications, and (2) whether researchers have a preference over where to give advice.

As for the third research question regarding the strength of health advice in abstracts and discussion sections, we compare two aspects: (1) we check whether the recommendations made in abstracts and discussion sections are semantically similar, discussing the same clinical or policy practice. (2) For semantically similar recommendations, we compare whether abstracts or discussion sections give stronger advice. Figure 1 below illustrates our process of analysis.

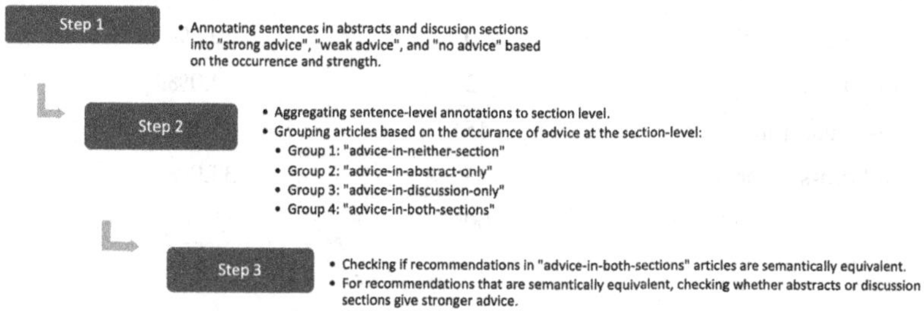

Fig. 1. An illustration of the analysis process.

4 Result

Table 2 shows the category distribution of sentences in abstracts and discussions. The average length of abstracts is 9 sentences. The average length of discussions is 39 sentences. Overall, the discussion sections contained a higher percentage of advice sentences (7.6% total, 3.5% strong, 4.1% weak), compared to that in abstracts (4.7% total, 1.7% strong, 3.0% weak). To calculate articles that gave advice and to compare the advice strength between abstracts and discussion sections, we then aggregated the sentence-level annotations into section levels.

Table 2. Advice sentence distribution in abstracts and discussion.

Advice type	Abstract	Discussion
No advice	890 (95.3%)	3635 (92.4%)
Weak advice	28 (3.0%)	162 (4.1%)
Strong advice	16 (1.7%)	135 (3.5%)
Total	934	3932

Table 3 shows the distribution of health advice after aggregating sentence-level annotations into section levels. The result shows that only 20% of articles did not give advice in either abstracts or discussions, suggesting that the majority of researchers embraced the practice of giving health advice in individual studies. However, only 2% (2/100) of articles gave advice in abstracts only, suggesting that most papers (78%) did not use abstracts as the main place to give advice. In fact, nearly half papers (45%) chose to give advice in discussion sections only, and 33% gave advice in both discussions and abstracts. Overall, researchers were much more likely to give advice in the discussions than in abstracts, and they rarely gave advice in abstracts only.

Table 3. Distribution of articles based on the practice of advice-giving.

Article type	Counts	Percentage
Advice-in-neither-section	20	20.0%
Advice-in-abstract-only	2	2.0%
Advice-in-discussion-only	45	45.0%
Advice-in-both-sections	33	33.0%
Total	100	

We then examined the strength of health advice in abstracts and discussions. Table 4 shows the advice types in abstracts and discussions for the 33 articles that gave advice in both abstracts and discussions: 9 gave weak advice in both sections; 12 gave strong advice in both sections; 12 gave strong advice in discussions but weak advice in abstracts. Interestingly, none of the papers gave strong advice in abstracts and weak advice in discussions. These results suggest that researchers were cautious in giving advice, especially strong advice in abstracts.

Table 4. Distribution of articles giving advice in both abstracts and discussions.

		Discussion	
		Weak advice	Strong advice
Abstract	Weak advice	9 (27%)	12 (36%)
	Strong advice	0	12 (36%)

To compare the content of different advice sentences in the same articles, we further checked the correspondence between the advice in abstracts and discussions. We paid particular attention to whether authors made multiple versions of the same recommendations with inconsistent strength levels. The result shows no strength inconsistency in the 12 articles that gave weak advice in abstracts and strong advice in discussions. Instead, we found two strategies that authors used to give different versions of advice. One strategy is to give weak and non-specific advice in abstracts, while using more sentences to give a completely different version of advice, which is stronger and more specific, in the discussions. This strategy occurred in 5 of the 12 articles. In the following examples, the authors gave a weak and non-specific recommendation for a protocol that is useful (sentence 1 in abstract). In comparison, they made a series of direct recommendations for specific clinical practice, adding a number of conditions required for the implementation (sentences 1–4 in discussion).

PMC: 5808411

Section: Abstract

1. Thus, a protocol for clinicians to manage the patient presenting with oligometastatic prostate cancer would be a useful clinical tool.

Label: weak advice

Section: Discussion

1. As in other settings, only those patients likely to suffer mortality or substantial morbidity due to their disease should be considered for aggressive treatment, which should only be offered in the setting of an institutional-review-board-approved clinical trial or prospective registry.

Label: strong advice

2. Patients must be fully informed of the potential risks and benefits associated with an aggressive approach; specifically, they must be made aware that data from appropriately conducted studies to demonstrate prolonged survival as a result of treatment is lacking.

Label: strong advice

3. Men who do undergo treatment should be assessed and treated in a multidiscipline-nary setting including medical oncology, radiation oncology, and urology.

Label: strong advice

4. Clinicians managing such patients should consider establishing a prostate cancer multidisciplinary clinic if not already present at their institution.

Label: strong advice

5. Finally, establishment of an institutional biorepository for banking of serum, urine, stool, and tissue samples should be considered — only with the committed and coordinated efforts of the entire health-care team will we find answers to the many questions that remain.

Label: strong advice

The other strategy was to use more sentences in discussions for stronger and more specific recommendations, but it would also include two paraphrased but semantically equivalent sentences in the abstract and the discussion sections (occurred in 7 of the 12 articles). The sentence examples below show a pair of semantically similar recommendations extracted from the abstract and discussion sections respectively.

PMC: 325258

Section: Abstract

Therefore, intraoperative antifibrinolysis may not be indicated in routine cardiac surgery when other blood-saving techniques are adopted.
Label: weak advice

Section: Discussion

Therefore, due to the cost, possible side effects, and the limited saving of homologous blood, intraoperative antifibrinolytic therapy may not be indicated in routine cardiac surgery.
Label: weak advice

Overall, when giving advice in both abstracts and discussions, authors tended to give weak and non-specific advice in abstracts, while giving stronger and more specific advice in discussions, where there is more room to lay out the conditions required for the strong recommendations.

5 Discussion and Conclusion

In this study, we conducted a content analysis of health advice made in medical research literature to understand health researchers' advice-giving behavior. Our results show that most authors gave advice in individual studies, but they rarely gave advice in abstract only. It is more common that they gave advice in discussion sections only, or in both abstracts and discussions. When giving advice in both sections, authors tended to give weak and non-specific advice in abstracts, usually in one sentence; however, they would use more sentences in the discussion sections to give strong and more specific advice, adding conditions required for the recommendations. The result suggests that most researchers support giving advice in individual studies, but they are generally cautious in giving advice in abstracts.

Our finding from the current analysis also indicates that health advice in abstracts, although widely accessible, does not contain details, such as the specific conditions required for recommended clinical practice. Therefore, readers of medical research publications are recommended to check the discussion sections in the full-text content for a thorough review of study implications. This finding also calls for open access to medical research publications such that researchers' contribution to the clinical and policy recommendations can be understood accurately by health professionals and the general public.

One limitation of our study is that the current sample size is small. However, the 4,866 manually annotated sentences could serve as training data for developing automated text classification models. The prediction model could be applied to a much larger corpus to further evaluate the generalizability of the findings from this study. We leave this to our future work.

Acknowledgement. This work is supported by the US National Science Foundation under grant 1952353, the Microsoft Investigator Fellowship program, and the Syracuse University CUSE Grant.

1. References

1. Cummings, P.: Policy recommendations in the discussion section of a research article. Injury Prev. **13**(1), 4–5 (2007)
2. Banerjee, R., Prasad, V.: Are observational, real-world studies suitable to make cancer treatment recommendations? JAMA Netw. Open **3**(7), e2012119–e2012119 (2020)
3. Prasad, V., Jorgenson, J., Ioannidis, J.P., Cifu, A.: Observational studies often make clinical practice recommendations: an empirical evaluation of authors' attitudes. J. Clin. Epidemiol. **66**(4), 361–366 (2013)
4. Wilson, M.K., Chestnutt, I.G.: Prevalence of recommendations made within dental research articles using uncontrolled intervention or observational study designs. J. Evid. Based Dent. Pract. **16**(1), 1–6 (2016)
5. Lazarus, C., Haneef, R., Ravaud, P., Boutron, I.: Classification and prevalence of spin in abstracts of non-randomized studies evaluating an intervention. BMC Med. Res. Methodol. **15**(1), 1–8 (2015)
6. Cooper, C.M., et al.: Evaluation of spin in the abstracts of otolaryngology randomized controlled trials. Laryngoscope **129**(9), 2036–2040 (2019)
7. Green, L.W., Glasgow, R.E., Atkins, D., Stange, K.: Making evidence from research more relevant, useful, and actionable in policy, program planning, and practice: slips "twixt cup and lip." Am. J. Prev. Med. **37**(6), S187–S191 (2009)
8. Sumner, P., et al.: The association between exaggeration in health related science news and academic press releases: retrospective observational study. BMJ **349** (2014)
9. Haneef, R., Lazarus, C., Ravaud, P., Yavchitz, A., Boutron, I.: Interpretation of results of studies evaluating an intervention highlighted in Google health news: a cross-sectional study of news. PloS One **10**(10), e0140889 (2015)
10. Titler, M.G.: The evidence for evidence-based practice implementation. In: Patient Safety and Quality: An Evidence-Based Handbook for Nurses (2008)
11. Thiese, M.S.: Observational and interventional study design types; an overview. Biochem. Med. **24**(2), 199–210 (2014)
12. Kabisch, M., Ruckes, C., Seibert-Grafe, M., Blettner, M.: Randomized controlled trials: part 17 of a series on evaluation of scientific publications. Dtsch. Arztebl. Int. **108**(39), 663 (2011)
13. Faraoni, D., Schaefer, S.T.: Randomized controlled trials vs. observational studies: why not just live together? BMC Anesthesiol. **16**(1), 1–4 (2016)
14. Song, J.W., Chung, K.C.: Observational studies: cohort and case-control studies. Plast. Reconstr. Surg. **126**(6), 2234 (2010)
15. Mann, C.J.: Observational research methods. Research design II: cohort, cross sectional, and case-control studies. Emerg. Med. J. **20**(1), 54–60 (2003). http://dx.doi.org/10.1136/emj.20.1.54
16. Schlesselman, J.J.: Case-control Studies: Design, Conduct, Analysis, vol. 2. Oxford University Press (1982)
17. Read, J., Velldal, E., Cavazza, M., Georg, G.: A corpus of clinical practice guidelines annotated with the importance of recommendations (2016)
18. Murad, M.H., Asi, N., Alsawas, M., Alahdab, F.: New evidence pyramid. BMJ Evid.-Based Med. **21**(4), 125–127 (2016)
19. Cohen, J.: A coefficient of agreement for nominal scales. Educ. Psychol. Meas. **20**(1), 37–46 (1960)
20. McHugh, M.L.: Interrater reliability: the kappa statistic. Biochemia Medica **22**(3), 276–282 (2012)
21. Shaqman, M., Al-Abedalla, K., Wagner, J., Swede, H., Gunsolley, J.C., Ioannidou, E.: Reporting quality and spin in abstracts of randomized clinical trials of periodontal therapy and cardiovascular disease outcomes. PloS One **15**(4), e0230843 (2020)

22. Boutron, I., Altman, D.G., Hopewell, S., Vera-Badillo, F., Tannock, I., Ravaud, P.: Impact of spin in the abstracts of articles reporting results of randomized controlled trials in the field of cancer: the SPIIN randomized controlled trial. J. Clin. Oncol. **32**(36), 4120–4126 (2014)
23. Hopewell, S., Eisinga, A., Clarke, M.: Better reporting of randomized trials in biomedical journal and conference abstracts. J. Inf. Sci. **34**(2), 162–173 (2008)
24. Condoravdi, C., Lauer, S.: Imperatives: meaning and illocutionary force. Empirical Issues Synt. Semant. **9**, 37–58 (2012)
25. Austin, J.L.: How to Do Things with Words. Oxford University Press (1975)
26. Lakoff, R.: Language in Context. Language 907–927 (1972)
27. Myers, G.: The pragmatics of politeness in scientific articles. Appl. Linguist. **10**(1), 1–35 (1989)
28. Hyland, K.: Hedging in Scientific Research Articles, vol. 54. John Benjamins Publishing. (1998)
29. Hyland, K.: Hedging in academic writing and EAF textbooks. Engl. Specif. Purp. **13**(3), 239–256 (1994)
30. Hyland, K.: Writing without conviction? Hedging in science research articles. Appl. Linguist. **17**(4), 433–454 (1996)
31. Anderson, L.B.: Evidentials, paths of change, and mental maps: typologically regular asymmetries (1986)
32. Searle, J.R.: A classification of illocutionary acts1. Lang. Soc. **5**(1), 1–23 (1976)
33. Faraoni, D., Schaefer, S.T.: Randomized controlled trials vs. observational studies: why not just live together? BMC Anesthesiol. **16**(1), 1–4. (2016)
34. Coyne, J.C., Tennen, H.: Positive psychology in cancer care: bad science, exaggerated claims, and unproven medicine. Ann. Behav. Med. **39**(1), 16–26 (2010)
35. Hopewell, S., Altman, D.G., Moher, D., Schulz, K.F.: Endorsement of the CONSORT statement by high impact factor medical journals: a survey of journal editors and journal instructions to authors. Trials **9**(1), 1–7 (2008)
36. Simera, I., Moher, D., Hoey, J., Schulz, K.F., Altman, D.G.: The EQUATOR network and reporting guidelines: helping to achieve high standards in reporting health research studies. Maturitas **63**(1), 4–6 (2009)
37. Shah, P., Michal, A., Ibrahim, A., Rhodes, R., Rodriguez, F.: What makes everyday scientific reasoning so challenging? In: Psychology of Learning and Motivation, vol. 66, pp. 251–299. Academic Press (2017)
38. Andrews, J., et al.: GRADE guidelines: 14. Going from evidence to recommendations: the significance and presentation of recommendations. J. Clin. Epidemiol. **66**(7), 719–725 (2013)
39. Yavchitz, A., et al.: A new classification of spin in systematic reviews and meta-analyses was developed and ranked according to the severity. J. Clin. Epidemiol. **75**, 56–65 (2016)

Professional Identity and Perceived Crisis Severity as Antecedents of Healthcare Professionals' Responses to Health Misinformation on Social Media

John Robert Bautista[1,2(✉)], Yan Zhang[1,2], and Jacek Gwizdka[1]

[1] School of Information, The University of Texas at Austin, Austin, TX 78701, USA
jrbautista@utexas.edu

[2] Center for Health Communication, Moody College of Communication and Dell Medical School, The University of Texas at Austin, Austin, TX 78712, USA

Abstract. This study aims to determine the extent to which human information agents, such as healthcare professionals, respond to health misinformation on social media (i.e., by correcting it using private priming, public priming, private rebuttal, and public rebuttal, including reporting misinformation). Moreover, guided by social identity theory (SIT) and situational crisis communication theory (SCCT), it also aims to determine whether professional identity, perceived crisis severity, and their interaction are associated with such responses. Online survey data among 377 US healthcare professionals (i.e., nurses and medical doctors) were collected in October 2020. Linear regression and structural equation modeling were performed to determine the association between professional identity, perceived crisis severity, and their interaction with each of healthcare professionals' responses to health misinformation on social media. Results show that most healthcare professionals responded to health misinformation on social media by performing public methods of correction, such as public priming and public rebuttal. Those with high professional identity were more likely to respond to health misinformation on social media. The interaction of professional identity and perceived crisis severity showed that those with high professional identity and high perceived crisis severity were likely to perform private priming, public priming, private rebuttal, public rebuttal, and report health misinformation. Overall, responses to health misinformation on social media, such as correcting and reporting misinformation can be explained using SIT and SCCT. Theoretical and practical implications are discussed.

Keywords: Information agents · Perceived crisis severity · Professional identity · Social correction · Social media

1 Introduction

Global health crises, such as pandemics, are also information crises [1]. In fact, the current COVID19 pandemic, a global health crisis considered also as an infodemic [2],

M. Smits (Ed.): iConference 2022, LNCS 13193, pp. 273–291, 2022.
https://doi.org/10.1007/978-3-030-96960-8_19

made international and national authorities fully recognize health misinformation as a public health crisis. In April 2020, the United Nations initiated an initiative to fight COVID19 misinformation with the justification that misinformation is harmful to people's physical and mental health [2]. In 2021, the U.S. Surgeon General [3] issued an advisory on slowing down the spread of health misinformation since it is a serious threat to public health. Although health misinformation is not an entirely new phenomenon, it has now become a greater threat to public health because it can now be easily transmitted on social media [4, 5]. In general, there is consensus that health misinformation, especially on social media, is a public health crisis that needs to be dealt with.

There are several ways to address health misinformation on social media. One of these involves social correction. For instance, the United Nations' [6] digital first responder initiative aimed at encouraging more people to be on social media to share correct information and provide corrections to misinformation. Although individuals have a role to play in addressing health misinformation (e.g., identifying and not sharing misinformation and engaging with friends and family on the problem of health misinformation), the US Surgeon General's [3] latest advisory also emphasized the need for healthcare professionals to perform social correction. Specifically, it encourages healthcare professionals to proactively engage with the public to combat health misinformation by using technology and media platforms (e.g., by sharing accurate health information on media outlets and social media).

Aside from it being a health crisis, healthcare professionals have been taking a stand against health misinformation on social media because it is in line with their professional oath. For instance, several reports show that healthcare professionals are fighting health misinformation on social media because it is an opportunity for them to project their professional identity by educating the public and to prevent harm due to misinformation [7–9]. Although correcting health misinformation on social media is not their legal obligation, healthcare professionals are encouraged to do it because it is their ethical obligation to convey truthful health information whether it is to patients or to the public [10]. Besides, as one of the trusted professionals to convey insights on health issues [11], healthcare professionals are in the position to lead as digital first responders to correct health misinformation on social media.

Currently, there is a limited understanding of relevant factors (e.g., professional identity and perceived crisis severity) associated with healthcare professionals' responses to health misinformation on social media. Recent work has mainly focused on factors that influence the general public to correct others [12–14]. Although Bautista et al.'s [15] recent work provides insights on intrapersonal factors that could affect healthcare professionals' responses to health misinformation on social media, that study is mainly qualitative, and additional research is needed to determine the applicability of those factors to a larger population of healthcare professionals. Besides, misinformation-related literature often describes information agents as organizational entities (e.g., health agencies or media companies) [16–19] rather than human entities, such as healthcare professionals.

To address the abovementioned research gaps, this study fulfills two research goals. First, it examines the extent of healthcare professionals' responses to health misinformation on social media, such as correcting (i.e., private priming, public priming, private rebuttal, and public rebuttal) and reporting misinformation. Second, it uses Tajfel and Turner's [20] social identity theory (SIT) with Coombs and Holladay's [21] situational crisis communication theory (SCCT) to explain whether professional identity and perceived crisis severity, including their interaction, predict healthcare professionals' responses to health misinformation on social media. There is a need to examine the roles of professional identity and perceived crisis severity in this study because recent reports suggest that healthcare professionals are motivated to respond to health misinformation because they believe that it is their obligation to do it and they consider health misinformation as a public health threat [7–9]. Thus, understanding this from both SIT and SCCT provides a good theoretical underpinning because healthcare professionals' responses to health misinformation on social media may depend on their professional identity and perceptions of health misinformation as a public health crisis. Overall, the findings provide a better theoretical understanding of factors influencing healthcare professionals' responses to health misinformation on social media. Besides, it can provide ideas for health organizations in instituting activities that can inspire more healthcare professionals to correct health misinformation on social media.

2 Literature Review

2.1 Responses to Health Misinformation on Social Media

Exposure to misinformation can trigger people to respond to it by correcting or reporting it [12–14, 22]. Although some studies do not specify how correction is performed [12, 13], current research [14, 22] shows that correcting others on social media can be done through priming (i.e., just sharing correct information with little to no reference of the misinformation as a means of prebunking [23, 24]) or rebuttal (i.e., responding to a misinformation post by replying the correct information). Besides, priming and rebuttal can be done on social media through private or public means [22]. In this study, corrections can be done by performing private priming (posting correct information that is not publicly visible on social media), public priming (posting correct information that is publicly visible on social media), private rebuttal (sending a private message to a person to provide the correction), and public rebuttal (replying to a public post to provide the correction). Although studies suggest that social correction (correction performed by other people) is an effective means of reducing misperceptions [25, 26], results from nationally representative surveys in the US (35.1%) [12] and Singapore (12.1%) [14] show that very few people correct someone who posts misinformation on social media.

Aside from providing correction, people can also respond to health misinformation on social media by reporting it [14]. Reporting a social media post that contains health misinformation reduces its spread and increases the chances of it being taken down on social media platforms [27]. To date, studies examining responses to misinformation on social media have used the general public as target responses [13, 14, 25] and none has yet examined it from the perspective of healthcare professionals. Therefore, RQ1 is proposed:

RQ1: To what extent do healthcare professionals respond to health misinformation on social media?

Aside from identifying the extent to which healthcare professionals respond to health misinformation on social media, it is also important to explore whether the extent of their responses differs based on their profile (i.e., age, sex, race, healthcare profession, years as a healthcare professional and years using social media). Studies show that demographics, such as age, education, race, and income, were associated with correcting others on social media [12, 13]. Thus, RQ2 is proposed:

RQ2: Are there differences in responses to health misinformation on social media based on healthcare professionals' profile?

2.2 Professional Identity

Professional identity is referred to as the sense of being a professional wherein one projects a self-image that allows the achievement of personal adequacy and satisfaction in the performance of the expected role [28]. Previous work suggests that a strong sense of professional identity among healthcare professionals is associated with improved work performance [29] and quality of care [30]. For healthcare professionals, one way that they can exhibit professional identity is through the performance of their role as information agents [31] – that is to deliver accurate and evidence-based health information that can lead individuals, groups, and communities to perform appropriate health behaviors [32, 33]. Although healthcare professionals primarily share health information during clinical encounters (e.g., patient visits to clinics or during clinical rounds), the rise of the Internet and social media platforms provide a new channel that allows healthcare professionals to convey such information to global audiences. In fact, healthcare professionals have been shown to use their social media platforms to spread accurate health information as means of fighting health misinformation on social media, most notably during the COVID19 pandemic [15, 34].

The link between professional identity and healthcare professionals' responses to health misinformation can be understood using SIT. SIT posits that an individual's identity is derived from group-based self-definitions [20]. In turn, such an identity derived from belongingness to a particular group can dictate the attitudes and behaviors toward an issue [20, 35, 36]. For example, being part of the healthcare profession, there is an expectation for healthcare professionals to adhere to the principle of nonmaleficence (i.e., to do no harm) [37]. That is why most nurses and medical doctors are likely to promote COVID19 vaccination and are likely to be vaccinated because them being part of the healthcare profession dictates their responsibility to protect others from harm (i.e., aside from protecting themselves, getting vaccinated reduces the chance of infecting others). Using the same logic, professional identity can also influence healthcare professionals' responses to health misinformation on social media (e.g., correcting and reporting health misinformation on social media can prevent harm). Aside from the theoretical applicability of using SIT to predict responses to misinformation, recent empirical studies support the use of SIT as a framework to examine the link between social identity and misinformation-related attitudes and behaviors[38, 39]. Thus, the following hypothesis is proposed:

H1: Professional identity is associated with healthcare professionals' responses to health misinformation on social media?

2.3 Perceived Crisis Severity

In response to crisis situations, entities perform actions in ways that can mitigate, if not eliminate, the crisis. In the context of widespread health misinformation on social media that is already recognized by authorities as a public health crisis, healthcare professionals can perform actions that could limit its spread [3, 15, 22]. Thus, there is a need to examine healthcare professionals' perceived severity of health misinformation as a public health crisis and its association with their responses to health misinformation on social media.

To examine the link between them, this study adopts Coombs and Holladay's [21] SCCT. One of the tenets of SCCT is that the crisis' severity has an impact on the actions taken by entities (e.g., the organization or the organization's spokesperson) who are asked to act on it [21]. Depending how severe that crisis is perceived to be, such entities have a variety of actions that they can execute to minimize or eliminate the negative impact of a crisis whether to themselves or others [21]. For instance, if healthcare professionals think that health misinformation on social media is a public health crisis that can harm others, they will be motivated to act by correcting or reporting it.

In this study, perceived crisis severity refers to the degree to which individuals assess a crisis to be intense [21, 40, 41]. It is important to note that perceived crisis severity is based on an individual's understanding of the crisis and may not correspond to the actual risk presented by the crisis [21, 40, 41]. While a potential predictor of responses to health misinformation on social media based on SCCT, studies have used this construct primarily as a dependent variable in misinformation correction [16, 42] and crisis communication [43–45] experiments. On the other hand, studies found that perceived crisis severity is a predictor of intention to adopt voluntary proximity tracing applications [40] and organizational reputation [46]. Based on the abovementioned details, the following hypothesis is proposed:

H2: Perceived crisis severity is associated with healthcare professionals' responses to health misinformation on social media?

2.4 Interaction of Professional Identity and Perceived Crisis Severity

Aside from examining the independent association of professional identity and perceived crisis severity with responses to health misinformation on social media, this study also explores whether the interaction of these two predictors is associated with such responses. Initial qualitative work involving healthcare professionals suggests that those who exhibit heightened professional identity (e.g., believing that correcting health misinformation is their public health duty) and high perceived crisis severity (e.g., believing that health misinformation needs to be dealt with since it is a public health threat) seem to perform corrections [15]. Theoretically, examining their interaction contributes to past efforts [47–49] that combines SIT with SCCT to better explain the mechanism by which individuals respond to risk information. Thus, RQ5 is proposed:

RQ3: Is the interaction of professional identity and perceived crisis associated with healthcare professionals' responses to health misinformation on social media?

3 Method

3.1 Sampling and Data Collection

After obtaining approval from the Institutional Review Board of The University of Texas at Austin (2020-04-0001), online survey data was collected in October 2020 through Qualtrics. The survey link was posted on several social media platforms, such as Twitter, Facebook, and LinkedIn. A combination of purposive and snowball sampling was used for recruitment. Purposive sampling was performed by targeting respondents who were (1) social media users, (2) healthcare professionals such as nurses and medical doctors, and (3) practicing in the U.S. (4) for at least a year. This study focused on nurses and medical doctors since they have been recognized as professionals with the highest ethical standard based on the 2020 US Gallup poll [11]. On the other hand, snowball sampling was performed by requesting potential respondents to share the survey link with their contacts.

Of the 885 respondents who answered the screening questions, 523 were eligible. After data cleaning (e.g., respondents who did not finish the survey or completed it within three minutes were removed), data from 377 respondents were retained. G*Power 3.1.9.2 (linear multiple regression: fixed model R^2 increase, effect size = .15, power = .95, number of tested/total predictors = 9) suggests that the current sample size (i.e., 377) exceeded the estimated sample size (i.e., 166) for the study [50].

3.2 Measurement

The items used in the survey were mostly derived from previous work. Table 1 provides a list of the items including descriptive results.

Responses to Health Misinformation on Social Media. The dependent variables are composed of six items that reflect responses to health misinformation on social media. These items were developed based on initial qualitative work [22] and a literature review [12, 14]. These responses include four methods of social correction based on Bautista et al. (2021), such as private priming (M = 4.02, SD = 1.35), public priming (M = 4.22, SD = 1.29), private rebuttal (M = 3.55, SD = 1.80), public rebuttal (M = 4.23, SD = 1.35), including other responses based on previous work (i.e., [14]; Tully et al., 2020), such as reporting health misinformation (M = 4.06, SD = 1.39). Respondents were asked to indicate their responses using a seven-point Likert scale (1 = "never" and 7 = "always").

Professional Identity. The nine-item Professional Identity Scale (M = 4.72, SD = .82) of Adams et al. [51] was used to measure professional identity. Of the nine items, three were negatively worded and were reverse coded. The wordings of the items were slightly modified to fit the context of the study. Respondents were asked to indicate their responses using a seven-point Likert scale (1 = "strongly disagree" and 7 = "strongly agree").

Table 1. List of items and descriptive results

Items	*M*	*SD*
Responses to health misinformation on social media (1 = "never" and 7 = "always")		
1. Privately post accurate health information on your own social media page to correct health misinformation. (correcting-private priming)	4.08	1.35
2. Publicly post accurate health information on your own social media page to correct health misinformation. (correcting-public priming)	4.22	1.29
3. Send a private message to the person who posted health misinformation to provide correction. (correcting-private rebuttal)	3.55	1.80
4. Post a public comment or reply that provides a correction to health misinformation. (correcting-public rebuttal)	4.23	1.35
5. Report the health misinformation post so it gets removed. (reporting)	4.06	1.39
Professional identity (1 = "strongly disagree" and 7 = "strongly agree")		
1. I am part of my healthcare profession	5.01	1.50
2. I have strong ties with members of my healthcare profession	5.04	1.30
3. I am often ashamed to admit that I am a member of my healthcare profession. (reverse coded; removed)	4.31	1.79
4. I find myself making excuses for belonging to my healthcare profession. (reverse coded; removed)	4.27	1.67
5. I try to hide that I am part of my healthcare profession (reverse coded; removed)	4.26	1.79
6. I am pleased to belong to my healthcare profession	4.87	1.49
7. I can identify positively with members of my healthcare profession	5.01	1.38
8. Being a member of my healthcare profession is important to me	4.88	1.53
9. I share similar characteristics with other members of my healthcare profession	4.85	1.12
Perceived crisis severity (1 = "strongly disagree" and 7 = "strongly agree")		
1. I care about health misinformation as a public health crisis	5.07	1.18
2. Further news about health misinformation as a public health crisis is of my interest	5.08	1.22
3. I hope to know more about health misinformation as a public health crisis	5.01	1.12
4. I think health misinformation as a public health crisis interests me	5.11	1.20
5. Health misinformation as a public health crisis increased my sense of stress	5.12	1.19
6. I feel anxious about health misinformation as a public health crisis	5.01	1.14
7. My apprehension grows as I knew more about health misinformation as a public health crisis	5.17	1.21
8. I'm worried about health misinformation as a public health crisis	4.96	1.14

(*continued*)

Table 1. (*continued*)

Items	*M*	*SD*
9. I feel affected by health misinformation as a public health crisis	5.07	1.19
10. I feel involved to solve health misinformation as public health crisis	5.25	1.35
11. I find health misinformation as a relevant public health crisis to me	5.12	1.16
12. Solving health misinformation as a public health crisis is meaningful	5.19	1.26

Kaiser-Meyer-Olkin (.75) and Bartlett's Test of Sphericity ($\chi2 = 688.95$, df = 36, $p < .001$) values suggest sample adequacy for exploratory factor analysis (EFA). EFA based on maximum likelihood and promax rotation showed a single factor construct (Eigenvalue = 2.74) that was able to explain 33% of the variance. Common method bias is not an issue since the variance is <50%. The three reversed items were removed due to poor factor loading (<.40). The remaining six items had adequate reliability (McDonald's $\Omega = .74$).

Perceived Crisis Severity. The 12-item Perceived Crisis Severity Scale ($M = 5.10$, $SD = .86$) of Zhou et al. [41] was used to measure perceived crisis severity. The wordings of the items were slightly modified to fit the context of the study. Respondents were asked to indicate their responses using a seven-point Likert scale (1 = "strongly disagree" and 7 = "strongly agree").

Kaiser-Meyer-Olkin (.95) and Bartlett's Test of Sphericity ($\chi2 = 2017.10$, df = 66, $p < .001$) values suggest sample adequacy for EFA. EFA based on maximum likelihood and promax rotation showed a single factor construct (Eigenvalue = 6.15) that was able to explain 47% of the variance. Common method bias is not an issue since the variance is < 50%. The items had excellent reliability (McDonald's $\Omega = .91$).

Control Variables. Respondents' profile, such as sex (female = 63%), age ($M = 33.45$, $SD = 6.07$), race (white = 79%), profession (nurse = 52%; doctor = 48%), years as a healthcare professional ($M = 8.67$ years; $SD = 5.95$), and years using social media ($M = 10.61$, $SD = 3.42$), were entered as control variables. Table 2 provides more information of the respondents' profile.

3.3 Data Analysis

IBM SPSS Statistics 26 (hereafter SPSS) and Mplus 7 were used to perform several data analyses in this study. Descriptive statistics were performed in SPSS to answer RQ1. T-test and ANOVA were performed in SPSS to answer RQ2. Hayes' PROCESS Macro (model 1) [52] (via SPSS) and structural equation modeling (SEM; via Mplus 7) was performed to test H1 and H2 and answer RQ3. Unstandardized coefficients based on 10,000 bootstrap samples are reported. For SEM, model fit parameters were based on Hu and Bentler's [53] guidelines. To prevent multicollinearity, mean centering was performed for the means of professional identity and perceived crisis severity before creating their

Table 2. Respondents' profile and responses to health misinformation on social media ($N = 377$)

Profile	N	%	Private priming		Public priming		Private rebuttal		Public rebuttal		Report	
			M (SD)	*P*	*M* (SD)	*P*	*M* (SD)	*p*	*M* (SD)	*p*	*M* (SD)	*p*
Sex												
Male	139	37	4.05 (1.30)	.71	4.23 (1.29)	.91	3.86 (1.78)	.009	4.32 (1.35)	.29	4.08 (1.36)	.83
Female	238	63	4.00 (1.39)		4.21 (1.30)		3.36 (1.79)		4.17 (1.35)		4.05 (1.41)	
Age												
< 35	146	39	3.76 (1.35)	.000*	3.96 (1.31)	.000*	3.10 (1.82)	.000*	3.97 (1.41)	.000*	3.81 (1.37)	.000*
≥35	231	61	4.42 (1.27)		4.64 (1.16)		4.25 (1.53)		4.64 (1.15)		4.45 (1.34)	
Race												
White	297	79	4.01 (1.34)	.95	4.20 (1.30)	.60	3.49 (1.86)	.22	4.19 (1.33)	.27	4.00 (1.37)	.10
Non-white	80	21	4.03 (1.40)		4.29 (1.27)		3.75 (1.59)		4.38 (1.43)		4.29 (1.45)	
Profession												
Doctor	181	48	3.85 (1.31)	.02*	4.06 (1.17)	.02*	3.18 (1.83)	.000*	4.14 (1.35)	.21	3.82 (1.42)	.002*
Nurse	196	52	4.17 (1.37)		4.37 (1.38)		3.88 (1.71)		4.31 (1.36)		4.28 (1.33)	
Years as a healthcare professional												
1–5	120	32	3.84 (1.30)	.012*	3.93 (1.27)	.000*	3.21 (1.72)	.000*	3.92 (1.36)	.000*	3.68 (1.32)	.001*
6–10	160	42	3.94 (1.48)		4.19 (1.33)		3.39 (1.95)		4.19 (1.43)		4.15 (1.40)	
> 10	97	26	4.36 (1.14)		4.63 (1.15)		4.22 (1.45)		4.67 (1.08)		4.37 (1.36)	
Years using social media												
< 10	137	36	4.06 (1.24)	.64	4.17 (1.28)	.58	4.01 (1.49)	.000*	4.22 (1.16)	.95	4.11 (1.24)	.58
≥10	240	64	3.99 (1.42)		4.25 (1.30)		3.29 (1.91)		4.23 (1.45)		4.03 (1.47)	

interaction terms. Results are statistically significant if $p < .05$. Respondents' profiles were used as control variables. A zero-order correlational analysis was performed for exploratory purposes (see Table 3).

4 Results

4.1 Responding to Health Misinformation on Social Media

Figure 1 shows the distribution of healthcare professionals' responses to health misinformation on social media. About 90% of the respondents responded to health misinformation on social media by performing public priming (91%) and public rebuttal (90%). Moreover, 89% and 88% responded by reporting the health misinformation and by performing private priming, respectively. About 70% indicated that they performed private rebuttal.

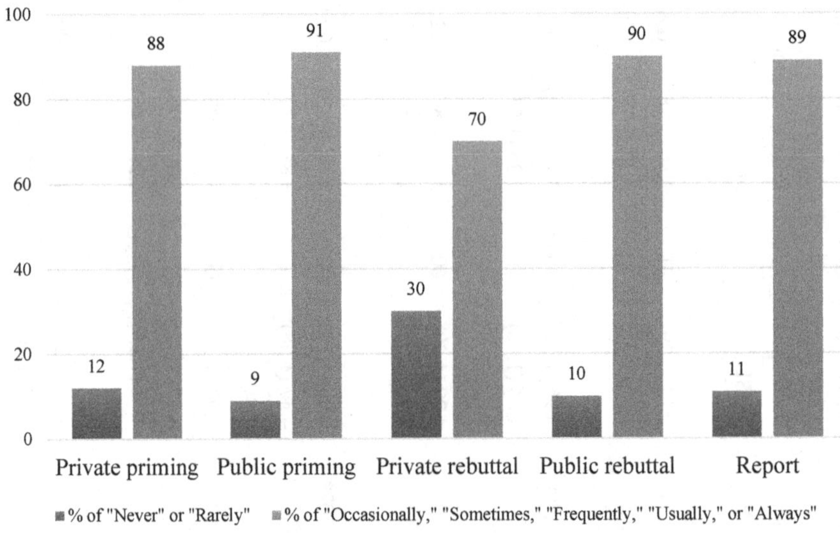

Fig. 1. Responses to health misinformation on social media

4.2 Differences in Responses to Health Misinformation on Social Media Based on Healthcare Professionals' Profile

Table 2 shows a summary of differences in responses to health misinformation on social media based on healthcare professionals' profile. Those who performed private priming and public priming as well as those who reported health misinformation were likely to be $\geq$35 years old, nurses, and >10 years in the profession. Moreover, those who performed private rebuttal were likely to be men, $\geq$35 years old nurses, >10 years in the profession, and social media users of < 10 years. Next, those who performed public rebuttal were

Table 3. Zero-order correlations

	1	2	3	4	5	6	7	8	9	10	11	12	13
1. Sex	1												
2. Age	−18*	1											
3. Race	.05	.05	1										
4. Healthcare profession	.42***	−.28***	−.02	1									
5. Years in profession	−.03	.80***	.02	−.11*	1								
6. Years using social media	.01	.08	−.11*	−.06	.10*	1							
7. Professional identity	.04	.18**	−.20***	.12*	.16**	.09	1						
8. Perceived crisis severity	.17**	.07	−.02	.11*	.02	.08	.50**	1					
9. Correct-Private priming	−.02	.19**	.00	.12*	.11*	−.05	.06	.11*	1				
10. Correct-Public priming	−.01	.20***	−.03	.12*	.12*	.05	.15**	.17**	.48***	1			
11. Correct-Private rebuttal	−.14**	.17**	−.06	.19***	.13*	−.09	−.13*	.23***	.51***	.47***	1		
12. Correct-Public rebuttal	−.05	.17**	−.06	.06	.14**	.04	.08	.10	.29***	.33***	.45***	1	
13. Report	−.01	.09	-.09	.16**	.08	.02	.07	.07	.43***	.40***	.53***	.33***	1

*** $p < .001$, ** $p < .01$, * $p < .05$.

likely to be ≥35 years old and >10 years in the profession. Finally, no significant differences were found based on race for all responses to health misinformation on social media.

4.3 Association of Professional Identity, Perceived Crisis Severity, and Their Interaction with Responses to Health Misinformation on Social Media

Table 4 summarizes the results of the regression analysis based on Hayes' Process Macro (model 1). After controlling for the effects of respondents' profile, results show that professional identity, perceived crisis severity, and the interaction of these two variables were able to explain 12%–33% of the variance for responses to health misinformation on social media.

Results show that those with high professional identity was associated with private priming (B = .23, p = .04), public priming (B = .39, p = .000), private rebuttal (B = .48, p = .000), public rebuttal (B = .27, p = .004), and reporting health misinformation (B = .28, p = .003). These results suggest that H1 is accepted since professional identity is associated with all responses to health misinformation on social media.

On the other hand, those with high perceived crisis severity were less likely to perform private rebuttal (B = -.79, $p < .001$). This result suggest that H2 is partially accepted since perceived crisis severity is only associated with one response to health misinformation on social media.

The interaction of professional identity and perceived crisis severity was associated with private priming (B = .40, p = .000), public priming (B = .37, p = .000), private rebuttal (B = .60, p = .000), public rebuttal (B = .31, p = .000), and reporting health misinformation (B = .42, p = .000). Moreover, Table 5 shows that only respondents with high professional identity and high perceived crisis severity were likely to respond to health misinformation on social media.

To determine the consistency of the regression results, structural equation modeling was performed (see Fig. 2). Results show that the model fits the data: $X^2 = 588$, df = 340, $X^2/df = 1.73$, CFI = .93, TLI = .91, RMSEA (90% CI) = .04 (.038, .050), SRMR = .059 [53]. Moreover, Fig. 2 shows that the statistically significant paths are consistent with the results presented in Table 4.

5 Discussion

This study examines the extent to which healthcare professionals responded to health misinformation on social media by correcting (i.e., private priming, public priming, private rebuttal, and public rebuttal) and reporting it. More importantly, the study adopts constructs from SIT and SCCT to determine whether professional identity, perceived crisis severity, and their interaction are associated with such responses. The following paragraphs discuss the key findings of the study.

First, the findings show that most of the respondents corrected health misinformation on social media using public methods, such as public priming (91%) and public

Table 4. Factors predicting responses to health misinformation on social media

Predictors	Responses to health misinformation on social media				
	Private priming B	Public priming B	Private rebuttal B	Public rebuttal B	Report B
Main variables					
Professional identity	.23*	.39***	.48***	.27**	.28**
Perceived crisis severity	.00	−.01	−.79***	−.01	−.07
Interaction					
Professional identity x Perceived crisis severity	.40***	.37***	.60***	.31***	.42***
Controls					
Age	.06**	.05**	.07**	.03	.02*
Sex (1 = female; 0 = male)	−.08	−.05	−.55**	−.17	−.14
Race (1 = white; 0 = non-white)	.07	.07	−.09	−.07	−.15
Healthcare profession (1 = nurse; 0 = doctor)	.33*	.22	.90***	.16	.37*
Years as a healthcare professional	−.04	−.02	−.02	.00	−.01
Years using social media	−.01	.00	−.02*	.00	−.00
Adjusted R^2	16%	21%	33%	12%	15%

B = unstandardized regression coefficients; *** $p < .001$, ** $p < .01$, * $p < .05$.

Table 5. Association of professional identity with responses to health misinformation on social media based on levels of perceived crisis severity.

Level of perceived crisis severity	Association of professional identity with...				
	Private priming B (95%CI)	Public priming B (95%CI)	Private rebuttal B (95%CI)	Public rebuttal B (95%CI)	Reporting B (95%CI)
Low (-1 SD)	−.12 (−.3617, .1265)	.08 (−.1470, .3065)	−.04 (−.3314, .2498)	.00 (−.2503, .2499)	−.07 (−.3292, 4220)
High (+1 SD)	.57 (.3550, .7807)*	.70 (.5085, .9040)*	1.00 (.7498, 1.2566)*	.53 (.3172, 7534)*	.64 (.4220, .8633)*

*The result is statistically significant if the 95% confidence interval does not cross zero.

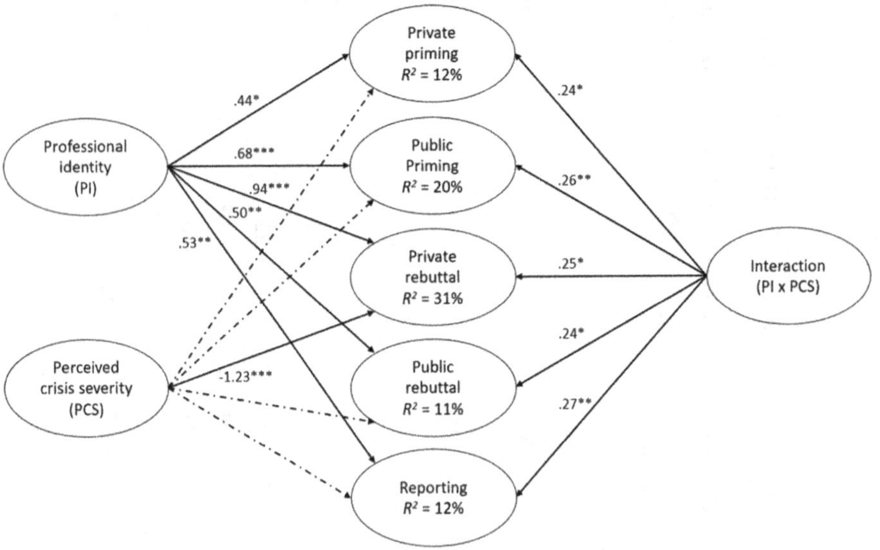

Fig. 2. SEM results.

rebuttal (90%). This is a welcome sign considering that the respondents of this study took proactive actions to correct health misinformation on social media. This contrasts with previous studies where that the general public is likely to ignore misinformation on social media [12, 14]. A potential explanation for this result is that healthcare professionals may have the knowledge and skills to make such corrections [15]. It is also important to note that there seems to be a preference to make publicly visible corrections. A potential explanation is that publicly visible forms of correction, such as public priming and public rebuttal, may increase the social utility of the correction [22]. In other words, publicly visible corrections can reach more audiences (e.g., can be seen and shared publicly) and has greater potential to educate the public via social learning.

To some extent, making the corrections publicly viewable can act as a digital receipt (i.e., a public record) of acting against misinformation, and such an online record can be used by healthcare professionals to enhance their professional identity and image on social media.

Second, age and years in the profession are related to correcting and reporting health misinformation on social media. Specifically, those who were 35 and older as well as those who were at least 10 years in their work were more likely to correct or report health misinformation on social media. Similar work involving US adults presents contrasting results. For instance, while Koo et al. [13] found that age is positively associated with correcting others, Bode and Vraga [12] found a negative relationship. In the context of this study, the positive relationship between age and years in the profession with correcting and reporting is reasonable because more established healthcare professionals (i.e., those who are older and have more years of work experience) might have accumulated clinical knowledge and skills through time, and this allows them to confidently correct or report health misinformation on social media.

Third, when examined independently, SIT's professional identity predicted all of healthcare professionals' responses to health misinformation on social media while SCCT's perceived crisis severity only predicted one response (i.e., private rebuttal). Nonetheless, it is also notable that the interaction of these constructs were associated all the responses and the regression results are consistent with the SEM results. Further examination of the significant interaction results revealed an interesting pattern wherein only those with high professional identity and high perceived crisis severity were likely to respond to health misinformation on social media by correcting and reporting it. The interaction results are consistent with SIT and SCCT since only those who hold a strong sense of identity as a healthcare professional (e.g., healthcare professionals need to provide evidence-based information) and those who think that health misinformation is a public health crisis were more likely to correct health misinformation on social media. Aside from supporting the theoretical assumptions of SIT and SCCT, these findings might also explain reports [15, 34, 54] on why some healthcare professionals choose to be on social media to correct health misinformation.

In general, the findings offer several theoretical and practical implications. Theoretically, this study demonstrates the applicability of combining constructs from SIT [20] (i.e., professional identity) and SCCT [21] (i.e., perceived crisis severity) to explain risk information behaviors [47–49]. It also contributes to a better understanding of factors that might influence information sharing in the context of correcting misinformation. On a practical note, the findings can provide insights on designing activities that healthcare professionals and students can take to be able to correct health misinformation on social media. For instance, activities that target the enhancement of professional identity, such as reflection, workshops, and working groups [55], can be performed. Aside from professional identity, these activities can provide an avenue to enhance healthcare professionals' awareness of the extent of health misinformation as a public health crisis.

5.1 Limitations and Future Research

There are several limitations in the study that can serve as future research directions. First, the results are non-generalizable since non-probability sampling techniques were used to recruit respondents. A nationally representative panel of healthcare professionals should be considered in the future to determine the consistency of the findings. Second, results are limited among nurses and medical doctors. Although they form the majority of the healthcare professionals in the United States [56], future research can improve the generalizability of the findings by including other healthcare professionals. Third, although the sample size is sufficient for the statistical analyses performed in this study, a sample size of at least 1,000 respondents should be aimed in future research to enhance generalizability. Finally, the predictors used in this study only accounted for less than 50% of the variance explained. This indicates that there are other factors that can predict responses to health misinformation on social media. Future research can add other factors in addition to the ones identified here.

6 Conclusion

Despite its limitations, this study is one of the first to describe the extent of healthcare professionals' responses to health misinformation on social media. Compared to surveys involving the general public [12, 14], healthcare professionals are more likely to respond to health misinformation on social media, particularly by making publicly visible corrections and reporting it to social media platforms. The study also contributes to the theoretical understanding of factors that affect health misinformation responses. Specifically, the study supports the applicability of SIT and SCCT when predicting the association of professional identity, perceived crisis severity, and their interaction with responses to health misinformation on social media. On the other hand, the findings of the study can serve as a starting point for health educators and institutions in developing activities that can encourage healthcare students and professionals to proactively respond to health misinformation. For instance, highlighting health misinformation as a public health crisis along with activities fostering greater professional identity could encourage more healthcare professionals to correct health misinformation on social media.

References

1. Xie, B., et al.: Global health crises are also information crises: a call to action. J. Assoc. Inf. Sci. Technol. **71**, 1419–1423 (2020). https://doi.org/10.1002/asi.24357
2. World Health Organization: Managing the COVID-19 infodemic: promoting healthy behaviours and mitigating the harm from misinformation and disinformation. https://www.who.int/news/item/23-09-2020-managing-the-covid-19-infodemic-promoting-healthy-behaviours-and-mitigating-the-harm-from-misinformation-and-disinformation. Accessed 07 Sept 2021
3. Office of the Surgeon General: Confronting Health Misinformation: The U.S. Surgeon General's Advisory on Building a Healthy Information Environment. https://www.hhs.gov/sites/default/files/surgeon-general-misinformation-advisory.pdf. Accessed 07 Sept 2021
4. Himelein-Wachowiak, M., et al.: Bots and misinformation spread on social media: implications for COVID-19. J. Med. Internet Res. **23**, e26933 (2021). https://doi.org/10.2196/26933
5. Wang, Y., McKee, M., Torbica, A., Stuckler, D.: Systematic literature review on the spread of health-related misinformation on social media. Soc. Sci. Med. **240**, 112552 (2019). https://doi.org/10.1016/j.socscimed.2019.112552

6. United Nations: UN launches new initiative to fight COVID-19 misinformation through 'digital first responders. https://news.un.org/en/story/2020/05/1064622. Accessed 03 May 2021
7. Corriel, D.: The Rise of the Social Media Doctor. https://www.self.com/story/social-media-doctors. Accessed 07 Sept 2021
8. Farr, C.: This doctor is recruiting an army of medical experts to drown out fake health news on Instagram and Twitter. https://www.cnbc.com/2019/05/31/doctor-recruiting-doctors-to-fight-fake-health-info-on-social-media.html. Accessed 07 Sept 2021
9. Varshavski: Physicians Must Meet Patients Where They Are, on Social Media—Physician's Weekly. https://www.physiciansweekly.com/physicians-must-meet-patients-where-they-are-on-social-media/. Accessed 07 Sept 2021
10. Wu, J.T., McCormick, J.B.: Why health professionals should speak out against false beliefs on the Internet. AMA J. Ethics **20**, 1052–1058 (2018). https://doi.org/10.1001/amajethics.2018.1052
11. Saad, L.: U.S. Ethics Ratings Rise for Medical Workers and Teachers. https://news.gallup.com/poll/328136/ethics-ratings-rise-medical-workers-teachers.aspx. Accessed 03 May 2021
12. Bode, L., Vraga, E.K.: Correction experiences on social media during COVID-19. Soc. Media Soc. **7**, 20563051211008828 (2021). https://doi.org/10.1177/20563051211008829
13. Koo, A.Z.-X., Su, M.-H., Lee, S., Ahn, S.-Y., Rojas, H.: What motivates people to correct misinformation? Examining the effects of third-person perceptions and perceived norms. J. Broadcast. Electron. Media. **65**, 111–134 (2021). https://doi.org/10.1080/08838151.2021.1903896
14. Tandoc, E.C., Lim, D., Ling, R.: Diffusion of disinformation: how social media users respond to fake news and why. Journalism **21**, 381–398 (2020). https://doi.org/10.1177/1464884919868325
15. Bautista, J.R., Zhang, Y., Gwizdka, J.: US physicians' and nurses' motivations, barriers, and recommendations for correcting health misinformation on social media: qualitative interview study. JMIR Public Health Surveill. **7**, e27715 (2021). https://doi.org/10.2196/27715
16. van der Meer, T.G.L.A., Jin, Y.: Seeking formula for misinformation treatment in public health crises: the effects of corrective information type and source. Health Commun. **35**, 560–575 (2020). https://doi.org/10.1080/10410236.2019.1573295
17. Nyhan, B., Reifler, J., Ubel, P.A.: The hazards of correcting myths about health care reform. Med. Care **51**, 127–132 (2013)
18. Nyhan, B., Reifler, J.: Does correcting myths about the flu vaccine work? An experimental evaluation of the effects of corrective information. Vaccine **33**, 459–464 (2015). https://doi.org/10.1016/j.vaccine.2014.11.017
19. Vraga, E.K., Bode, L.: Using expert sources to correct health misinformation in social media. Sci. Commun. **39**, 621–645 (2017). https://doi.org/10.1177/1075547017731776
20. Tajfel, H., Turner, J.C.: An integrative theory of inter-group conflict. In: The Social Psychology of Inter-Group Relations. pp. 33–47. Brooks/Cole, Monterey (1979)
21. Coombs, W.T., Holladay, S.J.: Communication and attributions in a crisis: an experimental study in crisis communication. J. Public Relat. Res. **8**, 279–295 (1996). https://doi.org/10.1207/s1532754xjprr0804_04
22. Bautista, J.R., Zhang, Y., Gwizdka, J.: Healthcare professionals' acts of correcting health misinformation on social media. Int. J. Med. Inf. **148**, 104375 (2021). https://doi.org/10.1016/j.ijmedinf.2021.104375
23. van der Linden, S., Roozenbeek, J., Compton, J.: Inoculating against fake news about COVID-19. Front. Psychol. **11**, 2928 (2020). https://doi.org/10.3389/fpsyg.2020.566790
24. van der Linden, S., Maibach, E., Cook, J., Leiserowitz, A., Lewandowsky, S.: Inoculating against misinformation. Science **358**, 1141–1142 (2017). https://doi.org/10.1126/science.aar4533

25. Bode, L., Vraga, E.K.: See something, say something: correction of global health misinformation on social media. Health Commun. **33**, 1131–1140 (2018). https://doi.org/10.1080/10410236.2017.1331312
26. Swire-Thompson, B., Lazer, D.: Public health and online misinformation: challenges and recommendations. Ann. Rev. Public Health **41**, 433–451 (2020). https://doi.org/10.1146/annurev-publhealth-040119-094127
27. World Health Organization: How to report misinformation online. https://www.who.int/campaigns/connecting-the-world-to-combat-coronavirus/how-to-report-misinformation-online. Accessed 07 Sept 2021
28. Paterson, M., Higgs, J., Wilcox, S., Villeneuve, M.: Clinical reasoning and self-directed learning : key dimensions in professional education and professional socialisation. Focus Health Prof. Educ. **4**, 5–21 (2002)
29. Mitchell, R.J., Parker, V., Giles, M.: When do interprofessional teams succeed? Investigating the moderating roles of team and professional identity in interprofessional effectiveness. Hum. Relat. **64**, 1321–1343 (2011). https://doi.org/10.1177/0018726711416872
30. Rasmussen, P., Henderson, A., Andrew, N., Conroy, T.: Factors influencing registered nurses' perceptions of their professional identity: an integrative literature review. J. Contin. Educ. Nurs. **49**, 225–232 (2018). https://doi.org/10.3928/00220124-20180417-08
31. Vila-Candel, R., et al.: Determinants of seasonal influenza vaccination in pregnant women in Valencia. Spain. BMC Public Health **16**, 1173 (2016). https://doi.org/10.1186/s12889-016-3823-1
32. Back, A.L., Fromme, E.K., Meier, D.E.: Training clinicians with communication skills needed to match medical treatments to patient values. J. Am. Geriatr. Soc. **67**, S435–S441 (2019). https://doi.org/10.1111/jgs.15709
33. Park, E., et al.: A train the trainer program for healthcare professionals tasked with providing psychosocial support to breast cancer survivors. BMC Cancer **18**, 45 (2018). https://doi.org/10.1186/s12885-017-3965-2
34. Jennings, R.: The rise of the nursefluencer. The doctor will fave you now. https://www.vox.com/the-goods/2019/5/10/18535853/doctor-instagram-nurse-doctor-mike-influencer. Accessed 03 May 2021
35. Harwood, J., Sparks, L.: Social identity and health: an intergroup communication approach to Cancer. Health Commun. **15**, 145–159 (2003). https://doi.org/10.1207/S15327027HC1502_3
36. Huddy, L.: From social to political identity: a critical examination of social identity theory. Polit. Psychol. **22**, 127–156 (2001). https://doi.org/10.1111/0162-895X.00230
37. Guharoy, R., Krenzelok, E.: Searching for COVID-19 treatments: first, do no harm. Am. J. Health. Syst. Pharm. **77**, 1899–1905 (2020). https://doi.org/10.1093/ajhp/zxaa257
38. Cohen, E.L., et al.: To correct or not to correct? Social identity threats increase willingness to denounce fake news through presumed media influence and hostile media perceptions. Commun. Res. Rep. **37**, 263–275 (2020). https://doi.org/10.1080/08824096.2020.1841622
39. Schulz, A., Wirth, W., Müller, P.: We are the people and you are fake news: a social identity approach to populist citizens' false consensus and hostile media perceptions. Commun. Res. **47**, 201–226 (2020). https://doi.org/10.1177/0093650218794854
40. Trkman, M., Popovič, A., Trkman, P.: The impact of perceived crisis severity on intention to use voluntary proximity tracing applications. Int. J. Inf. Manag. **61**, 102395 (2021). https://doi.org/10.1016/j.ijinfomgt.2021.102395
41. Zhou, Z., Ki, E.-J., Brown, K.: A measure of perceived severity in organizational crises: a multidimensional scale development and validation. J. Int. Crisis Risk Commun. Res. 2 (2019). https://doi.org/10.30658/jicrcr.2.1.3
42. Jahng, M.R.: Is fake news the new social media crisis? Examining the public evaluation of crisis management for corporate organizations targeted in fake news. Int. J. Strateg. Commun. **15**, 18–36 (2021). https://doi.org/10.1080/1553118X.2020.1848842

43. Hong, S., Kim, B.: Exploring social media use in university crisis communication: an experiment to measure impact on perceived crisis severity and attitudes of key publics. J. Conting. Crisis Manag. **27**, 61–71 (2019). https://doi.org/10.1111/1468-5973.12242
44. Hong, S., Len-Riós, M.E.: Does race matter? Implicit and explicit measures of the effect of the PR Spokesman's race on evaluations of spokesman source credibility and perceptions of a PR crisis' severity. J. Public Relat. Res. **27**, 63–80 (2015). https://doi.org/10.1080/1062726X.2014.929502
45. Lee, H., Jahng, M.R.: The role of storytelling in crisis communication: a test of crisis severity, crisis responsibility, and organizational trust. Journal. Mass Commun. Q. **97**, 981–1002 (2020). https://doi.org/10.1177/1077699020923607
46. Claeys, A.-S., Cauberghe, V., Vyncke, P.: Restoring reputations in times of crisis: an experimental study of the Situational Crisis Communication Theory and the moderating effects of locus of control. Public Relat. Rev. **36**, 256–262 (2010). https://doi.org/10.1016/j.pubrev.2010.05.004
47. Borden, J.: Effects of national identity in transnational crises: implications of social identity theory for attribution and crisis communications. Int. J. Commun. **21**, 10 (2016)
48. Ma, L.: How to turn your friends into enemies: causes and outcomes of customers' sense of betrayal in crisis communication. Public Relat. Rev. **44**, 374–384 (2018). https://doi.org/10.1016/j.pubrev.2018.04.009
49. Yoon, S.-W., Shin, S.: The role of negative publicity in consumer evaluations of sports stars and their sponsors. J. Consum. Behav. **16**, 332–342 (2017). https://doi.org/10.1002/cb.1636
50. Faul, F., Erdfelder, E., Buchner, A., Lang, A.-G.: Statistical power analyses using G*Power 3.1: tests for correlation and regression analyses. Behav. Res. Methods **41**, 1149–1160 (2009). https://doi.org/10.3758/BRM.41.4.1149
51. Adams, K., Hean, S., Sturgis, P., Clark, J.M.: Investigating the factors influencing professional identity of first-year health and social care students. Learn. Health Soc. Care **5**, 55–68 (2006). https://doi.org/10.1111/j.1473-6861.2006.00119.x
52. Hayes, A.: PROCESS macro for SPSS and SAS. http://processmacro.org/. Accessed 22 Nov 2021
53. Hu, L., Bentler, P.M.: Cutoff criteria for fit indexes in covariance structure analysis: conventional criteria versus new alternatives. Struct. Equ. Model. Multidiscip. J. **6**, 1–55 (1999). https://doi.org/10.1080/10705519909540118
54. Wong, Q.: Coronavirus pandemic gives health care workers a chance to shine on social media. https://www.cnet.com/tech/mobile/coronavirus-pandemic-gave-healthcare-workers-a-chance-to-shine-on-social-media/. Accessed 07 Sept 2021
55. Chandran, L., Iuli, R.J., Strano-Paul, L., Post, S.G.: Developing "a way of being": deliberate approaches to professional identity formation in medical education. Acad. Psychiatry **43**(5), 521–527 (2019). https://doi.org/10.1007/s40596-019-01048-4
56. Laughlin, L., Anderson, A., Martinez, A.: 22 Million employed in health care fight against COVID-19. https://www.census.gov/library/stories/2021/04/who-are-our-health-care-workers.html. Accessed 07 Sept 2021

"She Seems More Human": Understanding Twitter Users' Credibility Assessments of Dementia-Related Information

Fatimah Alhayan[1,2], Diane Rasmussen Pennington[1(✉)], and Ian Ruthven[1]

[1] University of Strathclyde, 26 Richmond Street, Glasgow G1 1XH, Scotland
{fatimah.alhayan,diane.pennington,ian.ruthven}@strath.ac.uk
[2] College of Computer and Information Sciences, Princess Nourah Bint Abdulrahman University, Riyadh 11564, Saudi Arabia

Abstract. The presence of incorrect, medically uncorroborated information on social media may be harmful if people believe it. The purpose of this qualitative study was to identify how Twitter users evaluate the credibility of dementia-related information sources. It used a think-aloud protocol via semi-structured interviews with 13 caregivers. It identified main credibility dimensions, including 13 factors. Participants deployed a combination of heuristics to assess information sources, and engaged in intensive systematic content review based on prior knowledge and relevance. The findings contribute to a nuanced understanding of how users evaluate Twitter sources in the health domain. Some of these are discussed in light of the MAIN Model, and prove significant in how practitioners and developers can better understand and help users evaluate information.

Keywords: Credibility · Health information · Twitter · Dementia · Bot

1 Introduction

Social media has become a common source of health information [1]. Despite social media promoting better health through increased communication, patient education, and professional development, unintended consequences can include professional image damage, violation of patient boundaries, privacy breaches, medical licensing and legal issues, poor information quality [2], and misinformation [3]. Health misinformation is defined by [4] as 'a health-related claim of fact that is currently false due to a lack of scientific evidence'. Different factors illuminate information quality, including credibility [5]. There is, however, no consensus on what constitutes credibility, a complex and intuitive concept involving accuracy, precision, objectivity, believability and informativeness [6].

Research on social media credibility has increased recently [12]. Twitter has emerged as a powerful and effective information dissemination source, but needs the application of credibility assessment methods. Most existing studies on Twitter credibility focus on domains such as news and politics. Health information impacts decision-making, and is therefore considered worthy of exploration [7]. There is growing attention on

M. Smits (Ed.): iConference 2022, LNCS 13193, pp. 292–313, 2022.
https://doi.org/10.1007/978-3-030-96960-8_20

analyzing the credibility of health-related tweets on crises such as Zika [8] and Covid-19 [9]. However, only a few studies have focused on people's reliability assessments of health-related information on social media [7], as opposed to the many studies on users' assessment of databases and static websites [10, 11]. The aim of this study is to identify factors affecting users' credibility assessment of dementia-related information on Twitter.

2 Background

2.1 Information Credibility Assessment

Social media credibility research has attracted interest from psychology, communication, information science, and human-computer interaction, each with different contexts and scopes [12]. In research at the confluence of computer science and information science, credibility is defined as a filter or qualifier between the impending task and user behavior in the context of information seeking [13]. Credibility is vital in decision-making, since it affects not just people's attitudes, but also how and whether the information or system is used [14].

Research on credibility assessment of social networks can be divided into machine-based and human-based approaches. With machine-based approaches, features such as source and content are used to predict credibility ratings of information, employing techniques like machine learning, encompassing both supervised and unsupervised algorithms. However, the accuracy of results from supervised approaches must rely on available ground truth information [15], which may or may not exist. Another critical component for predicting credibility is the set of features used, which varies among datasets. Human-based approaches employ cognition to assess the credibility of information sources or content and have attracted researchers from communication and information science. Several Twitter studies used a human-based approach to identify factors that influenced users' credibility judgements on either the source (profile) or content (tweets) [16–24].

However, most have used quantitative methods [7], employing surveys and questionnaires as the research instruments. The purpose of these methods is to develop or test theories. Since the constructs used to define credibility have no single definition, and the relation among variables is not clear, it is difficult to generate comprehensive and coherent results [25]. Participants in most existing studies were confined to providing specific answers to given questions. Although qualitative data can be produced by asking open questions to allow participants to express their opinions [26], it will not include all possible real-life influences.

Additionally, most previous studies have used screenshots of manipulated Twitter feeds rather than a live view [27, 28]. Viewing either a static view or a live view of the feed could lead to different perceptions [28]. This demonstrates the need to further examine participants' perceptions using live feeds. Also, more qualitative studies are required [25]. Most credibility studies have targeted politics [29] and news [30, 22]. Few researchers have looked at the credibility of specific health conditions on Twitter to comprehensively assess its health information credibility.

2.2 Credibility Assessment Frameworks

The main proposed theoretical frameworks for web credibility assessment have been summarized by [31] (Table 1). The frameworks share common aspects; however, the individual theoretical models have unique features depending on the focal point of each. Four major aspects (context, user characteristics, information characteristics, and process) were identified in them. Two emphasize the importance of classifying contextual factors: P-I Theory [32] and the Unifying Model [33]. Given that credibility assessment is based mainly on users' perception, most of the models (except the MAIN Model) consider user characteristics including demographics, user involvement, and information skills to theorize the process of web credibility assessment. Operationalization classifies how each model measures information credibility; namely, the cues that can be pinpointed in terms of source, message, and structural characteristics of web resources. Process classifies whether the framework is 'process-based' or 'judgment-based'. The former illustrates the entire process, whereas the latter focuses on particular factors affecting user perception [31]. Overall, variations in the models meet the needs of credibility operationalizations in various contexts. As new technology and information systems emerge on the web (e.g. social media platforms), there will be a continuous need for understanding credibility cues and heuristics. Most features of these platforms are static as on websites, yet social media are characterized by dynamic features such as numbers of followers.

Table 1. Web credibility assessment theoretical frameworks [31]

Model	Context	User characteristics	Operationalization	Process
P-I Theory [32]	√	√	√	√
Judgment Model [34]	√	√	√	√
MAIN Model [35]			√	√
Unifying Model [33]	√	√	√	√
Dual Model [36]		√	√	√
Revised-3S Model [37]		√	√	

2.3 Context: Dementia Information on Twitter

Two contextual factors have been established to develop models for credibility judgment, namely topic and platform type [38, 39]. This research selected these contexts. The rationale to select dementia as the topic and Twitter as the medium is reviewed here.

The rapid increase in the ageing population makes dementia a major public health concern, with new cases occurring every three seconds, affecting 50 million people worldwide [40]. People with dementia (PWD) access social media like blogs, Facebook, and Twitter to connect with others, seek support and share information [41–43]. Caregivers also take part in decision-making [44] and increasingly turn to the web for information and support. Existing research points to positive conclusions (e.g. increased knowledge, satisfaction, and involvement) among informal caregivers of critically ill patients in 16 out of 31 studies on the impact of social media interventions and tools [45], demonstrating improvement of confidence in technology-enabled interventions, including social media. Some 66% of UK dementia caregivers utilize the internet for dementia information; 76% use social media [46]. Dementia caregivers also use online tools such as blogs to seek and share information and social support [47].

On Twitter, dementia is among the top five most discussed health conditions [48]. PWD use it for fundraising, lobbying, increasing awareness, educating, providing support, challenging stigma [43], sharing their lived experiences, and advocating for social change. Caregivers use Twitter to expand their social networks, obtain support, learn about support structures [49], and share their caregiving experience [50]. Findings of [51, 52] emphasized stakeholder engagement, from patients to physicians, in the Twitter dementia community.

Prior studies have found caregivers use Twitter for various purposes, and it impacts the quality of available information regarding health and care of older adults, potential misinterpretation [51], and associated economic burden. Therefore, research is required to better understand how PWD and their caregivers use it. This research investigated the factors dementia caregivers employ to assess the credibility of dementia-related information sources on Twitter.

3 Methods

Data were collected through think-aloud protocols followed by semi-structured interviews.

3.1 Think-Aloud Protocol

Participants engaged in an approximately 15-min think-aloud session that entailed assessing Twitter profiles. This method is popular for exploring the thoughts and cognitive processes of participants during a task [53]. It is a non-directive technique in which participants are instructed only before the initiation of the task and only interrupted when participants stop verbalising [54]. The purpose is to gather the participants' immediate thoughts in real time, which allows greater richness in descriptions of user experience. Participants are not required to remember how they felt throughout the experience, but rather express themselves in real time [55]. It is commonly used to reveal possible factors influencing the credibility judgment of health-related information on websites and during online search [10, 56–58, 37].

3.2 Post-task Interviews

Participants next completed a semi-structured interview to further elaborate on their statements made during the think-aloud session to increase the depth of understanding about the participants' think-aloud experience. The participants were asked for their assessments of the profiles they did not select and what they felt constituted a credible source generally (e.g. In your opinion, what do you think about other accounts that you didn't select? Can you explain in your own words what a credible source is on Twitter?) Interviews lasted 15–20 min. Think-aloud sessions and interviews were recorded.

3.3 Participants

The researchers recruited a purposive sample of dementia caregivers aged 21 and older who live in the UK and use Twitter. The sample included six formal and seven informal caregivers for PWD at different stages: 12 females and 1 male, with ages ranging between 21–35 (3), 36–50 (2), and 51 +(7). Education levels spanned undergraduate (5), college (6), and postgraduate (2). Twelve participants had used Twitter for over a year. Their usage frequency was 8 daily, 1 weekly, 2 monthly, 1 occasionally, 1 not sure.

3.4 Recruitment

The researchers posted a flyer on Twitter with a link to the study registration form. UK dementia organizations were invited to share the flyer by retweeting or sharing by email. Participants read the information sheet, signed the consent form, and provided their preferred interview time and contact details. They received a confirmation email within 24 h, containing the interview date, time, and a secure Zoom link. Participants received a £20 e-gift voucher after completing the interview; this was later increased to £40 to encourage participation. Participants were recruited until data saturation was reached; the last two participants did not reveal new insights [59]. Rich and in-depth data are the focus of think-aloud studies, and sample sizes are fairly small [55].

3.5 Procedures

Participants received a link to an online questionnaire as well as Zoom interview instructions by email a day before the interview. The questionnaire gathered basic demographics, frequency of Twitter and other social media usage, and general questions regarding the profiles and information types usually read on Twitter.

Prior to the interviews, participants received a five-minute video with instructions on computer requirements and Zoom screen sharing. In each interview, the researcher first initiated discussion about the participant's questionnaire responses about their preferred Twitter sources, categories (e.g., organizations, professionals), and information types. The interviewer started the think-aloud task by sending a link via the chat box with a description of the task and instructions (Appendix 1). Participants then read the task scenario and instructions for a 15-min session that entailed assessing live views of Twitter profiles and had a chance to ask questions. Participants then shared their screen in order for the researcher to observe their interactions with the profiles.

The researchers had previously selected six profiles to ensure that (1) most tweets were dementia centric, as two independent assessors had already determined, and (2) there were two publically available profiles from each of the following categories: *Organizations*, *Professionals,* and *Individuals*. The researchers chose these because they embody the primary user types that tweet about dementia [52]. As self-identified in their profile descriptions, *Organizations* contained two dementia-related organizations, *Professionals* featured two dementia researchers, and two partners/caregivers of PWD comprised *Individuals*. In each category, one profile had an extremely high bot score and the other had an extremely low bot score as calculated by the BotOrNot API[1] [60]. Accounts with high bot scores mostly included automatically generated tweets or retweets. While some sources were reputable, other sources' posts had misleading information; for instance, how certain fruits or a particular exercise can prevent the risk of dementia or memory loss. Providing a chosen list of webpages is common in think-aloud web studies; for example, [58] selected eight search engine results page (SERP) listings (four credible, four non-credible) to study judgements of three controversial topics. The research presented in [56] also used SERP listings, representing either correct or incorrect information.

A sample screenshot of tweets from an individual profile with a high bot score appears in Appendix 2. BotOrNot computes scores that indicate the likelihood of a Twitter account being a bot: high scores for likely-bot, and low scores for likely-human accounts [60]. BotOrNot had been employed because an objective of the larger study is to determine individuals' perceptions surrounding the credibility of dementia-related bot profiles. This paper focuses only on how people assessed the credibility of dementia information, regardless of source.

All six profiles contained a biography, profile photos, location, the year the user joined Twitter, and dementia-related tweets. Participants were asked to think-aloud while assessing the pair of profiles in each category, potentially choosing one of the accounts as credible, and providing reasons supporting their choice. Participants were free to navigate the profile content without time constraints, reading as many tweets as they preferred, and going back to profiles whenever they wanted. The longest think-aloud session was about 15 min. Participants were also asked to rate each account's credibility on a Likert scale, with 1 being the least credible, and 7 the most credible, to align their justification with the rating to determine their confidence in choosing a profile.

3.6 Data Analysis

Data collected through the think-aloud sessions and semi-structured interviews were transcribed and analyzed using conventional qualitative content analysis, in which coding categories are gained directly from the text [61]. One researcher checked Zoom's automatically generated transcripts to ensure accuracy. The next step was open coding, and then lists of categories were grouped under higher level headings. Open coding started with four transcripts. Next, another researcher independently coded the four transcripts, and then they held a meeting to discuss the coding and reach a consensus on the main categories. Based on the discussion, both researchers used the scheme to code the four transcripts, reading each transcript line by line, and refined the coding scheme by discussing opinions immediately when any disagreements or discussion points emerged. They iterated this process until they agreed on the themes and codes [62]. Finally, they used the resulting scheme to code all the interviews. They made slight modifications to

[1] https://github.com/IUNetSci/botometer-python.

some codes' definitions, and added new sub-categories as they related to the evidence and variation under each category.

Table 2 displays the participants' credibility ratings. Significantly, a comparatively high number of profiles were rated from 3–5, indicating indecision. Fourteen human-likely profiles were rated as credible, and only 7 bot-likely profiles were rated credible.

Table 2. Participants' credibility ratings

Profile type	Ratings		
	Unsure (1–2)	Indecisive (3–5)	Sure (6–7)
Bot-likely	8	24	7
Human-likely	7	18	14

4 Findings

The analysis resulted in three main categories of credibility assessment dimensions: source, content, and user, as well as 13 subcategories that support different main categories. Figure 1 shows the proposed model based on this analysis.

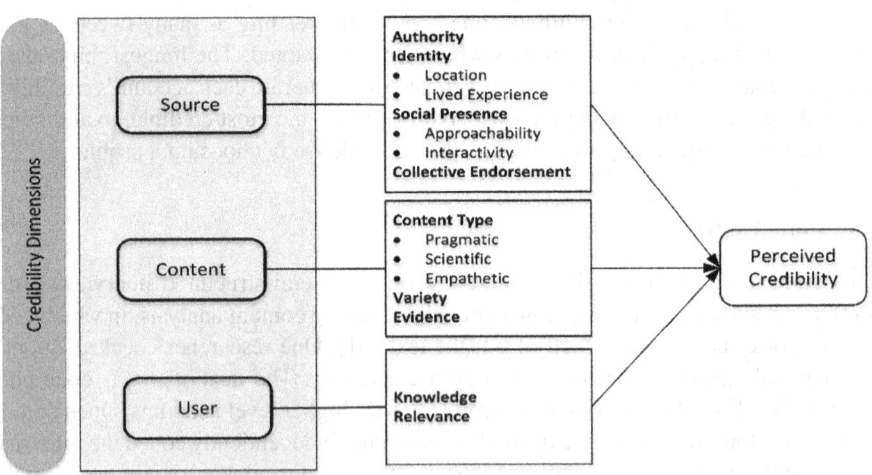

Fig. 1. Proposed model

4.1 Source

This category captures participants' assessment criteria for determining the credibility of the source as described in the sub-sections. *Source* refers to the Twitter profile based on features such as profile description, location and picture, the profile owner choosing which information to share publicly. A *source* can author tweets, retweet, quote other users' tweets, reply to tweets, follow others' accounts, be @mentioned in tweets, and be grouped into lists.

Authority

Ten participants considered the source as credible if they recognized the author of the tweets as an authoritative source. Participants expressed *authority* as subject-related experts with a scientific background and/or qualification, or an official entity; a well-recognized public account, including the blue badge or verified feature assigned by Twitter which validates an account of public interest as authentic. Some points of view on authority from participants were as follows. The + or – denoted after each quote indicates whether the related statement positively or negatively affected the participants' perception.

> *"I would find that less credible than someone with a qualification or a recognized organization." +(P6).*
>
> *"If it has a blue tick, then it's a credible account" +(P7).*
>
> *"Just to make sure that it was all credible. What their qualifications were. What they'd studied" +(P10).*

In general, authority had a positive effect on source credibility assessment.

Identity

Participants discussed *identity* when the source declared geographic location as well as lived personal experience as patient or caregiver.

Location is declared either in the source's profile or posts. The participants identified the accountholder's location as an identity cue when they browsed a profile. Nine participants believed that profiles of individuals and organizations from the same country are more credible.

> *"It seems credible source, but because it's not the UK. Wouldn't probably follow it." +(P8).*
>
> *"I wouldn't be interested in that because that was in the USA" (P6).*
>
> *"I would be more inclined to go for a UK based one" +(P10).*

A second type of identity cue is *lived personal experience*, defined as a caregiver or a PWD stated either in profile descriptions or posts. Six participants showed an interest in finding people with the same situation, either living with dementia or caring for a person with dementia.

"just because she seems to be dealing more with what I deal with on a daily basis" +(P3).

"I think perhaps in terms of experiences, personal experiences, I might go with it, who either has lived experience and has done something with that?" +(P5).

Collective Endorsement

Participants considered how other people view the source. It was measured by the number of followers the source has, who the followers are, the number of likes on the source's posts, if they have mutual friends, or even through a recommendation suggested by a trusted person offline. The endorsement could be from one user or a group of people:

> *"I think the more followers you have probably the more credible, the more reliable source" +(P1).*
>
> *"Number of followers is a factor. It's a conscious factor I should say that." +(P5).*

"If I go back a step, this profile followed by [redacted]. [Redacted] is a dementia expert by experience. He has dementia and I've followed him and attended some conferences he's spoken at prior to covid so that immediately I like in terms of reliability" +(P5).

Social Presence

Participants expressed the *social presence* of the source in two different ways: approachability and interactivity. *Approachability* is the feeling that the source is human and there is a possibility of direct interaction with the source. During think-aloud session, participants experienced greater feelings of social presence while evaluating a source in the *professional* category who was more likely to be perceived as a social actor. Some of the profile posts included their contact details (e.g. telephone number). Six participants shared consensus via comments while assessing that source:

> *"Okay, so she's posting things that make her more human." +(P5).*
>
> *"it's it sounds more friendly ... she said, you know, you can call you can chat. Which I think is good, whereas the others no. I didn't get that impression of the others." +(P9).*
>
> *"I like her approach. I like the fact that she was actually asking for experiences. It was much more tailored to the needs of someone caring for someone with dementia" +(P4).*

Interactivity is expressed in terms of constant tweeting activity, either writing one's own tweets or only retweeting. One participant felt stronger social presence when evaluating a user who tweets more than retweets:

> *"She seems more human. The other one a lot of retweets and not really about him, as such ... Can see human behind feed whereas other link has no personal feel ... whereas there further wasn't enough evidence of the human behind any of those accounts and that might suggest that it's a bot or not an actual human being and have a good thing about people that only retweet. I like people that give their own opinion" –(P11).*

In contrast, another participant did not sense a strong social presence from someone who tweets more than retweets:

"wouldn't say is particularly good because it's not taking into account like of a wide range of people's opinions." –(P2).

"Uses fellow colleges and alike as well as himself, not self-involved and purely wants good information out there ... It's not self-involved. So, it's, it seems more like actual information output rather than a personal account that's kind of trying to like glorify themselves." +(P2).

Other two participants experienced greater feelings of user presence from one who constantly tweets:

"Yet they haven't posted since June and July. So, I want to be kept up to date. They're not active, they're not recent" –(P7).

"A more credible account. Even though it was in Z. They are actively sharing information daily." +(P8).

4.2 Content

The posts on profiles were also valued and provide meaningful insight from the participants' credibility perspective. *Content* is the source timeline, or aggregated stream of tweets, retweets, replies, and tweets quoted by a user. A tweet is a message with a maximum text length of 280 characters, and may also contain photos or videos.

Content Type

Scientific, pragmatic, and empathetic *content types* contributed to source credibility assessment. Six participants showed interest in sources providing scientific information. In other words, most of the source's tweets included medical or scientific research findings. Generally, these tweets include links to external websites or cite information on external platforms.

"He would be the more credible source. He seems to be sharing, you know, this is sharing more of studies ... The other one just raising awareness." +(P12).

Contrary to pure scientific information in articles, seven participants showed interest in sources' pragmatic information. This means practical ideas or tips that can be usefully applied in caregivers' everyday lives.

"Account offers more practical ways of making life more bearable for people living with dementia" +(P7).

"Appears to share more practical information and tweets about own experience which may be more helpful than seeing scientific papers in second link" +(P11-T).

Participants also viewed sources providing empathetic contents as more credible. Empathetic content conveys expressions of emotion or feeling including caring, helping, appreciating, and supporting, as well as faith-based support.

"Going to assume an accredited account of course everything they have to say matters to me as a caregiver and especially because they are offering support for their carers" +(P7).

"We're here to help carry the burdens that would be brilliant" +(P10).

"the faith based one I liked, but I wasn't sure how applicable it would be to me because we have Christians and think that I would like a faith-based support, but what. there isn't a Christian tradition" +(P4).

Variety. Variety in the content refers to topic diversity, whether focused on one or several aspects. Two different points of view emerged about the content's variety. One participant showed interest in accepting an information source as credible if it is focused only on one topic rather than discussing a range of topics.

"I would pick him because it tends to be more of a focus on actual dementia." + (P12).

However, other participants expected a wide range of information from a source and rated the source as credible if the content covered different topics such as drugs and medicines or research articles.

"It just seems to focus on the one drug, and it doesn't seem to sort of focus on too many you know, other things" –(P10).

Evidence. Another criterion referred to evidence for scientific claims: if available within the content, the information source is deemed credible. Evidence refers to links (URLs) to other references supporting the information.

"Credible source showing links to other sources" +(P13).

"If someone's just saying, like, fruit can help prevent dementia. Well, I need to know why that you're saying that what's your rationale behind its kind of thing, where have they got this information from because the Internet is not reliable at all" +(P12).

Another group of participants questioned the quality and reliability of the provided references and links, believing that information based on authentic, reliable, high-quality sources, could be credible.

"She's posting information or links to information that looked like it would be very useful and that from reliable sources as well. So, I see University of [redacted], I recognize that name Centre for Dementia Studies, Alzheimer's Society. I know. So, I'm drawn to this" +(P5).

"links they are sharing and go to the links and see what the quality information that they were receiving; were the links they're sharing from credible sources?" +(P10).

Participants also mentioned that if the contents include links from the same source or website then these could not be trusted.

"Kind of links they have are from the same website...because if it's from the same websites. It's most likely the same people who are writing articles... It doesn't seem like a bad organization, in any way; it just seems as not as reliable as something else would be. I probably would not use it" –(P2).

4.3 User

This refers to the participant who has been asked to assess the profile; in this study, the users were the caregivers. Some characteristics related to the users were found as factors influence user assessment during the credibility, including relevance and prior knowledge. Relevance refers to the participant's interest in the content provided by the source. Relevance was frequently mentioned during profile assessments.

"They're that just too medical they're not they're not something that I'm that interested in to be honest. As I said, I am more interested about the care and support that one might need after diagnosis" –(P4).

Prior knowledge refers to the participant's ability to understand and interpret the content provided by the source.

"Interesting material that I have some knowledge of and can understand" +(P5).

Lack of knowledge was mentioned as a reason for not being able to understand the information; for example, scientific terms used in most of a profile's tweets:

"I wouldn't follow user1 purely and simply because I wouldn't have a clue what he's talking about and to be honest, I don't have the time to go in and look it up" –(P5).

"I would have difficulty making a decision whether that's credible ... it looks way above anything that I intellectually could understand" –(P13).

5 Discussion

The aim of this study was to understand factors that people employ to assess the credibility of health-related information sources on Twitter. The qualitative approach and think-aloud method enhance experimental studies by providing results that expand understanding of credibility assessments regarding health-related sources on social media.

Most source-related heuristics – authority, identity, collective endorsement, and social presence – were in line with the agency affordance heuristics provided in the MAIN model [35]. The MAIN model proposes four classes of technological affordances that can trigger cognitive heuristics which affect credibility judgments: Modality (M), Agency (A), Interactivity (I), and Navigability (N). Modality deals with the medium through which data is presented, Interactivity implies both interaction and activity with devices, and Navigability focuses on interface cues helping with navigation in cyberspace. The agency affordance deals with the source of information on digital media such as websites, a poll of friends on social media, or a person having a profile on any online platform. However, as the role of contents in credibility assessment and user characteristics are complementary to technological affordances in the MAIN Model [35], it is necessary to incorporate all these facets in order to understand participants' evaluations. Participants in this study identified a source as an authority when the source was a domain expert or an official entity [35]. This aligns with the general finding among credibility literature showing that authority impacts credibility evaluation [63, 64].

According to the MAIN Model [35], the identity heuristic is likely to be triggered whenever the user is able to express oneself through manipulating content. The user interface of social media platforms can be designed to generate different verifications of identity, and potential followers may use these for their own evaluation of a profile [35]. People can evaluate a source's name, place, profile photo, or other identifiers to verify the identity of a profile owner. Various identity-related parameters for credibility assessment have been used in prior research for different contexts, such as profile pictures for evaluating online news comments [65] and LinkedIn profiles [66]. Another identity cue, nationality, is used during online shopping; if someone from their own country has provided a review, it is trusted more than someone from a different nationality [67]. This study further showed identity was perceived in two forms: source location, and personal experience as a caregiver or PWD. All participants were UK residents, and they evaluated sources located outside of the UK as not credible.

Social presence as a concept means feeling the presence of other people irrespective of technology use [68]. Feeling social presence of other entities (human or machine) develops trust in the system [69, 70]. Social presence heuristics, triggered by agency cues, may provoke feeling the presence of another entity [35]. Prior studies demonstrated different cues of social presence on Twitter influencing users' credibility perceptions. During disaster situations, [71] identified Twitter account age as a cue for social presence. Other research investigated dynamic features, such as the relationship between levels of the source's timeline interactivity, as social presence cues: a high-interactivity source's timeline (a political figure) expressed by the number of replies provided to followers, resulted in greater social presence [72]. Dialogic retweets, or retweets of users who @mentioned the organization, produced a higher level of social presence compared to monologic or "one-way" tweets from the organization [73].

A key finding of this study was participants' use of social presence to detect human characteristics. It has extended past research by incorporating different perspectives on a source's profile interactivity and adding approachability as another lens for social presence. Interactivity involved frequent tweeting. Contradictory perceptions towards sources' tweeting interactivity were also revealed. For some participants, the source who tweeted more than retweeted generated a greater sense of social presence for some participants, whereas they did not for other participants. These varied perceptions of social presence should be further explored because bots can be set to retweet as well as automatically reply to tweets, pretending to be real people. Bots spreading false information could potentially negatively affect healthcare.

Sundar's [35] proposed bandwagon heuristic reflects a group endorsement of the source's reputation, which impacts on its credibility. Collective endorsement has been observed as a factor affecting credibility perception in news [74] and online health forums

[75]. Similarly, endorsement here included the number of followers the source has, who the followers are, the number of likes on the source's posts, and if they have mutual friends; however, one participant included a recommendation suggested by a trusted person offline.

Agency affordances [35] have been extensively utilized in investigations of credibility assessment [64, 76] to measure their relationship with source credibility perceptions in different contexts. Similarly, the study demonstrated agency affordance [35] on Twitter's structural properties and helped participants perform source assessment; however, the affordance is perceived by a person's subjective perception and understanding of external cues [77]. Thus, this study identified how these affordances were perceived differently in the context of health-related information. For example, this investigation presents a new understanding of how social presence could be formed in its particular context. It identified how technologies can virtually create and enhanced social realities.

The study found another dimension for credibility evaluation: content features. Participants also evaluated the profile based on content type, verity of content, and evidence. They marked empathetic content as an important cue for evaluation source credibility. Interestingly, faith-based content contributed to enhanced credibility perception. Although empathetic content has been identified as an important aspect in evaluating general web health information sources by studies such as [78], to the best of our knowledge, no work has directly examined the relationship between individual perception assessment of health information and faith-based content or religiosity on social media. Mixed perceptions were observed regarding the variety of contents. Although few participants were only interested in topic-focused information, some showed interest in multiple *types* of information. Participants also assessed content in light of evidence or references provided with the tweet. Some participants did not believe in the contents if they were posted by the same web source.

Users' knowledge and relevance of the contents also play a vital role in assessment. If the contents were related to the participant's needs or experiential background, they identified the source as more credible. This is unlike the results in [79], where knowledge did not impact the participants' credibility perceptions of search engine results, yet it agrees with topic knowledge of many credibility assessment models on the general web [80] and on Wikipedia [81].

Although some of these findings are common in the previously discussed models, this study cannot be directly connected to any one credibility assessment model. Offering participants to evaluate the full 'live' profile and content using the think-aloud methodology provided a means to observe that users do not only rely on source heuristics. The findings demonstrate the importance of qualitative studies that help establish the role of users' prior knowledge and relevance in information processing. It has also shown the necessity of adopting systematic processing metrics for credibility evaluation in health information on social media along with source heuristics. Most existing models and frameworks for credibility assessment have been developed with the perspective of information available through static web resources. The proposed model in this study can serve as a starting framework for further research on credibility of health information on social media.

6 Limitations

Because all participants were caregivers, the findings are not representative of all Twitter users seeking dementia information, so future studies should examine a greater variety of participants to compare credibility evaluations. Moreover, the potential influence of the participants' location and culture may limit the generalizability of the findings, as these factors influence people's perceptions. Also, the study focuses only on dementia information, so a study of how people evaluate tweets about other chronic health conditions would be useful. A broader understanding of how culture might factor into people's perceptions would be valuable as well. A final limitation is the small sample of profiles shown to the participants; future work should evaluate a broader set of profiles.

7 Conclusions

Despite the limitations, this study contributes to the field of information credibility research in social media significantly. Given the growing popularity of Twitter bots and users' ability to share content without gatekeepers' filters, it is imperative to understand how and why credibility assessments of information sources on social media are made. The study provided a step towards qualitative assessment of user perceptions of social media health information sources, and suggested a direction toward generalizing for other domains.

Appendix 1

(See Figs. 2 and 3).

Task:

Your partner has been diagnosed with dementia recently. You would like to help by finding out what is generally recommended for people in his /her situation. Six types of Twitter source (users) links are shown below. There are two users from different categories. Explore the users in each category and select which of these options you think will be a reliable source for the task.

Instructions :

1- Open both user links in each category.

2- Select the user(s) you think will be a reliable source for the task. You can select 'None", if you prefer neither.

3- Justify your selection for each in the text entry below the user link.

4- Rate the credibility of each user 1-7, least to best.

5- You are encouraged to think aloud while you are exploring the profiles.

Fig. 2. Study homepage (1)

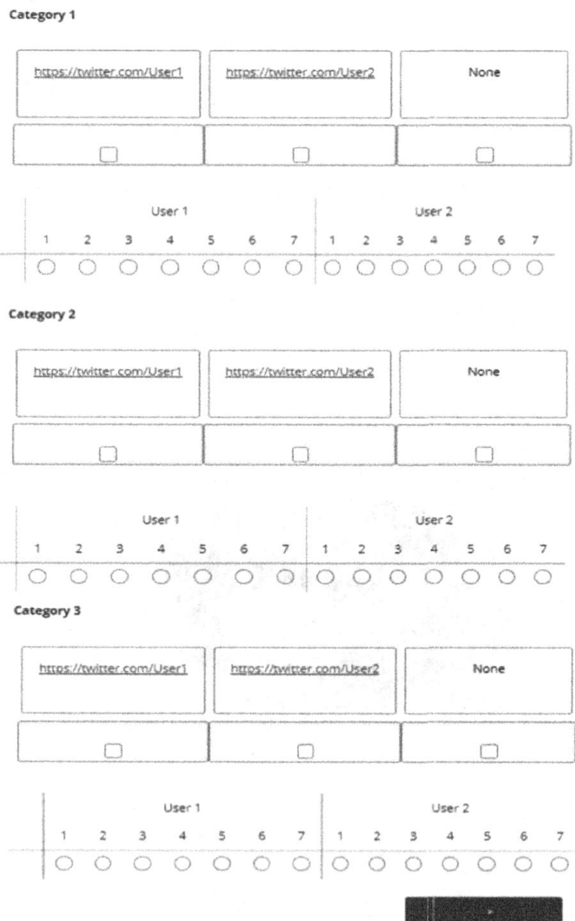

Fig. 3. Study homepage (2)

Appendix 2

(See Fig. 4).

Fig. 4. Profile with high bot score (screen name and photo are redacted)

References

1. Zhao, Y., Zhang, J.: Consumer health information seeking in social media: a literature review. Health Info. Libr. J. **34**, 268–283 (2017). https://doi.org/10.1111/hir.12192
2. Ventola, C.L.: Social media and health care professionals : benefits. Risks Best Pract. **39**, 491–500 (2014)

3. Suarez-Lledo, V., Alvarez-Galvez, J.: Prevalence of health misinformation on social media: Systematic review. J. Med. Internet Res. **23** (2021). https://doi.org/10.2196/17187
4. Chou, W.S., Oh, A., Klein, W.M.P.: Addressing Health-Related Misinformation on Social Media. Am. Sci. **320**, 2417–2418 (2018). https://doi.org/10.1511/2017.105.6.372
5. Stvilia, B., Mon, L., JeongYi, Y.: A model for online consumer health information quality. J. Am. Soc. Inf. Sci. Technol. **60**, 1781–1791 (2009). https://doi.org/10.1002/asi.21115
6. Rieh, S.Y.: Credibility and cognitive authority of information. Encycl. Libr. Inf. Sci. Third Ed. 1337–1344 (2009). https://doi.org/10.1081/E-ELIS3-120044103
7. Keshavarz, H.: Evaluating credibility of social media information : current challenges. Research Directions and Practical Criteria (2020). https://doi.org/10.1108/IDD-03-2020-0033
8. Sharma, M., Yadav, K., Yadav, N., Ferdinand, K.C.: American journal of infection control Zika virus pandemic — analysis of Facebook as a social media health information platform. AJIC Am. J. Infect. Control. **45**, 301–302 (2017). https://doi.org/10.1016/j.ajic.2016.08.022
9. AbdElminaam, D.S., Ismail, F.H., Taha, M., Taha, A., Houssein, E.H., Nabil, A.: CoAID-DEEP: an optimized intelligent framework for automated detecting COVID-19 misleading information on Twitter. IEEE Access. **4**, 1 (2021). https://doi.org/10.1109/access.2021.3058066
10. Klawitter, E., Hargittai, E.: Shortcuts to well being? Evaluating the credibility of online health information through multiple complementary heuristics. J. Broadcast. Electron. Media **62**, 251–268 (2018). https://doi.org/10.1080/08838151.2018.1451863
11. Liao, Q.V., Fu, W.T.: Age differences in credibility judgments of online health information. ACM Trans. Comput. Interact. 21 (2014). https://doi.org/10.1145/2534410
12. Alrubaian, M., Al-Qurishi, M., Alamri, A., Al-Rakhami, M., Hassan, M.M., Fortino, G.: Credibility in online social networks: a survey. IEEE Access. **7**, 2828–2855 (2019). https://doi.org/10.1109/ACCESS.2018.2886314
13. Ginsca, A.L., Popescu, A., Lupu, M.: Credibility in information retrieval. Found. Trends® Inf. Retr. **9**, 355–475 (2015). https://doi.org/10.1561/1500000046
14. Manfredo, M.J., Bright, A.D.: A model for assessing the effects of communication on recreationists. J. Leis. Res. **23**, 1–20 (1991)
15. Sikdar, S., et al.: Finding true and credible information on Twitter. In: 7th International Conference on Information Fusion (FUSION). pp. 1–8. IEEE (2014)
16. Aladhadh, S., Zhang, X., Sanderson, M.: Tweet author location impacts on tweet credibility. In: Proceedings of 2014 Australasian Document Computing Symposium - ADCS 2014, pp. 73–76 (2014). https://doi.org/10.1145/2682862.2682873
17. Chorley, M.J., Colombo, G.B., Allen, S.M., Whitaker, R.M.: Human content filtering in Twitter: the influence of metadata. **74**, 32–40 (2015). https://doi.org/10.1016/j.ijhcs.2014.10.001
18. Edwards, C., Spence, P.R., Gentile, C.J., Edwards, A., Edwards, A.: How much Klout do you have ⋯ A test of system generated cues on source credibility. Comput. Human Behav. **29**, A12–A16 (2013). https://doi.org/10.1016/j.chb.2012.12.034
19. Jahng, M.R., Littau, J.: Interacting is believing: interactivity, social cue, and perceptions of journalistic credibility on Twitter. Journal. Mass Commun. Q. **93**, 38–58 (2016). https://doi.org/10.1177/1077699015606680
20. Kang, B., Hölerer, T., O'Donovan, J.: Believe it or not? Analyzing information credibility in microblogs (2015). https://doi.org/10.1145/2808797.2809379
21. Morris, M.R., Counts, S., Roseway, A., Hoff, A., Schwarz, J.: Tweeting is believing ? Understanding microblog credibility perceptions. In: CSCW 2012 Proceedings of ACM 2012 Conference on Computer Supported Cooperative Work, pp. 441–450 (2012). https://doi.org/10.1145/2145204.2145274

22. Shariff, S.M., Zhang, X., Sanderson, M.: On the credibility perception of news on Twitter: readers, topics and features. Comput. Human Behav. **75**, 785–796 (2017). https://doi.org/10.1016/j.chb.2017.06.026
23. Westerman, D., Spence, P.R., Van Der Heide, B.: A social network as information: The effect of system generated reports of connectedness on credibility on Twitter. Comput. Human Behav. **28**, 199–206 (2012). https://doi.org/10.1016/j.chb.2011.09.001
24. Yang, J., Counts, S., Morris, M.R., Hoff, A.: Microblog credibility perceptions: comparing the USA and China. In: CSCW, pp. 575–586 (2013). https://doi.org/10.1145/2441776.2441841
25. Sbaffi, L., Rowley, J.: Trust and credibility in web-based health information: a review and agenda for future research. J. Med. Internet Res. **19**, 1–17 (2017). https://doi.org/10.2196/jmir.7579
26. Shariff, S.M.: A review on credibility perception of online information. In: Proceedings 2020 14th International Conference on Ubiquitous Information Management and Communication IMCOM 2020. (2020). https://doi.org/10.1109/IMCOM48794.2020.9001724
27. Spence, P.R., Edwards, A., Edwards, C., Jin, X., Spence, P.R., Edwards, C.: '\The bot predicted rain, grab an umbrella ': few perceived differences in communication quality of a weather Twitterbot versus professional and amateur meteorologists meteorologists. 3001 (2019). https://doi.org/10.1080/0144929X.2018.1514425
28. Edwards, C., Edwards, A., Spence, P.R., Shelton, A.K.: Is that a bot running the social media feed? Testing the differences in perceptions of communication quality for a human agent and a bot agent on Twitter. Comput. Human Behav. **33**, 372–376 (2014). https://doi.org/10.1016/j.chb.2013.08.013
29. Johnson, T.J., Kaye, B.K.: Credibility of social network sites for political information among politically interested internet users. J. Comput. Commun. **19**, 957–974 (2014). https://doi.org/10.1111/jcc4.12084
30. Granskogen, T., Gulla, J.A.: Fake news detection on social media: a data mining perspective. ACM SIGKDD Explor. Newsl. **19**, 22–36 (2017). https://doi.org/10.1145/3137597.3137600
31. Choi, W., Stvilia, B.: Web credibility assessment: conceptualization, operationalization, variability, and models. J. Am. Soc. Inf. Sci. Technol. **64**, 1852–1863 (2015). https://doi.org/10.1002/asi.23543
32. Fogg, B.J.: Prominence-interpretation theory: explaining how people assess credibility online. Conference on Human Factors Computing System – Proceedings, pp. 722–723 (2003). https://doi.org/10.1145/765891.765951
33. Hilligoss, B., Rieh, S.Y.: Developing a unifying framework of credibility assessment: construct, heuristics, and interaction in context. Inf. Process. Manag. **44**, 1467–1484 (2008). https://doi.org/10.1016/j.ipm.2007.10.001
34. Wathen, C.N., Burkell, J.: Believe it or not: factors influencing credibility on the Web. J. Am. Soc. Inf. Sci. Technol. **53**, 134–144 (2002). https://doi.org/10.1002/asi.10016
35. Sundar, S.: The MAIN Model: a heuristic approach to understanding technology effects on credibility. Digit. Media, Youth, Credibil. 73–100 (2008). https://doi.org/10.1162/dmal.9780262562324.073
36. Metzger, M.J.: Making sense of credibility on the web: models for evaluating online information and recommendations for future research. J. Am. Soc. Inf. Sci. Technol. (2007). https://doi.org/10.1002/asi.20672
37. Lucassen, T., Muilwijk, R., Noordzij, M.L., Schraagen, J.M.: Topic familiarity and information skills in online credibility. J. Am. Soc. Inf. Sci. Technol. **64**, 1852–1863 (2013). https://doi.org/10.1002/asi.22743
38. Flanagin, A.J., Metzger, M.J.: The role of site features, user attributes, and information verification behaviors on the perceived credibility of web-based information. New Media Soc. **9**, 319–342 (2007). https://doi.org/10.1177/1461444807075015

39. Rieh, S.Y.: Credibility assessment of online information in context. J. Inf. Sci. Theory Pract. **2**, 6–17 (2014). https://doi.org/10.1633/JISTaP.2014.2.3.1
40. World Health Organization: 10 facts on dementia, https://www.who.int/news-room/fact-sheets/detail/dementia. Accessed 01 Feb 2021
41. Rodriquez, J.: Narrating dementia : self and community in an online forum **23**, 1215–1227 (2013). https://doi.org/10.1177/1049732313501725
42. Strivens, E.: Innovation and translation facing the times: a young onset dementia support group: Facebook TM style. Australas. J. Ageing **35**, 48–53 (2016). https://doi.org/10.1111/ajag.12264
43. Talbot, C.V., O'Dwyer, S.T., Clare, L., Heaton, J., Anderson, J.: How people with dementia use twitter: A qualitative analysis. Comput. Hum. Behav. **102**, 112–119 (2020). https://doi.org/10.1016/j.chb.2019.08.005
44. Mackie, B.R., Mitchell, M., Marshall, A.P.: Patient and family members' perceptions of family participation in care on acute care wards. Scand. J. Caring Sci. **33**, 359–370 (2019). https://doi.org/10.1111/scs.12631
45. Cherak, S.J., et al.: Impact of social media interventions and tools among informal caregivers of critically ill patients after patient admission to the intensive care unit: a scoping review. PLoS One **15**, 1–19 (2020). https://doi.org/10.1371/journal.pone.0238803
46. French, T.: Dementia and digital: using technology to improve health and wellbeing for people with dementia and their carers 35 (2016)
47. Anderson, J.G., Hundt, E., Dean, M., Keim-Malpass, J., Lopez, R.P.: "The church of online support": examining the use of blogs among family caregivers of persons with dementia. J. Fam. Nurs. **23**, 34–54 (2017). https://doi.org/10.1177/1074840716681289
48. Zhang, Z., Ahmed, W.: A comparison of information sharing behaviours across 379 health conditions on Twitter. Int. J. Public Health **64**(3), 431–440 (2018). https://doi.org/10.1007/s00038-018-1192-5
49. Danilovich, M.K., Tsay, J., Al-Bahrani, R., Choudhary, A., Agrawal, A.: #Alzheimer's and dementia expressions of memory loss on Twitter. Top. Geriatr. Rehabil. **34**, 48–53 (2018). https://doi.org/10.1097/TGR.0000000000000173
50. Al-Bahrani, R., Danilovich, M.K., Liao, W.K., Choudhary, A., Agrawal, A.: Analyzing informal caregiving expression in social media. In: IEEE International Conference on Data Mining Work. ICDMW, pp. 342–349 (2017). https://doi.org/10.1109/ICDMW.2017.50
51. Robillard, J.M., Johnson, T.W., Hennessey, C., Beattie, B.L., Illes, J.: Aging 2.0: health information about dementia on Twitter. PLoS One. **8**, 1–6 (2013). https://doi.org/10.1371/journal.pone.0069861
52. Alhayan, F., Pennington, D.: Twitter as health information source: exploring the parameters affecting dementia-related tweets. In: ACM International Conference on Proceeding Series, pp. 277–290 (2020). https://doi.org/10.1145/3400806.3400838
53. Ericsson, A., Simon, H.: Protocol Analysis: Verbal Reports as Data. The MIT Press, Cambridge, MA (1984)
54. Eveland, W.P., Dunwoody, S.: Examining information processing on the World Wide Web using think aloud protocols. Media Psychol. **2**, 219–244 (2000). https://doi.org/10.1207/S1532785XMEP0203_2
55. Solomon, P.: The think aloud method: A practical guide to modelling cognitive processes (1995). https://doi.org/10.1016/0306-4573(95)90031-4
56. Ghenai, A., Smucker, M.D., Clarke, C.L.A.: A think-aloud study to understand factors affecting online health search. In: CHIIR 2020 – Proceedings of 2020 Conference on Human Information Interaction and Retrieval, pp. 273–282 (2020). https://doi.org/10.1145/3343413.3377961

57. Muntinga, T., Taylor, G.: Information-seeking strategies in medicine queries: a clinical eye-tracking study with gaze-cued retrospective think-aloud protocol. Int. J. Hum. Comput. Interact. **34**, 506–518 (2018). https://doi.org/10.1080/10447318.2017.1368949
58. Kattenbeck, M., Elsweiler, D.: Understanding credibility judgements for web search snippets. Aslib J. Inf. Manag. **71**, 368–391 (2019). https://doi.org/10.1108/AJIM-07-2018-0181
59. Reilly, M.O., Parker, N.: 'Unsatisfactory saturation': a critical exploration of the notion of saturated sample sizes in qualitative research. Qual. Res. **13**, 190–197 (2012). https://doi.org/10.1177/1468794112446106
60. Yang, K.-C., Varol, O., Davis, C.A., Ferrara, E., Flammini, A., Menczer, F.: Arming the public with artificial intelligence to counter social bots. Hum. Behav. Emerg. Technol. **1**, 48–61 (2019). https://doi.org/10.1002/hbe2.115
61. Hsieh, H.F., Shannon, S.E.: Three approaches to qualitative content analysis. Qual. Health Res. **15**, 1277–1288 (2005). https://doi.org/10.1177/1049732305276687
62. Gibbs, G.R.: Analyzing Qualitative Data (2007)
63. Rieh, S.Y.: Credibility and cognitive authority of information. In: Encyclopedia of Library and Information Sciences, 3rd edn, pp. 1337–1344 (2010). https://doi.org/10.1081/e-elis3-120044103
64. Lin, X., Spence, P.R., Lachlan, K.A.: Social media and credibility indicators: The effect of influence cues. Comput. Human Behav. **63**, 264–271 (2016). https://doi.org/10.1016/j.chb.2016.05.002
65. Lin, X., Kaufmann, R., Spence, P.R., Lachlan, K.A.: Agency cues in online comments: exploring their relationship with anonymity. South Commun. J. **84**, 183–195 (2019). https://doi.org/10.1080/1041794X.2019.1584828
66. Edwards, C., Stoll, B., Faculak, N., Karman, S.: Social presence on linkedin: perceived credibility and interpersonal attractiveness. Online J. Commun. Media Technol. **5**, 102–115 (2015)
67. Bracamonte, V., Okada, H.: Impact of nationality information in feedback on trust in a foreign online store. J. Socio-Inform. **8**, 1–12 (2015). https://doi.org/10.14836/jsi.8.1_1
68. Lee, K.: Presence, explicated. Commun. Theory **14**, 27–50 (2004)
69. Kim, K.J., Park, E., Shyam Sundar, S.: Caregiving role in human-robot interaction: a study of the mediating effects of perceived benefit and social presence. Comput. Human Behav. **29**, 1799–1806 (2013). https://doi.org/10.1016/j.chb.2013.02.009
70. Lu, B., Fan, W., Zhou, M.: Social presence, trust, and social commerce purchase intention: an empirical research. Comput. Human Behav. **56**, 225–237 (2016). https://doi.org/10.1016/j.chb.2015.11.057
71. Son, J., Lee, J., Oh, O., Lee, H.K., Woo, J.: Using a heuristic-systematic model to assess the Twitter user profile's impact on disaster tweet credibility. Int. J. Inf. Manag. **54**, 102176 (2020). https://doi.org/10.1016/j.ijinfomgt.2020.102176
72. Lee, E.J., Shin, S.Y.: Are they talking to me? Cognitive and affective effects of interactivity in politicians' Twitter communication. Cyberpsychol. Behav. Soc. Netw. **15**, 515–520 (2012)
73. Lim, Y., Lee-Won, R.J.: When retweets persuade: the persuasive effects of dialogic retweeting and the role of social presence in organizations' Twitter-based communication. Telemat. Inform. **34**, 422–433 (2016). https://doi.org/10.1016/j.tele.2016.09.003
74. Xu, Q.: Social recommendation, source credibility, and recency: effects of news cues in a social bookmarking website. Journal. Mass Commun. Q. **90**, 757–775 (2013). https://doi.org/10.1177/1077699013503158
75. Jucks, R., Thon, F.M.: Better to have many opinions than one from an expert? Social validation by one trustworthy source versus the masses in online health forums. Comput. Human Behav. **70**, 375–381 (2017). https://doi.org/10.1016/j.chb.2017.01.019
76. Lin, X., Spence, P.R.: Identity on social networks as a cue: identity, retweets, and credibility. Commun. Stud. **69**, 461–482 (2018). https://doi.org/10.1080/10510974.2018.1489295

77. Norman, D.A.: The Psychology of Everyday Things. Basic Books (1988)
78. Neal, D.M., McKenzie, P.J.: Putting the pieces together: endometriosis blogs, cognitive authority, and collaborative information behavior. J. Med. Libr. Assoc. **99**, 127–134 (2011). https://doi.org/10.3163/1536-5050.99.2.004
79. Unkel, J., Haas, A.: The effects of credibility cues on the selection of search engine results. J. Am. Soc. Inf. Sci. Technol. **64**, 1852–1863 (2017). https://doi.org/10.1002/asi.23820
80. Rieh, S.Y., Belkin, N.J.: Interaction on the web : scholars' judgment of information quality and cognitive authority. In: Proceedings of the Annual Meeting-American Society for Information Science, pp. 25–38. Information Today (2000)
81. Lucassen, T., Schraagen, J.M.: Factual accuracy and trust in information: the role of expertise. J. Am. Soc. Inf. Sci. Technol. **64**, 1852–1863 (2013). https://doi.org/10.1002/asi.21545

Hands-Free Electronic Documentation in Emergency Care Work Through Smart Glasses

Zhan Zhang[1(✉)], Xiao Luo[2], Richard Harris[1], Susanna George[2], and Jack Finkelstein[3]

[1] Pace University, New York, NY 10038, USA
zzhang@pace.edu
[2] Indiana University-Purdue University Indianapolis, Indianapolis, IN 46202, USA
[3] Interfaith Medical Center, New York, NY 11213, USA

Abstract. As U.S. healthcare system moves towards digitization, Electronic Health Records (EHRs) are increasingly adopted by medical providers. However, EHR documentation is not only time-consuming but also difficult to complete in real-time, leading to delayed, missing, or erroneous data entry. This challenge is more evident in time-critical and hands-busy clinical domains, such as Emergency Medical Services (EMS). In recent years, smart glasses have gained momentum in supporting various aspects of clinical care. However, limited research has examined the potential of smart glasses in automating electronic documentation during fast-paced medical work. In this paper, we report the design, development, and preliminary evaluations of a novel system combining smart glasses and EHRs and leveraging natural language processing (NLP) techniques to enable hands-free, real-time documentation in the context of EMS care. Although optimization is needed, our system prototype represents a substantive departure from the status quo in the documentation technology for emergency care providers, and has a high potential to enable real-time documentation while accounting for care providers' cognitive and physical constraints imposed by the time-critical medical environment.

Keywords: Smart glasses · Documentation · Electronic health record · Natural language processing · Emergency medical services

1 Introduction

As U.S. healthcare system moves towards digitization, Electronic Health Records (EHRs) have been widely adopted by medical providers. However, documenting patient data using EHR systems is a challenging and time-consuming task as it demands a significant portion of care providers' time and cognitive attention. Prior work has pointed out that the use of EHRs could lead to physician burnout, reduced patient care time, and compromised patient-physician relationships [1, 2]. In time- and safety-critical medical settings, such as emergency medical services (EMS) or pre-hospital domain, these challenges are exacerbated due to the dynamic, rapid, and high-stress nature of patient care

M. Smits (Ed.): iConference 2022, LNCS 13193, pp. 314–331, 2022.
https://doi.org/10.1007/978-3-030-96960-8_21

in the field, making the use of EHR systems challenging [3, 4]. For example, since EHR systems are often implemented on handheld devices, such as tablets, EMS providers may not be able to use such devices in real-time as they need to perform hands-on care to stabilize critical patients while processing various information and making sense of what they face [5–8]. Also, switching between patient and EHR could increase the chance of cross-contamination [9]. As such, jotting down notes on temporary artifacts, such as gloves, persists in EMS work practice [8, 10]. This workaround, however, is a barrier to implementing real-time clinical decision support systems. Therefore, it is more than evident that novel technologies are necessary to support real-time EMS documentation.

Prior work suggested that smart glasses—wearable technologies that superimpose information onto a field of view through transparent heads-up display—can potentially serve as an unobtrusive hardware platform to support timely documentation as they offer novel interaction techniques (e.g., voice control) [11–13]. They can be connected with EHR systems and vital signs monitor to facilitate information sharing and enable an integrated view of patient status. Since their introduction several years ago, smart glasses have been tested and used mainly as a telemedicine tool in various medical settings, such as surgical tele-mentoring [14], remote evaluation of acute stroke patients [15], and disaster telemedicine triage [16, 17]. The "hands-free" capability of smart glasses makes this technology of interest to EMS providers [18, 19]. However, to date, limited research has investigated the application of smart glasses in supporting real-time documentation during pre-hospital encounters.

To that end, we conducted an exploratory study to design and develop a smart glass application to automate EMS documentation. More specifically, we first conducted user studies with 13 EMS providers to elicit system requirements (Sect. 4.1). The findings of user studies informed the design of our smart glass application, including system features, interaction mechanisms, and system architecture (Sect. 4.2). Then we developed a system prototype that leverages natural language processing (NLP) techniques to process domain-specific, voice-based dictations (Sect. 4.3). Lastly, we conducted preliminary evaluations with EMS providers to measure system accuracy and gather user feedback (Sect. 5). To the best of our knowledge, this is the first smart glass system prototype developed to support documentation in time-critical medical settings. We conclude this paper by discussing lessons learned, limitations, and future work.

2 Related Work

In this section, we first review a set of literature on the use of electronic health records in time-critical medical settings to highlight research gaps. Then we discuss existing research on the application of smart glasses in medical work to highlight the novelty of this technology and its promising potential in supporting clinical documentation.

2.1 Electronic Health Records in Time-Critical Medical Settings

As prior work pointed out, the use of EHR systems in fast-paced, safety-critical medical settings could lead to decreased patient care time, inefficiencies, and incomplete data entry [20]. One main reason for these issues is the mismatch between the formal EHR documentation and actual clinical workflow, making it nearly impossible to complete numerous EHR data fields in a timely fashion [21, 22]. For example, in trauma resuscitation settings, Jagannath and Sarcevic [23] found that only 8% of verbally reported information was documented in near real-time, while 42% of verbal reports were not documented in the EHR system. Also, information was documented with a delay, which can be attributed to the current layout of the EHR system used by trauma teams, that is, the data fields were grouped following logical rather than context-driven structure [23, 24].

Our study context—EMS—faces even greater challenges because unlike other clinical teams which usually have a designated person (e.g., nurse recorder) in charge of documentation [25, 26], EMS teams do not have a dedicated role for the documentation task. EMS providers are constantly on the move at the point of accident while performing hands-on tasks to address life-threatening injuries or illnesses, leaving them with limited ability to use an EHR system in real-time [5, 10]. Even when used, EMS documentation is prone to erroneous and incompletion. For example, a study found that 40% of the data entered on EMS medical records were either left blank or filled in erroneously [6], while another study reported that 28% of EMS records were missing patient's physiological data values [7]. As pointed out by several studies [3, 4], many of these issues were caused by the gap between data entry methods and EMS workflow—complicated data entry across too many screens increased the cognitive and physical burden of using EHR [10]. It is, therefore, more than evident that novel technologies and modes of interaction are needed to improve data collection and documentation in time-critical and hands-busy critical care environments. Although some studies examined ways to automate the information extraction from the EHR clinical notes [27–29], few research has investigated how to facilitate and automate real-time data collection and documentation in fast-paced medical environment [30, 31].

2.2 Smart Glasses in Medical Work

Smart glasses have gained momentum in recent years because they offer hands-free operation through novel interaction mechanisms such as voice control [12, 13, 32, 33]. With a transparent screen and a video camera, smart glasses enable constant information presentation and allow local workers to project first-person point-of-view to a remote viewer. Given these benefits, researchers are increasingly interested in using smart glasses to support medical work, such as care management [13, 34–36], surgical tele-mentoring [14], disaster telemedicine triage [16, 17], and vital sign monitoring [18]. For example, one study [11] explored the feasibility of using smart glasses to capture visual information of a patient's wound and transfer it to the patient's EHR record through gestural and voice commands. Despite this prior work, how smart glasses can support real-time documentation during fast-paced medical work remains unanswered. In this study, we aimed to bridge this knowledge gap by designing and developing a smart glass application to augment real-time data capture and documentation.

3 Methodologies

3.1 Data Collection and Evaluation of System Prototype

We first conducted semi-structured interviews with 13 EMS providers recruited from four hospital-based EMS agencies in the U.S. Northeast region to elicit user needs and opinions for using smart glasses to facilitate their documentation task. The interviews focused on the challenges faced by EMS providers in collecting, documenting, and sharing patient data in real-time during pre-hospital encounters, and how smart glasses can help address these challenges. Based on the results of this user study, we designed and developed our system prototype.

We also conducted preliminary evaluations of our system. More specifically, we recruited two experienced EMS providers who have more than 30 years of experience to measure the accuracy of our system in processing and automatically documenting medical information. We also presented our prototype to 10 EMS providers who participated in the previous interview study. Following the presentation, we asked the EMS providers to express their opinions and concerns, identify unmet needs, and discuss opportunities for further improvement.

All interviews and evaluations were audio recorded and transcribed verbatim. The study was approved by the first author's university Institutional Review Board.

3.2 Data Analysis

We used an open coding technique [37] to analyze the transcripts. Two researchers generated and discussed a list of codes in an iterative manner until consensus was reached. Then the researchers used affinity diagrams—a common approach for finding patterns in the qualitative data [38]—to group all the codes under themes. This step allowed the researchers to identify high-level themes describing user needs regarding the use of smart glasses for automated documentation, and opinions and concerns about using the system in practice.

4 System Design and Development

In this section, we first describe the major technology requirements emerged through user studies, followed by an overview of the design of our system prototype. Lastly, we provide detailed description of how we leveraged NLP techniques to automate domain-specific information processing and documentation.

4.1 User Requirements

Through the interviews, four major technology requirements emerged, the details of which are described as follows:

(1) *Facilitate rather than replace the use of current EHR system.* As we learned from the discussion with EMS providers, the system should be designed to facilitate their documentation task instead of replacing current EHR system used in practice. As such, the smart glasses should be connected with an EHR system and function as a "facilitator" to quickly collect and integrate patient data and transfer that into EHR to reduce the time spent working on documentation. To achieve that goal, the system should allow EMS providers to dictate patient information to the smart glasses and have the smart glasses transcribe the dictation in real-time to text through voice recognition. Also, the system should be able to parse and extract key medical information from the transcript and populate the corresponding data fields in EHR.
(2) *Enable the "hands-free" paradigm of using smart glasses.* The default interaction technique is using the built-in touchpad and buttons to navigate the user interface embedded on the transparent heads-up display. However, this interaction modality requires physical touching and clicking on the device, which EMS providers would want to avoid. As such, participants expressed interest in using hands-free interaction mechanisms to interact with smart glasses.
(3) *Allow timely collection of medication information.* Collecting and documenting accurate medication information is a challenging and time-consuming task, especially under extreme time pressure. EMS providers expressed interest in being able to use the smart glasses to scan the barcode of the medication given to the patient so that the detailed information of the medication (e.g., name, dosage, etc.) can be automatically captured and saved to EHR. In addition, since some patients could take several medications due to, i.e., comorbidities, but EMS providers may not have sufficient time to complete detailed entry for each medication using EHR, the medication scanning feature enabled by smart glasses could also make the collection of patient's medical history much easier.
(4) *Ability to record and store visual information.* In most cases, EMS providers need to share information with the care providers in the receiving hospital (e.g., emergency department physician and charge nurse) en route to the hospital or during patient handoff. When doing so, EMS providers usually need to spend a significant amount of time describing the patient situation and mechanism of injury (e.g., what happened, how severe the accident was) with words. Aligning with previous work [39, 40], our participants mentioned that this practice is not only time-consuming but also vulnerable to miscommunication. Therefore, participants would like to use the smart glasses to take pictures or record short videos so that they can share such visual information with the receiving care team.

4.2 System Architecture

As our major goal is to augment rather than replacing the use of EHR during EMS care, we integrate the smart glasses with the EHR system used by EMS providers. Our system prototype consists of a pair of Vuzix M400 smart glasses, an Android-based EHR system, and a cloud-based backend (Fig. 1). The major functionality of this system prototype is allowing EMS providers to dictate patient information to the smart glasses and have the smart glasses transcribe the dictation in real-time to text, which will be saved in the "Narrative" section of EHR. Then, the system can process the transcribed narrative and extract key medical information to be saved into the corresponding EHR data fields.

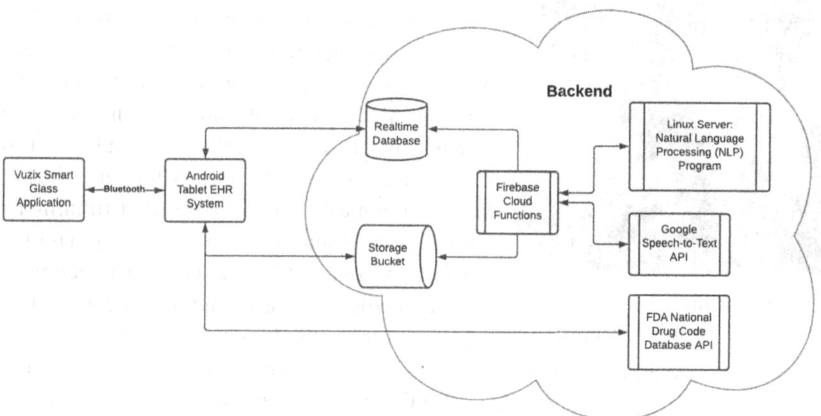

Fig. 1. System architecture

The Vuzix M400 is an ergonomically designed wearable device. It runs using an Android 9.0 based operating system. The camera on the device allows for still image capture or video recording, which can be saved for further use (e.g., sharing with the emergency care teams at the receiving hospital). Our application will allow the user to scan medical barcodes to capture information about patient treatments and medication. This is done by utilizing the National Drug Code database in the OpenFDA API. The device also has a transparent heads-up display, on which computer-generated or digital information can be overlaid and seen by the users. By default, users can use the touchpad and buttons to navigate the user interface (Fig. 2). But smart glasses can also offer hands-free user interaction through other novel mechanisms, such as voice commands and hand gestures. For example, we implemented voice commands (e.g., "take a picture," "dictate," etc.) using the Vuzix software development kit (SDK), and gesture-based controls using a third-party SDK (CrunchFish[1]).

[1] https://www.crunchfish.com/.

Since we need an EHR system for testing purposes, we developed a hypothetical, simplified EHR application based on a real system. This EHR application runs on Android mobile devices (e.g., a tablet) and contains five major sections to organize and record patient information (e.g., incident, demographics, assessments, vitals, and narrative), with each section contains a set of data fields.

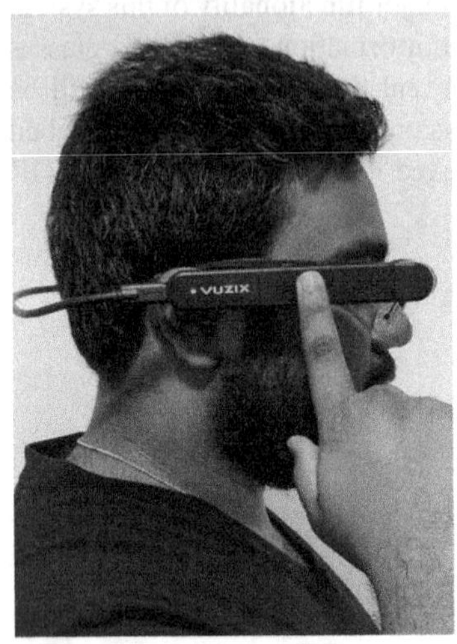

Fig. 2. Interacting with smart glasses via the built-in touchpad

The backend of our system consists of a Firebase real-time database, a storage bucket, Firebase cloud functions, and an external Linux server running our text analysis program. All application data regarding patient records are stored in the real-time database. Audio files created through dictation are stored in the storage bucket and the cloud functions monitor the bucket for new audio files. When the user completes a dictation, the audio file is saved and then transcribed using the Google Cloud Speech-to-Text API. When the transcription is completed, the text is written to the database and saved to the "Narrative" section on EHR. Afterward, the system makes a request to the Linux server running a program for text analysis (see Sect. 4.3). The textual analysis program utilizes a set of NLP techniques to extract medical concepts and return data that is categorized for each field of the EHR. Upon successful processing, the data produced will be written to the database and updated on the EHR application simultaneously, and the user will be able to review and make any necessary changes before closing out the patient record.

4.3 Automating Information Processing and Extraction from Transcribed Narratives

As the major functionality of our system prototype is allowing EMS providers to dictate to document patient data, in this section, we focus on describing how we implemented this feature to automate the extraction of domain-specific information from transcribed dictations. As shown in Fig. 3, we built an unsupervised NLP framework which consists of four major components: UMLS MetaMap [41], syntactic analysis [42], pattern matching, and Med7 [43]. The UMLS MetaMap is a tool developed by the U.S. National Library of Medicine (NLM), which makes use of various biomedical sources to map the phrases or terms in the input text to different semantic types. Figure 4 provides an example of mapping phrases to different semantic types using MetaMap. We used a set of semantic types of UMLS MetaMap to identify the relevant concepts to the EHR fields. For example, semantic type 'Body Part, Organ, or Organ Component' is used to identify whether a chunk of text mentioned lung, pupil, or any body organs. Then, the syntactic dependency tree generated by Stanford CoreNLP [44] is used to extract the information describing the conditions of the body organs or mental status. The negation detection and word sense disambiguation of MetaMap are configured to recognize negation context and determine the best matching sense of the concepts within the context. Pattern matching is a rule-based approach to identify gender information, blood pressure values, etc. Med7 is a refined named-entity recognition model which is mainly used to identify medication-related information mentioned in the dictation, such as medication names, route, usage frequency, suggested dosage, strength, form, and duration.

In this exploratory project, we demonstrate the feasibility of extracting information to populate 23 EHR data fields using the designed NLP framework, including gender, age, blood pressure (BP), pulse, oxygen saturation (SPO2), respiration rate (RESP), blood glucose levels (B.G.L), Glasgow Comma Scale (GCS), mental status, patient condition, patient medication, allergies, past medical history, pain, trauma scale, pupils, lung sounds, verbal, airway, injury, mechanism of injury, complaint, and treatment. Below we describe the information extraction techniques we used for each data category in greater details.

A 14 month old male who apparently has had a fall down a flight of steps, approximately seven steps.
Qualitative Concept
Injury or Poisoning

Fig. 4. Example of MetaMap processing and semantic types

***Age*:** To recognize patient age mentioned in the description, we used the name entity recognition module in the Stanford CoreNLP [44]. If a text is tagged as "Duration" with "PXX", shown in Fig. 5, it is extracted as age. "PXX" is the tag for person (P) entity with age value "XX". In this example, the age value is 14M – 14 months.

Fig. 5. Name entity recognition using Stanford CoreNLP

***Gender, BP, SPO2, RESP, B.G.L, GCS, Verbal, Trauma scale and Airway*:** We used pattern matching and syntactic dependency tree analysis to extract the information for these categories. First, we defined a set of terms for each field that are often used by EMS, such as "blood pressure" and related abbreviations for BP, to locate the relevant information within the context. Then, a set of regular expression rules based on the patterns and syntactic dependencies between the terms are used to extract the associated values for the fields, if there are any. As shown in Fig. 6, once "blood pressure" is identified using pattern matching rules, then syntactic dependency tree is used to identify whether there is a number tagged as Part-Of-Speech tagging "CD" has a direct or indirect dependent relation with one of the words in "blood pressure". If yes, regular expression is used to extract the numbers of the blood pressure. It is worth noting that since the recorded narratives are in spoken language, EMS providers may not necessarily follow the strict grammar. Hence, we also specified an additional set of regular expression rules to identify the numerical values corresponding to these fields when there are no dependent relations between the term and the corresponding numerical values.

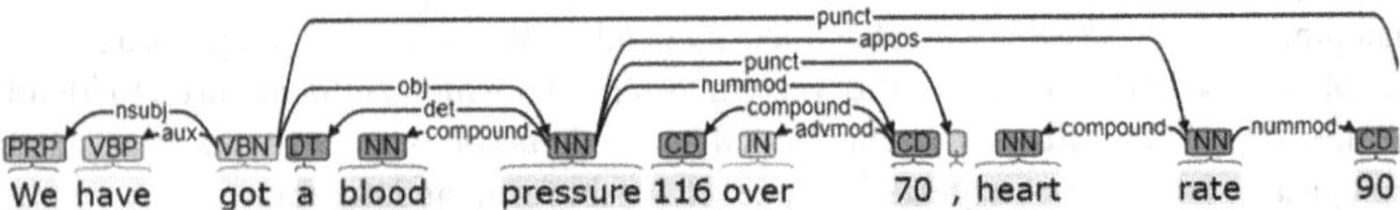

Fig. 6. Syntactic dependency analysis

Table 1. MetaMap semantic types used for the selected EHR fields

EHR fields	Semantic types
Mental status, patient condition, complaint	Finding
Lung sound, pupil, injury	Body part, organ, or organ component
Treatment	Clinical attribute, clinical drug, medical device
Allergies	Finding, pathologic function
Pain	Sign and symptom
Injury, mechanism of injury	Injury and poisoning

***Mental Status, Patient condition, Complaint, Lung sound, Pupil, Allergies, Pain, Treatment, Injury, and Mechanism of Injury*:** To process information for these fields, we first used MetaMap to identify the concepts of selected semantic types that are relevant to them. Then, we applied syntactic analysis to retrieve the context describing the status or conditions for these fields. Table 1 lists the MetaMap semantic types used for each field.

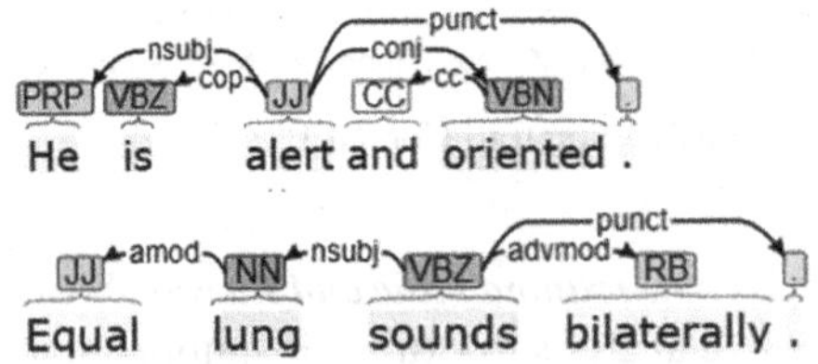

He is alert and oriented. Equal lung sounds bilaterally.
Finding
Body Part, Organ, or Organ Component

He is backboarded and collared and, but other than that no obvious injuries.
Medical Device
Medical Device

Fig. 7. An example to demonstrate the use of MetaMap with syntactic analysis

Since not all concepts tagged as semantic type 'Finding' is relevant to mental status or patient condition, we specified a set of terms often used by EMS providers and then refined the terms using syntactic dependency analysis to retrieve additional words that are syntactic modifiers or connected by conjunctions. Given the example in Fig. 7, the 'alert and oriented' is categorized as mental status. The 'oriented' is tagged as 'Finding' by MetaMap and it is in the set of terms we specified. The 'alert' is also extracted since there is a conjunction relation between 'alert' and 'oriented'. The 'equal' is extracted for lung sound field because 'lung' is identified by MetaMap as semantic type 'Body Part, Organ, or Organ Component', and there exists a modifier relation, such as adjective modifier (amod), between 'equal' and 'lung'. Lastly, 'backboarded' and 'collared' are both extracted as treatment since they are tagged as semantic type 'medical device' by MetaMap.

***Past Medical History*:** The patient's past medical history refers to chronic health conditions or surgeries that the patient has had previously. From the transcribed narrative, the information about past medical diseases or statuses is first located using MetaMap semantic types 'Finding', 'Clinical Attribute', 'Clinical Drug', and 'Disease or Syndrome'. Then, syntactic dependency is analyzed to confirm whether the described medical history is relevant to the patient.

***Patient Medication*:** This data category refers to the medications taken regularly by the patient as part of their care management, e.g., treating chronic conditions. We used Med7 to extract all the detailed medication information from the narrative. Then, syntactic dependency analysis is applied to confirm whether the medication is taken by the patient or given by the EMS practitioners. Given the example in Fig. 8, we first identified 'metformin' using Med7. Then through dependency analysis, we found that metformin is indirectly linked to 'patient' through the verb 'taken'. Hence, 'metformin' is extracted as patient medication.

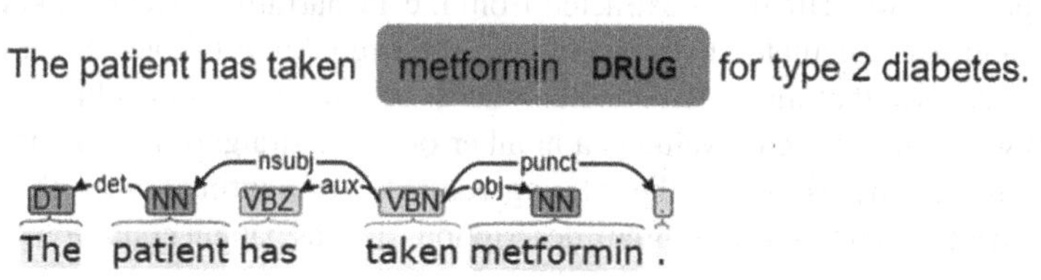

Fig. 8. An example of utilizing Med7 and syntactic analysis for medication extraction

5 Preliminary Evaluation

In this section, we describe the preliminary evaluations of our system prototype, including the accuracy of automated documentation and end-users' perceptions of using the system.

5.1 Measuring the Accuracy of Automated Documentation

The performance of the system, especially the accuracy in processing and extracting medical information from narratives, was evaluated independently by two experienced EMS professionals. Each evaluator was given 19 processed narratives and asked to evaluate the accuracy of each extracted information based on the content of the original

Table 2. Inter-rater reliability results

EHR field	Cohen kappa	EHR field	Cohen kappa
Age	1	Past medical history	0.944
Gender	0.889	Pain	0.889
BP	0.944	Trauma scale	0.780
Pulse	0.944	Pupils	0.944
RESP	0.889	Lung Sound	0.944
B.G.L	1	Verbal	0.889
SPO2	1	Airway	0.889
GCS	1	Injury	0.726
Mental Status	0.512	Mechanism of injury	0.460
Patient Condition	0.304	Complaint	0.726
Current Medication	0.889	Treatment	0.780
Allergies	1		

narrative. For each field, the evaluator needs to provide an answer as to whether the extracted information is correct or not. If it is incorrect or partially correct, the evaluator was asked to provide the correct information that should be extracted. Based on the expert inputs for all EHR fields extracted from the 19 narratives, Cohen's kappa value for each field was calculated to measure inter-rater reliability (Table 2). Based on the results, we can see that the inter-agreement between two evaluators is high on most of the fields when the extracted value is a number or some straightforward content, such as "clear" for airway. However, the inter-agreement is not optimal when the extracted value is expected to be a more complex description, such as patient condition and mental status.

To calculate the system performance, we used the fields of all narratives for which both evaluators have the same evaluation, which means they either both agree the extracted value is correct or incorrect. If they both agree that the extracted value is incorrect and provide the same correct information, the information provided by evaluators is used as ground truth. Two different evaluation metrics were used: exact match (EM) and fuzzy partial match (FPM) [45]. These metrics are often used in information extraction and name entity recognition tasks [46, 47]. The exact match counts an extracted field is correct only if the extracted content matches the ground truth exactly, whereas fuzzy partial match score measures the differences between the extracted content against the ground truth at the word level. Given a narrative "*…my patient is awake and alert, no crying, but he does smile and interact. 15 on GCS, he's got good pulse…*", the extracted mental status is "*awake and alert*", but the ground truth given by the evaluators is "*awake and alert, no crying, does smile and interact*". It is counted as incorrect if exact match is used but counted as partial correct with a fuzzy partial score. The fuzzy partial match score [48] is calculated using the fuzzy string matching based on Levenshtein distance [49]. The fuzzy ratio score is calculated using Eq. 1, where $|A|$ and $|B|$ are the lengths of string A and B, and L is the Levenshtein distance between A and B.

$$\frac{|A| + |B| - L}{|A| + |B|} \tag{1}$$

The fuzzy partial score is calculated by first finding the best matching sub-string between A and B. Then it calculates the ratio score between the sub-string and shorter string among A and B.

Figure 9 shows the performance evaluation using the average FPM and SM scores of all narratives on each field. The results show that for age, gender, B.G.L, SPO2, allergies, past medical history, and airway, our system can extract all the values correctly from the narratives. However, for mental status, patient condition, and mechanism of injury, the system gains relatively low FPM and SM scores. We also noticed that the inter-agreement values for those fields are not high, which means the information to be extracted for those fields varies based on human's understanding of the narratives. For example, given the following narrative, the first evaluator identified the patient mental status as "patient is awake and alert, not crying, but he does smile, and interact", whereas the second evaluator extracted "not crying, awake, alert, had started acting lethargic". The identified content by both evaluators is similar semantically, although not exactly the same.

> "*A 14 month old male who apparently has had a fall down a flight of steps, approximately seven steps. there's no LOC, no history, no medications, no known drug allergies. Our patient, came home, he was over at a friends house, he was brought back home, and apparently, had started acting lethargic and started shaking and convulsing. at this time, my patient is awake and alert, not crying, but, he does smile, and interact. 15 on the GCS, he's got a good pulse, everything's good. Little bump on the head, on the front of the head. he is backboarded and collared and, but other than that no obvious injuries.*"

The output of our system for patient mental status in the above narrative is "not crying, awake, alert, no LOC, had started acting lethargic and started shaking and convulsing". Compared with the identified content by both evaluators, our system successfully extracted most information related to patient mental status. However, according to the evaluators, "no LOC" and "started shaking and convulsing" should not be considered and extracted as part of the mental status. Nevertheless, our system was deemed to perform well in processing narratives to extract medical information to be saved in corresponding EHR data fields, despite optimization is needed.

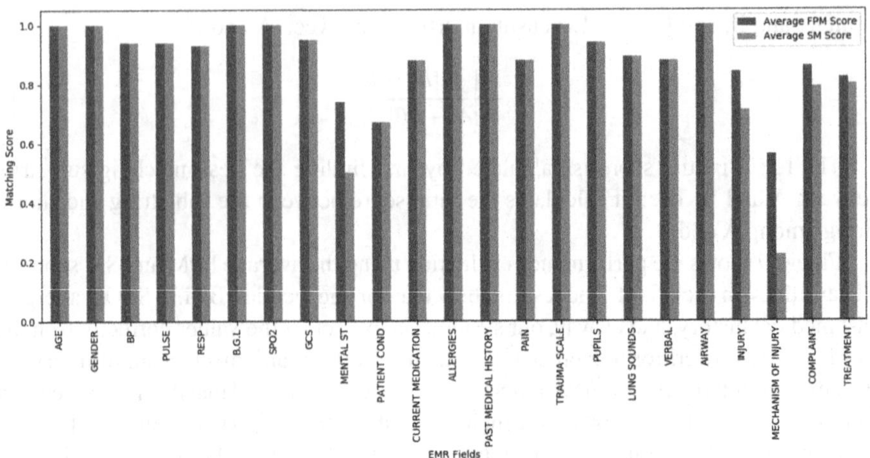

Fig. 9. System performance on information extraction

5.2 User Perceptions and Concerns

We also presented our system prototype to EMS providers (n = 10) to elicit their feedback. All participants considered our system useful in supporting their documentation tasks. Almost all of them (9 out of 10) expressed the willingness to use this system given its potential benefits: "*I think that would be very beneficial because it frees up our hands to do almost everything. If I would be able to say to narrative, I think that would be very helpful because that frees up not only one care provider, but two, so that two people can work on their patient and expedite the patient's care, which leads to a better patient outcome.*" [P7].

In addition, our participants believed that being able to document patient data in real-time could also facilitate patient handover between EMS providers and emergency care providers in the receiving hospital. As one participant explained: "*It saves time. When you get a trauma patient to the hospital, we have to stand in the middle of the emergency room or in the trauma bay, and we have to go over what happened to the patient and what we did step-by-step like at least three times because somebody is always walking in who wasn't there when we were giving our verbal report. If we can get the documentation relayed to the emergency doctor before we arrived, they can just play a voice record or read through our documentation, and they would have all of our primary impression regarding how we found the patient and all such. Everything would be right there for them and that could save a lot of time.*" [P7].

Despite the positive attitude, our participants shared some concerns in using this application in practice. First, pre-hospital environment is often very noisy, posing significant challenges in the effective use of the voice recognition feature of our system: "*The only thing that I am curious about is how sensitive it is to noise. For example, I have a patient who is yelling, and I am trying to dictate to document. How accurate will that be?*" [P9] Second, the work pace in EMS is very rapid, especially when patient acuity is high. In such cases, EMS providers are often both physically and cognitively overwhelmed as they need to multi-task—observing the scene, talking to partners or remote experts, while performing hands-on patient care tasks. As such, one participant had doubts about whether they can use the smart glass device in real-time: "*If I have somebody who got shot four times and I am trying to stabilize him, I'm not going to mess with that device [smart glass]. I wouldn't even bother documenting right away. I got to stabilize this person and after I get them stabilized, then I'll worry about the paperwork. [...] But I definitely see the benefit of it in jobs that are not crazy and hectic.*" [P11] However, this participant further explained that if there are multiple EMS providers on the scene in a high acuity situation, it is still possible for an EMS provider to use the smart glass device: "*If you are going to have two EMTs and two paramedics, not everyone is going to be doing all patient care. If any of these people that are on that scene can use a set of the smart glasses and just start getting information imported to the [EHR] data fields, I could see that being a huge benefit.*" [P11].

6 Discussion

The system prototype we developed allows EMS providers to complete documentation in real-time while accounting for their physical ability to use computing devices. Instead of replacing current EHR systems, our goal is to facilitate the use of EHR for real-time data collection and documentation through smart glasses. As such, we integrate smart glasses with EHR to allow EMS providers to dictate to smart glasses in a hands-free manner. The dictations then can be transcribed and processed to populate the data fields on EHR automatically. By doing so, the documentation work in time-critical medical settings that is often vulnerable to delayed or erroneous data entry can be semi-automated, thereby saving a significant amount of emergency care providers' time and effort.

Although a number of studies focused on developing techniques to automate the information extraction from the EHR clinical notes [27–29], few research looked at how to facilitate data collection and decision making in emergency medicine [30, 31]. To the best of our knowledge, our research is the first attempt at automating EMS documentation. This work is essential in that it can enable the deployment and use of decision support tools in EMS if real-time data collection and documentation can be accomplished. However, using smart glasses in EMS context has some challenges to overcome [50]. For example, the noisy and interruptive nature of the field could pose challenges in the effective use of the voice recognition feature of smart glasses. In recent years, novel techniques have been developed to address this issue, such as sensing and signal processing solution that enables high performance of automatic speech recognition of smart glasses [51]. To fully realize the use case of smart glasses in automating EMS documentation, future research is needed to systematically test the performance of smart glasses in transcribing medical procedures while EMS providers perform them in noisy, dynamic, and fast-paced environments.

Regarding our underlying NLP framework for EMS concepts extraction from transcribed narratives, one of the major challenges is the lack of EMS lexicon, annotated data, or ontology. Hence, it is difficult to systematically apply EMS domain knowledge or supervised information extraction algorithms. In this research, we choose to use unsupervised learning, with which we successfully extract the values for most data fields, including complex clinical information (e.g., treatments). However, we found that it is challenging to extract information for the fields that often contain longer and domain-specific content, such as mental status. In this research, we utilized a set of EMS terms to first locate the mental status content within the whole narrative, and then extract the negation words or dependent words to those EMS terms. The limitation of this approach is that if some terms or jargon used by EMS are not included in our list, we could miss the relevant content. On the other hand, through the dependency analysis, we might introduce words that are not standard terminologies in the EMS domain, although they are used to describe patient status. Hence, it is very important to incorporate the EMS domain knowledge, i.e., through building an EMS ontology, to optimize our NLP framework. More specifically, we will leverage the narrative data in the National EMS Database [52] to build an ontology to include the terminologies often used in the EMS domain for better information extraction. We will also create an annotated data set for the EHR fields with various and complex content, so that we can train supervised deep language models [53, 54] for those content recognitions.

Lastly, as shown in Table 2, the inter-agreement scores of some categories with long and complex descriptions, such as patient condition, are relatively low. This is because we applied word-based matching to calculate the inter-agreement scores. The calculation could be changed to segment based semantic matching, which means if the semantic similarities between segments of the annotations are high, the inter-agreement is high. Our system performance could also take advantage of the segment based semantic matching approach. Hence, instead of using the word level matching calculation, semantic based matching counts the correctness when the semantic meaning is very close. The semantic based matching could also improve the low performance categories listed in Fig. 9.

7 Conclusion

In this exploratory study, we first conducted an interview study with EMS providers to elicit user perceptions and needs with respect to using smart glasses to support their documentation work. Based on the user studies, we designed and developed a smart glass application to automate documentation during pre-hospital encounters. We also performed preliminary evaluations to measure system accuracy and gather user feedback for further improvement. Although optimization is needed, our system demonstrates its high potential in enabling hands-free, real-time documentation for emergency care providers. Our future work includes systematic evaluations of system usability and performance, and improvement of our underlying NLP framework.

Acknowledgement. This work was supported by National Science Foundation (NSF) Award #1948292. We would like to thank the ESO company for sharing their EHR system with us so we can create a hypothetical EHR system based on their design. We also want to thank our research participants for providing valuable feedback.

References

1. Downing, N.L., Bates, D.W., Longhurst, C.A.: Physician burnout in the electronic health record era: are we ignoring the real cause? American College of Physicians (2018)

2. Zulman, D.M., Shah, N.H., Verghese, A.: Evolutionary pressures on the electronic health record: caring for complexity. JAMA **316**(9), 923–924 (2016)
3. Tollefsen, W.W., et al.: iRevive: a pre-hospital database system for emergency medical services. Int. J. Healthc. Technol. Manag. **6**(4–6), 454–469 (2005)
4. Hertzum, M., Manikas, M.I., á Torkilsheyggi, A.: Grappling with the future: the messiness of pilot implementation in information systems design. Health Inform. J. **25**(2), 372–388 (2019)
5. Sarcevic, A., Burd, R.S.: Information handover in time-critical work. In: Proceedings of the ACM 2009 International Conference on Supporting Group Work, pp. 301–310 (2009)
6. Holzman, T.G.: Computer-human interface solutions for emergency medical care. Interactions **6**(3), 13–24 (1999)
7. Laudermilch, D.J., Schiff, M.A., Nathens, A.B., Rosengart, M.R.: Lack of emergency medical services documentation is associated with poor patient outcomes: a validation of audit filters for prehospital trauma care. J. Am. Coll. Surg. **210**(2), 220–227 (2010)
8. Zhang, Z., et al.: Data work and decision making in emergency medical services: a distributed cognition perspective. Proc. ACM Human-Comput. Interact. **5**(CSCW2), 1–32 (2021)
9. Momen, K.S.: Identifying nursing activities to estimate the risk of cross-contamination. University of Toronto, Canada (2012)
10. Pilerot, O., Maurin Söderholm, H.: A conceptual framework for investigating documentary practices in prehospital emergency care. Inf. Res. **24**(4), colis1931 (2019)
11. Aldaz, G., et al.: Hands-free image capture, data tagging and transfer using Google Glass: a pilot study for improved wound care management. PloS One **10**(4), e0121179 (2015)
12. Jonas, S., Hannig, A., Spreckelsen, C., Deserno, T.M.: Wearable technology as a booster of clinical care. In Medical Imaging 2014: PACS and Imaging Informatics: Next Generation and Innovations, pp. 90390F. International Society for Optics and Photonics, Washington, USA (2014)
13. Mitrasinovic, S., et al.: Clinical and surgical applications of smart glasses. Technol. Health Care **23**(4), 381–401 (2015)
14. Lee, J.-S., Tsai, C.-T., Pen, C.-H., Lu, H.-C.: A real time collaboration system for teleradiology consultation. Int. J. Med. Inform. **72**(1–3), 73–79 (2003)
15. Noorian, A.R., et al.: Use of wearable technology in remote evaluation of acute stroke patients: feasibility and reliability of a Google Glass-based device. J. Stroke Cerebrovas. Dis. **28**(10), 104258 (2019)
16. Cicero, M.X., et al.: Do you see what I see? Insights from using google glass for disaster telemedicine triage. Prehosp. Disaster Med. **30**(1), 4 (2015)
17. Broach, J., et al.: Usability and reliability of smart glasses for secondary triage during mass casualty incidents. In Proceedings of the Annual Hawaii International Conference on System Sciences, p. 1416. IEEE, New York (2018)
18. Schaer, R., Melly, T., Muller, H., Widmer, A.: Using smart glasses in medical emergency situations, a qualitative pilot study. In: 2016 IEEE Wireless Health (WH), pp. 1–5. IEEE, New York, USA (2016)
19. Schlosser, P., Matthews, B., Salisbury, I., Sanderson, P., Hayes, S.: Head-Worn displays for emergency medical services staff: properties of prehospital work, use cases, and design considerations. In: Proceedings of the 2021 CHI Conference on Human Factors in Computing Systems, pp. 1–14. ACM, New York (2021)
20. Saarinen, K., Aho, M.: Does the implementation of a clinical information system decrease the time intensive care nurses spend on documentation of care? Acta Anaesthesiol. Scand. **49**(1), 62–65 (2005)
21. Davidson, S.J., Zwemer, F.L., Nathanson, L.A., Sable, K.N., Khan, A.N.: Where's the beef? The promise and the reality of clinical documentation. Acad. Emerg. Med. **11**(11), 1127–1134 (2004)

22. Chen, Y.: Documenting transitional information in EMR. In Proceedings of the SIGCHI Conference on Human Factors in Computing Systems, pp. 1787–1796. ACM, New York (2010)
23. Jagannath, S., Sarcevic, A., Young, V., Myers, S.: Temporal rhythms and patterns of electronic documentation in time-critical medical work. In: Proceedings of the 2019 CHI Conference on Human Factors in Computing Systems, pp. 1–13. ACM, New York (2019)
24. Sarcevic, A., Ferraro, N.: On the use of electronic documentation systems in fast-paced, time-critical medical settings. Interact. Comput. **29**(2), 203–219 (2017)
25. Bossen, C., Pine, K.H., Cabitza, F., Ellingsen, G., Piras, E.M.: Data work in healthcare: an Introduction. SAGE Publications Sage UK, London (2019)
26. Sarcevic, A.: "Who's scribing?" documenting patient encounter during trauma resuscitation. In: Proceedings of the SIGCHI Conference on Human Factors in Computing Systems, pp. 1899–1908. ACM, New York (2010)
27. Meystre, S., Haug, P.J.: Natural language processing to extract medical problems from electronic clinical documents: performance evaluation. J. Biomed. Inform. **39**(6), 589–599 (2006)
28. Rosales, R., Farooq, F., Krishnapuram, B., Yu, S., Fung, G.: Automated identification of medical concepts and assertions in medical text. In: AMIA Annual Symposium Proceedings, p. 682. American Medical Informatics Association, Maryland (2010)
29. Li, Q., Wu, Y.-F.B.: Identifying important concepts from medical documents. J. Biomed. Inform. **39**(6), 668–679 (2006)
30. Preum, S.M., Shu, S., Alemzadeh, H., Stankovic, J.A.: Emscontext: EMS protocol-driven concept extraction for cognitive assistance in emergency response. In: Proceedings of the AAAI Conference on Artificial Intelligence, pp. 13350–13355. AAAI Press, California (2020)
31. Rahman, M.A., Preum, S.M., Williams, R., Alemzadeh, H., Stankovic, J.A.: GRACE: generating summary reports automatically for cognitive assistance in emergency response. In: Proceedings of the AAAI Conference on Artificial Intelligence, pp. 13356–13362. AAAI Press, California (2020)
32. Noma, H., Ohmura, A., Kuwahara, N., Kogure, K.: Wearable sensors for auto-event-recording on medical nursing-user study of ergonomic design. In: Eighth International Symposium on Wearable Computers, pp. 8–15. IEEE, New York (2004)
33. Klein, G.O., Singh, K., von Heideken, J.: Smart glasses—a new tool in medicine. Stud. Health Technol. Inform. **216**, 901 (2015)
34. Aungst, T., Lewis, T.: Potential uses of wearable technology in medicine: lessons learnt from Google Glass. Int. J. Clin. Pract. **69**(10), 1179–1183 (2015)
35. Yu, J., Ferniany, W., Guthrie, B., Parekh, S.G., Ponce, B.: Lessons learned from google glass: telemedical spark or unfulfilled promise? Surg. Innov. **23**(2), 156–165 (2016)
36. Klinker, K., Wiesche, M., Krcmar, H.: Digital transformation in health care: augmented reality for hands-free service innovation. Inf. Syst. Front. **22**, 1–13 (2019)
37. Holton, J.A.: The coding process and its challenges. The Sage Handbook of Grounded Theory **3**, 265–289 (2007)
38. Hartson, R., Pyla, P.S.: The UX Book: Process and Guidelines for Ensuring a Quality User Experience. Elsevier (2012)
39. Zhang, Z., Sarcevic, A., Bossen, C.: Constructing common information spaces across distributed emergency medical teams. In: Proceedings of the 2017 ACM Conference on Computer Supported Cooperative Work and Social Computing, pp. 934–947. ACM, New York (2017)
40. Zhang, Z., Sarcevic, A., Burd, R.S.: Supporting information use and retention of pre-hospital information during trauma resuscitation: a qualitative study of pre-hospital communications and information needs. In: AMIA Annual Symposium Proceedings, p. 1579. American Medical Informatics Association, Maryland (2013)

41. Aronson, A.R.: MetaMap: mapping text to the UMLS metathesaurus. Bethesda, MD: NLM, NIH, DHHS **1**, 26 (2006)
42. Sager, N., Lyman, M., Bucknall, C., Nhan, N., Tick, L.J.: Natural language processing and the representation of clinical data. J. Am. Med. Inform. Assoc. **1**(2), 142–160 (1994)
43. Kormilitzin, A., Vaci, N., Liu, Q., Nevado-Holgado, A.: Med7: a transferable clinical natural language processing model for electronic health records. Artif. Intell. Med. 102086 (2021)
44. Manning, C.D., et al.: The Stanford CoreNLP natural language processing toolkit. In: Proceedings of 52nd Annual Meeting of the Association for Computational Linguistics, pp. 55–60. Association for Computational Linguistics, Pennsylvania (2014)
45. Chinchor, N., Sundheim, B.M.: MUC-5 evaluation metrics. In: Fifth Message Understanding Conference (MUC-5): Proceedings of a Conference Held in Baltimore, Maryland (1993)
46. Zeng, X., Li, Y., Zhai, Y., Zhang, Y.: Counterfactual generator: a weakly-supervised method for named entity recognition. In Proceedings of the 2020 Conference on Empirical Methods in Natural Language Processing (EMNLP), pp. 7270–7280. Association for Computational Linguistics, Pennsylvania (2020)
47. Thieu, T., et al.: A comprehensive study of mobility functioning information in clinical notes: entity hierarchy, corpus annotation, and sequence labeling. Int. J. Med. Inform. **147**, 104351 (2021)
48. Sen, S., Ekbal, A., Bhattacharyya, P.: Parallel corpus filtering based on fuzzy string matching. In: Proceedings of the Fourth Conference on Machine Translation (Volume 3: Shared Task Papers, Day 2), pp. 289–293. Association for Computational Linguistics, Pennsylvania (2019)
49. Levenshtein, V.I.: Binary codes capable of correcting deletions, insertions, and reversals. Sov. Phys. Doklady **10**(8), 707–710 (1966)
50. Romare, C., Hass, U., Skär, L.: Healthcare professionals' views of smart glasses in intensive care: a qualitative study. Intensive Crit. Care Nurs. **45**, 66–71 (2018)
51. Maruri, H.A.C., et al.: V-Speech: noise-robust speech capturing glasses using vibration sensors. Proc. ACM Interact. Mob. Wearable Ubiquit. Technol. **2**(4), 1–23 (2018)
52. Dawson, D.E.: National emergency medical services information system (NEMSIS). Prehosp. Emerg. Care **10**(3), 314–316 (2006)
53. Li, J., Sun, A., Han, J., Li, C.: A survey on deep learning for named entity recognition. arXiv preprint arXiv:1812.09449 (2018)
54. Gehrmann, S., et al.: Comparing deep learning and concept extraction based methods for patient phenotyping from clinical narratives. PloS One **13**(2), e0192360 (2018)

Privacy Attitudes and COVID Symptom Tracking Apps: Understanding Active Boundary Management by Users

Jinkyung Park(✉), Eiman Ahmed, Hafiz Asif, Jaideep Vaidya, and Vivek Singh

Rutgers University, New Brunswick, NJ 0890, USA
jinkyung.park@rutgers.edu

Abstract. Multiple symptom tracking applications (apps) were created during the early phase of the COVID-19 pandemic. While they provided crowdsourced information about the state of the pandemic in a scalable manner, they also posed significant privacy risks for individuals. The present study investigates the interplay between individual privacy attitudes and the adoption of symptom tracking apps. Using the communication privacy theory as a framework, it studies how users' privacy attitudes changed during the public health emergency compared to the pre-COVID times. Based on focus-group interviews (N = 21), this paper reports significant changes in users' privacy attitudes toward such apps. Research participants shared various reasons for both increased acceptability (e.g., disease uncertainty, public good) and decreased acceptability (e.g., reduced utility due to changed lifestyle) during COVID. The results of this study can assist health informatics researchers and policy designers in creating more socially acceptable health apps in the future.

Keywords: COVID-19 · Symptom tracking · Privacy · Boundary management · Information boundary theory · Communication privacy management theory

1 Introduction

On March 11, 2020, the World Health Organization (WHO) declared the novel Corona Virus Disease 2019 (COVID-19) outbreak a global pandemic, [29] and as of September 15, 2021, approximately 22.5 million confirmed cases of COVID-19, including more than 4.6 million deaths were reported worldwide [28]. In the early months of the pandemic, the population testing for COVID-19 was deficient. The low population testing led to the lack of information necessary to track and curb the spread of the virus. To fill this information gap, many COVID-19 symptom

This material is in part based upon work supported by the US National Science Foundation (Grant #2027789) and National Institutes of Health.

M. Smits (Ed.): iConference 2022, LNCS 13193, pp. 332–346, 2022.
https://doi.org/10.1007/978-3-030-96960-8_22

tracking mobile applications (apps) were developed worldwide to generate real-time data about the spread of the virus. Since then, these apps have assisted in identifying specific symptoms of COVID-19 and predicting new hot spots five to six days in advance [8]. On the other hand, these apps collect and utilize peoples' private and sensitive information, raising serious privacy concerns. Therefore, in this work, we study people's privacy attitudes towards COVID-19 symptom tracking apps.

The use of mobile apps in fighting the spread of infectious diseases is not new or specific to COVID-19. In the past, mobile apps have been used to curb the spread of flu, SARS, and H1N1 [27,32]. Such mobile apps can be categorized into two types: symptom tracking apps and contract tracing apps—collectively, we refer to them as *disease monitoring apps*. A COVID-19 symptom tracking app collects self-reported personal information such as COVID-19 related symptoms, COVID-19 test results, demographic information, health history, and location from its users. It then uses this data to track the spread of the virus, identify emerging hot spots of COVID-19, and predict outbreaks [2,4,8]. A COVID-19 contact-tracing app, on the other hand, continuously tracks individuals (e.g., via Global Positioning System (GPS)) to identify and notify them about possible exposure to the virus [19]. Although the two types of apps work very differently, they share a common goal, i.e., to curb the pandemic.

Many users may have shared their information with these apps considering COVID-19 to be a "state of exception," [1] wherein temporary exceptions to existing rights (e.g., freedom of movement or some aspects of privacy) can be justified to preserve the health and security of citizens as a whole. At the same time, the general public and privacy-rights advocates raise concern for users' privacy due to the mass collection of sensitive health, demographic, and location data. They worry that the data collected via COVID-19 related apps could potentially be used for other purposes (e.g., health-insurance risk assessment) rather than to monitor the spread of the infectious disease [31].

Although disease monitoring apps claim to protect data through various privacy-preserving technologies [2,22], many research studies show that these apps fail to guard the privacy of all people [2,5,9,27]. For instance, Wen et al., [27] identified potential ways of re-identifying individuals in 41 different COVID-19 contact tracing apps. Asif [2] argued that symptom tracking apps that publicly release raw aggregates risk re-identification attacks. Even with advanced privacy-preserving technologies, COVID-19 monitoring apps could still raise individual users' privacy concerns.

In fact, privacy concerns among people are an essential factor in the adoption of disease monitoring apps, as indicated by several recent studies on COVID-19 contact tracing apps. Simko et al., [23] conducted a survey and found that the privacy concerns reduce the likelihood to install a new COVID-19 contact tracing apps. Another survey study by Kaptchuk et al., [10] found that both accuracy and privacy of COVID-19 contact tracing apps are significant influencing factors for their adoption. Williams et al., [30] conducted a focus group study in the

U.K. and discovered that privacy attitudes impacted people's willingness to use these apps.

While there is significant literature on users' privacy attitudes regarding health apps, *changes* that occur in individuals' privacy attitudes during pandemic (i.e., a public health emergency) settings are understudied. Hence, this exploratory study aims to understand users' privacy attitudes toward COVID-19 symptom tracking apps and how their privacy expectations change during the pandemic using focus group interviews in the U.S. The study uses communication privacy management as the underlying framework to examine elements of privacy that changed during the pandemic compared to a non-pandemic situation.

To do so, we focus on the notion of "informational privacy," which is concerned with controlling whether and how personal data can be gathered, stored, processed, and disseminated [11]. Furthermore, we focus on privacy attitudes rather than privacy concerns. Though closely related, they are different. Privacy concerns could be generic and, in most cases, are not bound to any specific context, while privacy attitudes refer to the appraisal of specific privacy behaviors in a particular context—here, COVID-19 symptom tracking apps [11].

2 Communication Privacy Management Theory

As online information can be easily obtained and integrated from disparate sources, research efforts have been conducted from various perspectives on informational privacy. Scholarly communities have utilized several theories concerning online information privacy research, including the theory of reasoned action [3], the privacy calculus theory [12], the social presence theory [20], and the protection motivation theory [21]. These theories conceptualize the formation of users' privacy concerns and their subsequent behaviors to provide personal information. Among existing theories of online privacy, a major stream of research that the current work builds upon is the communication privacy management theory (CPM) [16–18] and its adaptation as the information boundary theory (IBT) [24,25]. These theories are utilized in the present study as constructs of the theories (e.g., privacy turbulence) that offer natural ways to study changes in individuals' privacy attitudes under exceptional circumstances, such as the COVID-19 pandemic.

Using the metaphor of a "boundary," CPM [16] presents a psychological process in which individuals manage their desire for both communication and privacy. According to CPM, individuals balance the tension between intimacy (e.g., revelatory processes through which an individual becomes known to others) and autonomy (e.g., behaviors to protect and separate oneself from others) by negotiating psychological boundaries between themselves and others. In this context, a boundary serves as a "psychological contract" [24] or "ownership line" [17] between oneself and others concerning the amount, nature, and circumstances of requesting, sending, and receiving personal information [24].

The idea of boundary management has been applied across different contexts from early work that focused on communication in close relationships (e.g., marital relationships) [16] to later work that considered the role of information technology in social relationships [24]. Stanton [24] extended CPM to organizational settings and developed a synthesized theory called the information boundary theory. Using the same boundary metaphor, IBT focuses on individuals' motivations to disclose personal information via a given medium (e.g., messaging system) and in particular social environments (e.g., workplace). The extension of CPM to IBT indicates that individuals frame their use of information technology to transmit information in similar terms to those used in interpersonal relationships (e.g., telling about oneself to others).

CPM and IBT explicate that individuals' decisions on how privacy boundaries are regulated follow the rules for "boundary opening" and "boundary closure" [24], depending on the degree of risk associated with privacy. The boundaries are opened when there is a high probability that people will allow access to private information; hence, information flows freely. In contrast, boundaries are closed when people are less likely to reveal private information; hence, information flow is restricted [18]. In the context of the current study, "boundary" can be seen as an individual's willingness to use the COVID-19 symptom tracking apps. A boundary can be described as "opening" when an individual is more likely to use the apps. On the contrary, a boundary can be "closing" when an individual is less likely to use the apps.

According to CPM and IBT, individuals can articulate a personal "calculus of boundary negotiation" [25] regarding the conditions under which disclosure of personal information is acceptable or unacceptable. Often referred to as "privacy calculus," this mental calculus model suggests that individuals tend to weigh two competing factors (e.g., risks and benefits) associated with the transmission of personal information when they determine whether to disclose personal information [7]. The boundary negotiation processes are not static, but rather "dynamic psychological processes of regulation" [24] that allow people to control the flow of personal information. When privacy rules do not meet an individual's expectations anymore, they are adjusted according to individuals and other people [18]. According to CPM, "privacy turbulence" occurs when "normal" privacy rules no longer work to achieve the expected outcomes of privacy management [18]. In the context of the current study, COVID-19 can be seen as a unique privacy turbulence situation in which individuals' privacy rules no longer operate as they did before and need to be adjusted.

Prior studies of IBT and CPM elaborated several sources of motivation to disclose or withhold personal information. Stanton [24] investigated the use of monitoring and surveillance technologies within organizational settings and suggested that both boundary opening and closing are affected by organizational justice considerations such as mission-relatedness of the information. Recent work by Walters and Markazi [26] focused on the boundary closing resulting from privacy turbulence (e.g., privacy violation) with an individual's voice-activated phone. They reported that the conditions for boundary closing are not stemming from a particular information system but an overall lack of trustworthiness toward the information systems.

While previous research has conceptualized and applied boundary management in different settings, no study has looked into how an extreme health scenario, such as the COVID-19 pandemic, influences the way individuals shift their information boundaries online. Similarly, while some work is emerging on privacy attitudes and COVID-19 tracking app adoption, it has not been undertaken from the lens of CPM and the dynamic boundary management process. Thus, the present study presents the following research question:

RQ1: *How did users' privacy attitudes toward health symptom tracking apps change during the COVID-19 pandemic?*

RQ2: *How did users rationalize their boundary closing and boundary opening behavior during the pandemic?*

3 Methods

3.1 Recruitment and Participants

The present study reports an exploratory study involving three focus groups (N = 21) with United States-based residents aged 18 years or older. Participants were recruited from mailing lists (e.g., alumni mailing lists, community mailing lists, social media) based on their interest in participating in a study related to COVID-19 symptom tracking applications. Interested participants were asked to complete a pre-screening survey to determine their eligibility to partake in the study. Participants 18 years or older, comfortable speaking English, and residing in the United States were deemed eligible to engage in the research. Eligible individuals were sent consent forms and demographic information surveys before the focus group interviews. The authors' Institutional Review Board granted ethical approval for the study, and research participants were provided 50 U.S. dollars as compensation for participating in the study.

Focus group interview sessions with 6–8 participants were arranged on an online video conferencing platform (Zoom) for about an hour each in February 2021, when the United States was primarily still in lockdown and vaccines had yet to be administered to the general public. Participants were divided into three focus groups depending on their usage of symptom tracking apps to facilitate conversations. For instance, participants that had never used an application (group 3, n = 8) were placed into a different group than those who stated having used or currently using a COVID-19 symptom tracking application (group 1, n = 6/group 2, n = 7). The moderators (the research team) briefly reviewed ground rules before the interviews and informed participants that they could withdraw from the study at any point they wanted. The participants were also informed that they could request assistance in seeking counseling or mental health aid at any time during the focus group interviews. The moderators utilized semi-structured questions to ask participants about their relationship with symptom tracking applications, their symptom tracking application experiences, and the degree to which they feel either comfortable or uncomfortable sharing their personal health information on these applications.

The majority of participants were female (62%) with a mean age range of 18 to 21 (90%) and 1 to 3 years of college education (71%). In addition, most participants were either Asian or Asian American (48%) or Non-Hispanic or White (38%) residing in New Jersey and New York. The participants' family income ranged from less than $25,000 to $150,000 or more, with the median income range of $75,000 to $99,000. Finally, participants reported using four different COVID-19 symptom tracking applications (COVID Nearby, Pace Safe, COVID Alert NJ, My Campus Pass) that were recommended by friends, institutions, or the state.

3.2 Coding Process

The focus group interview questions were developed based on the detailed literature review and the study's goals. All the focus group sessions were video recorded and transcribed verbatim by the research team. The user numbers replaced participants' names to support confidentiality. Data were analyzed qualitatively; the research team compared participants' responses to uncover common themes. Finally, the team developed a coding scheme based on the iterative analysis. The final coding scheme consisted of 19 themes representing the main topics discussed from the three focus groups (see Table 1).

Once themes were established, the research team recruited a coder. Next, the team discussed the established themes with the coder over multiple iterations during March 2021. A sub-sample (10%) of the transcripts was selected to determine the reliability of the developed codes. Inter-coder reliability scores were calculated between the research team and the additional coder to ensure the consistency and validity of the uncovered themes. The average percent agreement was 0.87, and Krippendorff's alpha was 0.83. Both coefficients met the criteria suggested by the existing literature [12,15] for a good agreement. Finally, the research team and the coder coded the complete transcripts.

4 Findings

Participants from the three focus groups discussed their experience with COVID-19 symptom tracking apps. Given the focus of this study on the *changes* in privacy management during the COVID-19 pandemic, the discussion below focuses on two dimensions of privacy management (boundary opening and boundary closing), along with their central themes and sub-themes.

4.1 Boundary Opening

The first dimension of CPM and IBT explored was "boundary opening," in which individuals are more willing to share their personal information during the pandemic than non-pandemic situations. The five main themes that emerged from the focus group conversations were: (1) severity of the COVID-19 pandemic, (2) uncertainty of the COVID-19 pandemic, (3) protecting themselves and people around them, (4) contributing to the public good, and (5) mandatory use.

Severity of the COVID-19 Pandemic. Individuals considered the severity of the COVID-19 pandemic when deciding whether to open their privacy boundaries. One participant noted, *"with COVID it's a lot more deadlier so that's why, that was also one of my main reasons for why I downloaded it because I was just concerned with COVID (user 1, group 1)."* Another participant added that *"I think just because it's like all about COVID. That's why I'm more willing to use this app (user 2, group 1)."*

This major theme was closely related to the benefit factor in the boundary negotiation. The perceived benefit of sharing personal information (e.g., family safety) functioned as the decision criteria that individuals use to open their privacy boundaries. For example, one participant mentioned this change in privacy boundary: *"I don't think I'd use it to track like a cold or flu because like I'm honestly using the app to like, protect my family from like any, like, really severe illness (user 3, group 2)."*

Uncertainty of the COVID-19 Pandemic. Similarly, participants discussed the uncertainty of the COVID-19 pandemic as a criterion that they used to open their privacy boundaries. As an example of this theme, one participant said that *"I probably wouldn't have used anything else besides right now, because there's still so much uncertainty with the pandemic and the virus in general (user 4, group 1)."*

For some participants, the uncertainty related to the transmission of the virus was the primary motivation to use the COVID-19 symptom tracking app. As one participant elaborated: *"I'm afraid of possibly getting it or possibly giving it to someone else even walking by. So I'd be more compelled to use it (user 5, group 1)."*

Protecting Themselves or People Around Them. As the risk perception regarding the COVID-19 increased, it motivated personal- and family- safety-conscious individuals to open their privacy boundaries. Some individuals were more willing to use the COVID-19 symptom tracking app to safeguard their health. For example, one participant noted: *"I feel like it's a good thing to just have on your phone and for your for your own safety (user 6, group 3)."*

Participants were also willing to use COVID-19 symptom tracking apps to protect people around them (e.g., family members) from the pandemic. They mentioned that *"my family has some health issues and I just wanted to be on the safe side (user 3, group 2)."* *"I got kind of nervous because my mom is a high-risk patient. So, I started using it just to make sure that, what kind of cases are around me and what spots I should be careful at (user 1, group 1)."*

Table 1. Coding themes developed by the research team

Theme	Definition [example quotation]
Personal safety	*Safety of one's self* (health) ["I just wanted to be on the safe side and uh just know if anybody around me has COVID"]
Family safety	*Safety of family* (health) ["I also use uh the same app because um my family has some health issues and I just wanted to be on the safe side"]
Public good	*Using applications* (apps) *to contribute to the public good* ["try to contribute as much data as possible"]
Uncertainty	*Uncertainty related to spreading or risk of illness* ["I'm afraid of possibly getting it or possibly give, you know, possibly giving it to someone else even walking by"]
Severity	*Severity and danger of illness* ["It's not as deadly as like um COVID right now"]
Anonymization	*De-linking identity from person's shared data* ["As long as my name and identity remain anonymous, I will be okay with them"]
Data protection	*How data is protected from unauthorized access* ["Maybe emphasize that like your identity won't be shared with anybody else"]
Mandatory use	*Using apps because they are required* ["I'm contractually obligated to use it"]
Voluntary use	*Using apps out of own free-will* ["I just like use it to track the cases and everything"]
Normalization of Loss of Privacy	*Normalization due to society or other applications* ["I think um location tracking is kind of like normalized for me because there are like other apps that like Find my iPhone"]
Desire for control	*The desire for some control over personal information* ["I think I would want to have control over my own location... so like I'd want like an option for that"]
Transparency	*Clear communication of how data is protected* ["Be like upfront like this is exactly who um has access to your information and... tell us when our information is accessed also, and who accessed it."]
Accuracy	*Whether reported information is accurate* ["I don't know if I believe that every single person at Pace who walks in this building, isn't just like lying on these questions."]
Cost-benefit analysis	*Comparing the cost and the benefit of apps* ["Why give my location data if it's not going to benefit me"]
App-provided data coverage	*The scope of the data provided by the app* ["If ... everyone had to download the app and ... (get tested regularly) and then would have to put the results in the app. That'd be amazing"]
User-provided data coverage	*The scope of data collected by the app* ["It was a check-in or whatever and it just said: Do you have any symptoms, yes, no...and that was it. So it was not very comprehensive"]
Utility	*Usefulness of apps in everyday life* ["I don't really leave my house much, ... That's probably another reason but I'm not against it."]
Necessity	*Whether data collected is necessary for the app* ["It has to be relevant to you... If I'm shopping for something and they say, oh, can we access your camera? Then it's like, there's no point."]
Easy availability	*How easily understandable data protection process is* ["I guess like a short blurb or summary of like the data that they would probably collect"]

Contributing to the Public Good. The public good was another decision criterion that participants used to open their privacy boundaries. Some participants were willing to share their location and health information to contribute to the public's well-being. They noted that *"it would be good to just share location for that. Just because the intention is for the general health, and overall greater good (user 11, group 3)," and that "at least you know it benefits a large population of people in the end which is sick (user 2, group 1)"*.

Other participants mentioned that they decided to use the tracking app to provide their health and location data for research purposes with the hope of going back to normalcy: *"my health information could be used for um research purposes or just to help like you know extension of like scientific knowledge (user 5, group 1)." "you're taking the steps to try to help society, get back to some sort of normalcy (user 6, group 3)."*

Mandatory Use. Finally, mandatory use to support the community functioned as a decision criterion that participants used to open their privacy boundaries. For example, some participants used a COVID-19 symptom tracking app because they were required to use them for the well-being of their community during the pandemic.

> *"I also use the COVID app cause I also got a call from the state and they asked me to also use it ... in addition to that since I also work for *institution name*, they make me use the *name of the pass* ... I'd be more compelled to use it and make sure just try to contribute as much data as possible. Just to help them out (user 7, group 2)"*.

4.2 Boundary Closing

At the same time, multiple participants mentioned that they have become even less likely to install COVID-19 symptom tracking apps during the pandemic than before, which corresponds with the "boundary closing" dimension of CPM and IBT. The two main themes that emerged from the focus groups were: 1) lifestyle changes and 2) data quality. The theme of data quality included the sub-themes of user-provided data coverage and app-provided data coverage.

Lifestyle Changes. The lifestyle change was one decision criterion used to close their privacy boundaries. Participants mentioned that they were unwilling to use a COVID-19 symptom tracking app because their lifestyles had changed. Many felt as though tracking was not crucial since they did not engage with the "outside" world as much since the beginning of the pandemic.

One participant elaborated: *"I'm only going out like uh once or twice a month ... so it's not really worth me having to like manage a COVID tracking app for that one instance (user 8, group 3)."*

Another participant mentioned that the utility of the app decreased for them as the pandemic became more prominent, and they started spending most of their time in a lockdown: *"prior to this, I was using, I think it was called *name of an app* ... and I just stopped using it because um well I'm not on campus anymore so it's not really relevant (user 3, group 2)."*

Furthermore, some participants explicitly elaborated on the privacy calculus regarding the use of the COVID-19 symptom tracking app: *"I don't leave my house that much either unless it's for a necessity ... so why give my information and location data if it's not going to benefit me (user 9, group 3)."*

Data Quality. The data quality was another decision criterion that participants used to close their privacy boundaries. Participants were also less willing to use a COVID-19 symptom tracking app and share their personal information because they were skeptical about the quality of data provided by the app. There were two different scenarios described wherein the participants did not find the data provided by the application to be of high enough quality: app-provided data coverage and user-provided data coverage.

App-Provided Data Coverage. Some participants were unwilling to use a COVID-19 symptom tracking app during the pandemic because of the limited amount of data that an application provided. They felt as though applications did not always show enough statistics regarding COVID-related symptoms: *"for the *name of an app*, I think I ended up deleting it from my phone just because I didn't really see much stats within it. So I couldn't find it really useful." (user 2, group 1).*

Other participants pointed out that apps need to be used by many others to be beneficial enough for them to use: *"If we all use it, then it will be beneficial, and if not, then I don't think there's a lot of benefit to it (user 9, group 3)." "everyone needs to participate in it, in order to get like an accurate representation (user 10, group 3)."*

User-Provided Data Coverage. Some participants mentioned that they were even less likely to use the COVID-19 symptom tracking apps because they were not satisfied with the apps' questions. More specifically, they thought that many of these apps did not provide a comprehensive set of questions about the COVID-19 symptoms.

> *"I think it was like a check in or whatever and it just said: Do you have symptoms, yes, no and, just that was that was it. So it wasn't very comprehensive. So if it was like a little bit more detailed at least, then I'd be more inclined to use it but as of right now (user 11, group 3)."*

Other participants felt that the accuracy of self-reported health information that the users provided was not guaranteed: *"I think also along with that there's always going to be those people who don't really give the most like accurate representation or their symptoms (user 12, group 3)."*

5 Discussion

The first RQ for this work was: *RQ1: How did users' privacy attitudes toward health symptom tracking apps change during the COVID-19 pandemic?*

The focus group interviews provided strong evidence of changes in individuals' privacy attitudes during the pandemic. IBT suggests that boundary opening and closing are "dynamic psychological processes of regulation" [24] that allow people to control the flow of personal information to others in the social environment. The COVID-19 pandemic can be interpreted as a "privacy turbulence" in terms of the IBT/CPM since it affected how individuals closed/opened their information boundaries.

The current study captured the dynamicity in the processes of boundary management among the focus group participants. Besides multiple participants choosing to become less (or more) open with their boundaries, some participants went through cycles within the pandemic. One participant noted deleting a COVID-19 symptom tracking app they were using once they did not find it useful anymore. The participant mentioned that *"I think just because it's like all about COVID. That's why I'm more willing to use this app … I think I ended up deleting it from my phone just because I didn't really see much stats within it. So I couldn't find it really useful" (user 2, group 1).* In this conversation, the information boundary was first opened because of the severity of the pandemic and then closed due to a lack of utility to the app. Hence, acknowledging and understanding the dynamicity of privacy attitudes during health emergencies is a significant trend worth exploring further in future work.

As privacy turbulence, the COVID-19 pandemic had different meanings for different people. A clear variation in the needs and priorities of different users was observed. As reported in other areas, individuals' perceived risks and threats associated with the pandemic heavily influenced the risk-benefit ratio individuals used to regulate information boundaries during the pandemic.

The more risks individuals perceived, the more benefit they anticipated from sharing health and location information with COVID-19 symptom tracking apps. In this way, the risk perception regarding the pandemic and the benefit of sharing personal information went hand-in-hand. For example, participants described different levels of perceived risks of the COVID-19 pandemic; hence, different levels of perceived benefits of sharing personal information depending on their health conditions. For those who perceived that they were at a greater risk of contracting or being impacted by the pandemic, the benefit of having information that could aid them in staying safe was the primary decision criteria to open their information boundaries. One even called privacy concerns a "luxury" during the public health crisis. On the other hand, for those who perceived that they were not at high risk, the benefit of safety was not a significant motivator to modify their information boundaries. Those who did not perceive high risks from the COVID-19 pandemic prioritized other decision criteria (e.g., mandatory use, quality of the data, etc.) to open and close their information boundaries.

The second research question for this work was: *RQ2: How did users rationalize their boundary closing and boundary opening behavior during the pandemic?*

Boundary opening occurred when individuals were more willing to use health tracking apps than before, while boundary closing occurred when individuals were less willing to use health symptom tracking apps. Participants opened and closed their boundaries based on several decision criteria. The uncertainty and severity of COVID-19 posed an immediate and consequential risk to the health of individuals and their loved ones. The threat of COVID-19 and the benefit of having COVID-19 preventing information led users to engage in the increased act of boundary opening. These findings are consistent with recent work that suggests that perceived threats to life or health during a pandemic may be an important predictor of acceptance of potentially helpful yet controversial technologies such as COVID-19 tracking technologies [31].

Participants primarily opened their boundaries for information that they considered valuable. At the same time, participants closed their boundaries, which may have once been opened, if the information they received was no longer useful (e.g., due to lifestyle changes) or did not meet their expectations. These findings suggest that although users may open their privacy boundaries, these boundaries can just as quickly be closed and are contingent on the users' expectations, needs, and desires at any given time. In other words, boundaries may be both socially and contextually situated.

A lack of adoption by a critical mass was cited as a rationale for boundary closing, which connects with previous research on network externalities [14] discussing how reaching a critical mass of users in specific platforms incentives new users to join that platform. Hence, there is a need to explore ways for multiple stakeholders to identify ways to support privacy-aware data sharing mechanisms that can ensure high coverage of the apps. Similarly, the participants were well-informed about their requirements for adopting such apps and when/how they will consider opening their privacy boundaries to install them. Thus, the paradigm of participatory design [6] will be especially relevant in the creation of future symptom tracking apps.

Lastly, public good, which can be perceived as an individual's willingness to sacrifice one's privacy for the greater good, was identified as a key factor that led users to open their privacy boundaries. This finding connects with theoretical literature suggesting that privacy presupposes the existence of others and the possibility of a relationship between personal privacy and societal good [13,18,24]. Therefore, future apps can consider highlighting the social aspects (e.g., protecting those around them) and public good (e.g., helping science fight pandemics) in their descriptions and design to support better adoption.

The current study is considered to be exploratory and has some limitations. Participants consisted of 21 (majority young) individuals residing in the Northeastern U.S. Although they were diverse in race/ethnicity, they do not constitute a representative sample. Similarly, the current study discusses privacy concerns based on a small number of COVID-19 symptom tracking applications during a specific phase of the pandemic. Therefore, caution needs to be applied in interpreting the findings for other contexts.

Despite the above limitations, this study has important implications for both information privacy discourse and the specific instance of a public health emergency (COVID-19). The current study contributes to the IBT and CPM literature by (1) applying the theories to the context of public health emergencies such as COVID-19 and (2) empirically identifying conditions for privacy boundary opening and closing during health emergencies. For instance, it adds an interpretation of health emergencies as "privacy turbulence." The work also identified personal and social aspects of privacy boundary management and interconnections between the two. Similarly, it highlights the dynamic nature of the boundary management process. Thus, this work adds a new interpretation of boundaries and empirical evidence to CPM/IBT in public health settings. An improved understanding of privacy attitudes during the pandemic can motivate further research on similar topics in different contexts.

Many people are downloading and using tracking apps, and the privacy aspects of such apps are of great importance for the different stakeholders engaged with information systems. However, building apps serves little purpose unless the greater public adopts them. The current study identifies factors that will increase or decrease the adoption of such apps. Identifying these factors is vital for health policy designers (including US CDC, EU Information Commission), health professionals, and mobile app designers. Better health app design is also beneficial to the broader public and good for the health of society.

6 Conclusion

The primary purpose of the present study was to understand the changes in individual privacy attitudes toward mobile health apps during the COVID-19 pandemic. Drawing upon CPM and IBT, the study analyzed focus group interview inputs from 21 participants. The participants described the pandemic as a phenomenon that caused significant changes in their attitudes toward the acceptability of symptom-tracking health apps, which resonates with "boundary turbulence" in the CPM literature. Further, the participants identified multiple reasons for being more accepting ("boundary opening" as per CPM) and less accepting ("boundary closing") of the health apps. Rationales for the boundary opening included aspects like the severity and the uncertainty of the pandemic and contributing to the global good. Rationales for boundary closing included aspects like the reduced utility due to lifestyle changes and the quality of the data. The results can help policy designers and health information system designers understand the reasons for accepting and rejecting mobile apps in health emergencies. This knowledge can be vital for designing future health apps and supporting societal well-being.

References

1. Agamben, G.: The State of Exception. Duke University Press, Durham (2005)
2. Asif, H.: Chapter 7, Privacy or utility? How to preserve both in outlier analysis. Ph.D. thesis, Rutgers University-Graduate School-Newark (2021)
3. Azjen, I.: Understanding Attitudes and Predicting Social Behavior. Englewood Cliffs, Bergen (1980)
4. Berglund, J.: Tracking COVID-19: there's an app for that. IEEE Pulse **11**(4), 14–17 (2020)
5. Cho, H., Ippolito, D., Yu, Y.W.: Contact tracing mobile apps for COVID-19: privacy considerations and related trade-offs. arXiv preprint arXiv:2003.11511 (2020)
6. Davis, S., Peters, D., Calvo, R., Sawyer, S., Foster, J., Smith, L.: "Kiss myAsthma": using a participatory design approach to develop a self-management app with young people with asthma. J. Asthma **55**(9), 1018–1027 (2018)
7. Dinev, T., Hart, P.: An extended privacy calculus model for e-commerce transactions. Inf. Syst. Res. **17**(1), 61–80 (2006)
8. Drew, D.A., et al.: Rapid implementation of mobile technology for real-time epidemiology of COVID-19. Science **368**(6497), 1362–1367 (2020)
9. Gvili, Y.: Security analysis of the COVID-19 contact tracing specifications by Apple Inc. and Google Inc. IACR Cryptol. ePrint Arch. **2020**, 428 (2020)
10. Kaptchuk, G., Goldstein, D.G., Hargittai, E., Hofman, J., Redmiles, E.M.: How good is good enough for COVID19 apps? The influence of benefits, accuracy, and privacy on willingness to adopt. arXiv preprint arXiv:2005.04343 (2020)
11. Kokolakis, S.: Privacy attitudes and privacy behaviour: a review of current research on the privacy paradox phenomenon. Comput. Secur. **64**, 122–134 (2017)
12. Landis, J.R., Koch, G.G.: The measurement of observer agreement for categorical data. Biometrics **33**, 159–174 (1977)
13. Laufer, R.S., Wolfe, M.: Privacy as a concept and a social issue: a multidimensional developmental theory. J. Soc. Issues **33**(3), 22–42 (1977)
14. Lin, K.Y., Lu, H.P.: Why people use social networking sites: an empirical study integrating network externalities and motivation theory. Comput. Hum. Behav. **27**(3), 1152–1161 (2011)
15. Neuendorf, K.A.: The Content Analysis Guidebook. SAGE, New York (2017)
16. Petronio, S.: Communication boundary management: a theoretical model of managing disclosure of private information between marital couples. Commun. Theory **1**(4), 311–335 (1991)
17. Petronio, S.: Boundaries of Privacy: Dialectics of Disclosure. Suny Press, Albany (2002)
18. Petronio, S.: Communication privacy management theory. In: The International Encyclopedia of Interpersonal Communication, pp. 1–9. American Cancer Society (2015)
19. Ramakrishnan, A.M., Ramakrishnan, A.N., Lagan, S., Torous, J.: From symptom tracking to contact tracing: a framework to explore and assess COVID-19 apps. Future Internet **12**(9), 153 (2020)
20. Rice, R.E.: Media appropriateness: using social presence theory to compare traditional and new organizational media. Hum. Commun. Res. **19**(4), 451–484 (1993)
21. Rogers, R.W.: A protection motivation theory of fear appeals and attitude change1. J. Psychol. **91**(1), 93–114 (1975)
22. Sharma, T., Bashir, M.: Use of apps in the COVID-19 response and the loss of privacy protection. Nat. Med. **26**(8), 1165–1167 (2020)

23. Simko, L., Calo, R., Roesner, F., Kohno, T.: COVID-19 contact tracing and privacy: studying opinion and preferences. arXiv preprint arXiv:2005.06056 (2020)
24. Stanton, J.M.: Information technology and privacy: a boundary management perspective. In: Socio-Technical and Human Cognition Elements of Information Systems, pp. 79–103. IGI Global (2003)
25. Stanton, J.M., Stam, K.R.: Information technology, privacy, and power within organizations: a view from boundary theory and social exchange perspectives. Surveill. Soc. **1**(2), 152–190 (2003)
26. Walters, K., Markazi, D.M.: Insights from people's experiences with AI: privacy management processes. In: Toeppe, K., Yan, H., Chu, S.K.W. (eds.) iConference 2021. LNCS, vol. 12645, pp. 33–38. Springer, Cham (2021). https://doi.org/10.1007/978-3-030-71292-1_4
27. Wen, H., Zhao, Q., Lin, Z., Xuan, D., Shroff, N.: A study of the privacy of COVID-19 contact tracing apps. In: Park, N., Sun, K., Foresti, S., Butler, K., Saxena, N. (eds.) SecureComm 2020. LNICST, vol. 335, pp. 297–317. Springer, Cham (2020). https://doi.org/10.1007/978-3-030-63086-7_17
28. WHO: World Health Organization: Who coronavirus (COVID-19) dashboard. https://covid19.who.int/. Accessed 15 Sept 2021
29. WHO: World Health Organization: Who director-general's opening remarks at the media briefing on covid-19 - 11 March 2020. www.who.int/director-general/speeches/detail/who-director-general-s-opening-remarks-at-the-media-briefing-on-covid-19--11-march-2020. Accessed 15 Sept 2021
30. Williams, S.N., Armitage, C.J., Tampe, T., Dienes, K.: Public attitudes towards COVID-19 contact tracing apps: a UK-based focus group study. Health Expect. **24**(2), 377–385 (2021)
31. Wnuk, A., Oleksy, T., Maison, D.: The acceptance of COVID-19 tracking technologies: the role of perceived threat, lack of control, and ideological beliefs. PLoS ONE **15**(9), e0238973 (2020)
32. Yoneki, E., Crowcroft, J.: EpiMap: towards quantifying contact networks for understanding epidemiology in developing countries. Ad Hoc Netw. **13**, 83–93 (2014)

YouTube as a Helpful and Dangerous Information Source for Deliberate Self-harming Behaviours

Muhammad Abubakar Alhassan[1,2] and Diane Rasmussen Pennington[1(✉)]

[1] Department of Computer and Information Sciences, University of Strathclyde, Glasgow, UK
diane.pennington@strath.ac.uk

[2] Department of Computer Science, Federal University Dutse, Dutse, Nigeria

Abstract. Online social media platforms remain an excellent source of data for information scientists. Existing studies have found that people who self-harm find it easier to disclose information regarding their behaviour on social media as compared to in-person interactions. Due to the large and growing volume of user-generated content on YouTube, sources of videos presenting information concerning self-harm and discussions surrounding those videos could be hidden by other contents. By using a categorisation codebook and state-of-the-art topic and sentiment analysis techniques, the authors identified distinct groups of users who uploaded videos about self-harm on YouTube (n = 107) and uncovered the topics and sentiments expressed in 27,520 comments. In addition to other sources, our investigations discovered that 56% of the people uploading the examined videos are *non-professionals*, in contrast to the group of *professionals* with only 11% of the videos in the sample. In grouping comments based on similar topics, we discovered that *self-harming users*, *clean (recovered) users*, *at-risk audiences*, and *appreciative users* responded to the examined videos. Viewers responded more positively to '*recovered from self-harm*' and '*appreciative*' responses, as opposed to '*at-risk*' and '*self-harm*' comments with a high negative sentiments. These features could be used to build a classifier, although more research is needed to investigate self-injurious information to better support digital interventions for effective prevention and recovery.

Keywords: Social media · YouTube · Self-harm · Self-injury

1 Introduction

The ubiquitous nature of social media may create opportunities that could help in mitigating undiagnosed mental health problems. Many studies have explored social media use and its factors associated with mental well-being. Most focus on anxiety, depression and eating disorders [5,7], with less attention on self-harming behaviours [6,25]. In the last decade, as a response to a rising number of

M. Smits (Ed.): iConference 2022, LNCS 13193, pp. 347–362, 2022.
https://doi.org/10.1007/978-3-030-96960-8_23

case reports by physicians, schools and communities, investigating self-harming behaviours has gained more attention from researchers [23]. Self-harm is defined as intentional physical harm to oneself with no intent to end their life. This behaviour is most common among young people, and it usually involves cutting, carving, or burning of the skin [23]. Also, self-mutilation such as headbanging and bruising can be included in these harming behaviours as well [11].

In this study, we applied the definition of self-harming behaviour as reported by the Child and Adolescents Self-harm in Europe (CASE) research [16]. The study established criteria for identifying individuals who deliberately self-harm with a self-reported questionnaire to participants in six European countries. The authors constructed a standard definition that characterised deliberate self-harming (DSH) behaviours, including cutting oneself or ingesting dangerous substances, and developed a concrete approach for investigating the prevalence of self-harm. Many researchers use this definition as it entails most common forms of intentional self-injury [1,4]. Nevertheless, the stereotype and stigma surrounding DSH can make the Internet a stimulating space for those engaged in it. The anonymity and boundary-spanning of online networks can allow people greater freedom to convey views deemed hard to share [18]. In other words, online social networks connect people with commonalities much more than in offline social interactions [20,27]. Young people who self-harm are even more likely to participate in online activities than those who do not [22].

Some YouTube users record and share videos about their personal experiences or stories. YouTube is among the online platforms on which self-harming individuals share experiences, such as normalising self-harm (*dangerous*) or exchanging peer support (*helpful*) [12]. Further research is needed to understand the various sources of videos about self-harm on YouTube, as well as what viewers discuss and their opinions about the videos expressed through their comments. In line with this, our study aimed to answer the following research questions:

- *Who uploads videos discussing self-harm on YouTube, and how do viewers rate the videos?*
  With this question, we aimed to explore the groups of people involved in disseminating videos about self-harm on YouTube. Through exploring the characteristics of their videos, we wanted to understand how their audiences rated the videos on various channels.
- *What are viewers discussing concerning videos presenting self-harm information on YouTube?*
  Here, we sought to uncover hidden topics viewers discussed, and we grouped comments based on similar topics. Addressing this question increased our understanding of the conversations surrounding videos related to self-harm on YouTube.
- *What opinions do viewers communicate in their comments?* To answer this question, viewers' sentiments from the identified topics were examined. The opinions of the audiences viewing videos about self-harm is essential to explore. This will help to understand *dangerous* or *helpful* opinions to promote or prevent self-harm on YouTube.

However, this research paper is organised as follows; the next Section highlights the existing studies in this area, and Sect. 3 describes the approach adopted in the study. Section 4 explains our research findings, and the study's discussions and limitations are discussed in Sects. 5 and 6. The research conclusions and future directions are presented in the last section of this paper.

2 Deliberate Self-harm (DSH) and Social Media

An increasing amount of research reports that young people who self-harm frequently utilise the internet, with social media specifically being a preferred online communication mode [21]. Recent times have witnessed a growing body of research focusing around the impacts of social media on DSH, increasingly around user-generated content promoting DSH [17].

Many social media users who engage in DSH share content related to their self-harming behaviours, most of which is insufficiently explored through research[28]. One study investigated the differences in characteristics between self-harm and non-self-harm contents on Flickr [28]. Through analysing these and other features, a framework that can automatically detect self-harm content was proposed. Another comparative study investigated self-harm content from Tumblr, Twitter, and Instagram [21]. Using the '#cutting' hashtag, the researchers retrieved self-harm content and analysed 770 posts (333 from Tumblr, 78 from Twitter and 359 from Instagram). Instagram had more graphical content and more users with low self-esteem than Twitter. Furthermore, Twitter was found to have more DSH recovery-related posts than Instagram and Tumblr.

The qualitative study conducted by [8] uncovered attitudes and beliefs of DSH users on Twitter. The author demonstrated that self-harm is not treated lightly on Twitter, and also found posts that escalate the importance of celebrities' behaviour may influence followers' self-harming behaviours. Additionally, the study discovered that social media informs DSH personal stories through videos. In order to determine the potential risks associated with non-suicidal self-injury (NSSI) videos on YouTube, the work of [12] examined the comments made on those videos. Using coding rubrics, the researchers examined comments of the 100 most popular NSSI videos publicly available on YouTube. The authors discovered that the comments on the examined videos were predominantly on self-disclosure, and feedback was directed to the channel or the video uploader. However, the qualitative approach used by the investigators cannot be applied to a large volume of comments, and therefore likely missed crucial information within the comments.

Further effort is needed to understand viewers' opinions and discussions surrounding YouTube DSH videos on a larger scale [8,28]. This research investigation adds to the current research on the influence of social media in mediating or promoting self-injurious behaviour. We explored various sources of videos concerning self-harm on YouTube. While most of the examined videos were from non-professional YouTubers, we discovered that support organisations, news media agencies, government and non-governmental organisations, and medical and academic experts have contributed to sharing videos about self-harm on YouTube. Our research findings contribute to the body of knowledge on the views and opinions of people commenting on videos concerning intentional self-harm.

3 Methods

We adopted a mixed methods approach for this study. Choosing this depended mainly on the nature of our research questions and the type of data under investigation. In addressing the first research question, this study considered specific criteria explained in Table 1. Following a previous study on YouTube video authorship [19], we started with the author's approach, made a few changes, and then categorised the diverse group of channels included in our sample. We assessed viewers' interactions from each channel. We addressed research questions two and three using the *state-of-the-art* Python's natural language processing toolkit, topic modelling algorithm, and sentiment analysis technique.

Our research utilised the Natural Language Toolkit (NLTK).[1] It is a free and open source package available in Python that incorporates numerous tools for developing a programme and performing data classification tasks. Also, we used the Latent Dirichlet Allocation (LDA) technique, which is a popular probabilistic topic model that identifies similarities linking various data parts [2]. A specific part of the data in topic modelling is considered a textual document, which in our case is an individual comment on videos discussing self-harm. Similarly, we performed sentiment analysis of the video responses using the Valence Aware Sentiment Reasoner (VADER), which is a *rule-based* technique for conducting sentiment analysis of social media textual data [9] (Fig. 1).

Table 1. Source channel classification scheme

Category	Description	Code
Professionals	Professional individual(s) appeared in the video content and shared the video on their YouTube channels. Also, their channel's description may have contained information representing medical or academic experts such as psychologists and psychiatrists	001
Non-professionals	Channel(s) describing the YouTuber as a layperson who promotes mental health awareness, with the video presenter being a non-academic or non-medical expert	002
News media	This category includes channels maintained by traditional news media firms, such as local and international news organisations that have uploaded videos about self-harm	003
Government organisations	In this group, we included YouTube channels representing government institutions, such as educational or medical institutions	004
Private organisations	This group is mainly for video channels managed by private companies to promote mental health products, especially directed toward self-harming people	005
Support organisations	These channels belonged to support organisations, such as the UK-based Samaritans, which have produced videos concerning self-harm to increase awareness, promote support, and encourage recovery	006

[1] https://www.nltk.org/.

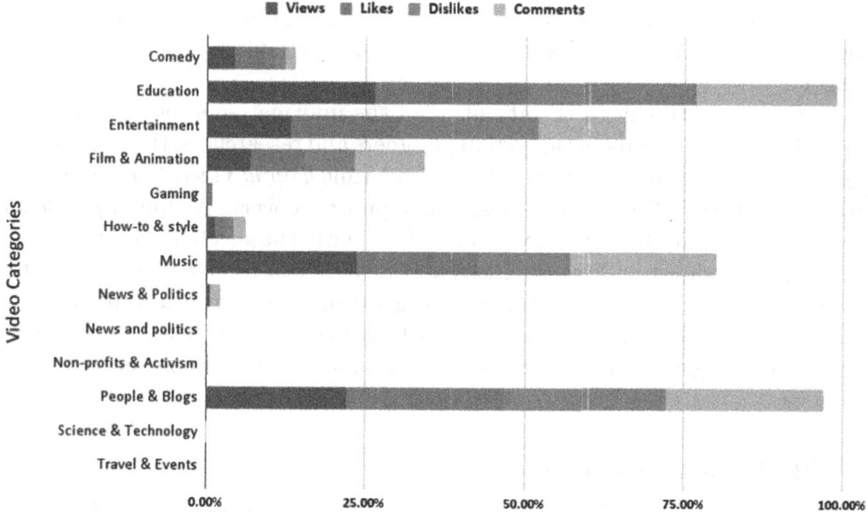

Fig. 1. Percentages of video categories.

3.1 Data Collection

As noted above, our approach was informed by previous studies that have investigated YouTube's DSH-related content. YouTube provides access for researchers to extract data via its Application Programming Interface (API). Previous studies used keywords such as 'self-cutting' and 'self-harm' to extract relevant data from YouTube. Our study searched the platform using (1) *'self-harm'*, (2) *'self-injury'*, (3) *'self-cutting'*, (4) *'non-suicidal self-injury'*, and (5) *deliberate self-harm'*. Per YouTube's data extraction limits, these terms returned 250 videos (with 50 from each query term) discussing self-harm. Duplicates and non-English videos were removed. This resulted in 172 unique videos uploaded between 2010 and 2020. We extracted a total of 37,100 comments from those videos, and removed duplicate comments or responses written in a language other than English. This produced a total of 27,520 responses from 27,510 unique users for analysis.

3.2 Data Analysis

Each of the videos examined featured one or more presenters. Similar to earlier research that demonstrated gender imbalance, showing how females self-harm at a higher rate than males [3, 24], our analysis found that female presenters appeared in 66.67% of the analysed videos, compared to male presenters who appeared in 24.56% of them. As we know, YouTube provides different video categories in which uploaders select the appropriate category related to their content. For example, a tutorial teaching people how to perform mathematical computations would likely be assigned to the *education* category. Therefore, our data analysis explored the categories assigned by the uploader to each of the videos. While video categories could be used to assist users to search specific videos, our analysis identified the most popular categories, including the number of views, likes, and dislikes for each category.

The idea was to call to the attention of the information science community, especially information retrieval system designers and researchers, the utilisation of these attributes to increase the ranking of relevant *helpful* videos for target audiences to increase self-harm awareness and support recovery. We found *people and blogs, education* and *music* to be the most frequently chosen channel categories in our sample, as shown in Fig. 1. Videos under *education* received fewer likes than those assigned under the *music* category, suggesting that viewers favour entertaining videos over educational videos. Regardless of the channel category, there was a high rate of engagement from viewers, as the videos in our sample received many comments.

3.3 Basic Text Processing

One of the critical steps of any natural language processing task is basic text processing. This study used Python's natural language toolkit and imported all the relevant libraries needed to clean and prepare the set of comments for topic modelling and sentiment analysis. In our analysis, we removed stopwords and created a document term matrix from the comments corpus. While this matrix was created using tokenization, it summarises the frequency of each term in every document. We also performed stemming, and lemmatization as the duo are crucial parts of every text pre-processing. Following that, we lemmatized each specific word to its base form, excluding nouns, adjectives, verbs, and adverbs. We retain these parts of speech tags since they are essential in understanding sentence meaning and context. Moreover, to effectively build the topic model, we created a dictionary and corpus.

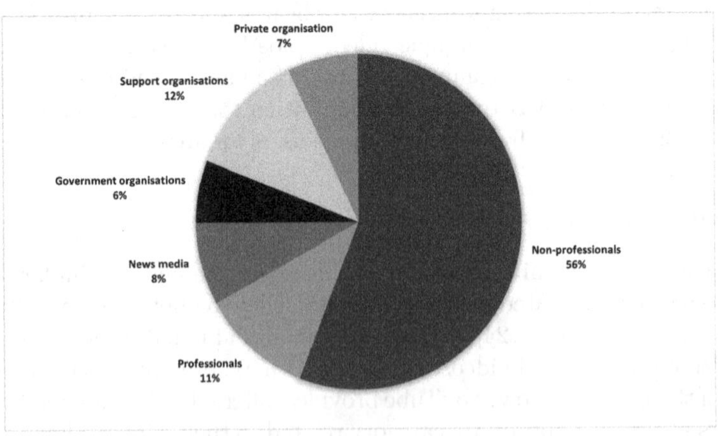

Fig. 2. Video authors' categories

4 Results

4.1 Users Sharing Videos About Self-harm

The present study classified YouTubers who shared videos concerning DSH using the criteria given in Table 1. The proportion of each category is depicted in Fig. 2. Non-professional individuals uploaded around 56% of the studied videos, compared to professionals, who authored only 11%. Support organisations accounted for up to 12%, whereas only 6% were from government organisations. Similarly, videos produced by news media organisations and commercial enterprises account for 6% and 7%, respectively. YouTube viewers engage with the platform in different ways. Firstly, in addition to subscribing to a video channel, there are options for viewers to rate a video through likes and dislikes. Secondly, viewers can interact by commenting on a video and liking or disliking a comment. Our study examined these interactions (except likes and dislikes of comments) from different channel cohorts, as shown in Fig. 3. Although all the categories of YouTubers had significant numbers of subscribers, it is apparent that the audiences favoured (liked) *non-professionals'* video content most.

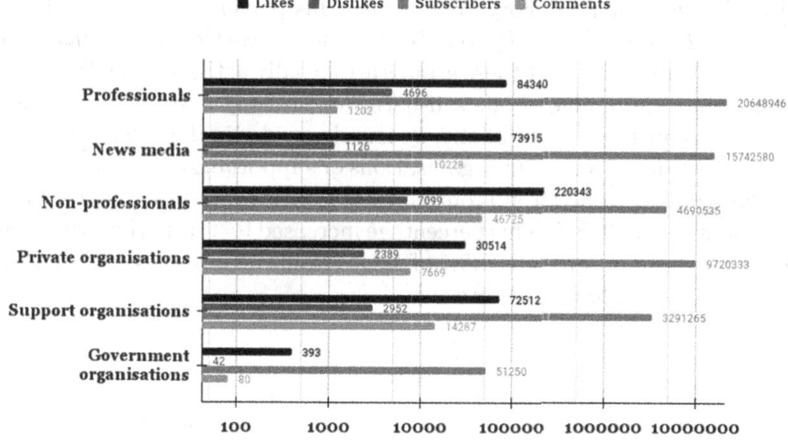

Fig. 3. Groups of users and the frequencies of interactions they received

Similarly, videos from these categories (except those from government institutions) encouraged interactions among viewers, and they received a large number of comments. In contrast to the rest of the categories, the rate of dislikes outweighed comments in the *professionals* group. This suggests that viewers possibly found videos from this group less engaging. Moreover, our analysis explored different video categories assigned by the group of video authors. The matrix table in Fig. 4 illustrates the percentage of video categories across the various uploaders' channels. Several channels assigned the *people and blogs* category to one or more videos.

Nevertheless, about 55.2% of the videos uploaded by the group of *non-professionals* were found in the *people and blogs* category. This implies that

	People & Blogs	Education	Entertainment	Film & Animation	Nonprofits & Activism	News & Politics	Music	Howto & Style	Science & Technology	Comedy	Gaming
Non-professionals	55.2	11.9	11.9	9.0			4.5	4.5		3	
Professionals	7.1	64.3	21.4	7.1							
News media	23.1		38.5		7.7	30.8					
Government organisations	12.5	75.0			12.5						
Support organisations	25.0	62.5			12.5						
Private organisation	33.3	16.7	16.7	16.7					16.7		

Fig. 4. Video uploaders and their channel categories

community members (especially those who had experienced self-harm) published videos to share their experiences and increase awareness about the behaviour. Similarly, videos uploaded in the *education* category appeared in all groups except *news media*, and up to 75% of the videos from *government organisations* were found in the *education* category. Meanwhile, this percentage reduced slightly to 64.3% and 62.5% in the *professionals* and the *support organisations* channels respectively. This shows that these groups are socially active on YouTube through educating the community about self-harm and raising awareness regarding its potential consequences. Additionally, we found no video in the *entertainment* category that was from government organisations or support organisations. Also, *news media* channels is the only group containing videos from the *news and politics* category, accounting for 30.8%. This percentage increased to 38% in the *entertainment* category. Surprisingly, around 38.5% of videos from the *news media* channels were assigned to the *entertainment* category.

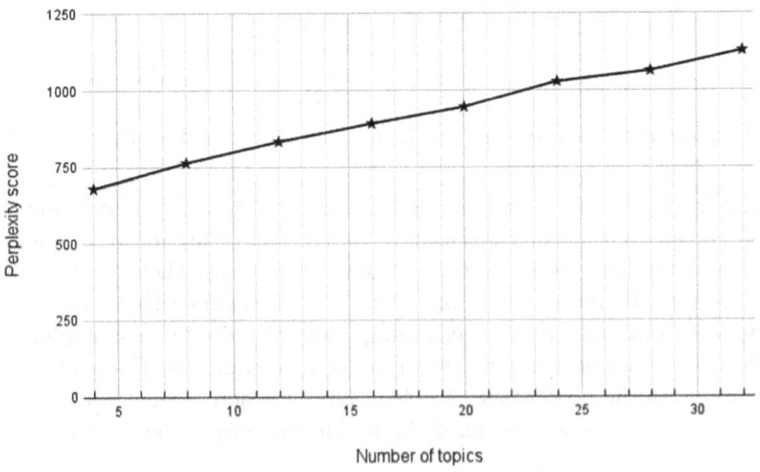

Fig. 5. Choosing appropriate number of topics

4.2 Themes Surrounding DSH Video Responses

To develop an LDA model, a sufficiently large dataset is essential. The minimum size required is determined by the document's attributes and average length - the more extensive the dataset, the more accurate the results due to the more significant number of observations [2]. Unlike tweets, YouTube comments can be long, reaching up to 10,000 characters. This paper examined 27,520 extracted comments.

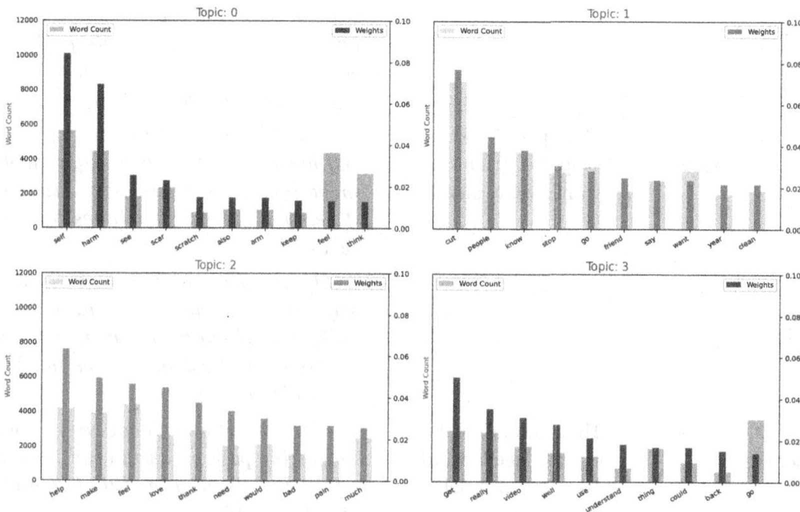

Fig. 6. Terms frequencies and their weights

However, although Latent Dirichlet Allocation (LDA) is one of the state-of-the-art techniques for topic analysis [10], determining the correct number of topics in which the LDA model predicts the topic is very challenging. To overcome this issue, we used *perplexity* and ran the model on different topics (4, 8, 16, 20, 24, 28, and 32). Intuitively, the lower the perplexity, the better the prediction [2]. After completing different rounds of experiments, a model with four topics produced the best prediction as shown in Fig. 5. Therefore, we applied this model and analysed the comments corpus, and identified essential topics surrounding videos presenting self-harm information. When interpreting topics, the keywords (unigrams) contained in the topics and their relevance (weights) is significant. The frequency in which the terms appeared in the comments is essential to explore. Intuitively, words that appeared in several topics, including those with a frequency higher than their weight, were considered less relevant as shown in Fig. 6. This study considered the first ten terms based on their weights, and interpreted the topics discussed by the viewers as presented in Table 2.

Table 2. Topic interpretations and examples of comments

Topic	Unigrams	Example comments
Topic 0: Self-harming users	Self, harm, see, scratch, also, arm, keep, feel, think	1. *"I'm 11 and so far I have cut all my arms, legs and the side of my throat! I'm not proud the scars and blood just show I'm still living and no one is right about me!"*
		2. *"I self harm and I often think of ways how to kill myself and how I can self harm even more. It's horrible but I have an addictive personality. My boyfriend self harms as well, we self harm together most the time."*
Topic 1: Clean (recovered) viewers	Cut, people, know, stop, go, friend, say, want, year, clean	1. *"I think I'm nearly a year clean from self harm and the kids at my school make fun of self harm all the time and it gets really hard sometimes not to relapse"*
		2. *"I think I'm nearly a year clean from self harm and the kids at my school make fun of self harm all the time and it gets really hard sometimes not to relapse"*
Topic 2: At-risk audiences	Help, make, feel, thank, need, would, bad, pain, much	1. *"Cuts, blood and then scars, it just makes the pain go away even for a little while. It tells me I'm still alive and can still feel pain"*
		2. *"I want to cut my self I use to be like this I wanna feel pain on my wrist."*
Topic 3: Appreciative users	Get, really, video, well, use, understand, thing, could, back, go	1. *"I really appreciate that you made this video I am always so worried if I can show my scars or not but this helped a lot so thanks"*
		2. *"This video literally changed my mentality so much on what I think off my scars wow, thank you I really needed to hear this from a different perspective."*

As seen in Table 2, the first column represents the topics that describe the entire set of comments: (1) *self-harming users,* (2) *clean (recovered) users,* (3) *at-risk audiences* and (4) *appreciative users.* In interpreting these topics, we grouped viewers based on similar themes. In doing so, this study identified the most discussed topics, as shown in Fig. 7. The clean (recovered) comments topic represents the most dominant topic of the discussion. This result is similar to previous research investigating responses to DSH videos on YouTube [12]. Topics

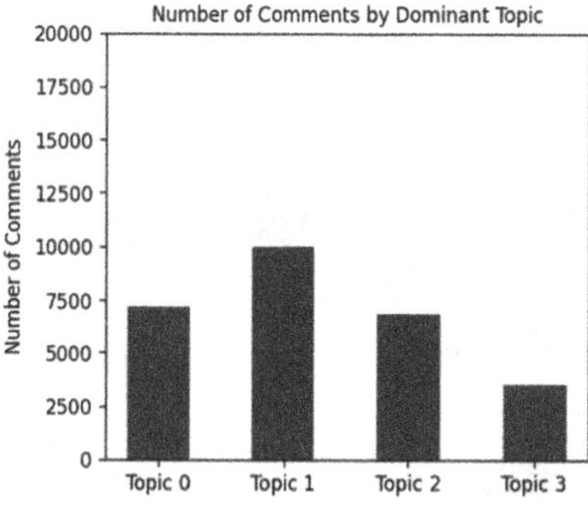

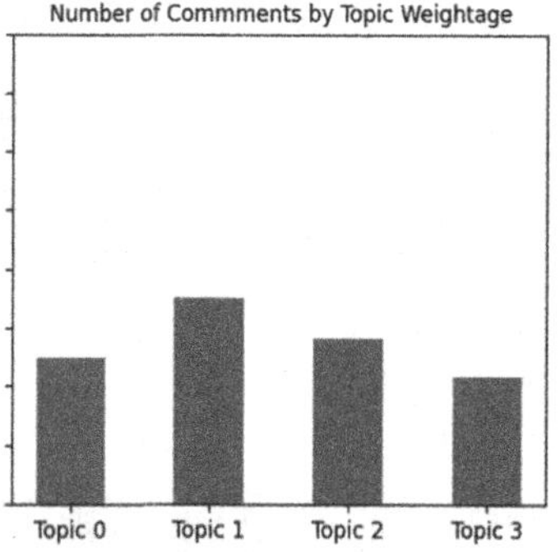

Fig. 7. Dominant topic of the discussion

about self-harm experiences and at-risk users were discussed at the same rate, while a few comments comprised a topic indicating appreciative responses.

4.3 Viewers' Opinions

Unlike other social media platforms such as Twitter, YouTube does not limit the length of viewers' comments. This allows broad audiences to discuss several topics about the video and express their opinions. This study applied VADER to compute the sentiment score of each comment. In other words, our experiment examined the rate of sentiments from the various topics discovered from the video responses. Figure 8 illustrates the percentage of positive, negative and neutral sentiments of each topic. In this bar graph, green represents positive comments, yellow denotes neutral responses, and red indicates the family of negative comments.

Notwithstanding, our investigation discovered mixed opinions across the topics. In the first topic, most of the viewers expressed negative opinions as opposed to positive sentiments. This could be a result of their discussion concerning self-harm experiences and associated difficult feelings. This is similar to the third topic, which consisted of more negative sentiments. While only a small number of viewers responded positively, some audiences remained neutral on both topics. In the same vein, topics two and four displayed a significant number of positive opinions. This shows how viewers in our sample encouraged positive peer support by inspiring others with their own recovery process. Also, they conveyed a positive tone in thanking the uploaders and acknowledging that the video contents were informative.

5 Discussion

The objective of the present study was to investigate the group of people involved in sharing videos about self-harm on YouTube, viewers' opinions on the videos,

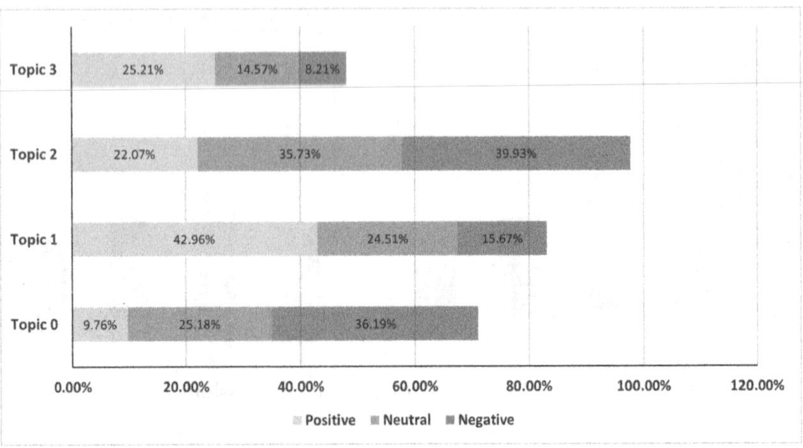

Fig. 8. Topics' sentiment analysis

and the nature of the discussions concerning those videos. Our findings demonstrated that only a small proportion of medical experts and professional bodies reach out to people struggling with self-harm on YouTube. Additionally, videos uploaded by these groups received fewer interactions among viewers and were less favourably viewed by the audiences. This indicates that healthcare and academic professionals need to reconsider the nature of video content preferred by self-injurers, as they favour entertaining videos over videos for educational purposes. The present investigation shows that individuals expressed their self-harming methods or behaviours, including the part of their body they injured, while commenting on the videos in our sample.

Using a statistical topic modelling technique, this study uncovered different topics from 27,520 comments on videos presenting self-harm information. Our analysis grouped viewers who participated in the conversation based on similar topics as one of the following: (1) *self-harming users,* (2) *recovered (clean) viewers*, (3) *at-risk audiences*, and (4) *appreciative users*. Moreover, based on the analysed video comments, many of those who participated in self-harm discussions engaged in sharing ideas and ways to recover from DSH. Existing research has demonstrated that self-harming individuals disclose their personal information on the internet to validate and accept their experiences [14] and receive peer support from members of the online community who are self-harming [13].

On the other hand, we found comments indicating some people accept DSH and normalise the behaviour while putting themselves at risk of potential harm. This finding is supported by existing studies that have explored self-harm content online [13]. Additionally, the comments from *appreciative users*, in which viewers were thanking the YouTuber for sharing a video, shows viewers found helpful information in the video. This is further supported by the high positive sentiments discovered in this group. Therefore, when *at-risk users* received helpful responses addressing dangerous behaviour, the information contained in the comment could be significant and therefore lead them toward recovery, especially if it is from a peer with relevant experience.

Furthermore, viewers had different opinions across the topics. Responses from recovered and appreciative themes attract more positive sentiments in contrast to comments from the topics representing at-risk and self-harming audiences. This result is similar to that of a study which investigated self-harm content on Flickr [28]. The sentiment cues from these topics and other related features can be used to build a machine learning classifier to detect users at risk of potential harm. Hence, to successfully target children and young self-harming individuals who use social media like YouTube and view videos about self-harm, it is essential to consider the content of such videos and their *positive* impact in an online community. One example could be providing innovative digital features to support vulnerable viewers and encourage help-seeking and recovery.

Although social media reveals the voices of people who self-harm, it is equally essential to consider self-harming users when designing and building digital interventions. Consequently, our findings add to the existing studies which demonstrate how young people who engage in DSH prefer YouTube as one of the online social spaces where they access information about their behaviour, interact with their peers with related issues, and exchange support [13].

6 Limitations

The current study has certain limitations. Firstly, our study retrieved and examined 107 videos discussing self-harm on YouTube. These videos do not represent the entire set of videos disseminating self-harm information on YouTube. Also, the video commentators do not represent the entire set of people that viewed the examined videos. This makes it hard to generalise our findings to the entire audience that watched the videos. Although the codebook used in categorising uploaders was reliable, it could be argued that the codebook may not be generalised, as it depicts the view of the researchers' practice. It is also likely that the categories we uncovered do not represent all YouTubers posting videos about self-harm; more research is needed to investigate other hidden categories or sub-categories.

Even though there are several ways to assess the impact of videos about self-harm, investigating the responses to those videos could be an effective strategy to determine the impact of those videos. While our analysis focused on only comments from the examined videos, it is apparent that not all viewers commented on the videos, based on the number of views compared to the number of comments. Therefore, the opinions of individuals who viewed without commenting could be another direction to explore. Secondly, the data we retrieved from YouTube does not incorporate demographic information of viewers who commented on the examined videos. Therefore, it is unknown whether most of those who commented were children, youth, or adults. However, we assume that most were young because of the existing evidence on youth internet use [26].

7 Conclusions and Future Work

Social media spaces like YouTube play a crucial role in disseminating information about mental health and well-being. The present research adds to the body of knowledge regarding the impact of social media concerning self-harm information. While other studies in this field concluded that social media could normalise or reinforce self-harm [15], our study shows the positive influence of social media content in increasing awareness about self-harm and promoting peer support. In response to our first research question, this study examined several channels and sources of YouTube videos presenting information about self-harm. Most of these videos were uploaded (and assigned to the *people and blogs* category) by the group of *non-professionals*. While audiences favourably responded to videos from experts and government institutions, there is a need for stakeholders to increase participation and engagement on social media to support vulnerable users at risk of DSH and consider how to design integrated online interventions.

We addressed the second and third research questions using natural language processing and computational techniques, specifically LDA and VADER. We examined topics from 27,520 responses of 107 videos presenting information about self-harm on YouTube. While viewers who participated in the discussion were grouped based on similar topics, our study found the following themes that described the entire comment corpus: (1) *self-harming users*, (2) *clean (recovered) viewers*, (3) *at-risk audiences* and (4) *appreciative users*. Additionally, topics representing *clean (recovered) viewers* was the most dominant theme among the discussions. The third research question was addressed by analysing the sentiment score of comments on each topic. Sentiment analysis revealed that *clean (recovered)* viewers and appreciative comments contained more positive sentiments than *self-harm* and *at-risk* comments. This is similar to findings of a previous study that examined Flickr content [28].

In addition to looking at other features, future studies should consider incorporating these sentiment-based features into a machine learning classifier to detect self-injurious or at-risk comments. Additionally, there is a need to determine the most effective online methods for reaching adolescents who self-injure, as young people prefer to acquire health information online and, when requested, prefer to receive NSSI assistance online. Medical clinicians supporting self-harming people need to consider investigating how self-harmers source or access information on social media during therapy sessions in order to help redirect their online activity toward positive content and interactions.

References

1. Arendt, F., Scherr, S., Romer, D.: Effects of exposure to self-harm on social media: evidence from a two-wave panel study among young adults. New Media Soc. **21**(11–12), 2422–2442 (2019)
2. Blei, D.M., Ng, A.Y., Jordan, M.I.: Latent Dirichlet allocation. J. Mach. Learn. Res. **3**, 993–1022 (2003)

3. Brunner, R., et al.: Life-time prevalence and psychosocial correlates of adolescent direct self-injurious behavior: a comparative study of findings in 11 European countries. J. Child Psychol. Psychiatry **55**(4), 337–348 (2014)
4. Cash, S.J., Thelwall, M., Peck, S.N., Ferrell, J.Z., Bridge, J.A.: Adolescent suicide statements on myspace. Cyberpsychol. Behav. Soc. Netw. **16**(3), 166–174 (2013)
5. Cosley, D., Forte, A., Ciolfi, L., McDonald, D.: Proceedings of the 18th ACM Conference on Computer Supported Cooperative Work & Social Computing. ACM Press (2015)
6. De Choudhury, M., Counts, S., Horvitz, E.: Social media as a measurement tool of depression in populations. In: Proceedings of the 5th Annual ACM Web Science Conference, pp. 47–56 (2013)
7. De Choudhury, M., Gamon, M., Counts, S., Horvitz, E.: Predicting depression via social media. In: Seventh International AAAI Conference on Weblogs and Social Media (2013)
8. Emma Hilton, C.: Unveiling self-harm behaviour: what can social media site twitter tell us about self-harm? A qualitative exploration. J. Clin. Nurs. **26**(11–12), 1690–1704 (2017)
9. Hutto, C., Gilbert, E.: VADER: a parsimonious rule-based model for sentiment analysis of social media text. In: Eighth International AAAI Conference on Weblogs and Social Media (2014)
10. Jacobi, C., Van Atteveldt, W., Welbers, K.: Quantitative analysis of large amounts of journalistic texts using topic modelling. Digit. J. **4**(1), 89–106 (2016)
11. Lehr, C.A., Tan, C.S., Ysseldyke, J.: Alternative schools: a synthesis of state-level policy and research. Remedial Spec. Educ. **30**(1), 19–32 (2009)
12. Lewis, S.P., Heath, N.L., Sornberger, M.J., Arbuthnott, A.E.: Helpful or harmful? An examination of viewers' responses to nonsuicidal self-injury videos on YouTube. J. Adolesc. Health **51**(4), 380–385 (2012)
13. Lewis, S.P., Heath, N.L., St Denis, J.M., Noble, R.: The scope of nonsuicidal self-injury on YouTube. Pediatrics **127**(3), e552–e557 (2011)
14. Lewis, S.P., Rosenrot, S.A., Messner, M.A.: Seeking validation in unlikely places: the nature of online questions about non-suicidal self-injury. Arch. Suicide Res. **16**(3), 263–272 (2012)
15. Lewis, S.P., Seko, Y.: A double-edged sword: a review of benefits and risks of online nonsuicidal self-injury activities. J. Clin. Psychol. **72**(3), 249–262 (2016)
16. Madge, N., et al.: Deliberate self-harm within an international community sample of young people: comparative findings from the Child & Adolescent Self-harm in Europe (CASE) study. J. Child Psychol. Psychiatry **49**(6), 667–677 (2008)
17. Marchant, A., et al.: A systematic review of the relationship between internet use, self-harm and suicidal behaviour in young people: the good, the bad and the unknown. PLoS ONE **12**(8), e0181722 (2017)
18. McDermott, E., Roen, K.: Youth on the virtual edge: researching marginalized sexualities and genders online. Qual. Health Res. **22**(4), 560–570 (2012)
19. McRoberts, S., Bonsignore, E., Peyton, T., Yarosh, S.: Do it for the viewers! Audience engagement behaviors of young YouTubers. In: Proceedings of the The 15th International Conference on Interaction Design and Children, pp. 334–343 (2016)
20. Mergel, I.: A framework for interpreting social media interactions in the public sector. Gov. Inf. Q. **30**(4), 327–334 (2013)
21. Miguel, E.M., et al.: Examining the scope and patterns of deliberate self-injurious cutting content in popular social media. Depress. Anxiety **34**(9), 786–793 (2017)
22. Mitchell, K.J., Ybarra, M.L.: Online behavior of youth who engage in self-harm provides clues for preventive intervention. Prev. Med. **45**(5), 392–396 (2007)

23. Nock, M.K.: Self-injury. Annu. Rev. Clin. Psychol. **6**, 339–363 (2010)
24. Nock, M.K., Holmberg, E.B., Photos, V.I., Michel, B.D.: Self-injurious thoughts and behaviors interview: development, reliability, and validity in an adolescent sample. Psychol. Assess. **19**(3), 309–317 (2007)
25. Pater, J.A., Haimson, O.L., Andalibi, N., Mynatt, E.D.: "Hunger hurts but starving works" characterizing the presentation of eating disorders online. In: Proceedings of the 19th ACM Conference on Computer-Supported Cooperative Work & Social Computing, pp. 1185–1200 (2016)
26. Rideout, V.J., Foehr, U.G., Roberts, D.F.: Generation m^2: Media in the Lives of 8-to 18-Year-Olds. Henry J. Kaiser Family Foundation, San Francisco (2010)
27. Rodriquez, J.: Narrating dementia: self and community in an online forum. Qual. Health Res. **23**(9), 1215–1227 (2013)
28. Wang, Y., et al.: Understanding and discovering deliberate self-harm content in social media. In: Proceedings of the 26th International Conference on World Wide Web, pp. 93–102 (2017)

Author Index

Printed in the United States
by Baker & Taylor Publisher Services